I met you in a story
Upon an autumn eve;
We built a treetop hideout
Among the russet leaves.

I met you in a story
Upon a snowy morn;
We wreathed a deer in holly
And fed him sweet white corn.

I met you in a story
Upon a summer night;
We took your sloop exploring
Through seas of silver light.

I met you in a story
Upon a rainy day;
We rode on armored stallions
Into the battle fray.

I met you in a story—
And, friend, I do believe
I'll meet you in that treetop
Another autumn's eve.
—Eileen M. Berry

Reading 4 Part 1
Teacher's Edition
Second Edition

BJU PRESS
Greenville, South Carolina

Consultants
from the administration, faculty, and staff of Bob Jones University
Philip D. Smith, Ed.D.
 Provost
Grace C. Hargis, Ph.D.
 Chairman, Department of English Education
Dan Olinger, Ph.D.
 Elementary Bible Consultant, BJU Press
James R. Davis, M.A.
 Director of Product Development, BJU Press
Vicky L. Burr
 Elementary Authors Project Director, BJU Press
Janice A. Joss, M.A.T.
 Professor of Reading, School of Education

NOTE:
The fact that materials produced by other publishers may be referred to in this volume does not constitute an endorsement of the content or theological position of materials produced by such publishers. Any references and ancillary materials are listed as an aid to the student or the teacher and in an attempt to maintain the accepted academic standards of the publishing industry.

READING 4 Teacher's Edition, Part 1
I Met You in a Story

Second Edition

Project Coordinators
 Vicky L. Burr
 Janice A. Joss
 Susan J. Lehman
Coordinating Writers
 Vicky L. Burr—Reader 4,
  I Met You in a Story
 Susan J. Lehman—Teacher's
  Edition
Writers
 Sarah Clayton
 Wendy M. Harris
 Aimee C. McDorman
 Debra L. Mills
Contributing Writers
 Peggy S. Alier
 Eileen M. Berry

 Grace Farr
 Shannon Hilton
 Dawn L. Watkins
 Susan W. Young
Project Editors
 Manda Kalagayan
 Sarah White
Computer Formatting
 Carol Larson
Designers
 Holly Gilbert—Reader 4,
  I Met You in a Story
 Elly Kalagayan—Reader 4,
  I Met You in a Story
 Patricia A. Tirado—Teacher's
  Edition

Graphics Coordinator
 Mary Ann Lumm
Graphics
 Daniel Van Leeuwen—
  Teacher's Edition
Photo Acquisition
 Cindy Mauk

© 2000 BJU Press
Greenville, South Carolina 29614

First Edition © 1985 BJU Press

Photograph credits appear on page 330.

ISBN 978-1-57924-457-6

15 14 13 12 11 10 9 8 7 6 5

Contents

Part 1

What better result could a teacher have than students who love to read—and who do read, thoughtfully and fluently? Because *READING for Christian Schools* emphasizes comprehension and develops phonics systematically, it

Introduction

What better result could a teacher have than students who love to read—and who do read, thoughtfully and fluently? Because *READING for Christian Schools* emphasizes comprehension and develops phonics systematically, it produces confident, eager readers who continue to read all their lives.

A skillful teacher can use these materials not only to teach reading well but also to encourage growth in Christian character. A variety of selections—family stories, adventure stories, Christian realism, historical fiction, Bible accounts retold, biographies, information articles, folktales, poems, and plays—offers delightful instruction, providing the student with both pleasure and understanding.

Goals for *READING for Christian Schools*

Teaches biblical principles and discernment for daily living

Bible Action Truths [BATs] and Bible Promises are integrated throughout lessons.

Reader selections reflect Christian truths.

Worktext pages provide practical application of biblical principles.

Develops higher-level thinking skills

Questions for lesson discussion go beyond facts and details to include appreciative consideration and critical reasoning.

Worktext pages evoke the use of higher-level thinking skills.

Builds skills needed for lifelong learning

Silent reading enables the student to focus on comprehending the author's message.

Oral reading is taught as a communication skill.

Reading strategies are emphasized to enhance independent reading.

Vocabulary instruction goes beyond memorizing word definitions to provide strategies for discovering word meanings.

Structural analysis is taught to facilitate word recognition.

Literary skills develop understanding and discernment in reading literature.

Study skills are introduced with relevant selections in the reader to strengthen and build comprehension.

Phonics skills equip students in lower elementary grades with tools for word recognition.

Phonics remedial review assists struggling readers in the upper elementary grades.

Fosters enjoyment and appreciation for reading and learning

Reader units contain a variety of genres from various cultures.

High interest, quality literature has been selected, including selections from classic authors.

Excerpts from junior novels pique student interest and encourage further reading.

Colorful illustrations add interest and enhance story content.

Meets the needs of individual teachers and students

Flexible teacher lesson format can be adapted easily to different reading levels of readers, group sizes, and time allotments.

Question-answer format promotes interactive teaching.

Worktext pages include review and application of skills as well as enjoyable, challenging activities.

Options are provided for verbal and written student evaluation.

Instructional Materials

Student Reader

I Met You in a Story

The colorful hardcover textbook contains a wide variety of inviting selections.

Teacher's Edition

Spiral-bound, two-volume teacher's edition includes complete lesson plans for teaching the reader selections. Questions and teaching strategies are printed beside each full-color, 75-percent-sized student page. Each reading lesson also focuses on one or more reading skills. An appendix provides support materials for instruction.

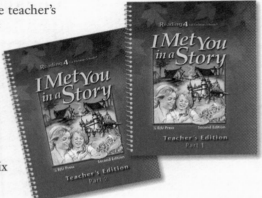

The weight of the skill teaching, however, is carried by special lessons on important skills. These lessons, planned for whole-class teaching, are supported by a Skill Station section in the student worktext.

Student Worktext

Colorful softcover worktext contains interesting activities to focus on specific reading skills. The Skill Station section includes systematic teaching of structural analysis, study skills, and literature skills. The Phonics section provides review for students who can benefit from remedial help.

Worktext Teacher's Edition

Spiral-bound copy of the student worktext includes answer overprint for the teacher. The "Useful for grading" label assists the teacher in selecting pages for evaluation. Pages labeled "optional" may be completed by advanced students, as a whole class, or not at all.

Teaching Visuals

Set of twenty-four colorful, attractive transparencies designed to be used on an overhead projector provides tools for teaching important skills: syllable division and accent rules, study skills, and literature skills. Included in the set is a full-color paper copy of each transparency, which can be used in the reading group setting. The full-color visuals are also available as a flip chart.

BJ BookLinks: Journey into Literature
Novels and teacher's guides

Sheriff at Waterstop by Andy Thompson, Level 1

Medallion by Dawn L. Watkins, Level 2

Mountain Born by Elizabeth Yates, Level 3

Supplementary novels broaden the reading opportunities for fourth graders. A copy is needed for each child in the instructional group.

Each teacher's guide includes a set of lesson plans for developing literature and comprehension skills through the reading of the novel. A folder with many ideas for student projects contains the set of lesson plans, including reproducibles, and a copy of the student book.

Sentence strips and pocket chart

Context sentences, used in nearly every lesson for teaching vocabulary, may be written on lined oak-tag strips. The sentence strips may be displayed in a pocket chart for teaching. These materials are available from BJU Press or any teacher supply source.

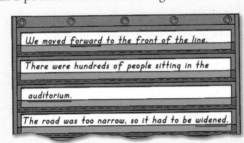

Sample Lesson

Bring each selection back to memory by reading the **short summary.** The summary should not be read to the students.

Know what items to collect ahead of time by simply glancing over the **list of materials.**

Enhance lessons by learning useful **additional information.** Use the information to liven discussions, but avoid reading the paragraph directly to the students.

Create interest and initiate comprehension by using the **short introductory activities.**

Use the **vocabulary sentences** to teach words that may hinder comprehension. Students gain the meaning of vocabulary through the context of the sentence.

Note: Display the sentences so that the reading group can see them easily.

WATCHING WALLACE

Ten whole dollars! But Timothy must overcome his fear of dogs to earn it. If he can take care of Mr. Parker's huge mongrel, Wallace, for a whole week, the money is his.

Materials
- Dog leash
- Vocabulary sentences prepared for display (e.g., on the chalkboard or on sentence strips)

Background information
Rabies—Some students may not be familiar with the disease of rabies. This infectious disease, transmitted through the bite of an infected animal, requires medical treatment. It is best to be cautious when near stray or wild animals, which may be infected with the disease.

INTRODUCTION
Vocabulary
Use the prepared sentences to introduce the vocabulary words in context.

Pet responsibilities
Display the dog leash.
▶ Have you ever been responsible for taking care of a pet?

What types of responsibilities did you have?

Have you ever had to take care of an animal that frightened you?

What are some ways that you can overcome your fears?

Lead the students to the conclusion that trusting in God will help us when we are afraid. God commands us to trust in Him and to have courage, not fear. [BAT: 8d Courage]

> The student should tear out and take home Worktext page 327, *A Message to Parents.*

Lesson	Reader pages	Worktext pages
1	2–5	1
2	6–9	2–4

VOCABULARY
LESSON 1
†Because Anna had kept thinking about the circus, she had not concentrated on her work. (p. 2)

If a dog's mother is a different breed from its father, the dog is a mongrel. (p. 3)

†The great expanse of land was enough to build two houses on. (p. 3)

†Animals that have the disease of rabies are very dangerous. (p. 4)

LESSON 2
†The items needed to bake the cake were in the pantry. (p. 8)

†The trees along the dark and lonely path loomed over him. (p. 9)

> † indicates the vocabulary word is found in the *Christian Student Dictionary.*
>
> A list of the remedial service words appears on Appendix page A6 of this teacher's edition. See also page xi in the Introduction for information about and activities for practicing service words.

Correlated Activities
- Vocabulary Box, Activity 1: Word Hunt
- Creative Writing, Activity 1: Runaway Writings

See "Classroom Management for Grouping" in the Appendix.

Watching Wallace

Lesson 1 . . . **3**

Make classroom management achievable by providing **enjoyable activities** for students to do while another reading group is being instructed. Corresponding instructions are given in the Appendix beginning on page A10.

Stimulate purposeful silent reading by asking questions before beginning to read. These **motivation questions** encourage students to look for an answer or think about an idea while they read. Avoid giving answers prior to reading.

Broaden and evaluate understanding of silent reading segments and objectives through **discussion.** The Overview and Follow-up discussion sections contain thought-provoking questions on the four levels of comprehension. See pages xiv-xv, Compreshension, for ideas on adapting the format to the student level.

Discuss the main ideas found throughout the assigned silent reading segment. The **Overview discussion** briefly establishes general information, such as main characters and setting, and examines the most important ideas.

Conduct a detailed discussion for each page of the reading segment by using the questions in the **Follow-up discussion.**

Be alert to **highlighted questions** that cover objectives and main ideas.

LESSON 1
THE AGREEMENT

COMPREHENSION

Objectives

The student will

- Evaluate character responses.
- Focus on the author's use of descriptive verbs.
- Identify problems and solutions.
- Note the author's use of flashback.
- Relate lesson content to personal experience.

Before silent reading: pages 2-3

Motivation

▶ Think about the dog leash and the story title. Who is Wallace?

Why could watching Wallace be a problem?

After silent reading

Overview discussion: pages 2-3

▶ [interpretive] Why is watching Wallace a problem? (Timothy doesn't really want to watch Wallace because he is afraid of the dog.)

[critical] Why is Timothy thinking about the time he was seven? (Accept any answer.)

▶ [appreciative] What kinds of things are you afraid of?

Essential questions for discussing the main ideas of the story and the lesson objectives can be found in the gold boxes. See the Introduction in the front of this manual.

Follow-up discussion: page 2

▶ [literal] Why does Timothy jump when he is with Mr. Parker? (Mr. Parker slaps Tim on the back and startles him.)

[critical] Do you think Mr. Parker startles Timothy on purpose? (Accept any answer.)

[literal] Why does Timothy concentrate on breathing normally? (so Mr. Parker will not know how startled he is)

▶ [critical] Why do you think Timothy agrees to take care of the dog? (Answers will vary. Elicit that Timothy probably doesn't want to admit he is scared to a man like Mr. Parker.)

Read aloud the conversation between Mr. Parker and Timothy, using Mr. Parker's booming voice and Timothy's shaky voice.

▶ [critical] Why isn't Timothy startled by his dad's voice? (Accept any answer.)

[interpretive] Does Timothy feel any different about the job after he knows he will get paid? Explain. (No, he still doesn't want to do it.)

Read aloud the sentences that tell how Timothy feels about watching Wallace even though he is getting paid.

4 . . . Unit 1

Exploits

Watching Wallace

Sharon Hambrick
Illustrated by Mary Ann Lumm

The Agreement

Timothy jumped when Mr. Parker slapped him on the back. Not that Timothy was a scaredy-cat, nothing like that—it was just that sometimes, if something jumped out at him or if someone shouted suddenly, he would jump.

"So, Tim, my boy," Mr. Parker's voice boomed in the late September afternoon, "what about it? What about watching Wallace for me while I'm gone?"

Timothy concentrated on breathing normally so Mr. Parker wouldn't know how startled he'd been.

"Okay," Timothy said. He hoped Mr. Parker wouldn't notice how his voice shook.

"Then it's settled," Mr. Parker said. "I'll leave Monday morning,

and I should be back Saturday afternoon."

Timothy nodded. Mr. Parker slapped him on the back again and tromped off to his house next door. He t...
bucks, Ti...
bucks for...

"Ten...
deep voic...
Timothy ...
kind face...

"I tol...
Dad," Tim...
shakiness ...
whole wee...

"Oh,"...
about this...

"No,"...

Timothy lay in bed that night, wishing he hadn't agreed to watch

2

> Adapt lessons so that focused instruction is suited to the student's level. Because each **silent reading segment** has motivation questions and an overview discussion, it can be treated as an independent lesson. See pages xiv-xv, Comprehension, for ideas on adapting silent reading segments to the student's level.

> Teach biblical principles and include Scripture during reading instruction. **Bible Action Truths** and **Bible Promises**, along with questions and answers, emphasize biblical principles that can be taught with the reading segments. Full explanations, including Scripture references, of the Bible Action Truths and Bible Promises are provided in the Appendix on pages A2-A4.

> Use the indicated **worktext pages** to reinforce and develop comprehension, vocabulary, and other skills.

> Enhance and nurture skills and creativity with enjoyable **elective activities.** These activities often incorporate writing.

"Come here, boy," he said. "Come here, Wallace."

Wallace ran wildly over the field. Timothy watched, feeling helpless. Wallace trotted toward him, then ran away. Timothy felt annoyed.

"Come here, Wallace!" Timothy shouted. "Come here!"

Wallace stopped, turned, and ran over.

Maybe he needs me to sound forceful, like Mr. Parker does, he thought.

"Sit!" Timothy said, as loudly and forcefully as he could. Wallace sat.

Timothy laughed. He grabbed the leash. "Now," he said loudly, "we are going home!" Wallace responded to Timothy's more demanding tone of voice. Maybe he just needed me to be in charge, he thought. Wallace pulled on the leash to go faster, but Timothy said, "No, boy!" and he slowed down.

The fence loomed in front of them. I *will* trust the Lord, thought Timothy. I *will not* be afraid. Carefully, he pulled up the fence to let the dog through. Then, holding as tightly as he could to the leash, he eased himself under the fence.

Then, covered with dirt and grass, and slowing Wallace's bounding pace to a walk by his firm commands, Timothy walked leash-in-hand down the sidewalk, all the way home.

Mr. Parker's van was in the driveway.

"Hey, Timmy, my man!" Mr. Parker's voice cracked the silence. "I'm home early. How's the old boy been treating you?"

Timothy smiled. "He's been great, Mr. Parker."

"Didn't jump all over you and scare you to death, did he?"

"Just a little."

Mr. Parker's booming laugh filled the whole neighborhood. He took the leash out of Timothy's hand and dug a ten-dollar bill out of his pocket with his other hand.

"Any idea what you're going to do with that money, Son?" he asked.

"Yes, sir," Timothy said, smiling. "I'm going to take it to the fair."

"The fair!" Mr. Parker shouted. "Good idea. Going to ride the Tingling Terror, are you?"

"Yes, sir," Timothy said. "I'm going to ride it with my mom."

Watching Wallace   9

Before silent reading: page 9

Motivation

▶ Will Wallace give Timothy any more trouble?

Do you think we will learn any more about why the author called this chapter "Taking Charge"?

After silent reading

Overview discussion: page 9

▶ [interpretive] Who seems to be "in charge" in this final part of the story? (Timothy—Wallace seems to be obeying him now.)

[interpretive] How does Timothy take charge? (He overcomes his fear of Wallace and orders Wallace to come to him.)

[interpretive] How does Timothy overcome his fear? (by trusting in the Lord) [BAT: 4d Victory]

[interpretive] How do other people in this story help Timothy overcome his fear? (Dad and Mom encourage him and guide him to verses; Mr. Parker shows that he trusts Timothy and can depend on him.)

Follow-up discussion: page 9

▶ [interpretive] Why doesn't Wallace slow down the first time Timothy tells him to? (Possible answer: Timothy does not speak firmly enough to Wallace.)

[interpretive] How does Timothy finally get Wallace to obey him? (He speaks to him firmly—he takes charge.)

▶ [interpretive] How does Timothy respond to Mr. Parker's question about how Wallace treated him? (He says Wallace was great, but he does admit that Wallace scared him a little.) [BAT: 4c Honesty]

▶ [interpretive] What does Timothy mean when he tells Mr. Parker he is going to ride the Tingling Terror with his mom? (Timothy expects his mother to keep her part of the bargain.)

▶ [critical] Do you think Timothy's mom will ride the Tingling Terror with Timothy? Why or why not? (Accept any answer, but elicit that she will keep her promise to Timothy.)

Worktext Objective

The student will

■ Sequence story events.

Comprehension: Worktext page 2

Watching Wallace

Lesson 2 . . . 11

Literature: Worktext pages 3-4

SOMETHING EXTRA

Write About It: My "Wallace" story

Direct the student to write about his own experience that left him afraid of something. Use the following questions as story starters.

▶ Did reading about Wallace make you remember a time that you were afraid?

What frightened you?

Did you think of a verse to help you when you were afraid?

12 . . Unit 1

Exploits

Unit theme discussion: page 1

▶ What is the title of the unit? ("Exploits")

Read aloud the following sentence:

The boy's exploit, rescuing the drowning child, took a lot of courage.

▶ What do you think *exploit* means? (Accept any answer, but explain that it is a special act or deed, usually one that is heroic or brilliant.)

What are some exploits or special deeds that you have read or heard about? (Answers will vary.)

What are some exploits that happened in the Bible? (Possible answers: David slew Goliath; Moses crossed the Red Sea; three men walked out of the fiery furnace.)

EXPLOITS

Joshua 1:9

Have not I commanded thee? Be strong and of a good courage; be not afraid, neither be thou dismayed: for the Lord thy God is with thee whithersoever thou goest.

The courage to accomplish great feats begins with a single step in the right direction. The young characters in "River's Rising," "Yukon Trail," and "Project Submarine" bravely take that step when unforeseen circumstances change their plans and, ultimately, their lives. Link courage with fantasy and the result will be "Pecos Bill Gets a Wife" or "A Wise King and a Wise Son." Reality checks in when facing and conquering the plummet of a roller coaster in "Over the Top" or coping with the unpredictability of animals in "Watching Wallace," "An Emergency," and "Lama Glama."

2 . . . Unit 1

Exploits

Follow-up discussion: page 5

▶ [interpretive] **How does Timothy's mom reassure him that he does not have to fear Wallace or getting rabies?** (Possible answers: She tells him that Wallace is a good dog who has had all his shots; she prays and sings with him; she tells him about a time when she was younger that left her afraid of roller coasters.)

[critical] **In what ways are Timothy's fear and his mom's fear the same?** (Answers will vary, but point out that both fears come from something that happened in the past.)

Read aloud Mom's description of her frightening experience. Read it like Mom says it—in a quiet voice.

▶ [literal] **What promise does Timothy's mom make to him?** (She promises to ride the roller coaster if he watches Wallace.)

[critical] **What does Timothy think about the possibility that his mom will ride the roller coaster?** (Accept any answer, but elicit that his mom is making a sacrifice and that he is excited.)

Looking ahead

▶ Do you think Timothy's mom will have to ride the roller coaster?

the charac- (Answers will way is to notice what the characters do an how they act.)

Write the word *actions* for display.

Discuss the characters from "Watc Wallace"—what they are like and h the story shows these traits (e.g., W lace: playful, energetic—gallops, ba Timothy: timid, afraid—is startled ily, shudders at the word *rabies*).

Read the instructions for the page to- gether. Direct the students to com- plete the page.

Lesson 1 . . . 7

Heritage Studies Connection

Lesson 8 can be linked to the study of map scale and map key.

Make a **connection between subject areas** for the students. Suggestions signal when other subject areas are referred to in the reading selections.

Note: This is not a direct correlation to specific lessons in other BJU Press textbooks.

The student will

■ Generalize about characters from actions.

Comprehension: Worktext page 1

Write the word *characters* for display. Read the word to the students.

▶ What are characters? (people or animals in the story)

Name the characters in "Watching Wallace." (Mom, Dad, Mr. Parker, Timothy, Wallace)

Who is the main character? (Timothy)

Watching Wallace

population, and rainfall maps).

re these maps the same?

How are these maps different?

Correlated Activities
• Word Work, Activity 2: Blooper Blurbs
• Spelling Practice, Activity 1: Spell Check
See "Classroom Management for Grouping" in the Appendix.

32 . . Unit 1

Exploits

Phonics

Say the word *phonics* in a crowd, and the definitions will be as varied as the people. Even educators vary in what they think phonics is and does.

Simply stated, phonics, the study of basic phonetics, is a tool for word recognition. The spellings of the forty-four sounds of the English language, presented in a variety of sequences and levels of intensity, make up the content of all phonics programs. How a teacher chooses to teach phonics reveals his definition of reading and also his understanding of how most children learn to read.

A phonics review section for remedial help can be found in the back of the student worktext.

The sounds

Students using Bob Jones University Press materials learn all forty-four sounds of the English language. Because of a strong emphasis on phonics teaching with songs and word family practice, most children by this grade level have a good working knowledge of phonics. For struggling readers or children new to a phonics-based reading program, phonics teaching is still beneficial.

The syllables

In every syllable (one "beat" of a word), there is a vowel sound. In English the vowel letters can represent many sounds. The choice of vowel sounds is greatly simplified when the student is taught to notice the pattern or setting for the vowel letter before he attempts to assign it a sound. This unique way of looking at phonics—a method as old as *The Blue Back Speller*—sets this phonics program apart from others. Looking at phonics as it appears in the syllables of the language has far-reaching rewards that continue to aid the student in the upper levels of reading.

Closed syllable pattern: The Short Family—A syllable that ends in one or more consonants is a closed syllable. The words *not* and *got* are closed syllables, as are *nest* and *best*. Both sets of syllables have one vowel letter. The first set ends in one consonant, the second set in two consonants. In this closed syllable pattern, the vowel letter nearly always represents the short sound.

In the BJU Press materials, the vowel patterns are represented by characters that help the students remember them. Mrs. Short represents the short vowel, which is followed by a consonant. She never appears without her husband, Mr. Short, who represents the consonant that always follows a short vowel. Sometimes Mrs. Short appears with both Mr. Short and his brother Uncle Short. Uncle Short represents the second consonant after a short vowel.

n o t
g o t

n e s t
b e s t

Open syllable pattern: Miss Long—In a syllable that ends with a vowel, the vowel nearly always represents a long sound. Miss Long, unlike Mrs. Short, may appear alone at the end of a syllable.

n o
g o
n o • b l e

Marker *e* pattern: Miss Long and Marker *e*, the dog—In a syllable with one vowel followed by one consonant and then the letter *e*, the first vowel is long and the final *e* is silent. The dog, Marker *e*, tags along behind Miss Long. He does not say anything, but she says her long sound.

n o t e
v o t e

Two-vowel pattern: Miss Long and Miss Silent—In a syllable that includes two vowels together, the first vowel often represents a long sound and the second vowel is silent. Sometimes Miss Long's friend Miss Silent is with her. Miss Silent never says anything, and she likes to stay close to Miss Long.

m e a l
p i e

R-influenced vowel pattern: Bossy R, the cowboy—In a one-syllable word or stressed syllable, when the *r* follows a vowel it usually modifies the vowel sound. A different vowel sound is heard instead of the short or long sound you would expect because of the pattern. There are several spellings for most of the *r*-influenced sounds.

Other patterns—Several other specific letter patterns represent five other sounds. These include two diphthongs: /oi/ as in *oil* and *boy* and /ou/ as in *loud* and *brown*. There are three other sounds: /o͞o/ as in *moon*, /o͝o/ as in *cook*, and /ô/ as in *paw*, *cause*, *lost*, and *ball*.

The process

Phonics skill is vital to every child. There are three key concepts to be applied to a balanced phonics program.

1. All phonics instruction must be linked to comprehension—the reading of real words.
2. The child needs to know the grapheme/phoneme relationships (letter-sound associations).
3. The child must tie these letter-sound associations to the rest of the word. Drill or practice focuses on word families. It is in the patterns that the letter-sounds are consistent.

From the key concepts listed above, some conclusions can be drawn about phonics teaching methods.

▸ *Avoid isolating sounds.* Never isolate a series of sounds while trying to decode a word (e.g., "/kuh/ /aah/ /tuh/"—*cat*). Weak readers find it hard to make a transition from this habit to natural (silent) blending. It creates a tunnel vision that does not teach the students to look at the syllable to find the pattern. Letters in isolation may represent a variety of sounds (e.g., the letter *o* in *not*, *note*, *north*, *noise*, *now*, *lemon*, *cost*, and *tractor*).

▸ *Never practice nonsense syllables.* Practicing nonsense syllables gives the child the idea that reading is the making of "word noises" rather than getting a message from print. Even when practicing word families, context sentences and discussion of word meaning should be part of the drill time.

▸ *Avoid overlearning any information that may change later.* Repeated practice of the onsets (initial consonant combined with a short vowel) often results in choppy reading when the student encounters the other pronunciations of the vowels (e.g., *la*, /lă/; *late*, /lāte/).

Word family practice

Most regular one-syllable words can be arranged into word families that provide a good basis for practice. A word family consists of a set of words that have a common phonogram—a combination of letters beginning with a vowel and proceeding to the end of the syllable. Phonograms are based on phonics generalizations and patterns.

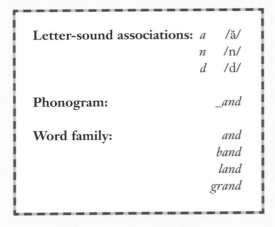

If a child struggles with reading one-syllable words, he would benefit from practice with word families. It is important to focus on comprehension while practicing word families. The child should be given opportunities to put these words into sentences correctly.

light—Please turn off the *light*.

fight—We had to hold the dogs to prevent a *fight*.

Practicing the word families will open the door to reading multi-syllable words. When the child comes to the new word *enlighten*, he will not go plodding across the word, one letter at time, saying "/eh/ /nuh/ /el/ /ī/ /guh/ /huh/ /tuh/ /eh/ /n/." He will see the syllables—en•light•en—and read the word with ease.

Structural Analysis

As part of the process in reading the syllables in a multisyllable word, a child may also put into use the things he has learned about the way words divide into syllables and which syllables are accented in words.

Syllable division rules

Rule 1: *VC/CV* pattern

Divide words with the *VC/CV* pattern into syllables between consonants, even when one of the consonants is written as a consonant digraph (*bas•ket, dol•phin*).

(Introduced in Lesson 22 with Visual 4, *California Challenge*.)

Rule 2: Compound words

Divide compound words into syllables between the base words (*base•ball, bas•ket•ball*).

(Introduced in Lesson 27 with Visual 5, *Dangerous Trails*.)

Rule 3: Words ending with a consonant + *le*

In most words ending with a consonant + *le*, divide into syllables before the consonant (*lit•tle, Bi•ble*).

In words ending with the consonant digraph *ck* + *le*, divide into syllables after the *ck* (*pick•le*).

(Introduced in Lesson 39 with Visual 8, *Eighty Stables*.)

Rule 4: Words with affixes

a. In words with prefixes, divide into syllables between the prefix and the base word (*un•load*).

b. In words with suffixes, sometimes divide into syllables between the base word and the suffix.

If the base word ends with /d/ or /t/, the suffix *-ed* is in a separate syllable (*hand•ed, plod•ded, rest•ed*).

If the base word ends with *ch, sh, s, x* or *z*, the suffix *-es* is a separate syllable (*church•es, wish•es, dress•es, box•es, buzz•es*).

(Introduced in Lesson 49 with Visual 9, *Ponies Carry the Mail*.)

Accent rules

Rule 1: Compound words

In compound words the primary accent falls on or within the first base word (*base´•ball*).

In compound words the secondary accent falls on or within the second base word (*bas´•ket •ball´*).

(Introduced in Lesson 27 with Visual 5, *Dangerous Trails*.)

Rule 2: Words with affixes

In words with affixes, the accent usually falls on or within the base word (*un•lock´•ing, ham´•mer•ing*).

(Introduced in Lesson 49 with Visual 10, *End of a Hard Ride*.)

Rule 3: Two-syllable words without affixes

In two-syllable words without affixes, the accent usually falls on the first syllable (*bas´•ket*).

In two-syllable words without affixes, the accent falls on the second syllable when that syllable contains two vowels (*col•lapse´*).

(Introduced in Lesson 49 with Visual 10, *End of a Hard Ride*.)

Rule 4: Schwa syllables

The accent never falls on a syllable with a vowel sound called a schwa—ə.

The schwa sound can be spelled many ways. Some common schwa syllables are *a-* (*again*), *con-* (*content*), *-le* (*little*), *-er* (*never*), *-ain* (*captain*), *-ous* (*famous*), and *-tion* (*nation*).

In words with the schwa ending /shən/, the accent usually falls on the syllable that precedes the ending (*va•ca´•tion*).

(Introduced in Lesson 56 with Visual 12, *A Special Mailbag*.)

Rule 5: Shift in accent

a. Adding suffixes to some words may affect where the primary accent falls. The accent often shifts to the syllable before the suffix (*ac´•ci•dent, ac•ci•den´•tal*).

b. A shift in accent often occurs when the meaning of a word changes (*per´•fect, per•fect´*).

(Introduced in Lesson 71 with Visual 15, *The Greatest Ride*.)

Vocabulary

Vocabulary development

New vocabulary—In each lesson a maximum of five words is listed for special study. These words are featured either because their meanings are unfamiliar or because their spellings are irregular.

In the following sentence most children can say the sounds of the word, but some do not know the meaning of the word used in a story.

bobbed—The boat *bobbed* up and down in the waves.

In another sentence most children have heard the word many times, but seeing the unusual spelling may inhibit comprehension of the story.

bouquet—Matthew brought a lovely *bouquet* of flowers to his grandmother.

In still another sentence both the spelling and the meaning of the word may be new.

pirogues—The Indians paddled down the river in their *pirogues*.

A context sentence is always given for each vocabulary word. As you present vocabulary words, follow these steps.

1. Write the sentence on a sentence strip, a chart, or the chalkboard. Underline the new word, but do not tell the students the word.
2. Ask the students to read the sentence silently and to think about the underlined word.
3. If it is a word like *bobbed*, guide a discussion that brings out the definition—"bounced about in the water."
4. If it is a word like *bouquet*, guide the use of context to help the children determine, by the syntax (word order) and the meaning of the other words, that *bouquet*—"an arrangement of flowers"—is the word they have heard often but may not have seen in print.
5. If it is a word like *pirogues*, guide a discussion of the definition and the pronunciation.

Vocabulary strategies

Context analysis—The chief vocabulary strategy used by literate adults is context analysis. Each reading lesson contains sentences with strong context to assist the reader in using interpretative thinking to aid in determining the meanings of the new words. Although this method of teaching requires some preparation and a little class time, learning how to determine word meaning is as important a vocabulary skill as learning specific meanings.

Morpheme analysis—Determining word meaning by looking at the meanings of parts of words to determine word meaning grows out of a knowledge of the meanings of prefixes and suffixes and of Greek and Latin roots.

Glossary use—Although many of the listed vocabulary words (marked *) appear in the glossary, use the glossary as only *one* of the vocabulary strategies. When the pronunciation is the issue, as it is for the word *bouquet*, the glossary is certainly useful.

Dictionary use—The ultimate vocabulary skill is a working access to word information in the dictionary. The listed vocabulary words that appear in *The Christian Student Dictionary*, available from BJU Press, are marked (†) to assist the teacher in determining appropriate times to use the dictionary as a strategy.

Remember that when you introduce vocabulary words in the manner described, you are teaching children strategies for learning words that will carry over into their independent reading. *Just telling them the meaning of a word does not teach these skills.*

Remedial vocabulary activities

Remedial service word review—Certain irregular, frequently used words need special attention. We call these words *service words*. A fluent reader is able to read these words instantly. Although phonetic analysis might give some hints about the word, such a word "breaks the rules" and therefore may need to be practiced by frequent exposure until the child can recognize it immediately.

A set of Service Word Cards is available from BJU Press for *READING 2 for Christian Schools*. On the back of each word card in the set there are three sample context sentences to use for practice. A list of the service words is included in the Appendix on page A7. The following activities can be used to provide additional practice.

Alphabet Soup
Materials
- Eight to twelve service word cards
- Large plastic bowl
- Stopwatch

Two students work together. Players place words in the plastic bowl and "stir." One player pulls out a word, reads it aloud, and begins placing the words in alphabetical order. He continues until all words are in alphabetical order. The partner times him. The players then switch roles. The player with the fastest time wins. (A student working alone may set a timer and keep records to try to beat his own time.)

Feed a Critter
Advance teacher preparation: *Decorate an empty shoebox to look like a critter such as a lion, a wide-mouth frog, or a pig. Cut a slit long enough for a word card to slide through one end of the box where the mouth of the critter will be.*

Materials
- Critter shoebox
- Ten to twenty service word cards

Students work in pairs or individually. The students place the service word cards word-side down in a pile. One student picks a service word card and reads it aloud. If the student reads the word correctly, he feeds the word to the critter. If he reads the word incorrectly he puts the card back into the pile. The students take turns until all the service word cards are fed to the critter.

Word Crunch
Materials
- Five service word cards for each student
- Writing paper

Students work in pairs or groups. Students place the service word cards word-side down in a pile. Each student chooses five service word cards. Each student writes as few sentences as possible while using all five words. The student with the fewest sentences using all five words wins. In the case of a tie, the student who finishes first wins. (A student working alone may simply try to see how many words he can get into a sentence, then read the sentence to someone else.)

Comprehension

Four levels of comprehension must be developed in young students. Every question in the comprehension section of the lesson plan is labeled with one of the levels.

1. *Literal*—The student locates and recalls information explicitly stated by the author.

2. *Interpretive*—The student draws inferences about what the author meant by what he wrote. He identifies concepts that the author implies about the characters, setting, or plot.

3. *Critical*—The student makes judgments about what the author said. He classifies information, develops the ability to relate the information read to other information, evaluates what is read, and draws conclusions.

4. *Appreciative*—The student responds to the content of the text and develops awareness of the author's skill with words and ideas.

Silent reading first

Teaching the life skill of reading silently for pleasure and understanding requires an emphasis on silent reading.

▶ Introduce the story and get your students thinking about it before you assign the silent reading.

▶ Before the silent reading, introduce any words that might stop a student's comprehension while he is reading silently.

▶ Base the length of the assigned silent reading portion on the reading ability of the students.

▶ Before your students read a portion silently, develop a purpose for reading by asking the motivation question in the lesson plan. Ask the question in a way that will make them anticipate something in the coming text.

Guided discussion (after silent reading)

To build comprehension, use the four levels of comprehension questions to guide discussion. In the lesson plan, questions that develop one line of thought are grouped to help the discussion flow naturally. The beginning of each group or cluster is indicated by an arrow.

▶ Each question should sound as though the teacher just thought of it as part of a natural conversation. (It should not sound like an oral quiz.) This atmosphere should generate thought, which is the foundation of comprehension.

▶ Not all of the questions need to be asked every day of every reading group. In circumstances where choices are appropriate, do not omit the questions that are highlighted. These highlighted questions are essential to building comprehension. If you ask only the highlighted question and the students cannot answer it, ask one of the questions preceding it or a question of your own to lead the students to answer the first question you asked.

▶ Use a variety of the comprehension levels. Each cluster of questions guides students to higher levels of thinking. Oral reading selections are included for the purpose of teaching students to

express the author's message to the audience.

▶ Answers provided to questions in the lesson plan are meant to serve as a guide and certainly do not have to be stated verbatim by the student. Instead, the answers should serve as guidelines for the teacher in eliciting responses. Cited Bible Action Truths and Bible Promises accompany questions that involve biblical or moral judgments. These aid the teacher in providing ways to guide children to God's truth.

Oral reading (with guided discussion)

Because writing is a code for speech, oral reading is more than just the decoding of phonemes. The oral reader is communicating the message of the author to an audience. The meaning and feeling of the text are expressed not only by the words but also by the tone, inflection, rhythm, pacing, and pitch of speech. For that reason the directed oral reading in the lesson is tied to the comprehension questions.

▶ Always let students read a word, a phrase, a sentence, or a page silently before you ask them to read it orally.

▶ Base your evaluation of a student's reading comprehension on how well he answers the comprehension questions rather than on his oral reading performance.

Although speech defects and certain word recognition skills can be diagnosed through oral reading, *evaluation should not be the main purpose of oral reading practice.*

Several plays in the student readers provide special opportunities for focus on building oral reading confidence. Children should enjoy reading aloud and do it with the purpose of communicating with the listener.

Flexible instruction

Because of the varying demands of reading groups, the lessons are designed to give the teacher flexibility during reading instruction.

Using the format of the questions

The lesson format includes Overview discussions and Follow-up discussions. The discussions can be tailored to meet the instructional level of each reading group.

Lower groups: Use the Overview discussion and all or most Follow-up discussion questions to develop students' awareness of main ideas and objectives.

Average groups: Because of time constraints, you may sometimes shorten the time in the reading group. Use the Overview discussion, the highlighted Follow-up discussion questions, and the read aloud requests with average readers. As necessary, use the other Follow-up discussion questions not highlighted to help students work up to critical ideas or objectives.

Upper groups: Because higher-level reading groups sometimes require less instruction, you may shorten the lesson from time to time by using the Overview discussion, a few of the highlighted Follow-up discussion questions, and some of the read aloud requests. This insures that the most important ideas are covered.

Note: When a reading group consists of exceptionally high-level readers or occasionally when the time is short, use only the Overview discussion questions and a few read aloud requests.

Using the silent reading segments

Some lessons contain more than one silent reading segment. The extra silent reading segment also allows the teacher to tailor the lesson to meet each reading group's needs.

Lower groups: Spend more time on lessons with struggling readers or lower groups. When a lesson contains more than one silent reading segment, take the first day to teach the first silent reading segment, and finish the lesson on the following day with the second silent reading segment. Review the vocabulary words for the lesson again on the second day of instruction.

Average groups: For average groups, complete the entire lesson in one day. Assign a silent reading segment, discuss it, then go on to the next silent reading segment in the lesson.

Upper groups: Higher-level reading groups could be assigned to read both silent reading segments in one sitting. In order to provide a purpose for reading both segments, first ask the Motivation questions from both silent reading segments.

Skill Station Days

Skill Station Days, designed for *whole-class* instruction, present focused teaching of the reading skills. Activities develop and apply comprehension, structural analysis, study skills, and literature skills. Listening activities provide background for teaching important comprehension skills and study skills.

Skill Station section of the Worktext

A special section in the worktext provides teaching material for the Skill Station Days. It is intended that this section remain in the worktext so that it also can be used as a reference for skill reteaching.

Skill Station lessons in the Teacher's Edition

As you proceed through the teacher's edition with your three ability groups of students, you may be flexible about when you teach a Skill Station lesson. The skill lessons appear in sequence with the reader lessons. If your advanced readers are far ahead of the other groups, you might want to wait and teach the skill lesson when the average group comes to it in the lesson sequence. You could also teach it on a day when scheduling constraints prevent you from devoting seventy-five minutes to reading instruction. (See the suggested daily schedule on page xxi.)

Teaching Visuals for Skill Station Days

Each Teaching Visual is introduced on a Skill Station Day. The Teaching Visual transparency is designed to be used with an overhead projector to introduce the entire class to the new skill. Later, when the same skill is reviewed in a reading group, it may be more convenient to use the paper copy that accompanies the transparency.

To extend the lifetime of the transparency, cover it with a clear acetate sheet and mark the acetate rather than the transparency when the lesson directs you to mark the transparency.

An index indicating the lessons in which each visual is used is available on Appendix page A7.

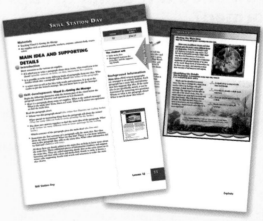

Ability/Achievement Grouping for Reading Instruction

Why group students for reading instruction?

Achievement grouping benefits all levels of readers in the class.

Limited readers

▶ Strengthen their skills as they progress at a pace that ensures success.

▶ Benefit from review and reteaching of subskills.

▶ Confidently interact and enjoy reading and discussion.

▶ Receive the additional time and guidance required for them to answer higher-level comprehension questions.

▶ Experience oral reading in the nonthreatening atmosphere of a smaller group.

▶ Benefit from additional class sessions. On whole-class lesson days (Skill Station Days) and other days when time constraints prevent all three reading groups from meeting, this group of readers may have a reading group lesson.

Average readers

▶ Receive more attention to their immediate and specific needs.

▶ Experience more participation in discussion.

Advanced readers

▶ Read and discuss at a level that challenges them.

▶ Direct their learning energy toward higher-level reading and thinking activities and enrichment experiences.

▶ Meet their needs *with greater dimensions of learning* rather than simply with a greater quantity of work.

Note that some students will be outside the continuum of groups, functioning above the highest level or below the lowest. It is possible for a student with very advanced reading ability to be instructed with the highest group of the class while receiving challenging projects in the areas where his interests lie. It is also possible for a reader who is more limited than the lowest level readers in the class to receive individual instruction in addition to reading with the lowest group.

How should reading groups be formed?

Use evidence from several sources to determine the grouping divisions in your class.

▶ Observe the silent reading skill of the student. The rate at which a child reads silently and finds the answer to an interpretive question tells you a great deal about how he will function in a group.

▶ Consult the test scores available to you in the student's permanent record. (These may overestimate actual instructional levels but will help you to look at a child in relationship to his classmates.)

▶ Administer an informal placement evaluation (IPE) such as the one provided in this teacher's edition. (See Informal Placement Evaluation on pages xxxvi–xxxviii.)

After you gather and record data, divide the students into temporary groups. Most classes divide naturally into three groups. (See previous note about students outside the continuum.) Usually efforts to have any more than three instruction groups result in frustration because of management concerns.

Start the school year by beginning all groups in the first lesson. As you determine the best instructional pace for each group, the advanced students will begin to move more quickly through the reader. The average students probably will complete a lesson a day. The limited students will move more slowly; it is important that they master the skills as they go rather than just "do the work" to keep up.

How should reading groups be managed?

Good classroom management is vital to the success of reading groups.

▶ Set aside a specific area of the classroom for group instruction. It should be out of high-traffic areas and away from the rest of the class. The teacher should be able to monitor the activities of the rest of the class without leaving the group.

▶ Arrange the reading group in a semicircle or at a table, facing the teacher. Students should also have a clear view of the chalkboard or a pocket chart.

▶ Provide adequate storage for materials near the reading area.

▶ Make a schedule. Reading groups may meet in succession or may be interspersed with other lessons, but the scheduled time and the duration should be as consistent as possible. Twenty-five to thirty minutes of instruction time for each group is a reasonable expectation. (See page xxi for a suggested daily schedule.)

▶ Establish routine behaviors for the reading group. Train the students to come and go promptly and quietly and to manage materials properly.

▶ Provide activities that profitably engage the other students in the class while you meet with reading groups. Each lesson plan refers to correlated activities located in the Classroom Management for Grouping section of the Appendix, beginning on page A10.

▶ Rotate activities for the three groups. Designate a specific activity for each group. One group is with you in the reading group area, another group does the correlated activities mentioned above, and the third group is at their desks with quiet work (worktext or independent reading). When you announce the next reading group, rotate the activities.

What cautions should be observed?

Grouping should be flexible. Some students will make substantial gains, and others will reveal some weaknesses as instruction progresses. Groups should be changed or varied accordingly. Despite any inconvenience, a student will benefit from being reassigned to a group that better suits his ability.

▸ Regrouping can be accomplished smoothly by observing the structure of the lessons and the natural divisions of the school year. Transition of individual students between groups may be accomplished smoothly by allowing the student to meet with both groups for a short time. He should not, however, be required to do the written assignments for both groups.

▸ The same time and attention should be given to planning and instruction for each group even though groups are reading different stories at different times. Lessons should be adapted to differing abilities. Likewise, each group should receive an equal amount of positive reinforcement.

▸ Grouping does not eliminate the necessity for addressing individual instructional needs. There will be occasions when it is desirable to challenge or provide remediation for some individuals in addition to their group instruction.

What about attitude and group placement?

Student attitude toward ability groups is influenced by the teacher. Social stigma and labeling of "smart" and "dumb" students are not inevitable, but these attitudes can be "caught" from the teacher. There are several things you can do to alleviate this.

▸ Think of the most limited readers as your "favorite" group. Save the best motivational ideas for when it is their turn to read the story. (For example, if you plan to bring cowboy items to introduce a story, save the hat or the silver spurs to show only to this group when they begin reading the story.)

▸ Transition of students between groups should be accomplished discreetly so that no student feels demoted.

Making reading group instruction and activities equally attractive to all the groups is of great importance. Plan exciting reading activities for each group to enjoy.

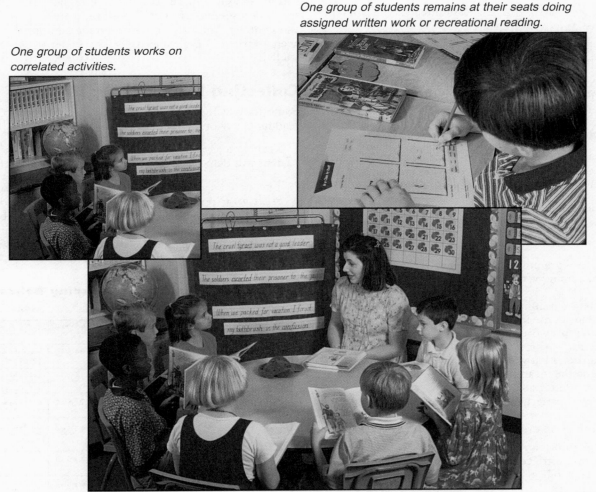

One group of students remains at their seats doing assigned written work or recreational reading.

One group of students works on correlated activities.

One group of students has the full attention of the teacher for guided reading.

Assessing and Evaluating Reading Progress

Every teacher struggles with the question "How do I arrive at a reading grade?" Grading reading is part of the big picture of evaluation, which is done for many reasons.

It is important to define some terms which are needed in any discussion of evaluation.

▶ *Assessment* is collecting evidence of learning.

▶ *Evaluation* is judging carefully all the evidence collected.

▶ *Grading* is assigning a mark that stands for a level of accomplishment. It often involves making a comparison to an accepted standard.

▶ *Reporting* is giving a presentation of the evidence of learning.

Who needs to know?

A good teacher evaluates constantly. At the beginning of the school year, assessments are carried out to determine grouping for instruction. (See pages xvi-xxii, Ability/Achievement Grouping for Reading Instruction.) As each teaching day comes to a close, the teacher may simply look at a set of student papers to determine whether or not his teaching has been effective. Finally, the teacher faces the challenging task of determining a grade for a report card or a permanent record for the purpose of documenting the progress of students.

Evaluation that leads to a grade communicates the student's progress to others.

▶ The *student* will understand his progress.

▶ The *parent* will understand his child's progress so that he can be supportive.

▶ The *administrator* will be able to interpret the process and product of assessment.

Silent reading—Why is it hard to evaluate?

Because silent reading is a skill that takes place in the mind it is not easy to evaluate. However, the teacher can observe oral and written responses that give clues to silent reading ability.

The teacher can observe whether the student

▶ Demonstrates apparent use of available cuing systems for unknown words.

1. Syntactic cues—grammar in a sentence
   Is this word a noun, verb, adjective, or other part of speech?
2. Semantic cues—meaning of other words in a sentence
   Are there clues in the meaning of words nearby to help me determine this word?
3. Schematic cues—prior knowledge about story content
   What background knowledge do I have that might help me determine the meaning of this word?
4. Phonics cues—letter-sound associations
   Do the phonics patterns and rules help me to determine this word?

▶ Evidences information processing.

1. Ability to get information from the text
2. Ability to store, retrieve, and integrate information
3. Ability to make logical predictions and inferences

▶ Applies metacognitive skills.

Simply stated, *metacognition is knowing about what you do and do*

not know. Does the reader have the ability to judge what he knows and does not know? Does the reader know when a word does not make sense, and does he self-correct? Does he know when to ignore and read on, when to form a prediction, when to reread the current sentence, and when to reread the previous context?

Oral reading—What do you look for?

When measuring oral reading, it is important to look at *communication* skills and not just *word recognition* skills.

Strong oral reading

▶ sounds like normal speech.

▶ demonstrates phrasing and pace that match the meaning of the text.

▶ uses pitch and tone that interpret the text.

Written responses

Most teachers rely on the student worktext for a portion of the reading grade. The teacher's edition of the student worktext indicates a variety of pages that are useful for evaluation. These pages have been selected at the point when mastery of a skill is expected rather than during the initial teaching of a skill. Worktext pages focusing on the literal and interpretive level are indicated for evaluation, as well as pages emphasizing higher-level thinking skills, such as cause-and-effect relationships, main idea, and comparison and contrast. You may choose to grade additional pages. Plan to keep a variety of evaluated pages in a folder or portfolio for each student.

Collecting the evidence

Some tools will help focus the teacher's observation on specific reading behaviors.

1. Keeping a *portfolio* or folder of these assessments for each student will help the grading process and parent conferences.

2. The dated comments on the *Informal Checklist of Reading Behaviors* (Appendix page A31) provide a framework for focusing your observations. Although this looks like a big task, most teachers can get adequate information by evaluating only a few students each day. (See the sample checklist below.)

Informal Checklist of Reading Behaviors

Name: Brian Hill Grade: 4 Reading Group: 1

Date	Skill	Task	Rating (10 is excellent)	Comments
			SILENT READING	
10/8	Literal thinking	Recalls explicitly stated facts, ideas, details, and sequence of events	1 2 3 4 5 6 7 8 9 ⑩	Brian's attention to details in life carries over into his reading.
	Interpretive thinking (vocabulary)	Explains word meaning in own words. Uses the four cuing systems to gain meaning of unknown words	1 2 3 4 5 6 7 ⑧ 9 10	After several scaffolding questions Brian figured out what a plaintiff is.
11/4	Interpretive thinking	Infers main ideas and key concepts in paragraphs and stories. Logically predicts coming events	1 2 3 4 5 6 7 ⑧ 9 10	It's hard for Brian to get past the stated details.
11/15	Critical thinking	Makes perceptive judgments about character thoughts, feelings, actions, and motives. Compares actions and thoughts of characters to biblical principles	1 2 3 4 5 6 7 8 ⑨ 10	Yes! Today Brian evaluated the main character's motive thoughtfully.
12/5	Appreciative thinking	Relates story events and characters to real life	1 2 3 4 5 6 7 8 9 10	
	Appreciative thinking	Is increasingly aware of the author's literary skill. Notices figurative language, vivid description, or compelling action	1 2 3 4 5 6 7 8 9 10	
			ORAL READING	
	Word recognition	Reads without defaults and self-corrects miscues smoothly	1 2 3 4 5 6 7 8 9 10	
	Communication	Conveys meaning of the text to listener(s)		

3. The dated observations on the *Individual Anecdotal Record* (Appendix page A32) provide less of a framework, but this tool allows more space for all your observations and impressions. Because of time constraints, most teachers use either a checklist or an anecdotal record, perhaps at different times during the school year. (See the sample record below.)

Individual Anecdotal Record

Name *Mary Knight*   Grade *4*   Reading Group *3*

Date	Comments	Prescription
9/11	*Unable to get the connection between a shoelace and the way an airstrip looked from the sky. (interpretive skill)*	*Use more concrete material (a map and shoelace)*
9/15	*Read mother's words with a "sigh" in her voice to show sadness (reading orally to communicate meaning)*	
9/22	*Mary did not know*	

What weight does each aspect have?

The teacher and administrator usually decide together what proportion of the grade to assign to each aspect of the reading process.

Silent Reading Comprehension

For observation of silent reading results, use the Informal Checklist of Reading Behaviors or the Individual Anecdotal Record.

Oral Reading

For observation of oral reading, use the Informal Checklist of Reading Behaviors or the Individual Anecdotal Record.

Written Responses

For assessment of written responses, use designated worktext pages.

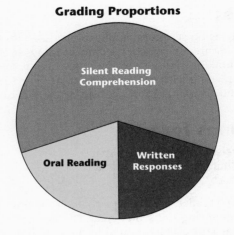

Grading Proportions

Silent Reading Comprehension

Oral Reading

Written Responses

Getting Parents Involved in Reading Development

How parents can help

What do you do when a parent asks, "How can I help my child become a good reader?" Reading outside the classroom is an essential ingredient for his success, but this extra reading does not need to take the traditional homework format. There are many suggestions you can give to all parents.

> *Read to your child.*
> *Visit the library.*
> *Read the newspaper with him.*
> *Ask your child to read to other family members.*
> *Encourage meaningful writing.*
> *Show interest in his school papers.*
> *Be enthusiastic about the stories in his reader.*
> *Talk about authors.*

A Message to Parents

The above list, accompanied by more specific ideas, is provided in "A Message to Parents" on page 327 of the student worktext. As a teacher you can encourage activities such as those given in the letter by following up on some of them at school. For book reports and class sharing, allow the children to use the books their parents have read to them. Invite the students to present to the reading group or the class the newspaper articles they have read with their parents.

What about homework?

After a student, especially a struggling reader, has finished reading and discussing a story in your class, send the story home with him. Include a note that tells which story the child should share. Include specific ideas of how the parent can best use the story at home.

▶ Encourage your child to read all or part of the story again silently for himself.

▶ Select parts with ample dialogue and read just the conversation with your child as a "play."

▶ Ask your child to read the most exciting paragraphs aloud. Praise him specifically if he makes you hear the character's voice, if he communicates fear or other emotions, or if he changes the pace or pauses to show suspense.

Parents are good partners. If you will recommend activities that become part of the family life rather than cause "school day" activities to spill over into the home and take from family time, most parents will eagerly cooperate with you.

BJ BookLinks

BJ BookLinks are individual units based on full-length, grade-level-appropriate novels published by BJU Press. They provide reading instruction and experiences that broaden and deepen the ability of students to comprehend, analyze, synthesize, and evaluate what they read.

Contents

- Pocket folder printed with complete directions for enrichment activities
- Teacher's guide with carefully planned lessons, enrichment activities, and reproducible work pages

Strategies

The lessons focus on scriptural applications that help build character and discernment, teach specific reading strategies and higher-level thinking skills, foster an appreciation for literature, and integrate reading with other subject areas. The suggested experiences include cooking, games, music, art, and crafts.

Suggestions for use

The three novels chosen for fourth grade represent a range of ability levels and literature genres. Several options may be considered for their use.

▶ The advanced readers read two or three of the novels at appropriate points during the school year, the average readers read the one or two novels most suited to their abilities at appropriate points, and the limited readers read only the least difficult of the novels (*Sheriff at Waterstop*) toward the end of the school year.

▶ All groups read the same novel at different points in the school year with adjustments in pacing and teaching strategies made for varying abilities.

▶ All groups read the least difficult novel at the end of the school year with appropriate adjustments made for varying abilities.

Sheriff at Waterstop, Level 1

It's 1870, and Bret Jensen and his parents have just arrived in the small town of Waterstop, Wyoming. Since Waterstop doesn't have a sheriff, it looks like Pa is the man to clean up the town. Watching Pa, Bret learns to appreciate his father's trust in the Lord, and he takes a guarded look at his own relationship with God. (BJU Press product numbers: novel—031443; teacher's set with novel—121046)

Medallion, Level 2

Sure of his rights to the throne and disgusted with the selfish uncle who reigns in his stead, Prince Trave must prove himself by winning the gold medallion. This fantasy adventure creates an avenue to address the themes of humility versus pride, reality versus appearance, and good versus evil. (BJU Press product numbers: novel—023523; teacher's set with novel—121020)

Mountain Born, Level 3

Wolves, weather, a black lamb, a trusty dog—all are part of Peter's life on a mountain farm. His best friend, Benj, a wise old shepherd, teaches Peter to care for a sprightly lamb. As the lamb grows into her place as leader of the flock, Peter grows too, learning the skills and joys of the shepherd's life. (BJU Press product numbers: novel—072108; teacher's set with novel—120618)

Suggested Daily Schedule

Time	Activity
15 minutes	Preparation for the day (attendance, lunch count, opening exercises)
30 minutes	Bible/Chapel
50-60 minutes	Reading: two groups (or a whole-class Skill Station lesson)
15 minutes	Recess, restroom
25-30 minutes	Reading: one group*
25-30 minutes	Spelling/Handwriting
25-30 minutes	Writing and Grammar
45 minutes	Lunch, restroom, recess
10-15 minutes	Read-aloud story time
35-40 minutes	Math
30 minutes	Heritage Studies/Science
30 minutes	Music/Physical Education/Art

*Weakest reading group (limited readers) meets every day, even Skill Station Days.

Table of Lesson Plans

Bible Truths	Comprehension Skills	Other Skills
2a Obedience 5a Love 6b Prayer 8a Faith in God's promises 8d Courage	evaluating character responses identifying problems and solutions relating lesson content to personal experience generalizing about characters from actions	**Literature:** focusing on the author's use of descriptive verbs noting the author's use of flashback

2c Responsibility
4c Honesty
4d Victory
5a Thankfulness
6b Prayer
8a Faith in God's promises
8d Courage
	drawing inferences from picture and text interpretation
	recognizing character growth and change
	relating story content to biblical truth: we can overcome fear
	    when we trust in God
	sequencing story events
		Literature:
		inferring differences between characters
		recognizing character development through actions and
		    speech

		Literature: recognizing free verse identifying figurative language identifying onomatopoeia noting author's choice of words classifying onomatopoeic words **Composition:** completing a free verse poem using onomatopoeia

		Literature:
		recognizing that the setting of the story tells where and
		    when the story takes place
		recognizing that the setting can affect the actions of the
		    characters

2e Work 5a Love 6b Prayer 7d Contentment 8a Faith in God's promises	developing an awareness of mood evaluating character responses identifying problems and solutions predicting outcomes identifying imagery inferring size relationships following directions	
2a Obedience 2b Servanthood 2b Helpfulness 3c Emotional control 6b Prayer 8a Faith in God's promises	noting how character actions reveal character traits evaluating emotional responses of characters relating story content to biblical truth: a Christian should love and help others identifying problems and solutions	**Vocabulary:** using context cues to determine word meaning
2b Teamwork 2e Diligence 2e Thoroughness 6b Prayer 7c Praise 8a Faith in God's promises	noting how character actions reveal character traits evaluating emotional responses of characters relating story content to biblical truth: a Christian should trust the Lord and ask Him for help during times of trouble identifying problems and solutions determining cause-and-effect relationships	**Study skills:** relating biblical truth to personal experience locating verses in the Bible relating to God's promises
	identifying main ideas distinguishing between relevant and irrelevant information identifying information explicitly stated reading for specific information	**Study skills:** reading a map scale determining distance using a map scale drawing a map that includes physical features, a map key, and a map scale
		Literature: defining plot as a sequence of events sequencing the events of a plot identifying the beginning, middle, and end of the story defining conflict as a problem in a story that must be solved identifying the conflict of a plot
5a Love 5a Kindness 5b Giving 5e Loyalty	determining the emotional responses of characters interpreting idiomatic expressions	**Literature:** noting the author's use of imagery **Vocabulary:** matching synonyms using context cues to determine meaning
5a Love 5e Friendliness	identifying character traits discerning motives of characters matching characters and dialogue	**Literature:** noting the author's use of foreshadowing

Bible Truths	Comprehension Skills	Other Skills
		Study skills: inferring main idea distinguishing between the main idea and the supporting details
2e Work 6b Prayer	determining sequence of events	**Literature:** recognizing the author's use of figurative language recognizing the author's use of humor **Vocabulary:** determining meaning from context matching words and definitions
	recognizing the setting through the author's description understanding characters' perspectives recognizing a simile's meaning recalling facts and details	**Literature:** determining conflicts and their solutions **Composition:** writing a solution to a conflict
3c Self-control 5a Kindness	identifying information not explicitly stated reading for specific information recalling likenesses and differences drawing conclusions	**Study skills:** writing and using captions to clarify content reading and organizing facts and details
4c Honesty		**Study skills:** identifying relevant and irrelevant information: words, topics, and sentences
	discerning characters' motives identifying characters' attitudes identifying place relationships interpreting a foreign setting inferring ideas not explicitly stated recalling facts and details	**Vocabulary:** developing vocabulary related to the Yukon
8a Faith in God's promises 8d Courage	predicting outcomes recognizing character growth and change drawing conclusions evaluating character motives and attitudes identifying cause-and-effect relationships inferring cause-and-effect relationships inferring unstated supporting details	**Vocabulary:** developing vocabulary related to the Yukon
	identifying exaggerations in a tall tale identifying fanciful elements in a tall tale interpreting an idiomatic expression recognizing the humor and fun in a tall tale identifying the conflict in a story plot matching story characters and dialogue predicting dialogue	**Vocabulary:** matching words and meanings developing vocabulary related to cowboy life
4c Honesty	developing a sense of literary heritage using comparisons to describe an object recognizing and identifying character traits and motives	**Literature:** identifying the elements of a tall tale developing an awareness of the author's use of imagery
2e Initiative 8d Courage	recognizing the motives of characters recognizing the character trait of courage predicting outcomes	**Literature:** sequencing story events identifying plot structure recognizing the author's techniques in revealing characters through their actions and dialogue
		Structural analysis: dividing words into syllables between the consonants in the *VC/CV* pattern identifying consonant digraphs recognizing that consonant digraphs are treated as one consonant in the *VC/CV* pattern
2c Faithfulness 2e Initiative 3b Mind 3c Emotional control 4c Honesty 8d Courage	identifying problems and solutions noting how character actions reveal character traits inferring unstated supporting details following directions	**Literature:** noting the author's use of descriptive words **Vocabulary:** defining vocabulary using context cues

Bible Truths	Comprehension Skills	Other Skills
		Literature: recognizing limerick form identifying rhyming words recognizing the poet's use of humor completing a limerick
		Literature: defining the term *moral* determining the moral of a story
2e Work 4c Honesty 4d Victory 5b Giving 5e Friendliness 6c Spirit-filled 6d Clear conscience 6e Forgiveness 8d Courage	demonstrating understanding of the author's message: it is never right to be dishonest identifying problems and solutions recognizing the changing of a character in the course of action inferring character motives evaluating character responses inferring unstated supporting details	**Oral reading:** reading orally with varied voice inflection to portray emotion
		Structural analysis: dividing compound words into syllables between the base words identifying primary and secondary accents in compound words placing the primary accent mark on or within the first base word of a compound word placing the secondary accent mark on or within the second base word of a compound word
1a Understanding Jesus Christ 1b Repentance and faith 2a Obedience 5c Evangelism and missions 6b Prayer 6c Spirit-filled 7a Grace 8a Faith in God's promises 8d Courage A. Liberty from Sin B. Guiltless by the Blood D. Identified in Christ H. God as Father	recognizing character growth and change understanding God's plan of salvation identifying facts and details	**Oral reading:** conveying the meaning of Scripture using volume and pacing to communicate meaning using tone of voice to convey emotion demonstrating self-confidence in oral reading **Literature:** discriminating between fiction and nonfiction
		Study skills: recognizing the dictionary as a valuable source of information identifying a biographical dictionary identifying a geographical dictionary identifying a Bible dictionary noting some special features of a dictionary
I. God as Master	appreciating the relevance of a story title developing a sense of history inferring the author's purpose reading for information identifying facts and opinions	**Structural analysis:** dividing compound words into syllables identifying the accented syllable of compound words
2d Dedication 2d Determination 3c Emotional control 5a Love 5a Compassion 5b Unselfishness 5c Evangelism and missions 5e Friendliness	determining emotional responses of characters inferring character traits from dialogue interpreting meanings of idioms recognizing the use of fiction to illuminate historical fact interpreting words in a nonliteral way interpreting dialect inferring facts and details	**Literature:** demonstrating an understanding of the author's use of colloquial language **Vocabulary:** matching words and meanings
		Study skills: recognizing the glossary as a valuable source of information recognizing the parts of a glossary identifying a pronunciation key using a pronunciation key

Bible Truths	Comprehension Skills	Other Skills
2b Helpfulness 2b Promptness 2c Faithfulness 2d Perseverance 3c Emotional control	noting elements of setting evaluating character responses predicting outcomes drawing inferences from picture interpretation and text recognizing facts and details inferring unstated supporting details	
2b Helpfulness 2b Teamwork 3c Emotional control 5a Love 5a Kindness 7d Contentment	identifying problems and solutions determining sequence of events interpreting actions of characters recognizing dialect as part of the setting identifying facts and details suggesting solutions to problem situations	
5a Love	evaluating emotional responses of characters developing an awareness of imagery developing an awareness of mood identifying cause-and-effect relationships recalling facts and details inferring unstated supporting details	
1a Understanding Jesus Christ 1b Repentance and faith 2f Cheerfulness 7c Thankfulness to God	recognizing folksongs as part of American literature heritage associating folksongs with cultural and regional groups interpreting the song "Were You There?" identifying facts and details relating types of folksongs to specific groups of people	
2c Responsibility 2d Goal setting 2d Perseverance 2e Diligence 2e Initiative 4c Honesty 6a Bible study 6d Clear conscience	interpreting the significance of the story title interpreting the motives of characters comparing a character's actions with his personal convictions evaluating character responses and choices noting how character actions reveal character traits	
2a Obedience 4c Honesty 6b Prayer 6d Clear conscience 6e Forgiveness 8a Faith in God's promises 8b Faith in the power of the Word of God C. Basis for Prayer	recognizing character growth and change relating story content to personal experience evaluating a character's response identifying with a character relating story content to biblical truth: it is always important to tell the truth recalling facts and details recognizing character traits	Study skills: locating Bible verses applying biblical principles
		Structural analysis: dividing into syllables words ending with a consonant + *le* dividing words with *ck* + *le* into syllables after the *ck* dividing words with the *VC/CV* pattern into syllables dividing compound words into syllables between the two base words
2b Teamwork 3a Self-concept	evaluating emotional responses of characters recognizing first-person point of view discerning motives of a character identifying conflicting points of view predicting outcomes	Study skills: using the glossary to build vocabulary
2a Authority 2c Responsibility 2d Goal setting 3c Flexibility 6c Patience	developing an awareness of a change in a character discerning the motives of characters recognizing character traits of leadership and responsibility identifying character traits making inferences applying punctuation	Literature: noticing the author's use of foreshadowing
3c Self-control 5a Kindness 5a Thoughtfulness 5e Friendliness 7d Contentment	evaluating the emotional responses of characters recognizing character growth and change relating story content to personal experience interpreting a cliché predicting outcomes recalling facts and details inferring unstated supporting details	Composition: writing and illustrating a description of a play

Bible Truths	Comprehension Skills	Other Skills
	determining whether statements are fact or opinion	
	perceiving time relationships inferring unstated facts and details recalling story details	**Study skills:** finding the main idea of a paragraph recognizing the main idea of a paragraph locating supporting details of a paragraph supplying supporting details in an outline
	recognizing a diagram noting the purpose for diagrams reading for information	**Study skills:** reading a diagram for information
2a Authority 5a Compassion 8d Courage	inferring attitude from the actions of the characters demonstrating enjoyment of fantasy distinguish between realistic fiction and fanciful fiction	**Literature:** recognizing the author's use of imagery understanding similes
2b Servanthood 4c Fairness 5a Love 5b Unselfishness 8d Courage	identifying fanciful elements in a story differentiating between realistic fiction and fanciful fiction identifying actions and traits of the characters in the story identifying conflicting points of view recalling facts and details	**Vocabulary:** matching words and definitions
2b Teamwork 5a Thankfulness	recognizing character growth and change	**Literature:** identifying characteristics of a fantasy **Vocabulary:** matching words and definitions
		Structural analysis: dividing words with affixes into syllables between the base words recognizing that the suffix -ed is in a separate syllable after base words that end with /d/ and /t/ recognizing that the suffix -es is a separate syllable after base words that end with ch, sh, s, x, or z placing the primary accent mark on or within the base word of a word with an affix placing the primary accent on the first syllable of a two-syllable word or on the second syllable when that syllable contains two vowels
2a Authority	relating story content to biblical truth: obey those in authority	**Literature:** recognizing the author's use of imagery to create setting recognizing the author's use of suspense to maintain the interest of the reader **Study skills:** reading a map using a map scale following directions
	determining the origin of the chapter title	**Literature:** noting the author's use of imagery to convey emotion **Structural analysis:** dividing words with the VC/CV pattern into syllables dividing words ending with a consonant + le into syllables **Vocabulary:** discerning meaning from context **Oral reading:** reading orally to convey emotion
8d Courage	recognizing the character trait of courage reading orally to convey the character's emotions identifying cause-and-effect relationships inferring unstated supporting details identifying facts and details following directions	**Literature:** noting the author's use of similes **Study skills:** reading a schedule

Bible Truths	Comprehension Skills	Other Skills
		Study skills: recognizing charts as a format for comparing information efficiently reading and interpreting information on a chart
	interpreting the concise language of haiku	**Literature:** recognizing the author's use of imagery recognizing the author's use of alliteration recognizing the elements of haiku **Composition:** writing haiku
1a Understanding Jesus Christ 5a Love 6b Prayer 7a Grace H. God as Father I. God as Master	identifying emotional responses of characters making comparisons relating story content to biblical truths: God gives grace to the needy; God is sovereign matching characters with actions and dialogue	**Literature:** recognizing first-person point of view
		Structural analysis: recognizing that schwa syllables have various spellings recognizing that the accent never falls on a syllable with a schwa sound identifying the accented syllable in words with a schwa sound dividing words with the *VC/CV* pattern into syllables dividing compound words into syllables dividing words with affixes into syllables dividing words ending with a consonant + *le* into syllables
5c Evangelism and missions 6a Bible study 6b Prayer I. God as Master	recognizing the use of fiction to illuminate historical facts recognizing the genre of biblical fiction	**Literature:** recognizing the author's techniques of revealing the characters through conversation and thoughts **Study skills:** locating verses in the Bible matching Bible characters with actions
2a Obedience 5a Kindness 6b Prayer 6e Forgiveness E. Christ as Sacrifice I. God as Master	demonstrating understanding of characters' perspectives discerning the motives of characters relating story content to biblical truths: God is holy; God forgives; God is just	
	recognizing the use of biblical fiction to illuminate biblical facts distinguishing biblical events from historical fiction details distinguishing biblical truth from error distinguishing fact from fiction	**Literature:** recognizing the author's use of details to create setting recognizing the author's use of historical research to plan a story plot recognizing that plot and setting build an understanding of Scripture in biblical fiction **Study skills:** completing a Venn diagram
2b Servanthood 2e Work 5a Love 7d Contentment	using a chapter title to predict story content	**Literature:** recognizing the author's use of the characters' speech and actions to reveal their traits **Study skills:** using a glossary labeling a diagram **Vocabulary:** matching words and definitions writing sentences to convey word meaning
2e Initiative 4a Sowing and reaping 4b Purity 4c Fairness 8d Courage	recognizing good and evil elements in a story recalling facts and details inferring unstated supporting details drawing conclusions	**Literature:** identifying the author's use of similes identifying good and evil in a story identifying the moral of a story **Study skills:** locating verses in the Bible **Oral reading:** reading orally to portray character traits
		Study skills: recognizing a time line as a concise, visual tool for organizing and recording time-related information demonstrating understanding of the term *interval* recognizing a time line as a way to relate one event to another interpreting time lines

Bible Truths	Comprehension Skills	Other Skills
2d Perseverance 6c Patience 8d Courage H. God as Father	demonstrating an understanding of the author's message: the people of France suffered during World War II drawing conclusions from information explicitly stated reading and writing captions recalling facts and details from expository writing	**Study skills:** reading a map
3c Emotional control 5a Love		**Literature:** identifying propaganda recognizing propaganda's impact on the reader
2b Teamwork 2c Responsibility 2e Initiative	inferring the motives of characters relating the story to World War II recognizing first-person point of view demonstrating understanding of the author's message: be responsible for your own work matching characters with dialogue	**Literature:** recognizing the author's use of simile and metaphor
8a Faith in God's promises 8d Courage H. God as Father	demonstrating understanding of biblical truths: trust God to take care of you; God loves you more than anyone else does	**Literature:** recognizing the author's techniques of revealing setting through characters' actions **Structural analysis:** dividing words into syllables between the base word and suffix placing the accent mark on the syllable preceding the ending *-sion* or *-tion*
7c Praise 8a Faith in God's promises 8d Courage I. God as Master	discerning the motives of characters demonstrating understanding of the author's message: obstacles can be overcome through faith in God identifying solutions to problems in the story	**Literature:** recognizing the author's use of simile **Vocabulary:** matching words and definitions determining word meaning from context
		Study skills: using an encyclopedia identifying the encyclopedia volume containing a keyword identifying parts of an encyclopedia article skimming to locate information determining a keyword for a given idea understanding the use of subtitles in expository writing matching subtitles with information developing skill for reading expository text
2a Obedience 2b Servanthood 2c Faithfulness 5b Unselfishness 5c Evangelism and missions 6a Bible study 6b Prayer 8a Faith in God's promises H. God as Father	comparing and contrasting information drawing conclusions using context to determine word meaning demonstrating understanding of the author's messages: missionaries desire to follow God's leading; missionaries are not "perfect" Christians locating information explicitly stated developing sentence closure	**Study skills:** reading a map
3e Unity of Christ and the church 5a Compassion 5c Evangelism and missions 6a Bible study 6a Reverence for the Bible 7a Grace 7b Exaltation of Christ 8a Faith in God's promises E. Christ as Sacrifice I. God as Master	demonstrating understanding of biblical truths: God is love; God is sovereign; God answers prayer recalling facts and details inferring unstated supporting details drawing conclusions	**Literature:** recognizing the author's use of description and imagery to create setting
		Structural analysis: recognizing that adding suffixes to some words may cause the primary accent to shift to the syllable before the suffix recognizing that a shift in accent often occurs when the meaning of a word changes

Informal Placement Evaluation (IPE)

IPE Instructions

For purposes of initial grouping, the informal placement evaluation (IPE) can be administered during the first few weeks of the school year. If necessary, another one may be administered about midyear.

Preparation

Gather the materials

▶ Prepare a copy of one of the reading passages on page xxxviii for the student to read. Use "Backpacking in Yellowstone National Park" at the beginning of the school year and, if needed, "Night Hunters" in the middle of the year.

▶ Prepare one copy of the corresponding Appendix page—A33 ("Backpacking in Yellowstone National Park") or A34 ("Night Hunters")—for each student. This will be the copy that you use for marking and recording results.

▶ Have available a cassette recorder to record the oral reading portion of the IPE (optional).

▶ Provide independent activities for the students while they wait their turn to be tested.

Prepare for miscue marking

Study the miscue markings given below so that you can mark the copy of the reading passage easily as each student reads. (You may prefer to record the students as they read orally and to mark the passage later. This method, however, adds to the time spent on evaluation.)

1. **Omissions:** Circle the word or letter(s) omitted.
   Example: *Child said, "The cat chased birds."*

   The cat chased ⟨the⟩ birds.

2. **Additions:** Insert word with a caret.
   Example: *Child said, "The cat he chased the birds."*

   The cat ^*he* chased the birds.

3. **Substitutions:** Draw a line through the word and write in the word that was substituted.
   Example: *Child said, "The cat caught the birds."*

   The cat ~~chased~~ *caught* the birds.

4. **Mispronunciations:** Draw a line through the word and write the mispronunciation above the word.
   Example: *Child said, "The cat chassed the birds."*

   The cat ~~chased~~ *chassed* the birds.

5. **Reversals:** Draw the transposition symbol.
   Example: *Child said, "The chased cat the birds."*

   The cat/chased the birds.

6. **Repetitions:** For two or more words, draw a wavy line under the repeated words.
   Example: *Child said, "The cat chased cat chased the birds."*

   The cat chased the birds.

7. **Words aided (defaults):** After five seconds, provide the word for the child and cross it out.
   Example: *Child said, "The cat . . ."*

   The cat ~~chased~~ the birds.

(*NOTE:* Do not mark a student's self-corrections that occur within five seconds or mispronunciations due to dialect or a speech impediment. Do not mark the same mispronounced word more than once in the passage.)

Administering the IPE

Beginning the testing session

▶ Allow enough time (approximately fifteen minutes per student) to administer the IPE.

▶ Make sure the other students are fully occupied and understand that they are not to interrupt while you are working with individuals.

▶ Set the student at ease. Make your marking and recording as unobtrusive as possible. If you are recording his oral reading, mention it casually.

▶ Place the copy of the reading passage in front of the student ("Backpacking in Yellowstone National Park" or "Night Hunters" from page xxxviii).

Part 1: Oral reading

▶ Ask the student to read the passage *orally*. Begin optional recording. As he reads aloud the passage, mark his miscues on the copy of the corresponding Appendix page (A33 or A34) that you have prepared for keeping his record.

▶ Count one point for each miscue.

▶ On the oral reading level form below the reading passage on the Appendix page, record the total number of miscues.

Part 2: Silent Reading/Comprehension

▶ Ask the student to read the passage *silently*.

▶ Ask the comprehension questions orally (from the Appendix page). The student should not have the opportunity to look back at the passage. Mark an *X* beside each question that the student answers incorrectly.

▶ On the comprehension level form at the bottom of the Appendix page, circle the total number of incorrect answers.

Using the results

Interpreting the IPE

The inventory should not be used for grading purposes, nor should it become a part of a student's permanent record. It is intended to be used as one of the tools the classroom teacher may use to group or regroup the students in the classroom for instructional purposes. It may also be used to determine whether a student needs individual help or referral for more formal testing. An explanation of the three reading levels, along with a sample of an individual student record, follows.

Reading Levels

▶ **Frustration**—the student has difficulty performing at the tested level.
▶ **Instructional**—the student performs at the tested level.
▶ **Independent**—the student performs with little help at the tested level.

Oral Reading Level Form

Oral Reading Level	Miscues Allowed	Actual Miscues
Independent	0-4	
Instructional: High	5-10	
Instructional: Average	11-16	
Instructional: Low	17-20	
(Frustration)	21+	*22*

Comprehension Level Form

# of incorrect answers	Comprehension Level
0	Independent at 4.0
1-2	Instructional at 4.0
(3+)	(Frustration) at 4.0

Comments ___*had trouble keeping the place*___

Check for tracking problems.

Forming the groups

Divide the students into groups according to reading level. As you evaluate the inventory results, factor in each student's speed of effective silent reading as you observed it. Keep in mind that the comprehension result should carry more weight than the oral reading result. A sample of a reading group list follows.

Student	Oral	Comprehension	Group
1. Scott	*Independent*	*Instructional*	*2*
2. Jesse	*Instructional: Average*	*Instructional*	*2*
3. Sarah	*Independent*	*Independent*	*1*
4. Katie	*Frustration*	*Frustration*	*3*
5. Lauren	*Instructional: Low*	*Frustration*	*3*
6. Amy	*Independent*	*Independent**	*1**
7. Justin	*Frustration*	*Frustration*	*3**
8. Rachel	*Instructional: Low*	*Instructional*	
9. Megan	*Independent*		
10. Paul	*Frustration*		
11. Jennifer	*Independent*		
12. Jonathan	*Instructional*		
13. Ben	*Independent*		

Note: The testing procedures described here are not to be confused with teaching strategies. *In the silent reading/discussion teaching strategy, a student never reads orally before he reads silently. When this teaching strategy is used, silent reading always precedes the discussion of the selection, and oral reading is an integral part of this discussion.*

Backpacking in Yellowstone National Park

Imagine camping in grizzly bear country. Bob and Sam Perry did. They went on a backpacking trip into the wilderness. The park ranger told them to hide all their food in a tree several hundred yards away from their tent. He also suggested that they sleep near a good climbing tree. Bob and Sam adhered to the ranger's advice and looked for good climbing trees. They never met a bear, but they did see bighorn sheep, elk, and three moose.

Each man carried a thirty-pound backpack while walking twelve miles a day. They had to battle rain and slick rocks. They faced light snow and winds up to forty miles per hour.

After a week in the wilderness, both were glad to see the ranger station. They could rest their sore muscles and aching feet. It was nice to get back to the comforts of modern life, but the backpacking trip was a great experience they will never forget.

Night Hunters

An owl's food source comes from hunting live prey. Rats, mice, and other small animals make up the owl's diet. Owls can eat over 2,000 rodents per square mile each year.

Part of the owl's success in hunting depends on its ability to fly silently. An owl's wings are very broad, allowing it to flap slowly while still maintaining speed. Slow-moving wings make very little sound. In addition, the main wing feathers have fringed edges to muffle any noise that might be made. These silent night hunters give no warning to the helpless animals, as they become the next meal.

Once captured, the small prey is swallowed whole by the owl. A larger rodent is torn to pieces before being swallowed. Owls spit up the fur and bones that cannot be digested. This ball of fur and bones is called a casting. By studying the castings, we can learn about the owl's eating habits.

Lesson Plans

Unit discussion: page 1

▶ What is the title of the unit? ("Exploits")

Read aloud the following sentence:

The boy's exploit, rescuing the drowning child, took a lot of courage.

▶ What do you think *exploit* means? (Accept any answer, but explain that it is a special act or deed, usually one that is heroic or brilliant.)

What are some exploits or special deeds that you have read or heard about? (Answers will vary.)

What are some exploits that happened in the Bible? (Possible answers: David slew Goliath; Moses crossed the Red Sea; three men walked out of the fiery furnace.)

EXPLOITS

Joshua 1:9

Have not I commanded thee? Be strong and of a good courage; be not afraid, neither be thou dismayed: for the Lord thy God is with thee whithersoever thou goest.

The courage to accomplish great feats begins with a single step in the right direction. The young characters in "River's Rising," "Yukon Trail," and "Project Submarine" bravely take that step when unforeseen circumstances change their plans and, ultimately, their lives. Link courage with fantasy and the result will be "Pecos Bill Gets a Wife" or "A Wise King and a Wise Son." Reality checks in when facing and conquering the plummet of a roller coaster in "Over the Top" or coping with the unpredictability of animals in "Watching Wallace," "An Emergency," and "Lama Glama."

WATCHING WALLACE

> Ten whole dollars! But Timothy must overcome his fear of dogs to earn it. If he can take care of Mr. Parker's huge mongrel, Wallace, for a whole week, the money is his.

Lesson	Reader pages	Worktext pages
1	2-5	1
2	6-9	2-4

Materials
- Dog leash
- Vocabulary sentences prepared for display (e.g., on the chalkboard or on sentence strips)

Background information
Rabies—Some students may not be familiar with the disease of rabies. This infectious disease, transmitted through the bite of an infected animal, requires medical treatment. It is best to be cautious when near stray or wild animals, which may be infected with the disease.

INTRODUCTION
Vocabulary
Use the prepared sentences to introduce the vocabulary words in context.

Pet responsibilities
Display the dog leash.

▶ Have you ever been responsible for taking care of a pet?

What types of responsibilities did you have?

Have you ever had to take care of an animal that frightened you?

What are some ways that you can overcome your fears?

Lead the students to the conclusion that trusting in God will help us when we are afraid. God commands us to trust in Him and to have courage, not fear. [BAT: 8d Courage]

The student should tear out and take home Worktext page 327, *A Message to Parents*.

Correlated Activities
- **Vocabulary Box, Activity 1: Word Hunt**
- **Creative Writing, Activity 1: Runaway Writings**

See "Classroom Management for Grouping" in the Appendix.

VOCABULARY
LESSON 1

†Because Anna had kept thinking about the circus, she had not concentrated on her work. (p. 2)

If a dog's mother is a different breed from its father, the dog is a mongrel. (p. 3)

†The great expanse of land was enough to build two houses on. (p. 3)

†Animals that have the disease of rabies are very dangerous. (p. 4)

LESSON 2

†The items needed to bake the cake were in the pantry. (p. 8)

†The trees along the dark and lonely path loomed over him. (p. 9)

---

† indicates that the vocabulary word is found in the *Christian Student Dictionary*.

A list of the remedial service words appears on Appendix page A7 of this teacher's editon. See also page xi in the Introduction for information about and activities for practicing service words.

Watching Wallace

Sharon Hambrick
illustrated by Mary Ann Lumm

COMPREHENSION

The student will

- Evaluate character responses.
- Focus on the author's use of descriptive verbs.
- Identify problems and solutions.
- Note the author's use of flashback.
- Relate lesson content to personal experience.

Objectives

Before silent reading: pages 2-3

Motivation

▶ Think about the dog leash and the story title. Who is Wallace?

Why could watching Wallace be a problem?

After silent reading

Overview discussion: pages 2-3

▶ [interpretive] Why is watching Wallace a problem? (Timothy doesn't really want to watch Wallace because he is afraid of the dog.)

[critical] Why is Timothy thinking about the time he was seven? (Accept any answer.)

▶ [appreciative] What kinds of things are you afraid of?

See the Introduction in the front of this teacher's edition for the explanation of highlighted questions.

The Agreement

Timothy jumped when Mr. Parker slapped him on the back. Not that Timothy was a scaredy-cat, nothing like that—it was just that sometimes, if something jumped out at him or if someone shouted suddenly, he would jump.

"So, Tim, my boy," Mr. Parker's voice boomed in the late September afternoon, "what about it? What about watching Wallace for me while I'm gone?"

Timothy concentrated on breathing normally so Mr. Parker wouldn't know how startled he'd been.

"Okay," Timothy said. He hoped Mr. Parker wouldn't notice how his voice shook.

"Then it's settled," Mr. Parker said. "I'll leave Monday morning, and I should be back Saturday afternoon."

Timothy nodded. Mr. Parker slapped him on the back again and tromped off to his house next door. He turned and shouted, "Ten bucks, Timmy! I'll give you ten bucks for it!"

"Ten dollars? What for?" a deep voice beside Timothy said. Timothy looked up into his dad's kind face.

"I told him I'd watch Wallace, Dad," Timothy said, not hiding the shakiness in his voice now. "For a whole week."

"Oh," said Dad. "You okay about this?"

"No," said Timothy.

Timothy lay in bed that night, wishing he hadn't agreed to watch

2

Follow-up discussion: page 2

▶ [literal] Why does Timothy jump when he is with Mr. Parker? (Mr. Parker slaps Tim on the back and startles him.)

[critical] Do you think Mr. Parker startles Timothy on purpose? (Accept any answer.)

[literal] Why does Timothy concentrate on breathing normally? (so Mr. Parker will not know how startled he is)

▶ [critical] Why do you think Timothy agrees to take care of the dog? (Answers will vary. Elicit that Timothy probably doesn't want to admit he is scared to a man like Mr. Parker.)

Read aloud the conversation between Mr. Parker and Timothy, using Mr. Parker's booming voice and Timothy's shaky voice.

▶ [critical] Why isn't Timothy startled by his dad's voice? (Accept any answer.)

[interpretive] Does Timothy feel any different about the job after he knows he will get paid? Explain. (No, he still doesn't want to do it.)

Read aloud the sentences that tell how Timothy feels about watching Wallace even though he is getting paid.

Wallace. Wallace was a huge mongrel dog whose tongue hung out slobbering. He never walked anywhere—he bounded. He didn't run. He galloped. He jumped. He barked.

"I will both lay me down in peace, and sleep," Timothy thought, remembering a Bible verse his mother had taught him long ago, "for thou, Lord, only makest me dwell in safety."

It didn't work. The more Timothy thought about Wallace, the more he could not sleep. He lay thinking about that other time, before, when he was seven.

Timothy had been walking home from school. He was in second grade then, and his mind was full of second-grade thoughts like adding two-digit numbers, writing in cursive, and playing first base for the city team. Timothy stopped at the edge of the empty field. Mom had told him to come home as fast as he could that day, but the field looked so inviting. He just had to crawl under the fence where it was loose. His backpack snagged for a minute on the metal chain links, but he managed to get it loose. Then it was just Timothy and the field, an open expanse of grass and weeds and dirt.

Watching Wallace 3

▶ [literal] What words does the author use to describe Wallace? (huge mongrel, tongue hung out slobbering, bounded, galloped, jumped, barked)

[appreciative] Do these words make the dog seem like one you would like?

▶ [interpretive] Does it help for Timothy to remember the Bible verse? Why or why not? (No; he keeps thinking about another time when he was seven.) [BAT: 8a Faith in God's promises.]

Read aloud from the story the verse that Timothy remembers.

▶ [interpretive] How does the author let you know that Timothy is thinking about a memory? (She mentions second grade.)

[critical] Why had Timothy gone under the fence? (Answers will vary, but elicit that he had probably been curious.)

Before silent reading: pages 4-5

Motivation

▶ What could have happened in second grade to frighten Timothy?

Who will help Timothy now?

After silent reading

Overview discussion: pages 4-5

▶ [literal] How did Timothy come to be afraid of dogs? (Timothy had been bitten by a dog and learned about rabies as he waited to find out if the dog that bit him had rabies.)

[critical] How does Timothy's mom help him now? (She prays with him and tells him about how she came to be afraid of roller coasters.) [BAT: 6b Prayer]

Follow-up discussion: page 4

▶ [critical] How could Timothy have prevented the dog bite he got when he was seven? (Possible answer: It might not have happened if he had obeyed his mother.) [BAT: 2a Obedience]

[interpretive] What does Timothy seem to fear even more than a dog bite? (getting rabies)

▶ [literal] Who tries to help Timothy feel brave about his task? (his mom) [BAT: 5a Love]

Read aloud the verse that Timothy's mother quotes to him.

Timothy didn't see the dog until it had knocked him down and was standing over him, teeth bared, a deep growl in its throat.

"Get off," Timothy screamed. "Help!" He struggled to free himself. Timothy pulled on his backpack, and the dog—a huge beast, just like Wallace—opened its powerful jaws and bit deep into Timothy's leg. Timothy screamed, struggled to his feet, and ran home, limping and sobbing.

Even now, two years later, he remembered his mother's frightened face as she washed off his leg and the white coat of the doctor who put in the stitches.

They had to catch the dog and watch it for two weeks to see if it had rabies. When Timothy heard the word "rabies" he shuddered. Even back in second grade, he knew that people didn't always recover from being bitten by a dog that had rabies. Timothy didn't want to die when he was seven. And he didn't want to die now.

His door opened. Mom came in and sat on his bed. She stroked his hair and kissed him. "It's very brave of you," she said.

"I'm scared. What if he bites me?"

"Remember Psalm fifty-six, verse three, 'What time I am afraid, I will trust in thee.' That means that anytime you are fearful, you can trust God to help you through the difficult situation.

4

Wallace has had all his shots, Tim," Mom said. "And he's a good dog. You won't be in any danger."

"I know."

Mom prayed with him and sang him a song. Even though he was almost ten years old, he liked it when Mom came in and sang. It was comforting at the end of the day.

"I know how you feel," Mom said.

"You do?"

"Yes." Mom's voice got quiet. "Once," she said, "when I was about your age, I went to a fair with my family. My sister and I got in a ride that spins around flat, and then goes up steeper and steeper, until you're spinning around suspended from the earth. We were at the very top of the ride, with our backs toward the ground, when the ride stopped. It was stuck. There I was, thirty feet off the ground, holding onto the handrail with hands that got sweatier and sweatier. I was sure I was going to slip out of the car and fall to the ground. We hung there for what seemed like hours.

It was the most frightened I've ever been in my life."

"Is that why you don't go on roller coasters now?"

"That's why. I know they're safe, but they terrify me."

"Like me and Wallace."

"Tell you what, Tim," Mom said. She took a deep breath. "You watch Wallace for the week, trusting God to take care of you, and I'll go on the biggest, twistiest roller coaster you can find."

"Wow!"

Timothy knew how frightened his mom was of roller coasters. Every year at the county fair, she'd wait, sipping a soft drink, while he and Dad stood in line for the loop-the-loop rides and the huge metal roller coasters that twisted back on themselves like snakes. Often he'd said, "Come on, Mom, it's fun!" and seen her shake her head no.

But now she had promised. If Timothy would overcome his fear of caring for Wallace, Mom would ride the Tingling Terror at the county fair with him this year.

Watching Wallace   5

Follow-up discussion: page 5

Follow-up discussion: page 5

▶ [interpretive] How does Timothy's mom reassure him that he does not have to fear Wallace or getting rabies? (Possible answers: She tells him that Wallace is a good dog who has had all his shots; she prays and sings with him; she tells him about a time when she was younger that left her afraid of roller coasters.)

[critical] In what ways are Timothy's fear and his mom's fear the same? (Answers will vary, but point out that both fears come from something that happened in the past.)

Read aloud Mom's description of her frightening experience. Read it like Mom says it—in a quiet voice.

▶ [literal] What promise does Timothy's mom make to him? (She promises to ride the roller coaster if he watches Wallace.)

[critical] What does Timothy think about the possibility that his mom will ride the roller coaster? (Accept any answer, but elicit that his mom is making a sacrifice and that he is excited.)

Looking ahead

▶ Do you think Timothy's mom will have to ride the roller coaster?

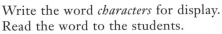

Worktext Objective

The student will

■ Generalize about characters from actions.

Comprehension: Worktext page 1

Write the word *characters* for display. Read the word to the students.

▶ What are characters? (people or animals in the story)

Name the characters in "Watching Wallace." (Mom, Dad, Mr. Parker, Timothy, Wallace)

Who is the main character? (Timothy)

How can you tell what the characters in a story are like? (Answers will vary, but elicit that one way is to notice what the characters do and how they act.)

Write the word *actions* for display.

Discuss the characters from "Watching Wallace"—what they are like and how the story shows these traits (e.g., Wallace: playful, energetic—gallops, barks; Timothy: timid, afraid—is startled easily, shudders at the word *rabies*).

Read the instructions for the page together. Direct the students to complete the page.

Objectives

COMPREHENSION

The student will

- Draw inferences from picture and text interpretation.
- Recognize character growth and change.
- Relate story content to biblical truth: We can overcome fear when we trust in God.

 Use the prepared sentences to introduce the vocabulary words in context.

Before silent reading: pages 6-8

Motivation

▶ Will Wallace give Timothy any trouble?

Why do you suppose the title of this chapter is "Taking Charge"?

After silent reading

Overview discussion: pages 6-8

▶ [literal] What kind of trouble does Wallace get into? (Answers will vary but should include that he jumps on Timothy and knocks him down and runs away into the open field.)

▶ [interpretive] Who seems to be "in charge" in this part of the chapter? (Wallace seems to be making up his own mind about jumping and running wherever he wants.)

▶ [critical] Is Timothy trying to overcome his fear of Wallace? How? (Yes; he prays to God and quotes Scripture verses.) [BATs: 6b Prayer; 8a Faith in God's promises]

Taking Charge

Mr. Parker left Monday morning. Monday after school, Timothy did his homework. Ate dinner. Brushed his teeth.

"Don't you think it's about time to feed that dog, Son?" Dad's voice broke through his thoughts.

"Yes, sir," Timothy said. He got Mr. Parker's key off the key rack and shoved his hands into his pockets. He looked at the floor.

"Will you go with me, Dad?"

Timothy scooped out Wallace's dog food. He poured clean water into his water dish.

"Mr. Parker said Wallace likes to be played with," Dad said.

Timothy reached out and touched Wallace's coat. It was soft and deep. When Wallace turned his head suddenly, Timothy pulled his hand away.

"Try again, Tim," Dad said.

Timothy petted the top of Wallace's head and scratched his neck. He ran his hands through his thick coat.

On Tuesday, Timothy asked, "Dad, will you go with me again?"

"Go alone, Son," Dad said. "You can do it."

Timothy shuffled to Mr. Parker's house, his hands shoved deep into his pockets. He thought back over the Bible lesson he'd heard in Sunday school this week. He thought about how Jesus had stood up in the boat and had said

6

Follow-up discussion: page 6

▶ [interpretive] How does the author let us know that Timothy is avoiding his job? (The author lists what Timothy does instead: finishes his homework, eats dinner, brushes his teeth.)

Read aloud what Dad asks about Timothy's job.

▶ [literal] What does Timothy ask Dad to do? (go with him)

[appreciative] Timothy is grateful that Dad agrees to go with him the first day. How should you respond when your parents do special things to help you? [BAT: 5a Thankfulness]

▶ [critical] Why does Timothy's dad mention that Wallace likes to be played with? (Accept any answer, but elicit that Dad knows Timothy is still afraid, that playing with Wallace might help dispel the fear, and that Wallace needs to be played with.)

Read the sentences that show how Timothy feels the first time he pets the dog.

▶ [interpretive] Why doesn't Timothy's dad go with him the second day? (He knows it is safe and that Timothy can go alone; he wants to help Timothy overcome his fear.)

to the wind and the waves, "Peace, be still."

"Lord," Timothy prayed, "make the wind and waves inside me be still."

Timothy's heart pounded as he turned the key in the lock.

He opened the door. "Wallace?" he called.

Out of nowhere, Wallace bounded, barking. He knocked Timothy over. Timothy's heart beat with fear. Wallace stood over him, slobbering wet drool onto his face.

"Jesus," Timothy whispered, "calm my heart. Help me not be afraid."

Wallace lowered his massive head right over Timothy's. And licked.

"Yuck, you old ugly dog," Timothy said, laughing.

He struggled up and—still shaking—scooped out Wallace's food and freshened his water.

"Good job, Son," Dad's voice startled him.

"Dad!"

"I came behind you," he said, "to make sure you were okay."

"You were here all the time?"

"Yep."

"Thanks, Dad. I was afraid."

"It's okay, Son."

On Wednesday, Timothy told Dad he would go alone. "I've prayed for a peaceful heart."

Mom stood behind Dad. "I'm not so sure I like this brave son thing," she said. Timothy smiled. He knew Mom was getting worried that she'd have to ride the Tingling Terror at the county fair. He smiled at Mom as he grabbed the key and headed out the door.

That day he watched Wallace play in the back yard. Dad watched over the fence.

On Thursday, Dad didn't watch anymore.

"Aren't you afraid of Wallace anymore, Timmy?" Mom asked at dinner Thursday night.

"No," he said. "Wallace is great. I took my Frisbee today and played catch with him. We had fun." Timothy dug into his mashed potatoes like a plow and shoveled a great load into his mouth.

"Do you think Mr. Parker would mind if I walked Wallace around the block today?"

Watching Wallace 7

Follow-up discussion: page 7

▶ [literal] What Bible lesson does Timothy remember from Sunday school as he walks to Mr. Parker's house? (the account of Jesus commanding the wind and waves to be still)

[interpretive] What does Timothy mean when he asks the Lord to make the wind and the waves inside him to be still? (Possible answers: He is nervous and wants the Lord to calm his nerves [Isa. 26:3]; he is trusting in the Lord to give him peace.) [BAT: 8a Faith in God's promises]

▶ [literal] How does Wallace greet Timothy? (He jumps up onto Timothy, knocking him over, and then licks his face.)

Read aloud the paragraphs that tell what happens when Timothy enters the house on Tuesday.

▶ [interpretive] Why does Timothy begin to laugh? (Possible answers: Wallace is probably tickling him as he licks and slobbers on him; Timothy is relieved that Wallace is being friendly.)

[interpretative] How do you know that Timothy is still afraid? (He shakes as he feeds and waters Wallace.)

▶ [critical] Why does Timothy have a peaceful heart even though he goes alone on Wednesday? (Answers may vary, but elicit that he is trusting the Lord this time.) [BAT: 8d Courage]

[interpretive] What clues does the author give to let you know that Timothy is overcoming his fears? (that Timothy plays with Wallace, says Wallace is great, and wants to take Wallace for a walk)

Read aloud what Timothy says that tells you he likes Wallace.

▶ [interpretive] Why is Wallace hard to walk? (He rushes out the door and down the sidewalk and tears the leash loose from Timothy's grip.)

Read aloud the section that describes Timothy's walk with Wallace. Help us see the action as you read.

▶ [interpretative] Why is Timothy hesitant to chase Wallace into the field? (Possible answer: This situation is similar to the time Timothy was bitten by a dog, and he is afraid it will happen again.)

[interpretive] What helps Timothy to have the courage to go under the fence? (praying and trusting in the Lord for protection) [BATs: 6b Prayer; 8d Courage]

[critical] Why is it all right for Timothy to go under the fence this time? (Accept any answer, but explain that he has a responsibility to take care of Wallace.) [BAT: 2c Responsibility]

Read aloud the verse Timothy says as he crawls under the fence (Psalm 56:3).

Timothy asked on Friday. "The leash is hanging up in the pantry where he keeps the dog food."

"Why not?" Dad said.

Timothy hooked the leash to Wallace's collar and opened the door. In a bound, Wallace was off—tearing off down the sidewalk. Timothy held onto the leash for dear life.

"Wallace, slow down!" Timothy called, trying to keep up.

His hands hurt as he held tight. Still the big dog raced, Timothy stumbling after him. He headed for the big field.

"Stop, Wallace, stop!" Timothy pleaded. But it was no use.

Wallace tore the leash out of Timothy's hand and scooted under the fence that surrounded the empty field. Timothy stood on the other side of the fence, shaking.

I can't go in there, he thought. He'll bite me. He ran his hand down his leg where he knew the scar was. He looked at the fence. He looked at Wallace.

"Help me, dear Lord. Help me get the dog back."

Slowly, Timothy lifted the loose part of the fence. He crouched down and slid his body beneath the chain links.

"What time I am afraid, I will trust in thee," he said aloud.

8

"Come here, boy," he said. "Come here, Wallace."

Wallace ran wildly over the field. Timothy watched, feeling helpless. Wallace trotted toward him, then ran away. Timothy felt annoyed.

"Come here, Wallace!" Timothy shouted. "Come here!"

Wallace stopped, turned, and ran over.

Maybe he needs me to sound forceful, like Mr. Parker does, he thought.

"Sit!" Timothy said, as loudly and forcefully as he could. Wallace sat.

Timothy laughed. He grabbed the leash. "Now," he said loudly, "we are going home!" Wallace responded to Timothy's more demanding tone of voice. Maybe he just needed me to be in charge, he thought. Wallace pulled on the leash to go faster, but Timothy said, "No, boy!" and he slowed down.

The fence loomed in front of them. I *will* trust the Lord, thought Timothy. I *will* *not* be afraid. Carefully, he pulled up the fence to let the dog through. Then, holding as tightly as he could to the leash, he eased himself under the fence.

Then, covered with dirt and grass, and slowing Wallace's bounding pace to a walk by his firm commands, Timothy walked leash-in-hand down the sidewalk, all the way home.

Mr. Parker's van was in the driveway.

"Hey, Timmy, my man!" Mr. Parker's voice cracked the silence. "I'm home early. How's the old boy been treating you?"

Timothy smiled. "He's been great, Mr. Parker."

"Didn't jump all over you and scare you to death, did he?"

"Just a little."

Mr. Parker's booming laugh filled the whole neighborhood. He took the leash out of Timothy's hand and dug a ten-dollar bill out of his pocket with his other hand.

"Any idea what you're going to do with that money, Son?" he asked.

"Yes, sir," Timothy said, smiling. "I'm going to take it to the fair."

"The fair!" Mr. Parker shouted. "Good idea. Going to ride the Tingling Terror, are you?"

"Yes, sir," Timothy said. "I'm going to ride it with my mom."

Watching Wallace   9

Before silent reading: page 9

Motivation

▶ Will Wallace give Timothy any more trouble?

Do you think we will learn any more about why the author called this chapter "Taking Charge"?

After silent reading

Overview discussion: page 9

▶ [interpretive] Who seems to be "in charge" in this final part of the story? (Timothy—Wallace seems to be obeying him now.)

[interpretive] How does Timothy take charge? (He overcomes his fear of Wallace and orders Wallace to come to him.)

[interpretive] How does Timothy overcome his fears? (by trusting in the Lord) [BAT: 4d Victory]

[interpretive] How do other people in this story help Timothy overcome his fear? (Dad and Mom encourage him and guide him to verses; Mr. Parker shows that he trusts Timothy and can depend on him.)

Follow-up discussion: page 9

▶ [interpretive] Why doesn't Wallace slow down the first time Timothy tells him to? (Possible answer: Timothy does not speak firmly enough to Wallace.)

[interpretive] How does Timothy finally get Wallace to obey him? (He speaks to him firmly—he takes charge.)

▶ [interpretive] How does Timothy respond to Mr. Parker's question about how Wallace treated him? (He says Wallace was great, but he does admit that Wallace scared him a little.) [BAT: 4c Honesty]

▶ [interpretive] What does Timothy mean when he tells Mr. Parker he is going to ride the Tingling Terror with his mom? (Timothy expects his mother to keep her part of the bargain.)

▶ [critical] Do you think Timothy's mom will ride the Tingling Terror with Timothy? Why or why not? (Accept any answer, but elicit that she will keep her promise to Timothy.)

Worktext Objective

The student will

■ Sequence story events.

Comprehension:
Worktext page 2

The student will

- Infer differences between characters.
- Recognize character development through actions and speech.

LITERATURE
Background information

Characterization—Authors use different ways to let us know about the characters in their stories. They tell about the characters through the characters' own speech and actions. Authors also reveal information about characters through what is said by other characters or by directly stating facts about the characters in the story.

Character development

▶ Listen to what the two characters do and say as I read this story.

"Worms yesterday, worms today, and it looks like worms tomorrow!" Roderick the chipmunk spit half a worm out of his mouth. "Being a traveling chipmunk salesman sure isn't what it's cracked up to be!"

Just then Frederick crept into the bottom of the musty mole hole. "I brought some half-eaten acorns that the squirrel's wife threw out," Frederick said, holding the bigger acorn out to Roderick.

As he took the acorn, instead of saying "thank you" he grumbled, "And why do we have to stay in this mole hole? Couldn't you have found an empty rabbit hole or something?"

Frederick shrugged. "We couldn't afford to rent a rabbit hole." He smiled at his younger chipmunk friend and curled up on the floor beside him. "I'm going to take a little nap before we get back on the path. My blanket's big enough for both of us if you want to take a nap, too!" And with a smile, Frederick drifted off to sleep.

▶ Based on what they did and said, are the chipmunks alike or different? (different)

How would you describe Roderick? What made you think that about him? (Grumpy, unthankful, complaining; he spits, grumbles, and complains about where they are staying and what they are eating.)

How would you describe Frederick? What made you think that about him? (Happy, content, kind even when not treated with kindness; he smiles, he is willing to share his blanket, he is content to eat the acorns he found.)

▶ We learn about characters through their actions and words.

Literature: Worktext pages 3-4

SOMETHING EXTRA
Write About It: My "Wallace" story

Direct the student to write about his own experience that left him afraid of something. Use the following questions as story starters.

▶ Did reading about Wallace make you remember a time that you were afraid?

What frightened you?

Did you think of a verse to help you when you were afraid?

OVER THE TOP

Lesson	Reader pages	Worktext pages
3	10-11	5-6

Experience the thrill of the roller coaster in this action-packed account.

Materials
- Picture of people riding a roller coaster (optional)
- Bible
- Vocabulary sentences for display (e.g., on the chalkboard or on sentence strips)

Background information

Centrifugal force—The force that causes an object to flee the center of its circular path is called centrifugal force. For example, when someone swings a bucket of water around himself, the water stays in the bucket.

Free verse—Poetry that does not conform to a regular pattern of rhyme or meter is called free verse. In free verse, the poet often takes liberties with conventional spelling, punctuation, and word arrangement.

Onomatopoeia—The use of words that sound like what they mean is onomatopoeia. The words imitate the sounds associated with the objects or actions they refer to.

INTRODUCTION

Vocabulary

Use the prepared sentences to introduce the vocabulary words in context.

A roller coaster ride

Display the picture of people riding a roller coaster.

▶ If this picture had sound, what would you hear? (possible answers: screaming, laughing, music)

Have you ever ridden a roller coaster? If so, what was it like?

Would you ride a roller coaster again? Why or why not?

VOCABULARY

LESSON 3

The driver must engage the clutch to make the truck start. (line 5)

In science class, we studied centrifugal force in which objects seem to move away from the center of their circular path. (line 19)

*†The reckless driver skidded around the corner and collided with a tree. (line 23)

---

* indicates the vocabulary word is found in the Reader 4 glossary.

Correlated Activities
- **Vocabulary Box, Activity 1: Word Hunt**
- **Connections, Activity 1: Fact or Fiction Destinations**
See "Classroom Management for Grouping" in the Appendix.

COMPREHENSION

The student will

- Recognize free verse.
- Identify figurative language.
- Identify onomatopoeia.

Before listening

▶ What sounds does a roller coaster make? Try to hear these sounds as I read the poem aloud.

Listening: pages 10-11

Read aloud the entire poem on pages 10 and 11 to the students.

After listening

Discussion: lines 1-11

Explain that although the poem is in free verse, it does follow a form of its own. Point out that this poem copies the look of a roller coaster in its arrangement of the lines on the page. Read aloud lines 1-11 again.

▶ [literal] What does the first word mean? (to move with a jerk)

[appreciative] What words make you feel you are going up a long, slow incline? (Answers may vary but should include *clickety, rickety, cranking, cheakle, crawling, hauling, groaning.*)

▶ [literal] To what does the poet compare the roller coaster's progress up the hill? (a caterpillar crawling up a mountain and hauling gravity)

▶ [critical] Why do you think line 11 ends with *o-* ? (Accept any answer, but lead the students to understand that the syllable *o-* imitates the sound the riders might make as the coaster goes over the top and pauses a moment before making the descent.)

Read aloud the first eleven lines again.

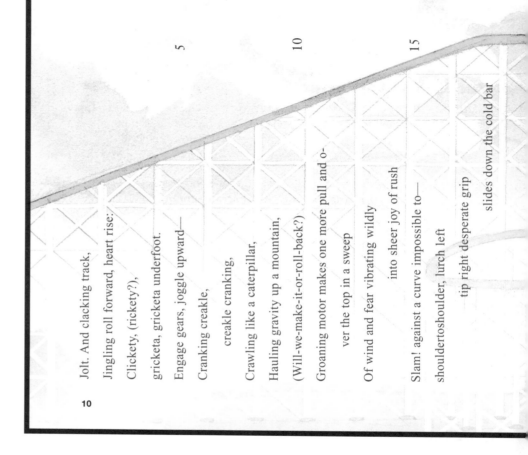

Over the Top

Dawn L. Watkins
illustrated by Preston Gravely Jr.

Jolt. And clacking track,
Jingling roll forward, heart rise:
Clickety, (rickety?),
gricketa, gricketa underfoot.
Engage gears, joggle upward—
Cranking creakle,
creakle cranking,
Crawling like a caterpillar,
Hauling gravity up a mountain,
(Will-we-make-it-or-roll-back?)
Groaning motor makes one more pull and o-
ver the top in a sweep
Of wind and fear vibrating wildly
into sheer joy of rush
Slam! against a curve impossible to—
shouldertoshoulder, lurch left
tip right desperate grip
slides down the cold bar

10

Discussion: lines 12-18

Read aloud lines 12-18.

▶ [appreciative] What words give you the feeling of speed? (Answers may vary but should include *sweep, rush, lurch, slides.*)

▶ [interpretive] What words appeal to the sense of touch? (*wind, slam, rush, vibrating, shouldertoshoulder, lurch, grip, cold*)

[critical] Why do you think the poet left out the spaces in the phrase "shouldertoshoulder"? (Accept any answer, but lead the students to conclude that the poet wanted to show how riders are thrown against each other on curves.)

Read aloud lines 12-18 again.

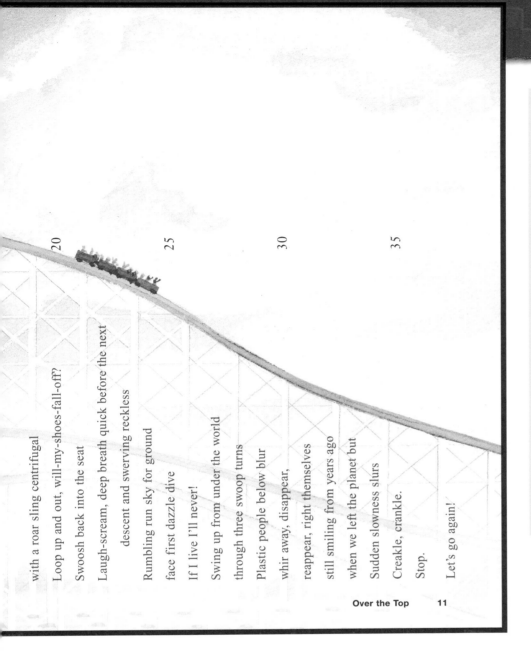

20
with a roar sling centrifugal
Loop up and out, will-my-shoes-fall-off?
Swoosh back into the seat
Laugh-scream, deep breath quick before the next
descent and swerving reckless

25
Rumbling run sky for ground
face first dazzle dive
If I live I'll never!
Swing up from under the world
through three swoop turns

30
Plastic people below blur
whir away, disappear,
reappear, right themselves
still smiling from years ago
when we left the planet but

35
Sudden slowness slurs
Creakle, crankle.
Stop.
Let's go again!

Over the Top   11

Discussion: lines 19-37
Read aloud lines 19-37.

▶ [interpretive] What do you think a "laugh-scream" is? (a laugh that ends in a scream)

[appreciative] Can you demonstrate a laugh-scream?

▶ [interpretive] Which words or phrases show the rider's thoughts? (Will my shoes fall off? If I live I'll never!)

▶ [critical] What do you think the poet means by "still smiling from years ago / when we left the planet"? (Accept any answer, but lead the students to understand that the experience was so unusual and exhilarating that it made the rider lose her sense of time and place.)

[interpretive] How do you know that the rider liked the experience? (She says, "Let's go again!")

Choose several students to read the entire poem aloud again, encouraging the students to imagine that they are riding the roller coaster.

The student will

- Note the author's choice of words.
- Classify onomatopoetic words.
- Complete a free verse poem using onomatopoeia.

LITERATURE

Onomatopoeia

Instruct the students to choose words from "Over the Top" that sound like what they mean. (possible answers: *clacking, clickety, cranking, creakle, crankle, gricketa*)

▶ Can you think of other words that sound like what they mean? (possible answers: *bang, pop, squeak, snap, knock, tap, rattle*)

Explain that the use of words that sound like what they mean is called onomatopoeia.

▶ Authors often use onomatopoeia to paint pictures for the reader. Listen to the word *pitter-patter*. Can you imagine tiny footsteps as I say the words several times?

Repeat "pitter-patter" several times with a rhythm that sounds like footsteps.

Literature: Worktext page 5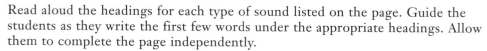

Read aloud the headings for each type of sound listed on the page. Guide the students as they write the first few words under the appropriate headings. Allow them to complete the page independently.

Literature: Worktext page 6

Explain the directions for the two activities.

Help the students finish the free verse sound poem at the bottom of the page.

Materials

- Three letters from Appendix page A35
- The following headings displayed in a row (e.g., on the chalkboard or sentence strips):

  Maine: September 1910   *Alaska: September 1950*   *Florida: September 1990*
- *These Are My People* by Milly Howard (BJU Press) (optional)

SETTING

(2) Skill development: Discussion

▶ The setting of the first paragraph is a gas station at night.

What is the setting of the second paragraph? (Grandma's bakery early in the morning)

What information is learned from the setting of a story? (when and where a story takes place)

In some stories the author gives a specific setting because it affects the characters' actions. He might say the story takes place in Philadelphia in the year 1776.

In other stories the setting is not important because it does not affect the characters' actions. In the next story in your reader, "River's Rising," the author gives a general setting. The story takes place at a river. But we are not told where the river is or the date when the story takes place because that is not really important.

Was the setting for "Watching Wallace" specific or general? (general)

Was the setting important or unimportant to the story? Why? (The setting was unimportant to the story. The story could have taken place in almost any neighborhood and at almost any date.)

(3) Skill development: Critical thinking

Display the three letters from Appendix page A35.

▶ I've found three letters in an old chest in the attic. They seem to have been written by three different young boys. Each comes from a place and time very different from the others.

Read each letter aloud and let a student place the letter, according to the character's actions, beneath the appropriate setting heading. (Maine: September 1910—Joel's letter; Alaska: September 1950—Shawn's letter; Florida: September 1990—Kyle's letter) Discuss the difference in each character's actions and the reasons for the differences.

▶ Why didn't Joel have to go to school five days each week? (Accept any answer, but mention that there was no law requiring attendance then.)

Why didn't Shawn ride the bus to school? (Accept any answer, but mention that in 1950 in Alaska buses weren't always available. Usually students had to walk or ski.)

What are some differences between Kyle's school and Joel's school? (possible answers: a one-room schoolhouse—five sixth-grade classes; open windows—air conditioning; no attendance requirements—required attendance)

The setting of a story often affects the actions of characters.

Lesson	Worktext pages
4	208-11

The student will

- Understand that the setting of the story tells where and when the story takes place.
- Recognize that the setting can affect the actions of the characters.

Background information

Setting—Setting is the time and place of a story. Sometimes a specific description of the setting is necessary to understand the events of the story, such as in historical selections. In other instances the setting is unimportant to the story. The author can help us see the setting through the characters—what they see, hear, say, and do.

(1) Introduction

Read the following paragraphs aloud. Ask where each event occurs and what time each event takes place. Do not use the word *setting* during this activity.

▶ Your dad pulls up and turns off the lights and the engine. You lean out the window to watch the numbers scroll upward in the slots on the pump. You wrinkle your nose at the smell of gasoline. You notice the dollar amount on the pump as your dad goes to pay the cashier.

Where in the world are you? What time is it? (gas station, nighttime)

▶ Your grandma is the best baker in the world! Even though the sun hasn't come up yet, there are already racks full of delicious breads, cakes, and pastries. Already, two customers have bought sweets for their breakfast. The smell of the apple fritters makes your stomach growl.

Where in the world are you? What time is it? (Grandma's bakery, early morning)

4 **Skill application:**
Worktext page 208

Find the Setting

▶ Read along silently as I read the story aloud. Find words that give clues to the story's setting.

Which of the words listed below the story are clues to the setting? (sea gull, waves, cliff)

Circle those words; then read the setting choices for the next question and mark the correct one. What is the setting? (the ocean)

Think It Through

▶ Some settings are very important and determine the kinds of actions characters perform. Other settings are not important at all. Read the first selection and think about whether the setting is important and why it is or is not. (The setting is important because this story could take place only at a space center and the characters' actions are more limited by the space center setting.)

Guide the completion of the page.

5 **Skill practice:**
Worktext page 209

6 **Skill application:**
Worktext pages 210-11

Direct attention to the story on page 210. Explain that it is taken from the book *These Are My People* by Milly Howard.

▶ Have you ever been to a foreign country?

How would you feel if the people didn't like you?

Read to find out what happened to one young woman in China. Then answer the questions on page 211.

When and Where

▶Find the Setting
Read the story and answer the questions.

Lost Dog

"Scotty!" Carl shouted as he struggled up the rocky path to the cliff. At the top, he braced himself against the wind and shouted again and again. Only a lonely sea gull answered, squawking miserably as it fought its way through the storm-gray sky. Carl walked to the jagged rocks that edged the cliff. He called again, as loudly as he could. Over the crashing of the waves below, he heard a sharp bark. He looked down. On a ledge about a quarter of the way down the cliff crouched a tiny black dog.

1. Circle the words below that are clues to the setting.
   shout   (sea gull)   (waves)
   dog   (cliff)   through

2. Circle the setting of "Lost Dog."
   (ocean)   pond
   town   forest

▶Think It Through
Read each selection and decide if the setting is important or unimportant to the action that is taking place. If it is important, put an *I* in the blank. If it is unimportant, put a *U* in the blank.

___*I*___ 1. "Mission Control here. All systems are go. Ready for countdown." All eyes at NASA were glued on the huge rocket ship as the timer ticked off the seconds.

___*U*___ 2. Dan and Tim stood in their back yard, glaring at each other. "You used my bike without asking me!" Tim yelled. "And now it has a flat tire!"

___*I*___ 3. The coach lifted his whistle. At the edge of the pool, the boys leaned forward, ready to hit the water in a clean dive. They tensed. The whistle shrilled. In a flash every one of them pushed off into the water and began racing to the other side.

> The **setting** of a story tells where and when the story takes place. Sometimes the setting is important because it affects the characters' actions. At other times it is not important because it does not affect the characters' actions.

208

Note: The selection on worktext page 210 is taken from *These Are My People* by Milly Howard (BJU Press). You may wish to obtain a copy for your classroom.

SOMETHING EXTRA

Write About It:
Where in the world

Display three magazine pictures of people eating, portraying different eating styles of countries such as America, China, and India. Discuss the fact that although all three pictures show people eating, the settings are different because the peoples' customs are different. Ask each student to write a description of the setting of one of the pictures. Allow the students to share the descriptions.

Fishing, crabbing, and boating are part of the daily routine for Josh and his family. Life on the houseboat is a smooth-sailing adventure until the floodwaters swell the river, and their home tears away from its moorings.

Lesson	Reader pages	Worktext pages
5	12-15	7
6	16-19	8
7	20-22	9-10

Materials

- Newspaper clippings or pictures of flooded areas
- A Bible for the teacher and each student
- Vocabulary sentences for display (e.g., on the chalkboard or on sentence strips)

INTRODUCTION

Vocabulary

Use the prepared sentences to introduce the vocabulary words in context.

Famous floods

Show news reports or pictures of places that have flooded.

▶ Have you been in a flood, or do you know someone who has?

▶ What was the biggest flood in history? (the Flood of the whole earth during Noah's time)

Has there ever been a flood of the whole earth since then? (no) Why not? (Refer to Genesis 9:11-17.)

Do you think that Noah trusted the Lord for protection during that flood? [BATs: 6b Prayer; 8a Faith in God's promises]

VOCABULARY

LESSON 5

*Since it was raining outside, he put his slicker on to keep his clothes dry. (p. 13)

*†Ray tied up the boat and stepped onto the landing. (p. 14)

LESSON 6

*†The mooring lines kept the boat from floating downstream. (p. 17)

*†The current was so strong it swept their little raft down the river. (p. 18)

*The four lanes of traffic moved to one lane, creating a bottleneck. (p. 19)

*†The debris of the bombed city lay everywhere. (p. 19)

*†While swimming underwater, my body was completely submerged. (p. 19)

LESSON 7

*They swam out to the sandbar and rested upon it before they swam back. (p. 20)

*†Using the tiller, he steered the boat away from the rocks. (p. 20)

*Although the rudder is very small, it turns the largest ships. (p. 22)

*†They were able to salvage most of their things after the tornado. (p. 22)

Correlated Activities

- **Vocabulary Box, Activity 1: Word Hunt**
- **Word Work, Activity 1: Comic Connection**

See "Classroom Management for Grouping" in the Appendix.

COMPREHENSION

The student will

- Develop an awareness of mood.
- Evaluate character responses.
- Identify problems and solutions.
- Predict outcomes.
- Identify imagery.

Before silent reading: pages 12-13

Motivation

▶ How do Ma, Pa, and Josh like living in a houseboat when it rains?

After silent reading

Overview discussion: pages 12-13

▶ [interpretive] As the story begins, how does the author make the mood of the story peaceful? (Possible answers: Josh is reading and falls asleep; Ma is humming; Pa is reading; Ma says the rain is "like music," and the fire sends a "cozy warmth throughout the houseboat.")

▶ [interpretive] Why does Ma and Pa's calm attitude change about the rain? (The current rain and the large amount of snow and rain earlier in the year may cause a bad flood.)

[literal] What is Josh's response to Pa's comments about the river? (He is happy because he thinks there will be no school if the river overflows.)

[critical] Does Pa think Josh has the right attitude about the river's rising? Why do you think so? (No; answers may vary but should include that Pa explains to Josh that floodwater can be deadly.)

[interpretive] Does Josh believe that floodwaters are as dangerous as his Pa makes them sound? Why or why not? (No; Josh remembers that grownups watch the water level while letting children play in the water, and he has never been afraid of high water.)

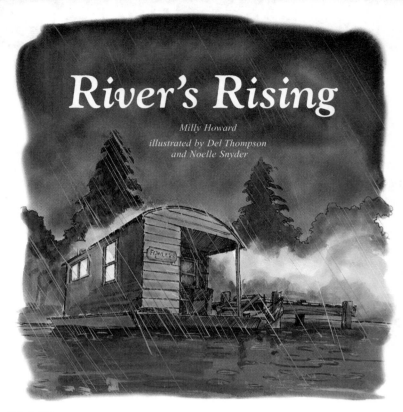

River's Rising

Milly Howard

illustrated by Del Thompson and Noelle Snyder

High Water

Josh Fowler lay on the braided rag rug in front of the big pot-bellied stove. He marked his place in the book he was reading and looked up. Ma was rocking Buddy, gently humming "Rock of Ages." Pa was sitting at the table, reading the Bible, a mended fishnet at his feet.

Behind the curtains, April rain slashed at the windows. It drummed on the tin roof of the houseboat. Josh rolled over, listening.

Ma stopped humming to listen too. "There's nothing like rain on a tin roof," she said softly. "It's like

12

Follow-up discussion: page 12

▶ [literal] Why does Ma stop humming? (to listen to the rain)

Read aloud what Ma says that tells you how she feels about the rain.

music, first soft, then loud, then soft again."

Josh nodded, eyes half closed. The low fire in the stove had sent a cozy warmth throughout the houseboat. The rain slowed, settling into a slow drizzle, gently pinging the roof. Josh yawned and closed his eyes.

When he awoke, lamplight spread a golden circle across the room. Josh lay for a moment, watching shadows moving across the ceiling. Behind him he heard quiet clinks as Ma set the table for supper. "Stew," he thought hungrily, taking a deep breath. He could hear Pa outside on the deck, moving toward the door. Pa's footsteps stopped, and Josh knew he was hanging his slicker on the peg beside the door.

Josh was on his feet when the door opened. He watched as Pa ran his hand over his wet hair. Ma handed him a towel and gave him a questioning look. Pa nodded in answer to her unspoken question.

"River's rising," he said.

"Bad?" Ma asked anxiously.

"Can't tell yet," Pa replied as he sat down at the table, "but there was a heap of snow this winter and too much rain this spring. Wouldn't be surprised if the Reedy River really leaps the banks this time."

"Won't be any school in the morning then," Josh said, grinning. He sat down.

"You've never seen a real flood, Son," Pa said. "The Reedy's a right friendly stretch of water most times, but floodwater's deadly. We rivermen move carefully when the water's rising."

Mr. Fowler waited until Ma sat down across from him and then bowed his head. "Let's pray."

Josh listened as his father prayed for God's mercy on the land. High water had always been a part of Josh's life. Almost every spring the river and the streams that fed it would overflow their banks. When the water covered the bridges, the buses would stop running, and school would be let out until the water went back down. The grownups kept a careful eye on the water level while the children splashed happily through their holiday. No, high water had never held terror for Josh.

Follow-up discussion: page 13

▶ [interpretive] What time is it when Josh wakes up? (suppertime)

Read aloud the paragraph describing the sounds and smells that tell Josh it is suppertime.

▶ [interpretive] Why is Pa out in the rain? (possible answer: to check the water level and the boat)

[critical] Why does Ma give Pa a questioning look when he comes in from outside? (Possible answers: Maybe Pa looks worried; Ma is worried.)

[interpretive] How do Ma and Pa speak to each other without using words? (facial expressions; "questioning look"; nodding)

Read the dialogue among Ma, Pa, and Josh. Read to show Ma and Pa's concern and Josh's cheerfulness about the river's rising.

▶ [critical] Why does Pa pray for God's mercy on the land? (Answers may vary, but elicit that Pa prays because of a possible flood and trusts the Lord to answer his prayer.) [BATs: 6b Prayer; 8a Faith in God's promises]

Before silent reading: pages 14-15

Motivation

▶ How do the Fowlers prepare for a possible flood?

After silent reading

Overview discussion: pages 14-15

▶ [interpretive] Is Josh excited about a possible flood now? How do you know? (No; he does not sleep well; he listens to the boat creak and feels it move against the landing.)

[appreciative] Are there times when you don't sleep well at night? Why don't you sleep well?

▶ [literal] What do Pa and Josh do to protect their family and houseboat from the possible flood? (They tie the houseboat to an old oak tree and clear the landing and dock of anything that could float away.)

[critical] Why is it important to tie the houseboat to the old oak tree? (Answers should include that the old oak is strong enough to keep the houseboat from drifting away.)

▶ [interpretive] How do you know Josh and his family love each other? (Possible answers: Ma and Pa tease each other; life flows smoothly; Ma sings as she does her work; they smile; they help each other.) [BAT: 5a Love]

But when bedtime came, even Josh could tell this time was going to be different. He could feel the Reedy moving under the houseboat.

"It's rising fast," Pa said the last time he came in. "A foot since sundown. She'll be over the banks by dawn."

Josh hardly slept that night. He lay in his bunk, listening to the creaking as the river rocked the houseboat against the planks of Fowler's Landing.

When he awoke early the next morning, Josh eased out of bed quietly. Trying not to awaken Buddy and Ma, he pulled on his clothes and tiptoed to the door. Pa was already outside, walking along the dock. He had rope coiled around his shoulder and was measuring the distance from the boat to the oak tree nearest the riverbank.

Josh didn't have to use the ladder to reach the dock this morning. Water lapped at the top rung, and the houseboat rode high against the landing. Josh leaped across and ran barefoot along the planks to his father.

"What are you doing, Pa?" he asked.

"River's still rising, Son," his father answered. "It's already over the low banks downstream, and it'll soon be over the landing. Help me tie the boat to this old oak. It'll hold the boat fast."

As Josh helped Pa wind the ropes around the trunk of the tree he asked, "Are the trees on Crab Island as old as our oak?"

"Probably older," his father grunted, giving the rope one last hard pull. "That ought to do it. Run and bring me the rope from the landing."

Josh ran back down the dock and untied the rope that held the houseboat. Holding one end of the coiled rope, he walked back along the dock to the big tree. The houseboat swung away from the dock and drifted closer to the tree. Pa and Josh pulled steadily, bringing the houseboat gently to the bank. With swift movements Pa tied that rope too.

"Now she'll stay," he said in satisfaction. "And the landing will protect her from floating branches. I've never seen the

14

Follow-up discussion: page 14

▶ [interpretive] How does Pa know the water will be over the bank by dawn? (It is rising so fast; it has risen quickly overnight.)

[literal] What is Pa already busy doing when Josh wakes up? (measuring the distance from the boat to the oak tree before tying the boat to the tree)

[interpretive] Why doesn't Josh have to use a ladder to get to the dock this morning? (The river is already at the top of the ladder.)

Read aloud the paragraph that tells how Josh reaches the dock and meets his father.

▶ [interpretive] What makes Pa feel their houseboat is safe? (It is tied to a strong tree, and the landing will protect it from floating branches.)

Read aloud Pa's statement, showing his satisfaction that the boat will stay and be protected.

river rise much higher than our landing anyway."

"How's it going?" Ma called.

"You up already?" Pa called back, teasing. "I thought you were going to sleep till noon."

Josh grinned. His folks were always teasing each other. Life on the houseboat flowed as smoothly as the Reedy River usually did. Ma cooked and took care of Buddy, singing as she did her work. Pa was a fisherman, just as Grandpa had been. When school was out Josh went with him, crabbing and fishing off Crab Island. Then they brought the day's catch home to sell in the little fish and bait house above Fowler's Landing.

Ma gave them a good-natured smile and went back inside. Josh and Pa cleared the landing and dock of anything that would float away; then they went to eat breakfast.

▶ [interpretive] To what does the author compare life on the houseboat? Why? (Reedy River; to show how calm life on the houseboat usually is)

Read aloud the paragraph that describes the Fowlers' life on the Reedy River.

[critical] Why are the Fowlers so happy living on a houseboat, especially when they know there could be a flood soon? (Accept any answer, but point out that they are content and believe they are prepared for a flood.) [BAT: 7d Contentment]

▶ [literal] What is happening in the picture? (Pa and Josh are clearing the landing and dock.)

[interpretive] Why is it important that the landing and dock be clear? (so the Fowlers' belongings do not float away)

[critical] How do Josh and his dad demonstrate diligence? (by working hard to prepare the houseboat before the possible flood comes) [BAT: 2e Work]

Looking ahead

▶ Will all the Fowlers' preparation keep them safe from a possible flood?

Worktext Objectives

The student will
- Infer size relationships.
- Follow directions.

Comprehension:
Worktext page 7

The Phonics Fitness unit of the worktext, beginning on page 273, provides a systematic review of phonics skills. These pages may be used during reading groups or for individual instruction. The teacher determines how and when to implement these pages.

COMPREHENSION

The student will

- Note how character actions reveal character traits.
- Evaluate emotional responses of characters.
- Relate story content to biblical truth: a Christian should love and help others.
- Identify problems and solutions.

Use the prepared sentences to introduce the vocabulary words in context.

Before silent reading: pages 16-19

Motivation

▶ What happens to the Fowlers as the river continues to rise?

After silent reading

Overview discussion: pages 16-19

▶ [interpretive] Why does Pa leave his family on the houseboat? (The sheriff asks him to help others get to high ground, and he thinks the houseboat and his family are safe.) [BAT: 2b Helpfulness]

[critical] Does Pa make the right decision to leave the houseboat and help others? Explain your answer. (Yes; the Bible tells believers to love their neighbors as themselves, and he trusts Josh to handle things while he is away.) [BAT: 2b Servanthood]

▶ [literal] What does Pa trust Josh to do while he is gone? (take care of the family and the houseboat by checking the mooring lines)

[critical] Why is it important to check the mooring lines? (The lines are the only things keeping the houseboat from floating away.)

Shifting Current

Josh and Pa spent the rest of the morning securing everything on the houseboat. Anything that might tip over or fall was lashed down. Loose things were taken inside to be stored. Pa went over every inch of the houseboat. He was checking the roof to see if it needed any repair work when the sheriff called from the bank.

"Hello, Fowlers!" He nodded in approval when he saw the boat secured to the tree. Glancing at the water that now covered the landing, he said, "Looks like you're all set for a while."

"Reckon so," Pa replied, reaching out a hand to help the sheriff aboard. "How's things going?"

The sheriff nodded at Ma and ruffled Josh's hair. He grinned when Josh ducked. "If your family's going to be all right for a while, I could use your help," he said to Pa. "The lower part of town's already flooded, and the farms north of us are half buried under floodwater. We need every man we can get that knows the river. We've got to bring those people to high ground."

16

▶ [interpretive] How do Ma and Josh feel about Pa's being gone? (Possible answers: They are worried about him; Josh is scared and eager for Pa to come home; Ma trusts the Lord to take care of them.)

▶ [literal] What happens to the houseboat while Pa is gone? (The mooring lines break, and it begins drifting downstream.)

[interpretive] What is dangerous about the houseboat's drifting downstream? (It will probably be wrecked in the bottleneck between the cliffs, and the family could be injured or could die.)

Follow-up discussion: page 16

▶ [literal] What are Josh and Pa doing when the sheriff arrives? (securing everything on the houseboat and checking the roof)

[interpretive] Why does the sheriff ask Pa to help bring people to high ground? (The sheriff sees that Pa's houseboat and family are prepared for the flood, and Pa knows the river.)

Read aloud how the sheriff tells of the town's need for help. Read with a sense of urgency.

Pa nodded. "Been expecting that. My boat's secure, and my people will be all right."

After the sheriff had left, Pa kissed Ma and Buddy and motioned for Josh to follow him to the back of the houseboat. "The water's rising faster than I've ever seen it, " he said quietly. "There's going to be a lot of people stranded, and I won't be back anytime soon. You have to take care of Ma and Buddy."

Josh swallowed, "We'll be all right, Pa."

"Just remember to check those mooring lines," Pa said as he untied the rowboat. "The current is sweeping close to shore."

"Okay, Pa," Josh said. He went back to stand beside Ma and Buddy. They waved until Pa rowed out of sight.

The rest of the day dragged by. Ma went about her work quietly, and Josh could tell she was praying for Pa and the people caught in the flood. Even Buddy played quietly, running his wooden train around the braided rug.

Josh checked the water every hour. And every hour he shook his head at Ma's look. "Still rising, " he said at last. "It's over the high banks now."

Night came, and Pa was still gone. At suppertime Ma wordlessly handed the Bible to Josh. He read a chapter slowly, stumbling over some of the words. Then he tried to pray as his father did, speaking to the Lord as a friend. Suppertime was quiet. The fish and cornbread were soon removed from the table, almost untouched.

Josh checked the mooring lines again while Ma did the dishes. He held the lantern high, peering toward the bank. The water was more than a foot over the bank now, churning around the roots of the old oak. Pieces of broken branches tumbled over the landing and swept under the mooring lines. The water was too far over the landing for it to offer any protection to the houseboat.

"Oh Pa," Josh thought, "come home!" He went back inside and set the lamp down on the table.

Ma touched his arm gently. "The Lord will take care of us," she said quietly.

River's Rising   17

Follow-up discussion: page 17

▶ [interpretive] Why does Pa expect the town to flood? (He is an experienced riverman and knows the river is rising faster than ever before.)

▶ [critical] Why does Pa call Josh to the back of the boat to talk to him? (Answers may vary but should include that Pa does not want Ma to hear what he says because then she might worry.)

[interpretive] How do you know Ma is concerned about Pa? (Possible answers: She prays for Pa and the people caught in the flood; she is quiet at suppertime; she does not eat much.)

Read aloud the paragraph that shows that Ma trusts the Lord with her concerns and wants Josh to also. Read it quietly like Ma speaks.

[critical] When should Christians trust the Lord? (Answers may vary but should include all the time.) [BAT: 8a Faith in God's promises]

▶ [interpretive] In what ways does Josh try to take care of the family and fill Pa's place? (Possible answers: He checks the mooring lines; he reads the Bible to the family; he prays to the Lord as a friend.) [BATs: 2a Obedience; 2b Helpfulness; 6b Prayer]

▶ [interpretive] What danger does Josh find when he checks the mooring lines? (The landing cannot offer any protection to the houseboat because the water is too far over it.)

Follow-up discussion: page 18

▶ [interpretive] Why does Ma read *David Copperfield?* (to pass the time and help Josh relax because they cannot sleep)

[literal] What makes Ma stop reading? (The houseboat trembles.)

[literal] What does Josh discover when he goes outside to find the cause of the tremble? (He finds that the current has shifted and thinks a branch probably got tangled in the mooring lines.)

[critical] Is the change of the current's direction dangerous to the Fowlers? Why or why not? (Yes; accept any answer, but elicit that it is pulling the houseboat out into the river, away from the shore.)

▶ Read aloud the paragraph that describes what happens as Josh starts to go back inside. Read to show Josh's fear.

[interpretive] How are we shown that Josh is scared? (Possible answers: He spins around; his heart is thudding; he holds his breath.)

[critical] What do you think Josh is afraid of? (Accept any answer, but point out that the mooring lines could break, sending the houseboat downriver to the bottleneck.)

When Buddy was asleep, Ma sat down beside Josh. "Like me to read to you?" she asked, picking up *David Copperfield.*

Josh nodded, knowing that neither of them would sleep until Pa came home. Ma read page after page, but still there was no homecoming shout from the river. Unexpectedly, the houseboat trembled under them, rocking on the water. Ma stopped reading.

Josh reached for the lamp and stepped outside. Holding the lamp up, he looked at the mooring lines. They were only inches above the rising water that stretched out into the night. The current had shifted, pulling them away from the tree.

"A branch must have tangled for a moment," Josh called back to Ma. He had turned to go back inside when a grinding crash came from the direction of the submerged landing. He spun around, heart thudding. A large shape had lunged out of the night and smashed into the landing. Josh held his breath, listening to the creaking and grinding. Then there was a splintering noise.

18

"The landing's breaking up," he cried.

"Come inside! Now!" Ma grabbed his arm and pulled him back inside, slamming the door behind them.

The houseboat shuddered as the broken mass hit the back of the boat. Then, with a jerk, the boat began to move.

Josh stared at Ma. "The lines broke. We're loose!"

"The current'll take us to midstream," she said, her face pale. "We'll just drift downriver."

Josh's eyes met hers for a moment before he looked away. Five miles downriver cliffs crowded the edge on both sides. Tonight the cliffs would form a bottleneck for the rushing water and floating debris. There was no way off the river. He couldn't take the boat across the fields. It would be wrecked on submerged fences and sheds. What could they do? Josh's mind searched his memory of the river for an answer.

Follow-up discussion: page 19

▶ [interpretive] Why does Ma pull Josh inside? (She is trying to protect him, because the landing is breaking up.)

[interpretive] How does Josh know the mooring lines broke? (He feels the houseboat begin to move.)

▶ [critical] Why does Josh look at Ma for only a moment? (Answers may vary, but elicit that he is searching his mind for a solution, he is worried, and he does not want Ma to panic.)

[interpretive] How does the author let you know Ma is scared? (Her face is pale.)

Read aloud the paragraph that describes how Josh tries to think of a solution.

[appreciation] How would you react if this were happening to you?

[critical] Is it important for Ma and Josh to stay calm? Why or why not? (Yes; answers should include that they need to think of a solution quickly.) [BAT: 3c Emotional control]

Looking ahead

▶ Do you think Josh will be able to think of an idea to save the houseboat and the family?

Worktext Objective

The student will

■ Use context clues to determine word meaning.

Vocabulary:
Worktext page 8

Display the sentence with the vocabulary word *current*. (See Vocabulary section on page 19.)

Review the technique of using sentence context to help determine the meaning of a word.

Direct the students to read the paragraphs and then to think about how the words are used in the sentences as they complete the worktext page.

Objectives

COMPREHENSION

The student will

■ Note how character actions reveal character traits.

■ Evaluate emotional responses of characters.

■ Relate story content to biblical truth: A Christian should trust the Lord and ask Him for help during times of trouble.

■ Identify problems and solutions.

 Use the prepared sentences to introduce the vocabulary words in context.

Before silent reading: pages 20-22

Motivation

▶ Will Josh, Ma, and Buddy avoid the bottleneck?

After silent reading

Overview discussion: pages 20-22

▶ [literal] What is Josh's plan to save the houseboat and family? (slow the houseboat on Crab Island's sandbar and tie lines from the boat to the oaks)

[interpretive] What preparations does Ma make before jumping into the river to help Josh? (Possible answer: She tucks blankets around Buddy, tucks her skirt around her, ties new ropes to the houseboat, and prays.) [BATs: 2e Thoroughness; 6b Prayer]

▶ [critical] Why do Josh and Ma laugh and cry after tying the lines? (Accept any answer, but elicit that they are thankful and relieved to be safe.)

▶ [literal] After comforting Buddy, how do Ma and Josh show they trusted the Lord to help them tie the lines? (They kneel beside Buddy's crib and thank the Lord for saving their lives.) [BATs: 7c Praise; 8a Faith in God's promises]

Crab Island

"Crab Island," he said thoughtfully.

At his mother's questioning look, Josh said, "We can use the current itself to swing us into the south end of the island!"

"But that's a sandbar!"

"Not anymore," Josh said. "It'll be covered with water just like everything else around here. Only that sandbar is good and high. The water'll be shallow."

"And the island will block the current," Ma whispered.

"Partly," Josh said. "Anyway, I think the boat'll slow down long enough for us to get some lines around the live oaks. You'll have to help, though, Ma. We'll need to get two lines tight at once."

Ma nodded. "I'll get ready."

Josh went outside as Ma tucked blankets around Buddy. She stuffed extra ones down the side of the crib for padding. Leaning down, she kissed him softly and then went to the door. Outside, Josh was at the tiller, dodging floating logs and planks whenever he could. Ahead, the black mass of Crab Island loomed out of the dark.

Quickly Ma tied new ropes to the ends of the houseboat, leaving them in neat coils. She tucked her skirt around her legs and tied it tightly.

The boat slid swiftly along the island. Josh edged in closer, letting underbrush and branches drag at the sides and roof. The boat slowed slightly as it neared the south end of the island.

"Ready, Ma?"

Josh saw Ma glance back at the door. If the boat got away from them, Buddy would go through the bottleneck alone. Ma's lips moved, and Josh knew she was praying.

Josh shoved the tiller hard. He heard a sharp crack as the houseboat swung to the right with a jar that almost took Josh to his knees. It slid across the sandbar into shallow water.

"Now, Ma!"

Josh and Ma grabbed the coils of rope and jumped. Water splashed into Josh's face as he plunged toward shore. Behind him he could feel the houseboat turning slowly as the current

20

▶ [interpretive] What does Josh do the next morning? Why? (He repairs the boat; the boat is in poor shape.)

▶ [interpretive] Why isn't Pa angry about the cracked rudder? (He thinks his family is more important.)

[interpretive] How do you know Pa is proud of Josh? (Possible answers: He puts his arm around Josh; he thanks God for Josh's clear thinking; he calls Josh a real riverman; he puts his cap on Josh.)

Follow-up discussion: page 20

▶ [interpretive] Why does Ma think going to Crab Island is a bad idea but then changes her mind? (Usually the south end is a dangerous sandbar, but it is covered with floodwater now and will help to slow the houseboat.)

Read aloud the dialogue between Ma and Josh concerning Crab Island.

▶ [interpretive] What makes Ma glance at the door before jumping into the river? (She is worried that Buddy will go through the bottleneck alone if the houseboat gets away.)

(continued on bottom of next page)

from the other side of the island reached for it.

Josh ran desperately, fighting the water. He reached the first tree and flung his rope around it. Two, three times, he wound the rope before tying it. Then he scrambled across the wet underbrush to Ma. Struggling, they tied the last knot. The houseboat steadied, rocked gently, and was still. Josh and Ma fell into each other's arms, laughing and crying at once.

When they scrambled back onto the boat, Buddy was screaming. Ma took the crying baby out of the crib and held him. When his crying had settled into hiccups, she knelt beside the crib and began to thank the Lord for saving their lives. Josh knelt beside her, weak and shaky with relief.

After he had checked the lines once more, Josh lay down on the rug and slept. He did not awake again until he felt the morning sun dancing on his face through the window.

"You were so tired, I let you sleep," Ma said. Buddy padded over and tumbled on Josh. "Up," he gurgled. "Up."

"Come look," Ma said. Josh stood up and followed her to the door. Water covered the land around them as far as they could see. To the south of them the river flowed swiftly but more calmly than before. Sunlight glinted off the water and off bits and pieces carried by the current. "It's quit rising," Ma said softly. "Pa'll find us as soon as he can. He'll be proud of you, Son."

River's Rising   21

Follow-up discussion: page 21

▶ [appreciative] Have you ever tried running through water that is waist high? Is it hard or easy?

▶ Read aloud the paragraph that describes how Ma and Josh tie the ropes.

[appreciative] Would you stay calm and trust the Lord in a similar situation?

▶ [literal] What does Ma want Josh to see the next morning? (that the river has stopped rising)

▶ [critical] **Why does Ma think Pa will be proud of Josh?** (Answers may vary but should include that Josh acted responsibly and protected the family.)

Read aloud the sentence telling how Josh knows Ma is praying before they jump.

▶ [interpretive] **Can Ma or Josh tie the lines alone? Why or why not?** (No; they need to tie the two ropes at the same time.) [BAT: 2b Teamwork]

[interpretive] **Why do Josh and Ma have to hurry to get the ropes around the trees?** (because the boat will float away and Buddy will go with it)

River's Rising

Follow-up discussion: page 22

▶ [literal] As Josh repairs the houseboat, what is he thankful for? (that the rudder is only cracked, not broken)

Read aloud the paragraph that describes Josh's repairs on the boat. Read to show his diligence toward work and his excitement at seeing Pa coming. [BAT: 2e Diligence]

▶ [literal] How does Pa know where to find his family? (He figures it out when he sees their broken landing and remembers that someone told him there was a boat at Crab Island.)

▶ [critical] What is Pa thinking as he looks over the mooring lines? (Answers may vary, but elicit that he might be looking to make sure the houseboat is secure.)

▶ [critical] Do you agree with Pa that Josh is a real riverman? Why or why not? (Answers may vary, but elicit that rivermen know the river very well and that Josh knew the river well enough to save the family and the houseboat.)

▶ [critical] Could this story have really taken place? Why or why not? (Accept any answer.)

Worktext Objective

The student will

■ Determine cause-and-effect relationships.

Comprehension:
Worktext page 9

Josh turned his head. "I'd better repair the boat then. I thought it was going to rip apart when I ran it under the trees."

Josh spent the rest of the morning repairing the boat. First he hammered back the boards that had been torn by the branches. Then he patched jagged edges and loose shutters. Josh knew that the sharp crack he had heard had been the rudder. He could do nothing about that, except be thankful that it had only cracked, not broken. It was late afternoon when Josh saw a boat approaching. Quickly he called to Ma. "Pa's coming!"

Ma, Josh, and Buddy were calling across the water as soon as Pa came within hearing distance. Pa was grinning as he tied up next to the boat. "Hold on," he said. He looked over the mooring lines without speaking. Then he said, "Somebody told me this morning there was a houseboat down here. I figured out what had happened when I saw the landing."

He listened to Ma's account of the night and then put his arm around Josh. "Son, thank God you kept a clear head."

Josh hesitated. "I broke the rudder."

Pa began to laugh. "What's a rudder compared to my family? You can help me start on a new one tomorrow."

"Come in and eat," Ma said. "You look like you can hardly stand up. "

"I'm tired all right," Pa said, "but we got everybody moved. When the river settles a little more, I'll go back and help the folks salvage some of their things." He removed his cap and put it on Josh's head. "And Josh can go with me. It'll be good to have a real riverman along!"

22

STUDY SKILLS

Locating verses in the Bible

Allow the students to tell about some times when they were afraid.

▶ Did you ask God for help?

What are some verses in which God promises to help us? (Answers may include Psalm 23:1, Psalm 91:2, Psalm 121:1, Isaiah 26:3-4, Isaiah 43:2, Romans 8:28, Philippians 4:6-7, Hebrews 4:16, and Hebrews 13:6.)

As the students give verses, allow them to look up the verses in their Bibles. Choose students to read or say the Scripture aloud.

▶ God is everywhere, even in times of trouble. He promises us in His Word that He takes care of those who love and honor Him. [BAT: 8a Faith in God's promises]

Study Skills: Worktext page 10

Guide the students in looking up the first two verses.

Discuss the answer to each question before the students write it.

Allow the students to complete the page independently.

SOMETHING EXTRA

Write About It: Rainstorming words

Instruct each student to write a paragraph describing a rainstorm. Tell him to describe the way the rain looks, feels, smells, tastes, and sounds. Encourage him to use a thesaurus to find interesting new words. Direct him to underline his favorite or most descriptive sentences and to share them with others.

SKILL LESSON: MAP READING

Lesson	Reader pages	Worktext pages
8	23-26	11-12

VOCABULARY
LESSON 8

†The bucket and spoon are symbols for the drinking fountain and picnic areas on the park map. (p. 23)

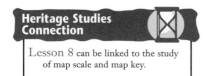

Heritage Studies Connection

Lesson 8 can be linked to the study of map scale and map key.

Connections are designed to provide ideas to connect themes in Reading with other subject areas. These do not correlate with specific lessons in other BJU Press products.

Materials
- Various types of maps (United States, road, physical, world, natural resource)
- Ruler for each student
- Vocabulary sentences for display (e.g., on the chalkboard or on sentence strips)

Background information
Political map—This map identifies political units and boundaries such as counties, states, and national divisions of continents.

Physical map—This map identifies physical features such as land elevation, rivers, and bodies of water.

State/city/county maps—These maps identify state boundaries, transportation routes, cities, towns, rivers, and geographical subdivisions.

Special-purpose maps—These maps identify temperature, climate, vegetation, and economic activities such as agriculture, manufacturing, population density, and transportation.

INTRODUCTION
Vocabulary

Use the prepared sentence to introduce the vocabulary word in context.

Taking a trip
▶ Let's pretend we are taking a trip across the country. On our trip, we will visit some famous land formations and bodies of water.

Where would you like to go?

List for display several places mentioned.

▶ What will we need to help us find our way as we are traveling to our destinations? (maps)

Have you used a map to help you find your way somewhere? (Suggest mall maps or park maps.)

Would a map be useful to you if you did not know how to read one? (no)

Name one of the destinations and hold up a map that would not help one to reach that destination (e.g., destination—Niagara Falls; map—Florida).

▶ Will this map help us find our way? Why not?

▶ Not all maps show the same information.

Show several different types of maps (e.g., political/physical, product, natural resource, population, and rainfall maps).

▶ How are these maps the same?

How are these maps different?

Correlated Activities
- **Word Work, Activity 2: Blooper Blurbs**
- **Spelling Practice, Activity 1: Spell Check**
See "Classroom Management for Grouping" in the Appendix.

SKILL LESSON:

Map Reading

• Maps

Maps come in different shapes and sizes and can give the reader many different types of information. Some maps include roads and highways to help the map reader find his way in unfamiliar territory. Other maps may show the boundaries of countries, states, or counties. Another type of map may emphasize the physical features of an area of the world. Many kinds of information can be shown on a map, and sometimes more than one type of information may appear.

In order for anyone to make use of the information given on a map, the mapmaker must provide a legend or a key to explain the symbols and colors used to identify the different kinds of information. In order for the map reader to understand the size of the area being shown or the distance from one place to another, the mapmaker must provide a scale which can be used to measure those distances.

Skill Lesson: Map Reading   23

COMPREHENSION

The student will

- Identify main ideas.
- Distinguish between relevant and irrelevant information.
- Identify information explicitly stated.
- Read for specific information.

Objectives

Before silent reading: pages 23-26

Motivation
▶ What types of maps are there?
▶ What helps us to read a map?

After silent reading

Overview discussion: pages 23-26

▶ [interpretive] Why are maps useful? (Possible answers: Maps help you find your way in unfamiliar territory; they show boundaries of countries and show states or counties; they emphasize physical features.)

▶ [interpretive] What two parts of a map make it easier to read? (a key and a scale)

[interpretive] Why is a scale on a map useful? (It helps you to measure the distance between features on a map and to understand the size of the area shown.)

[interpretive] Why is a key on a map useful? (It helps you interpret the symbols representing the physical features on a map.)

Follow-up discussion: page 23

▶ Read aloud the paragraph that describes different types of maps.

[critical] If you were traveling across several states, what type of map would be most helpful? (Accept any answer, but point out that a road map would be most helpful.)

▶ [critical] Why wouldn't you put all types of information on the same map? (Answers may vary, but elicit that it would be confusing to read.)

▶ [literal] What does a mapmaker include on a map to make it possible to read and use the information given? (a legend or key)

▶ [literal] What does a mapmaker include to help you understand the size of an area or the distance from one place to another on a map? (a scale)

Follow-up discussion: page 24

▶ [literal] What does the map on this page show? (Reedy River, the river where Josh's adventure took place; farmland; Brackenville; Crab Island; and Bottleneck Cliffs)

▶ Read aloud the sentence that tells why a scale is useful to the map reader.

[literal] Look at Map A. An inch on this map represents how many miles? (five)

[interpretive] Using your ruler and the scale on Map A, measure the distance from Brackenville to Crab Island as if you were going down the river. How far is it? (approximately ten miles)

[critical] If you did not have a scale, how would you find the distance between objects or places? (Answers may vary, but elicit that measuring distances with a scale and a map is more practical than measuring the distance at the actual place.)

• **Map Scale**

If Josh drew a map of the river where his adventure took place, his map might look like Map A.

To help someone reading the map to measure the correct distances, Josh would include a scale.

A map scale compares the distances on the map to the actual distances on the earth. Often the scale is shown by a straight line which may be divided into smaller parts. Each section stands for a certain number of miles. For example, one inch may represent one mile, or one inch may represent five miles, depending on the size of the map. The map reader

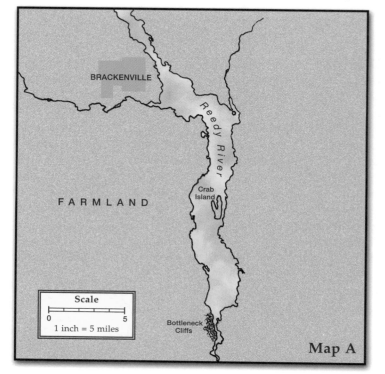

Exploits

can then use this scale to measure the exact distance between two points on the map.

Next Josh might draw a map of the section of the river where his adventure actually happened. His drawing might look like Map B.

Because of the difference in the area shown, a different *scale* is needed for each map. The scale for Map A is smaller—one inch equals five miles. If the drawing of the river is five inches long on the first map, then the real river is twenty-five miles long. On Map B, one inch equals one mile. Crab Island is two inches long on this map, so the island itself is two miles long.

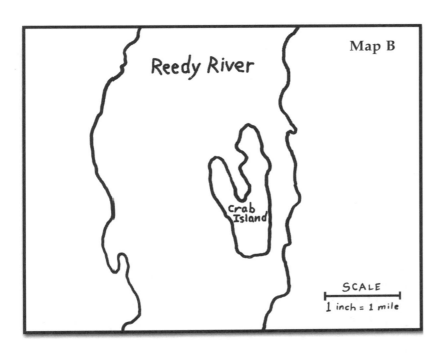

Map B

Reedy River

Crab Island

SCALE
1 inch = 1 mile

Follow-up discussion: page 25

▶ [interpretive] What would be the problem if Josh used the same scale from Map A for Map B? (Measurements would not be accurate.)

▶ [literal] One inch on Map B represents how many miles? (one)

[interpretive] Using your ruler and the scale on Map B, measure the widest part of the river. How wide is it? (two and a half to three miles)

Follow-up discussion: page 26

▶ [literal] On a map, how are physical features shown and made understandable to a map reader? (They are shown with symbols and colors and made understandable with a key.)

▶ [literal] Why would Josh want to include physical features on his map? (to identify characteristics important to his story)

[literal] What physical features are shown on Josh's map? (water, farmland, unfarmed land, oaks, sandbar, and current)

[interpretive] On this map, how can you find the sandbar and oaks that saved Josh's family? (Look at the key to find the symbol and color representing the sandbar and oaks and find those on the map.)

[interpretive] Does this map help a map reader to see Josh's adventure on the flooded river more clearly? How? (Yes; elicit that the map makes it easier to see what happened by using the colors and symbols to mark the physical features.)

[critical] Do you think the symbols and colors are appropriate for the physical features they represent? Why or why not? (Answers may vary, but elicit that the colors and symbols are similar to the real physical features.)

• **Map Keys**

Although Map B shows where the island is located on the river, it does not show the physical features of the area. Josh may wish to identify the characteristics that are important to his story.

He could do this using colors or symbols. Finally, Josh would need a key so anyone reading his map could understand at a glance the markings he used. His finished map might look like Map C.

Josh's knowledge of the river would help him draw a map of the river and the surrounding area. By identifying and labeling the features on the map, he would be able to help his teacher see more clearly exactly what had happened. And by providing a scale he could show the exact distance from place to place.

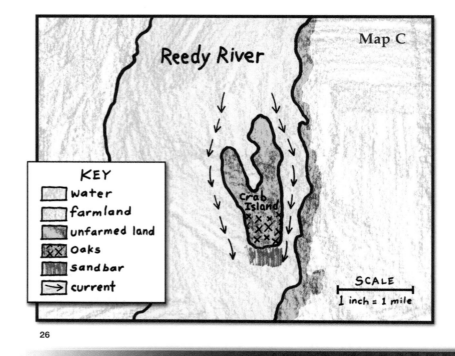

STUDY SKILLS
Map scales and keys

▶ On a map, what helps you measure distances between places? (a map scale)

What helps you understand the size of the area shown on a map? (a map scale)

▶ What helps you understand the physical features on a map? (a map key)

What shows you what the symbols and colors on a map represent? (a map key)

Study Skills: Worktext page 11

▶ Look at the map on the page. The map is similar to one we looked at in our reader. What is the scale for this map? (1 inch=4 miles)

Let's use our rulers to measure the distance across the river near Welcome City.

Demonstrate to the students how to measure the number of inches from one dot to another as they measure the distance on their pages.

▶ How many inches is the distance on the map? (about ¼ inch)

▶ Place the ¼ inch on your ruler below the map scale, lining up the left edge of the ruler with the 0 on the scale.

How many miles is the distance across the river near Welcome City? (1 mile)

Write the answer in the blank.

Guide the students in completing the page if necessary.

Study Skills: Worktext page 12

▶ What are some physical features that could be on a map? (possible answers: mountains, lakes, rivers)

How would these features be shown on a map? (symbols, colors, shading)

Allow the students to draw their own maps, including a map key and a map scale if they wish.

SOMETHING EXTRA
Write About It: Mapmakers

Challenge each student to make a map of his neighborhood, a room, or the school grounds. Help the student to include an accurate scale (one inch equals a specified number of feet) and key. An estimate may be used if the student is not able to actually measure the distances. Display a real map of a city or school for reference. Remind the student to use symbols and/or colors to represent various objects or places on the map. Instruct the student to exchange maps with another student and see if each student can figure out the place the map represents.

Objectives

The student will
- Read a map scale.
- Determine distance using a map scale.
- Draw a map that includes physical features, a map key, and a map scale.

Lesson	Worktext pages
9	212-15

Objectives

The student will

- Define plot as a sequence of events.
- Sequence the events of a plot.
- Identify the beginning, middle, and end of the story.
- Define conflict as a problem in a story that must be solved.
- Identify the conflict of a plot.

Background information

Plot and conflict—Plot is the order of action in a story. A story has three parts—beginning, middle, and end—with the conflict, or problem of the plot, revealed at the start of the middle and solved at the close of the middle.

1 Introduction

▶ Every story tells about certain events. In "River's Rising," we read about a family living on a houseboat. Name some events from that story. (Possible answers: A flood came; the houseboat broke loose; Josh helped with the boat, his mom, and his little brother.)

Write the named events for display. Discuss the order in which they occurred.

▶ Related events and their order make up the plot of a story.

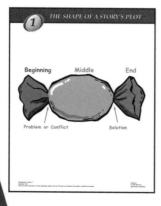

Materials

- Pocket chart
- Overhead marking pen
- Teaching Visual 1: *The Shape of a Story's Plot*
- Sentence strips for the following sentences:

  Ralph was a knight.
  Ralph had to help rid the country of dragons.
  Ralph met a dragon and was going to kill it.
  The dragon promised to pack up and leave the country if Ralph wouldn't hurt it.
  Ralph let the dragon go.
  Ralph continued to search for other dragons.

PLOT AND CONFLICT

2 Skill development: Sequencing

Read aloud the following story, "Ralph and the Dragon."

Ralph was a knight. He was required by law to help rid the country of all the dragons. Ralph started out on his horse to find a dragon. He was loaded down with a sword, two muskets, and a small cannon. Ralph met a dragon and was preparing to kill it. The dragon saw Ralph and begged not to be killed. It promised to pack up and leave the country, provided that Ralph didn't try to hurt it. Ralph let the dragon go after it promised to go to a faraway country. Ralph continued his search for other dragons.

Display the prepared sentence strips out of order. Guide students in sequencing them correctly.

3 Skill development: Visual 1—*The Shape of a Story's Plot*

▶ A story plot has a definite shape and parts, like this piece of candy.

Draw attention to the labels on the visual. As answers are given to the questions about "Ralph and the Dragon," write them in the appropriate parts of the visual.

▶ What kind of information might you find out in the *beginning* of a story? (possible answers: names of characters or what the story is about)

What information did you find out in the beginning of "Ralph and the Dragon"? (Ralph was a knight.)

▶ The largest part of a story is its *middle*. The middle begins when we learn about the story's problem. Can you guess when the middle part of a story ends? (when the problem is solved)

The problem can also be called a *conflict*. What is a conflict? (a fight, struggle, or problem)

What was the problem or conflict in the story about Ralph? (Ralph, the knight, has to help get rid of all the dragons in his country.)

When did the middle of the story about Ralph begin? (when we learned that Ralph had to get rid of dragons)

When did the middle part end? (when Ralph agreed to let the dragon go to a faraway country)

▶ What kind of information might be told at the end of a story? (possible answer: what happened to the characters later in life or how other people react when the conflict is solved)

What was told at the end of the story of Ralph after the conflict or problem was solved? (Ralph continued to search for other dragons.)

▶What's the Problem?

Read this paragraph. Then number the events in order. Circle the event that tells what the problem or *conflict* is.

Rapunzel was a very happy girl. But one day a wicked woman locked her in the top of a high tower without any food or water. Happily, the prince from next door wanted to rescue her. He was not only a prince but also a captain of the local volunteer firemen's brigade. So he called his men together. They drove the fire truck to the tower and used the big ladder to bring Rapunzel down. The prince married Rapunzel and they lived happily ever after.

__3__ The prince called his men together.

__2__ Rapunzel was locked in the top of a high tower without any food or water.

__4__ The prince and his men drove the fire truck to the tower and rescued Rapunzel.

__5__ The prince married Rapunzel.

__1__ Rapunzel was a very happy girl.

▶Find the Parts of the Plot

Write the number of the event that fits the beginning.
Write the numbers of the events from the middle.
Write the number of the event that belongs at the end.

Beginning   **Middle**   **End**

1   2, 3, 4   5

All the necessary events in a story are called the **plot**.

212

---

④ Skill application:
Worktext page 212

What's the Problem?
Direct the students to read the paragraph silently. Guide them in numbering the events in order and circling the conflict.

Find the Parts of the Plot
Guide the students in completing the activity as you ask the following questions.

▶ Now let's identify the three parts to the plot of this short story. Which sentence stated something in the beginning of the plot? (Rapunzel was a very happy girl.)

▶ Which sentences tell something from the middle of the plot? (Rapunzel was locked in the top of a high tower without any food or water; the prince called his men together; the prince and his men drove the fire truck to the tower and rescued Rapunzel.)

▶ Which happened at the end of the plot? (The prince married Rapunzel.)

⑤ Skill practice:
Worktext page 213

---

⑥ Skill practice:
Worktext pages 214-15

▶ Have you ever wanted something so much that it would be a dream come true if you got it?

▶ Bill (Scruggs) Grady, a foster child, is close to having his dream come true—a home of his own in Peabody, Wisconsin, with Mrs. Bennett, a lady in his church.

In this cutting from *A Dangerous Game*, Scruggs arrives home from church on the church bus one Sunday morning and finds a visitor with his foster parents, the Wilsons. It seems that they have news for him.

Direct the students to read the selection silently to find out if Scruggs's dream comes true.

▶ All stories have conflict. What is the problem or conflict in *A Dangerous Game*? (Scruggs does not want to go live with his aunt.)

After the big problem is told, other problems may be added to make the first problem even bigger or more complicated.

▶ *A Dangerous Game* is one book in a series of six called the Peabody Series, by Jeri Massi. Other books from this series are pictured on page 215.

Answer the questions about *A Dangerous Game* and then read to find out what kinds of conflicts are found in the other books. Think of possible problems to add to them.

Note: The selection on worktext page 214 and the summaries on worktext page 215 are taken from books in the Peabody Series by Jeri Massi (BJU Press). You may wish to obtain this series of six books for your classroom.

A WISE KING AND A WISE SON

Lesson	Reader pages	Worktext pages
10	27-31	13
11	31-35	14

The old king seeks an heir to rule his kingdom and to marry the beautiful princess. Three brothers try to pass the test that the king sets forth. While each of them works at the task diligently, only the youngest demonstrates the wisdom the king seeks.

VOCABULARY

LESSON 10

*†Because of our lack of practice, our victory astounded the coach. (p. 27)

*†The king sat on his throne holding his royal scepter. (p. 28)

*Lost in the wilderness, the puppy had to fend for himself. (p. 30)

After studying all night long, Trent's eyes looked red and bleary. (p. 30)

LESSON 11

*The carpenter's son had wielded a hammer since he was ten years old. (p. 31)

†After cutting the stalks of wheat, he gathered and tied them into shocks to dry. (p. 32)

Materials

- Bag of wheat
- Picture of a scythe
- Vocabulary sentences for display (e.g., on the chalkboard or on sentence strips)

INTRODUCTION

Vocabulary

Use the prepared sentences to introduce the vocabulary words in context.

Making flour

Display the bag of wheat flour and the picture of a scythe.

▶ How do you think this flour was made? (Accept any answer, but point out that flour is made by harvesting the grain, separating it from the chaff, and grinding the seeds into flour.)

How did people harvest wheat before machinery was invented? (Accept any answer, but elicit that a scythe was used to cut the wheat.)

Characteristics of a play

Direct the students to page 27.

▶ What does the heading "Cast" mean on this page? (the group of actors or characters in the play)

Do you know what is meant by "Act I"? (the first part of the play)

How do you know when a different character is speaking in a play? (The character's name is in bold lettering before the words he speaks.)

Correlated Activities
- **Vocabulary Box, Activity 1: Word Hunt**
- **Creative Writing, Activity 2: Senses in Setting**
See "Classroom Management for Grouping" in the Appendix.

A Wise King and a Wise Son

*adapted by
Kristin Lehman
and Karen Wilt*

*illustrated by
Justin Gerard*

Cast

Narrator #1	Youngest Son
Narrator #2	Blind Man
King	Lame Man
Princess	Guard
Mother	Herald
Oldest Son	Clerk
Second Son	

Act I

Narrator #1: A long time ago, in a faraway land, there ruled a wise king. His great wisdom astounded the people of his kingdom, and they honored him faithfully. It put fear into the heart of every enemy, for none of them could do anything to harm him or his kingdom. During the years of his reign, wisdom came to be valued more than the brightest diamonds or the purest gold.

Narrator #2: The wise king often journeyed through his kingdom to listen to the folk who served him, and many said that each mile he rode multiplied his wisdom. His young daughter always traveled with him, winning the peasants' hearts with her charming smile and gracious heart.

A Wise King and a Wise Son   27

COMPREHENSION

Objectives

The student will

■ Determine the emotional responses of characters.
■ Interpret idiomatic expressions.
■ Note the author's use of imagery.

Before silent reading: pages 27-31

Motivation

▶ Who thinks this king is wise? Why?

What does the wise king do to show his wisdom?

After silent reading

Overview discussion: pages 27-31

▶ [literal] What do the people think of their king? (He is wise and they honor him faithfully.)

[interpretive] How does the king show he is wise? (He rides through the kingdom, listening to his people.)

▶ [critical] Why do you think the king's contest is so important to the people of the kingdom? (Accept any answer, but elicit that the people need a future king.)

▶ [critical] How do you think the widow feels when she sees her sons go off to answer the king's challenge? (Accept any answer.)

Follow-up discussion: page 27

▶ [interpretive] What does the author write to let you know this story is make-believe? (It starts out, "a long time ago, in a faraway land.")

▶ [literal] What is valued more than diamonds or gold in this kingdom? (wisdom)

[interpretive] Why do the people honor the king so faithfully? (because his great wisdom astounds them) [BAT: 5e Loyalty]

[interpretive] What makes you think that the wise king cares for his subjects? (He often journeys through the kingdom to listen to those who serve him.)

▶ [literal] Who travels with the king? (his daughter)

[interpretive] How is the princess like her father? (Possible answers: She travels through the kingdom; she is kind.)

A Wise King and a Wise Son

Follow-up discussion: page 28

▶ [literal] What do the people begin to wonder about their king? (They wonder who will reign when the king can no longer raise his scepter.)

[interpretive] When will the king no longer raise his scepter? (when he is too old or when he dies)

[critical] Do you think the king is disappointed that he doesn't have a son to take his place on the throne? Why or why not? (Accept any answer.)

▶ [interpretive] How does the king answer the questions in the people's minds? (He sends heralds through the kingdom to announce a trial for men who wish to marry the princess.)

Pretend you are the herald and read aloud the king's challenge. Be sure the crowd can hear you!

Narrator #1: But as the years passed, the king grew old. Many times the good people of the kingdom wondered who would reign when the king could no longer raise his scepter. No royal son had been born to take his place.

Narrator #2: The wise king knew the thoughts of his subjects. One day in late summer the heralds of the throne rode through the kingdom, spreading news that answered the question.

Herald: *(reading from a scroll)* Hear ye, hear ye. Be it known that His Majesty, the king, desires a worthy man to marry his daughter, the princess, and to reign as king in his stead. His Majesty has planned a trial to determine the worthiness of each young man who seeks the hand of the princess.

Narrator #1: Many young men of the kingdom heard the proclamation and flocked to the palace to answer the king's challenge. One by one they failed and returned home.

Narrator #2: Meanwhile, in a far corner of the kingdom there lived a widow and her three sons. The sons plowed their stubborn corner of land, raising just enough wheat to feed themselves through the winter. The widow gave her sons all the schooling they required. Many of the villagers could not read as well as the three boys or figure half so quickly.

Narrator #1: In the middle of the harvest, the youngest boy drove the yearling calf to market to sell it. There he came upon a group of townsfolk gathered around a public notice board.

Clerk: *(whispering)* Can you read it, lad?

Youngest Son: *(standing up proudly)* Yes, sir. "Be it known that His Majesty, the king, desires a worthy man to marry his daughter, the princess, and to reign as king in his stead. His Majesty has planned a trial to determine the worthiness of each young man who seeks the hand of the princess."

Clerk: Ah me, imagine that. I'm off at once to try for such a prize! Care to join me?

Youngest Son: Oh, I'd love to try. I saw the princess once from a long distance. She's fairer than the morning sunshine on a field of honeysuckle. But alas, I have a job to do here and cannot leave my widowed mother. The best to you, sir. *(He waves farewell.)*

Narrator #2: After supper that evening, the widow's three sons discussed the notice.

Youngest Son: *(turning to his mother)* What do you think, Mother? You always give us good advice.

Mother: *(smiling)* Well, my sons, you have served me as good children and cared for me for many a long year. Soon you must go out and seek your fortunes. My blessings go with you in whatever you decide.

Oldest Son: *(jumping up from the table)* Then I'll be off at once. You'll hear news of me within the week.

A Wise King and a Wise Son   29

Follow-up discussion: page 29

► [critical] Why do many men flock to the palace to answer the king's challenge? (Answers will vary, but elicit that they want to marry the princess and someday become the king.)

[critical] Why do you think so many of the men of the kingdom fail the king's challenge? (Accept any answer.)

► Read aloud what is happening in another corner of the kingdom.

[interpretive] Why do you think the author describes the sons' land as "stubborn"? (Elicit that it is hard to plow.)

► [critical] Why does the clerk whisper to the youngest son when he asks if he can read the notice? (Accept any answer, but suggest that he might be embarrassed that he cannot read the notice himself.)

► Read aloud with awe the youngest son's description of the princess.

► [interpretive] How do you know that the youngest son values his mother's opinion? (He asks for her advice.)

[interpretive] Why does the mother feel that she can give her blessing in whatever her sons decide to do? (because her sons have cared for her for many years, and soon they must seek their own fortunes)

[interpretive] Which son seems to be the most excited about trying his hand at the king's challenge? How do you know? (the oldest son; because he leaves right away)

Follow-up discussion: pages 30-31

▶ [literal] Why doesn't the youngest son leave at once to try the king's task? (He does not want to leave his mother to fend for herself.) [BATs: 5a Love; 5b Giving]

[appreciative] How do you show your parents that you care about them?

▶ [literal] What is the task that the king requires? (He wants the oldest son to harvest wheat until noon the next day.)

Read aloud the conversation between the king and the oldest son as if you were a wise king commanding a task and a young man answering with a proud attitude.

▶ [interpretive] How do you know time is passing as the oldest son works? (Possible answers: The sun begins to set; the children run home to dinner; he works all through the night.)

[interpretive] Is the oldest son more concerned about protecting the wheat or helping the blind man? (protecting the wheat)

▶ [critical] What could the oldest son have done to show the blind man kindness? (possible answers: helped him to the castle, asked him if he was all right) [BAT: 5a Kindness]

▶ [critical] How do you think the oldest son feels as he finishes harvesting the wheat just as the king drives up in the coach? (Accept any answer, but suggest that he feels proud and happy that he finished harvesting all the wheat.)

[critical] Do you think the oldest son is surprised when the king tells him that he failed the test? Why or why not? (Accept any answer.)

Read aloud with regret the king's dismissal of the oldest son.

Looking ahead

▶ Will the king find a man worthy to marry the princess?

Who will that man be?

Second Son: *(rising from the table)* I must try also, Mother. I believe I'll be off in the morning.

Narrator #1: So in the early morning light of the next day, the youngest son waved good-bye as his brother set out on the same road the oldest son had traveled.

Youngest Son: *(taking his mother's arm)* Mother, I cannot leave you to fend for yourself. I shall wait and see what may come to pass.

Narrator #2: The oldest brother arrived at the palace at noon. Dust rose from his shoes at each footfall, and his eyes were bleary with lack of sleep.

Oldest Son: *(boldly to the guard)* I have come to take the test for the hand of the princess.

Guard: Come this way. *(The guard leads the way to the king.)*

Narrator #1: The guard ushered him into the throne room where the king offered him meat and drink.

King: The task I require is not difficult. Yonder is a field of wheat. *(He points out a window.)* You must harvest the wheat until

noon tomorrow. If you do well, the princess will be wed to you.

Oldest Son: *(smiling)* I have harvested wheat each fall since I was old enough to hold a scythe. Perhaps such a trial is too easy.

King: *(crossing his arms)* We shall see.

Narrator #1: The oldest son raced to the field. Over and over he swung the scythe, cutting the wheat. Then he bundled it in sturdy stacks and stood them on the edge of the field. The sun began to set as he worked on. Children laughed and ran home to dinner, but still he worked. All through the night the young man worked. By morning he had only a corner of the field left. Suddenly a blind man stumbled into the field.

Oldest Son: *(running to the man)* Be careful; you'll crush the grain.

Narrator #2: He lifted the man awkwardly by the arm and set him on the road.

Blind Man: Can you direct me to the palace?

Oldest Son: Yes, straight down

30

The student will

■ Match synonyms.

■ Use context clues to determine meaning.

Vocabulary:
Worktext page 13

▶ What are synonyms? (words that have the same or similar meanings)

Write the following columns of words.

foe	*rule*	*job*	*travel*
reign	*enemy*	*journey*	*task*

Guide the students in matching the above synonyms before they complete the page independently.

the road and to the left.

Blind Man: Thank you. *(He shuffles away.)*

Narrator #1: The oldest son increased his pace, swinging, cutting, and bundling until the field stood clean. At the last swoosh of his scythe, he saw the king drive

up in his coach.

King: *(leaning out the window)* A fine job, my son, but I'm sorry you did not pass. You have done better than most, but alas, the trial requires more.

Narrator #1: And so the oldest son returned home.

Act II

Narrator #2: The second son reached the palace as the bells chimed for dinner. He was ushered into the dining room to eat with the king.

King: *(pushing his plate back)* Your trial, as all the others have been, is to harvest a field of wheat for me until dinner tomor-

row. You must do well.

Second Son: *(rubbing his hands together)* Indeed, a simple task. I have wielded a scythe since I left the cradle.

King: *(wisely)* We shall see.

Narrator #1: The second son flew at once to the task of clearing a great portion of his field

A Wise King and a Wise Son 31

Follow-up discussion: page 31

▶ [interpretive] How is the second son like the oldest son when he hears the king's task? (He thinks the task is too easy.)

COMPREHENSION

Objectives

The student will

- Identify character traits.
- Discern motives of characters.
- Note the author's use of fore-shadowing.

 Use the prepared sentences to introduce the vocabulary words in context.

Before silent reading: pages 31-35

Motivation

▶ What is the king really trying to find out with the task he requires?

After silent reading

Overview discussion: pages 31-35

▶ [critical] What was the king really trying to find out about the men by giving them the task? (Accept any answer, but point out that he is trying to find out if they would be kind to the blind and the lame and show wisdom in their work.)

[interpretive] Why does the king choose the youngest son to marry his daughter? (because the youngest son is kind to the blind man and the lame man and because he takes responsibility for his work)

[appreciative] How would you react to the blind man and the lame man?

Follow-up discussion: page 32

▶ [interpretive] What makes you think that the second son might win the hand of the princess? (He works even more quickly than his brother does.)

[literal] How does the second son treat the blind man differently than his older brother did? (Instead of just pointing the blind man in the direction of the castle, he leads the man there himself.)

Read aloud the conversation between the second son and the blind man. Show the impatience of the second son.

▶ [critical] How do you think the second son feels when the king tells him that he too has failed the test? (Accept any answer.)

▶ [interpretive] What does the mother say the youngest son has learned that hints or foreshadows what might happen? (The mother says, "You have learned well the ways of wisdom. Now take your things and be off. Put your learning to use.")

before dark. On through the night he worked, even more quickly than his brother. As dawn broke, a blind man stumbled across his path.

Second Son: *(taking the blind man's arm)* What do you here?

Blind Man: I seek the palace.

Second Son: I have just time to guide you there, and then I must hurry back to my task. *(He leads the blind man away.)*

Narrator #2: The second son led the blind man to the palace gates, bade him farewell, and returned to the wheat field. Just as the last wheat fell, a lame man hobbled up.

Lame Man: Can you direct me to the palace?

Second Son: *(pointing in the direction of the palace)* Yes, straight ahead and to the left.

Narrator #1: The second son pulled the last shocks into a bundle and began tying it as the lame man stumbled away. Minutes later the king drove up in his coach.

King: *(looking over the field)* A very fine job, my son. Better than anyone before you. But

32

alas, you too have failed. I am very sorry. *(He pats the boy on the shoulder.)*

Narrator #2: And so the second son followed the path of his brother and returned home.

Narrator #1: Both brothers told their adventures to their mother and bade the youngest brother attempt the task.

Mother: *(putting her hand on his shoulder)* Perhaps it is your turn to try your hand.

Youngest Son: Thank you, Mother. I have waited to make sure you were well cared for.

Mother: You have learned well the ways of wisdom. Now take your things and be off. Put your learning to use.

Narrator #2: Before long, the guard at the gate was leading the youngest son to the throne room. The king and his daughter sat at a game of chess. The young man stood at the door, his heart melting at the sight of the lovely princess.

Princess: *(pouting)* Father, you shall put me in check no matter where I move!

Youngest Son: *(stepping forward)* Your Highness, you do have one move that could win the game.

Princess: *(picking up a chess piece)* Why, yes, of course. I see it now. Thank you, kind sir.

Youngest Son: *(blushing and looking away)* You're welcome.

Narrator #1: The young man's heart pounded so hard in his own ears that he stepped back, fearing that she would hear it beating.

Narrator #2: When the game was over, the king set it aside and explained the trial to the boy. Bowing, the youngest son hurried to begin the task.

A Wise King and a Wise Son 33

Follow-up discussion: page 33

▶ [interpretive] How does the youngest son help the princess? (He shows her how to win the chess game.)

▶ [interpretive] How does the author let you know that the youngest son likes the princess? (He blushes and his heart pounds when she speaks to him; his heart melts at the sight of her.)

Read aloud what the youngest son feels after helping the princess.

Follow-up discussion: page 34

▶ Read aloud in a steadfast voice the narrator's description of the youngest son as he cuts the field of wheat.

▶ [literal] What does the youngest son do when he sees the blind man and the lame man? (runs to help them)

[interpretive] How are the youngest son's actions different from the actions of the two other sons? (He takes the blind man and the lame man to the castle and talks with them along the way.) [BATs: 5a Love; 5e Friendliness]

[critical] How do the youngest son's actions show more kindness than the actions of the two older sons? (Answers may vary, but elicit that he does more than he has to.)

Read aloud what the youngest son does when the lame man approaches.

Narrator #1: The scythe flew as he harvested the grain, but the field stretched on and on. The king had given him the largest field of all to cut. The young man worked on through the night. The morning came and passed, and he continued working. The heat of noon beat down, and he worked on still.

Narrator #2: As evening approached, a blind man came stumbling down the road. The boy saw him from a distance and ran to help him.

Youngest Son: *(helping the man)* Where are you going, good sir?

Blind Man: To the palace.

Youngest Son: Let me guide you there.

Narrator #1: The two laughed and talked along the way.

Blind Man: My blessing on you, my son.

Youngest Son: Fare thee well. *(He runs in the direction of the field.)*

Narrator #1: He ran back down the road to the field and continued to cut the wheat. Soon a lame man approached. Again the boy ran to help, offering his shoulder and joking and talking as he led the man to the palace.

Lame Man: My blessing to you, Son. *(He sits down beside the gate.)*

Youngest Son: *(waving farewell)* Thank you and farewell.

34

Narrator #2: In the field the golden wheat bent and swayed with the breeze. Barely half of it lay in bundles. And far up the road, the coach of the king raised dust as it approached. The boy fell to cutting more quickly than he had ever done before, but it was too late. The coach drew to a stop.

Youngest Son: *(kneeling before the king)* I am sorry, Your Highness. I have failed to complete the task, but I thank you for the opportunity.

King: *(helping the boy to his feet)* My son, you alone have passed the test. Not only did you deal kindly with the blind man and the lame man but you also answered for your work with wisdom, showing that you alone are responsible for it. I told you only to harvest the wheat in the field. I did not say how much of the field was required.

Youngest Son: *(stammering)* Your Highness, did those men speak with you?

King: *(pointing to himself)* I was those men! Now come with me. You have yet more to learn in the ways of ruling a kingdom.

Follow-up discussion: page 35

▶ [critical] How do you think the youngest son feels when he sees the king's coach coming but only half of the wheat is done? (Accept any answer.)

[interpretive] How does the youngest son answer for his work with wisdom, showing that he is responsible? (He says he is sorry for not finishing the task and thanks the king for the opportunity to try.)

[interpretive] What makes you think that the youngest son is surprised that he passes the test? (He stammers when the king congratulates him on passing the test.)

Read aloud with kindness what the king says to the youngest son about passing the test.

▶ [critical] Why do you think the king dresses as the blind man and lame man? (Accept any answer.)

Worktext Objectives

The student will

■ Match characters and dialogue.

Comprehension: Worktext page 14

Before the students begin the page, elicit that true riches are not the physical things around us that we can buy but those things that cannot be bought, such as family, friendships, and God's love.

A Wise King and a Wise Son

SOMETHING EXTRA

Write About It: Fortune by foot

Explain that each of the three sons set out on a journey by foot to find his fortune and to gain the princess's hand in marriage. Direct each student to trace his own foot and write (within the outline) a short story about a journey of his own and whether he found his fortune or was forced to return home.

Read It: Play performance

Guide the students as they read and act out the play together.

Materials

- Teaching Visual 2: *Getting the Message*
- Art supplies such as colored pencils, markers, crayons, colored chalk, water-colors

Lesson	Worktext pages
12	216-17

MAIN IDEA AND SUPPORTING DETAILS

1 Introduction

Draw attention to the various art supplies.

▶ If I asked you to write a paragraph about these items, what would you write about? (possible answers: an artist, art class, instructions for a project)

▶ It is possible to write many different kinds of paragraphs from one idea. Who decides which idea a paragraph will be about? (the writer of the paragraph)

▶ A writer tries to tell us his idea with words and sentences. It is up to the reader to get the writer's message. Do you know how to get the message?

2 Skill development: Visual 2—*Getting the Message*

Begin the following discussion with the bottom part of the visual below the paragraph covered. Uncover each question as it is discussed.

▶ Here is a paragraph about some art supplies. What is the author's message? What is the main idea? First, listen as I read. Then we'll answer two questions to find the main idea.

Read the paragraph aloud.

▶ Whom was this paragraph about? (the artists that illustrate our reading books)

What special or interesting thing does the paragraph tell about the artists? (They use many different tools to create paintings for the books.)

▶ Put these two answers together to find the main idea of the paragraph. What is it? (Artists use many different tools to create paintings for the reading books.)

Which sentence of the paragraph gives the main idea? (the first one)

▶ Sometimes the first sentence of a paragraph tells the main idea. But what about the other sentences? What are they for? There is a lot more information in this paragraph that adds to the main idea. What other information did we find out? (Answers will vary.)

All these facts are details added to the main idea to help us know more about the main idea. These additional pieces of information reinforce and support the main idea. They are called *supporting details*. Just as the artist draws an illustration and then adds colors and draws little details to make it better, a writer adds supporting details with words and sentences to make the main idea clearer.

The student will

- Infer main idea.
- Distinguish between the main idea and the supporting details.

Objectives

Background information

Main idea—Well written paragraphs are arranged in an orderly fashion. Each paragraph has a main idea and information that supports that idea. If the main idea is not specifically stated, it can be determined by answering two questions: Whom or what is the paragraph about? What is special about this subject?

3 Skill development:
Worktext page 216
Finding the Main Idea
▶ Sometimes it is difficult to tell the difference between the main idea and supporting details. Let's read a paragraph from "Skill Lesson: Map Reading" and identify the main idea and the supporting details. Then we'll look at the difference between them.

Read the paragraph aloud.

▶ What is the main idea of the paragraph? Think about whom or what it is about and what is special about them in this paragraph. (Maps come in different shapes and sizes and can give the reader many different types of information.)

▶ What supporting details are added to make the information about maps clearer? (Possible answers: Some maps show roads; some maps show boundaries; some maps show physical features.)

▶ Why would finding your way in unfamiliar territory not be the main idea? (Accept thoughtful answers, but point out that it tells about only one part of the kinds of information maps give.)

▶ When you decide what you think the main idea is, check to see if it tells about the entire paragraph. Any information that gives details that add to or describe the main idea is a supporting detail.

Identifying the Details
Guide the students in reading the paragraph and distinguishing between the main idea and the supporting details.

4 Skill practice:
Worktext page 217

Which Is It?

▶ Finding the Main Idea
Read the following paragraph. Underline the main idea.

<u>Maps come in different shapes and sizes and can give the reader many different types of information.</u> Some maps include roads and highways to help the map reader find his way in unfamiliar territory. Other maps may show the boundaries of countries, states, or counties. Another type of map may emphasize the physical features of an area of the world. Many kinds of information can be shown on a map, and sometimes more than one type of information will appear.

▶ Identifying the Details
Read the paragraph. If the statement is the main idea, write *M*. If it is a supporting detail, write *S*.

Sharks can be identified in various ways. One way to distinguish a shark from another fish is by looking at the gill openings. A shark has five or more gill openings. The openings look like slits on each side of the shark's body. Also, the shark's skin is not scaly but is covered with tiny, hard bumps. Most fish have one row of teeth. The shark has two! Since you have to be close to see these differences, identifying a shark is much safer when it is in an aquarium!

___S___ A shark's body is covered with tiny, hard bumps.

___S___ It is safer to identify a shark in an aquarium.

___M___ There are several ways to identify a shark.

___S___ Sharks have five or more gill openings.

The **main idea** tells about the whole paragraph, and the **supporting details** describe the main idea.

216

AN EMERGENCY

> Penny, Jack, and the Ericsons think they have a problem when they discover the open pasture gates and realize their forty llamas have escaped. They know they have a problem when Ticktock is found with her nose buried in a store's licorice barrel.

Lesson	Reader pages	Worktext pages
13	36-40	15
14	41-45	16-18

Materials

- Pictures of a porcupine and a skunk
- Vocabulary sentences for display The Shape of a Story's Plot
- Teaching Visual 1: *The Shape of a Story's Plot*

Background information

Llamas on the Loose—This selection has been taken from *Llamas on the Loose* by Jeri Massi (JourneyForth). This book is part of the Peabody Series, named for the imaginary town of Peabody, Wisconsin. The books center on a group of young people who attend the same school and church. Each novel presents a new adventure as told by one of the members of the youth group.

INTRODUCTION

Vocabulary

Use the prepared sentences to introduce the vocabulary words in context.

Did you know?

Display the pictures of a porcupine and a skunk.

▶ Did you know that a porcupine can roll itself up into a tiny ball when it is in danger?

Did you know that a skunk releases a strong-smelling liquid when it is frightened?

Why do you think these animals do these strange things? (Accept any answer, but point out that it is their way of protecting themselves.)

What are some other forms of defense that animals use?

▶ In the story you will begin reading today, you will find out about another animal with a unique way to defend itself.

Head note

Read the head note on reader page 37 aloud.

▶ Who is going to an unusual farm? (Penny and Jack)

What are Penny and Jack to be prepared for? (an emergency)

VOCABULARY

LESSON 13

*†Dr. Lewis received money in the form of a grant to continue research of a fatal disease. (p. 37)

†She went to the barn to groom her horse before the state competition. (p. 37)

Baby llamas are called crias. (p. 37)

*A yearling animal is one year old. (p. 37)

*†Jake slipped the halter over the horse's head so it could be led to the pasture. (p. 38)

*†He lifted his chin indignantly after being falsely accused of cheating. (p. 39)

LESSON 14

We drove on the causeway over China Lake. (p. 41)

†The veterinarian placed straps around the dogs' muzzles so they could not bite. (p. 41)

†Karen bought a bag of black licorice at the candy store. (p. 42)

The pungent odor of the onion made him wrinkle his nose. (p. 42)

Correlated Activities

- **Vocabulary Box, Activity 5: Puzzle Pastime**
- **Recreational Reading, Activity 1: Board Game**

See "Classroom Management for Grouping" in the Appendix.

COMPREHENSION

Objectives

The student will

- Determine sequence of events.
- Recognize the author's use of figurative language.
- Recognize the author's use of humor.

Before silent reading: pages 36-40

Motivation

▶ What is the emergency?

After silent reading

Overview discussion: pages 36-40

▶ [literal] What animals are in this story? (llamas)

[appreciative] Is this the type of animal you think of when you hear someone talk about a farm?

▶ [interpretive] Who is telling the story? (Penny)

▶ [critical] Do you think Jack and Penny enjoy working on the llama farm? Why or why not? (Answers will vary.)

[literal] What big emergency happens on the llama farm? (The gate is left open and the llamas escape.)

[critical] Why is that an emergency? (Possible answers: The llamas might get lost; the llamas might hurt themselves.)

Follow-up discussion: page 36

▶ [interpretive] Look at the picture. What do you think Jack and Penny are doing? (trying to get the halter off the llama)

[critical] By the expressions on Jack's and Penny's faces, do you think that they are having fun? Explain your answer. (Accept any answer.)

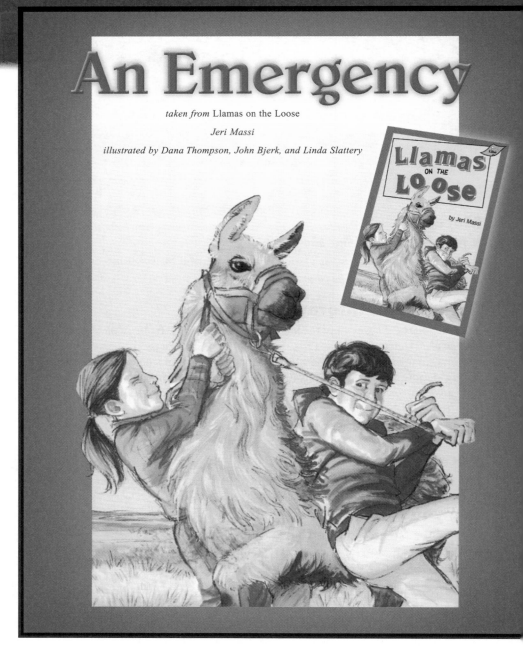

An Emergency

taken from Llamas on the Loose

Jeri Massi

illustrated by Dana Thompson, John Bjerk, and Linda Slattery

A visit from one of Dad's old friends, Doc Ericson, sends Penny and her brother Jack on an adventure. After Dad agrees to let Penny and Jack work on Doc Ericson's unusual farm, strange things begin to happen. Doc Ericson teaches Penny and Jack about the curious animals they raise and teaches them to work hard. "Beware of wild animals," Doc Ericson warns. "If the dinner gong rings and the floodlights shine, be prepared for an emergency!"

The Great Escape

Doc Ericson had to make our visit educational so he could qualify for a research grant, and during that week he taught us a lot about the history of llamas in the U.S. We also learned how to groom them and how to mix their feed.

There were forty llamas in all, thirty-four adults and six crias. There was one special male, Jock, who was boss of the herd. He took charge of all the females and every now and then had a spit-fight with the two other yearling males to remind them who was boss. Male llamas do have fangs to bite with, and if they get in a real fight, you'll see them leap up and come down on each other, biting, slashing with their hooves, trying to knock each other down, and spitting quarts at each other. But usually the lead male only has to let loose a couple of pints of spit at the other males to let them know he's still in charge.

Since female llamas don't have any upper teeth, their number one defense is to spit. And when a llama spits at you, you can consider yourself—in no uncertain terms—spit upon. They can reach right down into their stomachs to spit, unlike people, who use only their throats.

So in a sense, llamas are pretty well defended. They can sense intruders at a distance, and they will instinctively aim for an attacker's face to spit at, in order to blind him.

On the other hand, if a llama senses an approaching attacker but is trapped in a fenced pasture,

Follow-up discussion: page 37

▶ [critical] What kind of doctor do you think Doc Ericson is? (Accept any answer, but elicit that he is a veterinarian.)

[literal] How does Doc Ericson make Jack and Penny's visit educational? (He teaches them about the history of llamas in the U.S., how to groom llamas, and how to mix llama feed.)

[interpretive] What does it mean to groom an animal? (to clean and brush it)

[critical] How do you think Doc Ericson uses the research grant? (possible answers: to repair the farm, to buy food and necessities for the llamas, to complete his research on llamas)

▶ [literal] What makes the male llama Jock so special? (He is boss of the herd.)

[interpretive] What does the author mean when she says that the males spit quarts at each other? (Llamas spit so much it seems like quarts of spit.)

Read aloud the paragraph in which Penny describes the female llamas. Remember that she is disgusted at being spit on.

▶ [interpretive] From what Penny says, do you think she and Jack have learned a lot about llamas? (Answers will vary, but suggest that her giving so much information about llamas indicates that she has.)

Follow-up discussion: page 38

▶ [literal] What else do Penny and Jack *supposedly* learn? (how to halter a llama)

▶ [critical] What trainer's manual are Jack and Penny referring to? (Accept any answer, but elicit that they might have been given a manual to read before handling the llamas.)

[interpretive] Do you think Jack is serious when he suggests that Ticktock should read the trainer's manual? Why or why not? (No; it would be absurd to expect an animal to read. Elicit that the author is using humor.)

Read aloud Penny and Jack's conversation with exasperation as if you were trying to halter a llama.

[interpretive] How do you know that Jack is afraid of being hurt by Ticktock? (He says sarcastically, "Sure it's a game—Kill the Kid!")

he can't get away. And a llama under attack by more than one creature is pretty helpless. Two medium-sized dogs can pull down a full-grown llama. That was why Dr. Ericson had the whole place hog-wired.

Supposedly we also learned how to halter a llama, if you want to count it that way. What actually happened was that Jack got his arms 'round Ticktock's neck, and she bucked him all over the barnyard for about ten minutes. Then, when she was exhausted and wanted a drink, I got the harness around her nose and Jack fastened it before she could buck again.

"If we were taller and heavier, we could do it," Jack said. "But I can hardly reach her nose unless she keeps her head down."

"Look, two of us ought to be smarter than one of her," I told him. "Size has nothing to do with it. Even the trainer's manual says that."

"Well, I wish Ticktock would read the manual, then." But at the challenge in my words, he came up to Ticktock again and got his arms around her neck to get her

38

halter off. We were in the barnyard. Ticktock had been nibbling up some spilled grain. She took one look at Jack and started jumping again, taking him with her.

His legs swung up one way and then the other as she jumped and turned and bucked.

"All I want to do is get your halter off!" he yelled.

"She must think it's a game!" I called as I chased them around, trying to get a way to jump in and grab her 'round the neck on the other side.

"Sure it's a game— Kill the Kid!" Jack yelled. "Would you

do something?" But Ticktock turned away and jumped. I saw Jack's legs swing out past her. He tried to get his footing to brace himself. "Penny!" he called. I shut my eyes and jumped in.

Ticktock snorted indignantly, as though she thought I was cheating. "Quick! The buckle's on your side," I said. A second later the halter came off.

Ticktock stopped and stood stock-still.

"She does think it's a game!" Jack exclaimed. We let the tired llama go back to the pasture. "Boy," Jack said. "I'm glad Doc gets the grant just for teaching us. Because if it depended on how much we learned, I'm not sure he'd get enough to cover postage."

Of course, along with the fun stuff, we also "learned" to pick up rocks in the pasture, scrape paint on the outside of the bunkhouse, and weed the garden in the front of the house. In fact, most of what we did was just plain old work, but it was nice to have Jack there to talk to.

On our second Saturday we hurried to get the chores done early so that we could leave for home right after lunch.

"Now, you two be sure to bring Scruggs with you next Friday," Mrs. Ericson said as we sat down to eat. "We certainly can use him."

"Sure!" Jack exclaimed. I only nodded.

"And your sister Jean, too," Doc Ericson added.

Jack hesitated, looking glum, and I said, "She's not back from Alabama yet."

"Maybe next time then," Mrs. Ericson said. "Be nice to have two boys and two girls, because then nobody gets picked on and nobody gets left out."

Well, it was obvious that she didn't know Jean. Jean was just born with the tendency to get picked on and left out. I sighed heavily.

"You two eat up," Doc Ericson told us as he stood up. "I want to get the crias out to the Nursery before we leave for Peabody. The yearling males are too rough with them."

We nodded and he went out. A minute later the dinner gong that

Follow-up discussion: page 39

▶ [critical] Why does Penny think that Ticktock would think Penny is cheating? (Accept any answer, but point out that it is now two against one.)

[interpretive] What gives Jack and Penny the impression that Ticktock is playing a game? (As soon as the halter comes off, she stops jumping around and stands still.)

▶ [literal] What else do Penny and Jack "learn" on the farm? (to pick up rocks, scrape paint, and weed the garden) [BAT: 2e Work]

[critical] Why do you think there are quotation marks around the word *learned?* (Accept any answer, but elicit that this is probably not the type of learning Penny and Jack were expecting to do.)

Follow-up discussion: page 40

▶ [interpretive] Who is ringing the dinner gong? (Dr. Ericson)

[interpretive] Why do Jack and Penny assume that the dinner gong means trouble? (because it is ringing so furiously)

[interpretive] As Penny and Jack look around, do you think they immediately know what the problem is? Why or why not? (Possibly not; everything is silent.)

Read aloud the first thing Penny and Jack see as they burst out the door.

▶ [interpretive] Why is it bad that everything seems quiet? (because the llamas are gone)

[interpretive] What word does the author use to describe the way Doc uses his glasses? Why? (*Sweep;* answers may vary, but elicit that it gives a picture of looking back and forth.)

▶ Read aloud with haste what the Ericsons, Jack, and Penny do after realizing the llamas are gone.

[appreciative] What could you have done before rushing out to find the llamas? (Elicit from the students that they could have prayed and trusted God to help them.) [BAT: 6b Prayer]

Looking ahead

▶ Will the Ericsons, Jack, and Penny be able to locate the llamas?

hung on the porch started banging furiously.

Jack and I looked at each other and we both said, "Trouble!" at the same time before we rushed out. Mrs. Ericson followed.

"Look! Look!" Dr. Ericson cried as we all came bursting out the door. We looked. Everything was silent. A faint breeze kicked up dust in Pasture 1.

"Everything seems quiet," Jack said.

"Seems quiet!" Dr. Ericson exclaimed. "The llamas are gone! Gone!"

We ran down the steps.

"The gate's open," I said and pointed at the wide pasture gate. Mrs. Ericson squinted and said, "The gate to Pasture 2 is open, too."

Dr. Ericson ran back into the house and came out with his field glasses. He used them to sweep over the pastures. "All the gates are open! Quick, get in the truck!"

We scrambled for the pickup. Jack and I hopped into the truckbed, and the Ericsons got into the front. With a mighty jerk of the gears, we took off.

40

Worktext Objectives

The student will

■ Determine meaning from context.

■ Match words and definitions.

Vocabulary:
Worktext page 15

Ticktock on the Loose

Pasture 1 had the gate most often used as an exit gate. By that I mean that Pasture 4's gate led into the pasture alongside it. Pasture 3's gate led into Pasture 2, and Pasture 2's gate led into Pasture 1. But Pasture 1 had a gate that opened into the barnyard, and the barnyard gate opened to the dirt road. There was an exit gate on the far side of Pasture 4, but we never used it much because it was so far from the barns, and I'm not sure the llamas even knew it was there.

We jolted down that dirt road, headed for the causeway. A welcome sight met us as we came down the bank.

The llamas stood on either side of the causeway, knee-deep in shallow lake water. Most of them ignored us. They were busy drinking or browsing at some of the plants on the banks or lifting their muzzles to catch the smells. The two yearling males were having a spit fight. Mrs. Ericson hopped out of the cab and Jack jumped out of the back. I started to follow, but Dr. Ericson yelled, "I'll get the sheriff!" and took off again before I could get out.

Jack and Mrs. Ericson nodded and waved. I don't think Doc Ericson knew I was still in the truck until we pulled into town. But he was so flustered at the llamas having been let out that he simply parked and said, "I'll get the sheriff!"

And he rushed up the sidewalk.

I felt kind of blank myself. I hopped out of the truck and looked around.

Winneca certainly wasn't a big or a busy town. Right across the street was a big warehouse-type building that said "Ernie's Everything Outlet" on it.

Instead of regular doors like any other store, it had huge garage doors that opened onto the street. The effect was that the whole front of the store seemed to be opened for the public to walk in and out. But at the moment nobody was walking out of Ernie's Everything Outlet. Instead, a huge crowd seemed to be pushing to get in.

An Emergency   41

Follow-up discussion: page 41

▶ [literal] Which gate did the llamas escape through? (the gate in Pasture 1)

[interpretive] Why is the gate in Pasture 1 most often used as an exit gate? (It is the only gate leading into the barnyard.)

[literal] Where are the Ericsons, Penny, and Jack headed when they see a welcome sight? (to the causeway)

[critical] What is a causeway? (Accept any answer, but explain that it is a raised road that extends over water or marshland.)

▶ [critical] When he sees the llamas, why is Doc's first reaction to get the sheriff? (Accept any answer, but suggest that there may be a bad reason behind the llamas' escape. Explain that the book tells the reason for this mysterious emergency.)

[appreciative] What would you do in this situation?

The student will

- Recognize the setting through the author's description.
- Understand characters' perspectives.
- Recognize a simile's meaning.

 Use the prepared sentences to introduce the vocabulary words in context.

Before silent reading: pages 41-45

Motivation

▶ Do you think Penny, Jack, and the Ericsons will be able to find and return the loose llamas?

Will Penny and Jack learn anything new about the llamas?

After silent reading

Overview discussion: pages 41-45

▶ [literal] Where are the llamas? (on either side of the causeway)

[critical] How do you think the llamas got out of the pasture? (Accept any answer, but elicit that someone must have opened all the gates. Suggest that if students want to find out, they should read the book *Llamas on the Loose*, which tells the rest of Jack and Penny's adventure.)

[interpretive] Are Penny and Jack able to help get the llamas back? How? (Answers will vary, but elicit that the other llamas are probably returned the same way Ticktock is returned.)

[critical] How do you know that Penny has learned more about llamas from Dr. Ericson than she realizes? (Accept any answer, but point out that Penny knows what to do with Ticktock and how to get her out of the store.)

Follow-up discussion: page 42

▶ [interpretive] Why does Penny get a sinking feeling? (She hears people talking about a baby camel at Ernie's Everything Outlet, and she is sure it's a llama.)

[interpretive] How does the author help you paint a mental picture of what the scene looks like? (by describing the store in detail)

Read aloud in a narrative voice the description of what Penny finds as she enters the store.

▶ [literal] Where does Penny find Ticktock? (with her muzzle buried in black licorice bits)

[interpretive] What gives the impression that Ticktock is not surprised to see Penny at the store? (She looks at Penny and goes back to the licorice.)

Somebody was yelling, "Stay back, folks! It may bite!" That was why the crowd couldn't get in.

I walked across the street in time to hear someone say, "Looks like a Shetland pony to me."

"It's a baby camel, I tell you."

I started to get a sinking feeling. I pushed through the crowd to where the store manager was keeping everyone back.

The inside of the store was vast and cluttered. A pile of baskets lay here, a bundle of blankets there. Crates and cartons had been stacked to make aisles, and there was a candy center. There were crates of boxed candy all stacked together and several open bins of penny candy under a sign that said, "Take Your Pick, Penny Candy only $1.00 a pound."

And there, with her muzzle buried in the black licorice bits, was Ticktock. She lifted her head and looked over at me.

I'm not sure that Ticktock actually ate any of the licorice, but I think the pungent smell must have fascinated her. She put her muzzle back into the bin.

"Mister," I said. "I know that llama."

42

"Is it yours?" the manager asked me.

"Well no, but I'm a friend of the family, you might say."

"Can you get it out of here?" he asked.

"If you've got a rope," I told him.

"This is a store!" he exclaimed. "What would we do with rope?"

"The sign says it's an everything store."

"Everything but rope," he told me.

"How about a dog leash?" I asked.

"Ninety-nine cents and it's yours."

"I don't have ninety-nine cents," I told him. "And I only want to borrow it."

He went and found a dog leash. I tied a knot in it about a third of the way from the end, and walked up to Ticktock.

"That kid must be from the circus," someone guessed. "She knows how to handle a baby giraffe."

"Ticktock," I said, holding the leash behind my back. "Ticktock."

The llama looked up at me. There were black smudges on her nose.

The manager crowded up behind me. "A whole bin of candy, ruined!" he exclaimed. "Ruined by a baby giraffe!"

Ticktock put her banana ears back and raised her muzzle, eyeing him sideways.

"Stop," I said to him in a soft but urgent voice. "You're scaring her." And I halted where I was. He bumped into me.

"Scaring her!" he exclaimed. "She's eating my candy!"

"Don't!" I said as her eyes widened. "Oh no!" I covered my face with my hands and ducked.

Ticktock missed me when she spit, but I'm afraid she got the manager. He yelled, and she wheeled and raced up one of the aisles.

"Rabies! It's got rabies!" he yelled.

I ran after her.

She wasn't in sports shoes or baby clothes. I decided to look at the food aisles, and I soon found them.

A scream from the back of the store led me to her.

An Emergency   43

▶ [interpretive] Why does Penny need a rope from the store manager? (to get Ticktock out of the store)

Read aloud the conversation between Penny and the store manager. Remember that Penny is trying to hurry to get Ticktock out of the store.

[interpretive] Why does someone think Penny is from the circus? (She knows how to handle Ticktock.)

▶ [interpretive] Does the store manager make a good decision by not listening to Penny's warning? Why or why not? (No; his yelling scares Ticktock, and she spits at him.)

[critical] Why does the manager think Ticktock has rabies? (Accept any answer.)

▶ [interpretive] Why do you think someone screams at the back of the store? (probably someone is frightened by the llama)

Follow-up discussion: page 44

▶ [critical] Why do you think the florist holding the bouquet is so nervous? (Accept any answer, but elicit that she is probably unfamiliar with llamas.)

Read aloud the paragraph that tells what Penny does to capture Ticktock.

▶ [literal] What does the florist ask Penny? (if Ticktock is Penny's)

[critical] Why does Penny say that she is "just her maid"? (Accept any answer, but suggest that Penny is always cleaning up the messes that Ticktock makes.)

▶ [interpretive] Why is the manager mopping his face as he comes down the aisle? (because Ticktock spit on him)

▶ [critical] What do you think the store manager has to say to Doc Ericson? (Accept any answer.)

[literal] Why doesn't Doc Ericson mind what the store manager says to him? (He is just relieved that Ticktock is okay.)

[critical] Do you think Doc is proud of Penny? (Answers will vary, but suggest that he is.)

▶ [interpretive] What does the author mean when she describes Ticktock as "mild as milk"? (Elicit that the phrase is a simile meaning that Ticktock behaves well.)

The wholesale flowers were back there. One lady—a customer—rushed past me, but when I got there I saw the florist lady nervously holding out a bouquet to Ticktock. The llama gently sniffed along the tops of the carnations and took a nibble of baby's breath.

"She won't hurt you," I said. Ticktock glanced at me and went back to browsing. "Ticktock," I said, and put my free hand out to her.

She really wanted me to leave her alone, but as long as she had the flowers, she decided not to resist. I slipped my arm around her neck. While I talked to her I got the dog leash onto her neck and fastened it above the knot I had tied in it. That way the lead couldn't get too tight and choke her.

44

"Whew!" I said.

"Is she yours?" the florist lady asked me.

"No, I'm just her maid." And I laughed a little.

Just then Doc Ericson, the sheriff, and the store manager (who was mopping his face) came up the aisle. Doc Ericson was so glad that Ticktock was okay that he didn't mind how much the store manager had to say to him. He paid for the licorice and the flowers. I took the bouquet, and with that and the lead, I got the llama to come with me.

Ticktock was as mild as milk once we got her out of the store. She gladly hopped into the pickup on command. I followed her.

An Emergency   45

Follow-up discussion: page 45

▶ [interpretive] Which man in the picture is the store manager? How can you tell? (The man behind Penny; he is wiping his forehead and looking a little upset.)

▶ [critical] By looking at the expression on Penny's face, how do you think she feels? (Accept any answer.)

The student will

- Determine conflicts and their solutions
- Recall facts and details

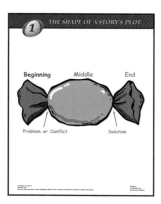

LITERATURE

◄ Teaching of conflict was presented in Lesson 9.

Conflict and solution

Display Teaching Visual 1, *The Shape of a Story's Plot.* Point out *Conflict* and *Solution* as you elicit from the students that a *conflict* in a story is a problem that must be solved and that a *solution* is an action or event that solves the problem.

► Most stories are about how a main character solves a problem.

► Think back to "Watching Wallace." What was the conflict and solution in the story? (Timothy was afraid of Wallace. He learned to trust the Lord.)

► In "River's Rising," what was the conflict and solution? (The houseboat broke loose. Josh and Ma secured the houseboat to trees on an island.)

Read the following situation to the students.

Danny's clock is old and unreliable. This morning he slept late and now has only fifteen minutes to get ready for school and walk three blocks to the bus stop.

► What is Danny's conflict? (He overslept and may be late.)

► How might he solve the conflict? (possible answers: skip breakfast, ask his mother to drive him to the bus stop)

Literature: Worktext pages 16-18

SOMETHING EXTRA

Write About It: Watch out!

Provide sources (e.g., books, magazines, encyclopedias, Internet access) of information about animal defense mechanisms. Instruct each student to record as many defense mechanisms as possible. Hold a contest to find the funniest, most interesting, or scariest animal defense mechanisms.

LAMA GLAMA

Humans are curious about the gentle llama. This piece offers fascinating details concerning the creature's unique makeup, helpfulness to man, and natural protective devices.

Lesson	Reader pages	Worktext pages
15	46-50	19-20

Materials

- Picture of llamas (optional—use the picture on reader page 46)
- White lab coat (optional)
- Note pad
- Pictures with captions from an encyclopedia, dictionary, newspaper, or magazine
- Vocabulary sentences for display (e.g., on the chalkboard or on sentence strips)

Background information

Llamas—These animals can carry loads that weigh up to 130 pounds, and they can travel fifteen to twenty miles a day with a full load. They are inexpensive to keep, needing only grass and low shrubs to feed on. The average llama is four feet tall at the shoulders. Native South Americans first used llamas that were untamed, and since then llamas have gradually come to be domesticated animals. The scientific name, *lama glama*, has a spelling slightly different from that of the common name, *llama*.

INTRODUCTION

Vocabulary

Use the prepared sentences to introduce the vocabulary words in context.

Lama glama science

Wear a lab coat if one is available.

Have your note pad visible as if you are ready to write down observations.

▶ Today we will be making scientific observations about the *lama glama*. *Lama glama* is the scientific name, but this animal also has a common name. Your formal name would be your first, middle, and last name; your common name would be what people call you, perhaps a nickname. Just as your full or formal name tells people which family you belong to, the scientific name *lama glama* tells us which family llamas belong to.

Show a picture of llamas.

▶ We can make observations with our senses. Let's make observations based on this picture of llamas, and then we will compare our observations to the information in the article we will read today.

Make a large, visible list of the students' observations. After the students finish reading the article, you may want to add to the list new information that was learned and delete from the list information that was found not to be true.

VOCABULARY

LESSON 15

The dog is named Spot for the irregular splotches of color on his coat. (p. 46)

†The hungry cows were led to the field of grass to graze. (p. 47)

†Several goats began to browse on the leaves of the young plants. (p. 47)

†The domesticated llamas seem content to live with and be used by people. (p. 47)

Correlated Activities

- **Word Work, Activity 3: The Title Match**
- **Connections, Activity 2: Dreamy Domains**

See "Classroom Management for Grouping" in the Appendix.

Objectives

COMPREHENSION

The student will

■ Identify information not
  explicitly stated.
■ Read for specific information.
■ Recall likenesses and
  differences.
■ Draw conclusions.

Before silent reading:
pages 46-50

Motivation

▶ What makes the *lama glama* a unique
  and useful animal?

  Where can llamas be found?

After silent reading

Overview discussion:
pages 46-50

▶ [literal] Where are llamas originally
  from? (South America)

▶ [literal] Where would it be easiest to
  find llamas? (possible answer: on
  llama farms and in zoos around the
  United States and Canada)

▶ [interpretive] What are llamas generally used for? (carrying loads)

▶ [appreciative] Why do you think
  llamas are interesting?

Lama Glama
by Wendy Harris

What has a head like a camel and ears shaped like bananas? What is white with splotches of color but can also be all black or white or brown? What has thick wool like a sheep and feet with toes? What chews its cud like a cow and hums when it's content? What can be kept as a pet but will spit on you if made angry? What is it? It's a *lama glama*.

46

Follow-up discussion: page 46

▶ [interpretive] How does the author
  make you curious about the llama
  and at the same time describe the
  lama glama? (by asking a lot of questions in the first paragraph)

  Read this page aloud as if you were
  asking your friends a riddle.

Lama glama is the scientific name for a large plant-eating animal from South America. Its common name is *llama*. Llamas are mammals that graze on grass and browse on low bushes. At one time these woolly animals lived wild in herds. Today no more wild llama herds roam over the mountains and highlands of South America. They live with, work for, and are cared for by man. They are domesticated.

Llamas are ruminants like cattle. Ruminants have stomachs with different parts, or chambers. One chamber stores food that has already been chewed and swallowed. The stored food is called *cud*. Cud can be coughed up by the llama and chewed again.

What does the llama look like? Many people think that the llama looks like a camel. Its face is shaped like a camel's. It has large eyes, long eyelashes, and a split

Follow-up discussion: page 47

▶ [interpretive] How is the scientific name *lama* different from the common name? (The common name is spelled with two *l*s and the scientific name has only one *l*.)

▶ [interpretive] Why are there no more wild llama herds today? (Llamas have been cared for by man; they have become a domesticated animal.)

▶ [literal] What characteristics do ruminants have? (They have several chambers in their stomachs; one chamber is used for storing food.)

[literal] What kinds of food would you see a llama eating? (grass and low shrubs)

▶ [interpretive] A llama could be mistaken for what animal? (a camel)

Lama Glama

▶ [interpretive] What are the similarities and differences between llamas and camels? (Both have large eyes, long eyelashes, split upper lips, and long necks; both can go for days without food. The llama's body is smaller and woollier; the llama does not have a hump and needs water every day.)

[literal] How do llamas usually behave? (They are usually calm and quiet.)

[literal] To what does the author compare the sound of a calm llama? (the purr of a cat)

[critical] Does the comparison of a purring cat help you to hear the sound of a calm llama in your mind? Why or why not? (Answers will vary.)

[interpretive] What would cause a llama to spit at a person? (Accept answers that include the llama's being frightened or angry.)

Read aloud the paragraph that tells about the llama's behavior.

▶ [interpretive] What is the disadvantage of using a llama to carry heavy loads? (When llamas get tired they lie down, refusing to get up; and they spit if they are forced to get up.)

[critical] If you saw a llama with a heavy load lying at the side of the road and a very angry owner, what advice would you give the owner? (possible answers: to have patience with the llama; not to make the llama angry; to lighten the load on the llama) [BATs: 3c Self-control; 5a Kindness]

Read aloud the ways that llamas can be used.

upper lip. The llama's long neck looks like a camel's too. But its body is smaller and woollier, and it does not have the camel's hump.

Like the camel, llamas can go without food for several days. Do you remember the chambered stomachs? If a llama has no food, it simply coughs up some cud. It chews the food again for another meal. Llamas do not drink much water. But unlike a camel, they cannot go for days without a drink. Llamas need water every day.

How do llamas behave? Llamas are usually calm and quiet. A contented llama can make a humming noise that sounds a little like the purr of a cat. But llamas will also spit a smelly, green liquid when they are angry or when they are afraid. Usually they spit at other llamas, but if you frighten one, watch out! Llamas have great aim!

The llama's long neck is similar to a camel's, but the llama is woollier than a camel and has no hump.

What good are llamas? Thousands of years ago, native South Americans discovered the usefulness of the gentle llamas. With little training the male llamas would carry heavy loads of goods from the mountain highlands to the lowlands for trading. Each male could carry about one hundred pounds. However, if a llama was overloaded or became too tired, it would lie down and refuse to get up. If the llama driver tried to make the llama get up, he was spit upon.

48

Follow-up discussion: page 49

▶ [interpretive] What do you think this woman is using the llama for? (possible answer: to carry a load)

▶ [critical] Where do you think this picture was taken? (Answers may vary, but point out that it was probably taken in South America.)

Lama Glama

▶ [interpretive] Why would a person find a llama useful to own? (Someone living in a rural area might need an animal that can travel rocky, slippery paths with heavy loads.)

[appreciative] Do you know anyone who has a pet llama?

▶ [literal] Why would llamas be better than other animals for our country's wilderness areas? (They do not ruin the land with their soft padded feet, unlike animals with hard hooves that do tear up the land.)

Read aloud the section that tells why a llama is a better pack animal than a donkey.

▶ [critical] What do you think would be the benefits of owning a llama? (Accept any answer.)

[critical] What are some problems you might have if you owned a llama? (Answers will vary.)

The female llamas were kept for their wool and for raising more llamas. The wool could be spun into yarn for weaving clothing and rope. The female llamas gave birth to a baby, or *cria,* every two years. The llama's hide could be used to make sandals. Its meat could be eaten or dried and stored. The native South Americans also used the llama's bones to make tools and its fat to make candles. Very little of the llama could not be put to good use.

Some llamas are kept for their wool and for raising more llamas.

50

Why were llamas brought to North America? Llamas proved so useful as pack animals in South America that they were imported to North America. Today there are thousands of them scattered across the United States and Canada. Some are found in zoos, but most are kept as pets and pack animals.

Do you know why someone would want a llama for a pack animal instead of a horse or donkey? The feet of the llama make it an excellent pack animal. The bottoms of the two-toed feet are covered with a soft pad. These pads do not slide on slippery, rocky paths. And the soft pads do little damage to wilderness areas our country wants to preserve. Horse and donkey hooves are hard. Hard hooves are more likely to slip on slick paths. They also wear and cut paths of dust in the land.

What is one of the most interesting animals you could ever learn about? *Lama glama,* of course!

STUDY SKILLS

Captions

Show several pictures with captions. Allow the students to look at the pictures as you choose students to read the captions aloud.

▶ The information given with each picture is called a *caption*. A caption is a title, short explanation, or description that explains a picture or illustration.

▶ Why are captions useful? (They are brief or short; they give specific information; because they are set apart, they are easier to read; they highlight story or article content.)

Read and discuss the captions in "Lama Glama."

Study Skills: Worktext page 19

Organizing information

Study Skills: Worktext page 20

Read and discuss the headings given for the facts about a llama before the students complete the page.

Note: Worktext page 20 will help to prepare the students for the skill of outlining in Lesson 44.

SOMETHING EXTRA

Write About It: Llama brief

Tell each student to write a brief description of a llama as if the person who will read it does not know much about llamas. Instruct him not to use either name, *llama* or *lama glama*, in his description. Encourage the student to have his parents or friends read it and see if they can determine what animal is being described.

Write About It: Description board

Direct each student to write a description of something (an object or animal) of his choice. Instruct him to include many details but not to reveal the identity of the object. Permit him to trade his description with another person, having that person draw what was described. If enough details are used, the person should be able to draw the correct object. If not, it's back to the "description board"!

Objectives

The student will
- Write and use captions to clarify content.
- Read and organize facts and details.

The last activity on Worktext page 19 is a composition to be done on the student's own paper. Worktext pages 319-24 have been designed to use for this purpose.

SKILL STATION DAY

Lesson	Worktext pages
16	218-19

Objective

The student will

■ Identify relevant and irrelevant information: words, topics, and sentences.

① Introduction

Draw attention to the columns of words.

▶ One word in each column does not belong with the others. The word that doesn't belong is related to a different subject or topic. But the other three words are related to each other. Which words do belong? Why? (Possible answers: *Truck, airplane,* and *car* are types of transportation run by a motor; *jacket, sweatshirt,* and *sweater* are clothing worn on the top half of our bodies; *water, lemonade,* and *milk* are drinks.)

Choose students to cross out the words that do not belong.

▶ Why don't the words *bicycle, pants,* and *ice cream* belong in these groups? (A bicycle does not have a motor. Pants are clothing worn over legs. Ice cream is eaten, not drunk.)

Write *relevant* and *irrelevant* above the columns of words.

▶ Two words that tell whether there is or is not a relationship between subjects are *relevant* and *irrelevant.* Which do you think means that two things are related? (relevant)

Name words from the lists that are relevant to each other. (possible answer: truck, airplane, car)

▶ Which word means "unrelated"? (irrelevant)

Which words from the lists are irrelevant to the other words in the lists? (bicycle, pants, ice cream)

Materials

- Globe (optional)
- A Bible
- Overhead marking pen
- Teaching Visual 3: *Relevant or Irrelevant?*
- The following columns of words for display:

truck	*jacket*	*ice cream*
bicycle	*pants*	*water*
airplane	*sweatshirt*	*lemonade*
car	*sweater*	*milk*

RELEVANT AND IRRELEVANT INFORMATION

② Skill development: Discussion

▶ When using an encyclopedia for research, it is helpful to know whether information given is relevant or irrelevant to your topic. Looking up several relevant entries will give more information about the topic.

▶ For example, if you were doing a report on motor transportation, you could find relevant information under the topics of trucks, airplanes, and automobiles.

Would you find relevant information about motor transportation under bicycles? (no) Why not? (Bicycles don't have motors.)

▶ If you were to write a report on sleds, under what topics do you think you would find relevant information? (possible answers: sleds; sled dogs; huskies; malamute; Alaska; Canada)

Would you look under the topics of airplanes or service dogs? Why or why not? (No; those topics are irrelevant to sleds.)

③ Skill development: Visual 3—*Relevant or Irrelevant?*

Call attention to the picture of the Royal Canadian Mounted Police.

▶ Who is in this picture? (possible answers: soldiers; Royal Canadian Mounted Police)

Point out Canada, the Northwest Territories, and the Yukon on the globe.

Read aloud the RCMP's motto, "Maintain Right."

▶ What is a motto? (a saying expressing what is important to a group of people)

Read the paragraph aloud.

▶ This is almost a well-written paragraph. There are a few problems with it. Did you recognize the problems?

What is the paragraph about? (the RCMP)

All sentences in this paragraph should be relevant to the RCMP. Were there any irrelevant sentences? (yes)

Which sentences are irrelevant or unimportant to the subject of the paragraph? (sentences 4 and 9)

Cross out these irrelevant sentences.

(continued on top of next page)

▶**Read and Identify**
Read the selection.
Cross out the one sentence in each paragraph that is irrelevant.

Sled Dogs

Sled dog breeds are excellent at pulling sleds. The most well-known sled dog breeds are the Alaskan Malamute, the Samoyeds, and the Siberian Husky. These breeds are considered part of a larger group of purebred dogs called the working group. But not all working dogs could pull sleds across the snow and ice in the Arctic, the Yukon, and Alaska. ~~The poodle came from Germany.~~

Sled dogs are specially made for the job they do. Their great strength is very valuable. They are large, rugged dogs. Speed and quickness are their greatest assets. These dogs weigh about 40-80 pounds and stand two feet high at the shoulder. ~~The fox hound is related to the beagle.~~ They have two coats of fur, the outer coat and the undercoat. The undercoat of fur allows them to be able to sleep outside in temperatures as low as seventy degrees below zero.

Dogsled racing is a very popular sport. The dogs race side by side. For short distances, the teams include 3 to 10 dogs. They travel at a speed of about 20 miles per hour. Long-distance racing teams travel 500 to 1,170 miles. ~~The malamute has a bushy tail.~~ Races last one to two weeks and require 10 to 20 dogs. The sleds also carry 300 to 600 pounds of food and equipment.

Sled dogs are used in other ways too. From 1873 to 1969, sled dogs were used by the Royal Canadian Mounted Police for patrolling. In addition to police patrol, sled dogs have been used for mail delivery. ~~Some dogs in Mexico have no fur on their bodies except small bunches on top of their heads.~~ They also make great companions.

> **Relevant** information is important to a particular subject. **Irrelevant** information has no connection or importance to a subject.

218

▶ Read aloud II Corinthians 8:21— "Providing for honest things, not only in the sight of the Lord, but also in the sight of men." How does this verse relate to the RCMP? (The Native Americans respected them because they were fair and just in their dealings.) [BAT: 4c Honesty]

4 **Skill application:**
Worktext page 218

◀ Teaching of main idea was presented in Lesson 12.

▶ What does the main idea of a paragraph or article tell? (what the paragraph or the article is about)

An article with several paragraphs may have several main ideas. But all sentences in a paragraph should give relevant information about that paragraph's main idea.

What is the difference between relevant and irrelevant information? (Information that is important to the topic is relevant. Information that is unimportant to the topic is irrelevant.)

Read the directions and complete the page together. Discuss why each irrelevant sentence is considered unrelated or unimportant to that paragraph in the article about sled dogs.

5 **Skill practice:**
Worktext page 219

3 RELEVANT OR IRRELEVANT?

"MAINTAIN RIGHT"

Royal Canadian Mounted Police

The Royal Canadian Mounted Police (RCMP) is the national police force in Canada. The Mounted Police was first formed in 1873. The men traveled on horseback through northwestern Canada, keeping peace between the new settlers and the Native Americans. Many Native Americans owned horses too. The Mounted Police also kept order during the Yukon gold rush. Today, they make sure that the national laws in Canada are obeyed. The Royal Canadian Mounted Police are known for their scarlet red tunics. The Native Americans considered scarlet a symbol of "justice and fair dealing," and they had great respect for those who wore the color. American policemen wear navy blue. This uniform color has remained unchanged over the years, along with the RCMP motto, "Maintain Right."

Lesson	Reader pages	Worktext pages
17	51-55	21
18	56-59	22

Steve is excited to be leaving the orphanage and heading to the Yukon where he will live with his uncle, the "Flying Doctor." He doesn't expect to lose his guide and be alone on the last leg of the long trip though. Can he control the sled dogs over days of snowy travel? Can he find his way to the small settlement of Unison?

VOCABULARY

LESSON 17

*†The lowering sky was a warning of the approaching thunderstorm. (p. 51)

*The dogsled trail over the snow turned out to be the longest mush ever! (p. 52)

*†As Steve traveled over the tundra, he noticed that there were no trees and that the ground was permanently frozen. (p. 52)

*The light brown, tawny-colored dog appeared to be the meanest. (p. 53)

*†He decided not to venture onto the thin ice for fear of falling into the lake. (p. 55)

LESSON 18

*†Standing at the edge of the bluffs, he could look down on the tops of the trees. (p. 56)

*†The husky's massive head went well with his giant body. (p. 56)

*Without thinking he instinctively pulled the little girl out of the freezing lake. (p. 58)

*An early settler of northwest Canada is called a sourdough. (p. 59)

*†His contempt toward his brother was evident in his disrespectful attitude. (p. 59)

Heritage Studies Connection

Lessons 17 and 18 can be linked to the study of Canada's Yukon Territory.

Materials
- A suitcase
- Map of northwest Canada
- Vocabulary sentences for display

Background information
The Yukon—The Yukon, located in northwest Canada, has an arctic climate with a rough terrain of mountains and plateaus. In this climate the treeless ground, or tundra, is permanently frozen and can support only low-growing vegetation. Because of the rough terrain, helicopters and light aircraft are used for transportation to many parts of the Yukon. Some people still use dogsleds as their means of transportation. Huskies and malemutes have double coats of fur to keep them warm in the severe cold. They can pull a sled all day if they are well fed and cared for.

INTRODUCTION
Vocabulary
Use the prepared sentences to introduce the vocabulary words in context.

An Alaskan trip
As you show the suitcase, pretend you and the students are taking a trip to Alaska. Show a map that includes northwest Canada, and locate the Yukon. Ask the following questions as you use the background information given to discuss the physical features of the Yukon.

▶ What will we need to know before going? (possible answers: weather; mode of transportation)

How will weather and transportation affect what we take? (They will affect the kind of clothes we pack, how much we can take, and how it is packed.)

What problems will we encounter as a result of long winters and frozen ground? (Possible answers: Construction of any kind is difficult, and the vegetation is scarce.)

How will traveling by dogsled differ from the way we travel?

Correlated Activities
- **Vocabulary Box, Activity 3: Glossary Day**
- **Spelling Practice, Activity 2: Spelling Makes Cents**
See "Classroom Management for Grouping" in the Appendix.

Yukon Trail

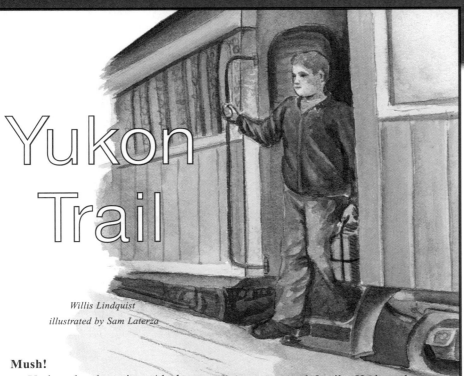

Willis Lindquist
illustrated by Sam Laterza

Mush!

Under the lowering Alaskan sky young Steve Woodford stepped from the train at the snow-covered outpost of Nenana. He looked anxiously around for his Uncle Jim, the famous "Flying Doctor" of the Yukon of whom he had boasted so much at the orphanage.

For years he had dreamed of going to the Yukon. Now he was on his way and he was happy. He was going to have a real home and belong to a real family. He hoped Uncle Jim and Aunt Bess would like him.

The young Indian who came up grinning couldn't have been over sixteen. "You're Steve?" he asked in perfect English. "Well, I'm Sam Ketchum. I've got a letter for you. There's been a lot of sickness up in the Yukon, and your uncle couldn't fly down for you."

Steve's heart sank as he took the letter. It was short. Uncle Jim

Yukon Trail   51

COMPREHENSION

The student will
- Develop vocabulary related to the Yukon.
- Discern characters' motives.
- Identify characters' attitudes.
- Identify place relationships.
- Interpret a foreign setting.
- Infer ideas not explicitly stated.

Before silent reading: pages 51-55

Motivation

Read aloud the title of the story.

▶ How does Steve choose to travel to the Yukon?

What happens while Steve travels to the Yukon?

After silent reading

Overview discussion: pages 51-55

▶ [literal] What does Uncle Jim think of Steve? (He thinks he is a "soft" boy from civilization.)

[interpretive] What is Steve trying to prove to his uncle by choosing to mush? (that he is strong enough to survive in the Yukon)

▶ [interpretive] Why is it important for Steve to hold on to the sled? (If he loses the sled, he could die.)

Follow-up discussion: page 51

▶ [literal] Whom is Steve Woodford looking for as he steps off the train? (Uncle Jim)

[interpretive] How does the author let us know that Steve is excited about going to live with his aunt and uncle? (He had bragged in the orphanage about his uncle, the famous "Flying Doctor," and had dreamed of this for years.)

[critical] Do you think Steve's aunt and uncle will like him? Why or why not? (Answers may vary.)

[literal] How does Steve find out that his uncle will not be able to meet him at the train? (A young Indian named Sam meets him with a letter from his uncle.)

Read aloud Sam's explanation about why Uncle Jim could not meet Steve.

▶ [interpretive] Why does Steve read the letter several times? (He is upset that his uncle calls him "soft.")

Read aloud in a determined voice what Steve tells Sam when he joins him for dinner.

▶ [critical] Is Steve obeying his Uncle Jim? (Answers may vary, but elicit that Uncle Jim left the decision up to Steve.)

▶ [interpretive] Why is it important that Steve learn about dogs? (His uncle uses dogs in his work and Steve will need to know how to handle dogs to be able to help him.)

wrote about how busy he was and that he might not be able to fly down for two or three weeks.

"Sam Ketchum is a young Indian guide who works for me," the letter went on. "I've told him to make you comfortable at the hotel. In a day or two he will be starting back for the Yukon with my new dog team. You could go with him if you wish, but I would not advise you to do so. It is a 350-mile mush through wilderness and tundra, and it would be a hardship for a boy accustomed to the soft life of civilization."

Steve read the letter several times at the hotel. It disturbed him that his uncle should think he was soft.

When he joined Sam for a dinner of venison roast he said, "I

wanted to come up here last year, Sam. But Uncle Jim wouldn't let me. He wrote that I was too young. He said that the Yukon was a man's country and it was no place for a boy. So he made me wait a year. And now he thinks I'm soft. I'm going to show him, Sam. I'm going with you and the dog team."

Sam laughed. "It won't be easy," he warned. "But you have to learn about dogs sometime if you're going to be of any help to your uncle. We'll start at dawn."

It frightened Steve to think of the trip when he went to bed. He had never seen the big sled dogs. Some were part wolf and said to be dangerous.

It was still dark when the hotel man came with a set of fur

52

breeches and a hooded parka, fur boots, and a fur sleeping bag. Sam was waiting for him at the sled, with eleven mighty huskies straining at their harnesses, anxious to be off.

"Better meet some of your dogs," Sam said. "This first one, your leader, is Mutt. He's been to the Yukon before, and he knows the trail."

The tawny big brute lowered its head and watched Steve with suspicion. Steve fought down his fear and leaned over to pet the dog. Its fangs bared in a snarl.

"Not too close," Sam warned. "Mutt doesn't know you yet. And you better stay clear of Kooga—this big malemute. He's a real troublemaker."

Yukon Trail   53

Follow-up discussion: page 53

▶ [interpretive] Why does Steve need fur-lined clothing and a fur-lined sleeping bag? (to be prepared for the cold Yukon temperatures)

▶ [interpretive] Why is Steve afraid of Mutt? (Possible answers: he has never seen the dog before; the dog does not appear to be friendly)

[critical] Do you think Steve will be able to survive on the mush? Why or why not? (Answers will vary.)

Read aloud Sam's warning to Steve.

► [interpretive] How does the author let us know the dogs run fast? (He tells us that they race at full gallop and that the sled bounces and flies.)

[literal] What warning does Sam give Steve about the dogsled? (He tells him not to fall off the sled, or he will lose the dogs and all his food and possibly die.)

Read aloud the paragraph as if you are Sam warning Steve of the danger.

"Why is the sled tied to a tree?" Steve asked.

"Because otherwise they'd be off like a flash and we couldn't stop them," Sam explained. He pointed to an iron rod suspended above the ground at the rear of the sled. It looked like a narrow rake. "That's your brake. You step on it and the prongs dig into the snow and stop the sled."

They packed, and Steve got on top of the sled.

"Hold on!" Sam warned as he untied the rope from the tree.

The dogs were off, eleven big brutes, harnessed in pairs except for Mutt, who took the lead. They raced over the snow in full gallop. The sled bounced and flew, and it took all Steve's strength to hold on.

Standing on the runners in back, Sam gave a hearty laugh.

"Dogs are always wild to get started. They'll soon slow down."

They did. For hours they went, skirting great slopes of spruce and Norway pine, and on and on into the still white wilderness.

At midday they stopped for a few minutes' rest and a bite to eat.

"Now you drive," suggested Sam. "I'll run behind for a while to get warm. But whatever you do, don't fall off the sled. You'll not be able to stop the dogs, and you'll lose them and the sled and all your food. It's not a good way to die."

Steve leaped on the runners. "Get going!" he shouted. Mutt

54

turned his head back and looked at him, but nothing happened.

"Holler *mush*," Sam suggested. "When you want to go right, holler *gee*, and for left *up*. And swing the sled around corners so it doesn't tip."

Steve nodded. "Mush!" he screamed. It worked. He stood proudly on the runners. He was driving a dog team!

There was real work to it, he soon discovered. Keeping the sled upright at curves was tricky, and he had to be careful to avoid stumps and rocks that might smash the sled. On the down slopes he stood on the brake to keep from running over the dogs.

But suddenly it happened. He made the mistake of looking back too long at Sam, who was jogging half a mile behind them. He hit a slope, and his feet slipped from the runners. But he held on, dragging as the sled gathered speed downhill until it pushed the dogs into a wild, scrambled heap. Then the sled tipped.

It started one of the wildest dogfights Steve had ever seen. Each seemed to be blaming the others for what had happened, and they snarled and slashed with white-fanged fury.

"Stop them! Stop them!" Sam yelled.

Steve stood frozen with fear. He didn't move. He didn't dare venture close.

Yukon Trail   55

Follow-up discussion: page 55

▶ [interpretive] How do we know that driving a dogsled is not as easy as it sounds? (because Steve has to learn to keep the sled upright at curves, avoid stumps and rocks, and remember to use his brake down the slopes)

[appreciative] Do you think there should be a driving test for dogsleds?

[interpretive] What causes the sled to tip? (Steve is looking back at Sam and not paying attention to what he is doing.)

Read aloud the paragraph describing the dogfight as if you are retelling the story to your friends.

[appreciative] What would you do to stop the dogs from fighting?

Looking ahead

▶ Do you think Steve will learn how to handle the dogs?

Comprehension:
Worktext page 21

COMPREHENSION

The student will

- Develop vocabulary related to the Yukon.
- Predict outcomes.
- Recognize character growth and change.
- Draw conclusions.
- Evaluate character motives and attitudes.
- Identify cause-and-effect relationships.

Use the prepared sentences to introduce the vocabulary words in context.

Before silent reading: pages 56-59

Motivation

▶ How will Steve reach his uncle?

Do you think Steve will be more responsible after his experience in the Yukon? Why or why not?

After silent reading

Overview discussion: pages 56-59

▶ [appreciative] How would you react to the possibility of driving a dogsled over the tundra alone?

[critical] Where should our confidence be? (Answers may vary, but elicit that our confidence should be in the Lord.) [BATs: 8a Faith in God's promises; 8d Courage]

▶ [interpretive] How is the branch incident similar to the first incident when the sled tipped over? (Both times Steve became careless and was not paying attention to what he was doing.)

▶ [critical] Does Steve's dream of finding a family and a home in the Yukon come true? Why or why not? (Answers will vary.)

Alone on the Tundra

Sam came up full speed, screaming at the dogs. He pried them loose one by one with a snowshoe, and straightened up their harnesses, which had become badly tangled. Then he mopped the sweat from his face.

"You'll have to learn how to do that quick," he gasped. "If you don't, you'll lose a dog or two before you know it."

For five days they went on, and then Sam began to have chills and fever. "I was in the hospital for a week before you came," he explained. "Maybe I left too soon. It's coming back."

By noon he was groaning with pain and could not leave the sled. "There's a settlement over on Carlson Creek," he whispered. "You'd better get me there fast."

Steve reached the hollow among the bluffs in three hours, but only the women and children were there to meet them. The men were out on a week-long hunt.

"This one needs the doctor," said an old woman.

Steve went cold with dread, but he knew what had to be done.

"Sam says my lead dog knows the trail well. I'll go get the doctor."

Sam mumbled in protest, "You'll stay here," he gasped. "Your uncle flies to this settlement every so often for a check."

"It might be weeks," said the old woman. "There is much sickness."

"I'll go," said Steve. He had no choice. Soon he found himself alone on the trail with a fierce pack of malemutes and Eskimo huskies, and he felt panic rising within him. He wondered if he could handle the team.

He began talking to the dogs, calling them by name as Sam had told him to do. He stopped for the night under a sheltering cliff near a staggering thicket of birches. Now the moment he dreaded had come. He had to handle the big dogs.

Steve tried not to show his fear. The big leader dog watched with yellow eyes as he approached, its ears flattened to the massive head. As Steve reached down to unfasten the harness, the wolf dog snarled.

56

Follow-up discussion: page 56

▶ [critical] Why does Sam break up the dogfight and not scold Steve? (Answers will vary, but elicit that he probably knows Steve is afraid and inexperienced, and scolding Steve would not help.)

Read aloud Sam's advice about losing a dog. Read it as though you are out of breath.

▶ [literal] What circumstances force Steve to face the tundra alone? (Sam gets sick, and Steve takes him to the nearest village. The men are out on a week-long hunt, and someone has to get the doctor. Steve knows he is the only able person and volunteers to go.)

[interpretive] What does Steve remember to do that helps him handle the dogs? (He remembers that Sam told him to talk to the dogs and call them by name.)

Read aloud in a fearful voice the paragraph describing how Steve approaches the lead dog.

"Easy, Mutt!" Swiftly, Steve unharnessed the dog and led it to the nearest birch tree and tied it up. He came away weak but bursting with a happiness he had never known. He could do it! The other dogs, even the big malemute Kooga, were easy after that.

One day followed another with perfect weather. The dogs were beginning to know him; some even licked his hand. But Mutt, the leader, remained sullen.

Then he saw the plane in the sky one morning. It circled above him; his uncle waved, and Steve, forming big letters in the snow, told him to go to Sam at Carlson's Settlement.

A howling Arctic blizzard started that night and kept him in his sleeping bag for two days. The third morning dawned clear, and he looked out on a white world. No dogs were in sight. They had all been buried by the snow.

As they mushed north that afternoon he became careless. He did not see the low branch until it struck him with a stunning blow in the face. He was falling. "Don't lose your sled or you die!" Sam's words came roaring back to his ears.

With all his strength he tried to hold on. But it was no use. His fingers slipped and he lunged headlong into the snow. He floundered. He tried to rise to his feet, but the earth seemed to tilt on end, and he couldn't tell which side was up.

Yukon Trail 57

Follow-up discussion: page 57

► [interpretive] Why does Steve feel the dogs are easier to handle now? (He begins to gain confidence in himself, and the dogs are feeling more comfortable with him.)

[interpretive] How does the author let us know that Steve and the dogs are getting along better? (Some of the dogs lick Steve.)

► [interpretive] Why does Steve write a message in the snow to his uncle? (It was the only way Steve could let his uncle know that Sam needed help.)

► [critical] Do you think it is difficult for Steve to keep warm in his sleeping bag for two days? Why or why not? (Answers may vary.)

Read aloud in a terrified voice what Steve remembers Sam saying about falling off the sled.

► [critical] Has Steve learned the lesson of responsibility yet? How do you know? (Accept any answer, but point out that he was not paying attention for the second time now, so he hasn't learned the lesson yet.)

▶ Read aloud what Steve cries out to make Mutt return.

[interpretive] In what ways does Steve respond correctly? (He keeps a clear head and does not panic. He uses the information that he has been taught to help him get the sled back.)

[literal] Why does it seem to Steve that a miracle has occurred? (Mutt, the lead dog, had been sullen but now is licking his face.)

▶ [interpretive] Why does Steve think his uncle and the people of the village will like him now? (because he drove a dog team all by himself and survived in the wilderness)

Read aloud the paragraph that explains the reason for Steve's great excitement.

[literal] How does the village respond to Steve's arrival? (They cheer, wave, and smile.)

The dogs and the sled were speeding away. He could see them vaguely. In a few moments they would be gone. There was nothing he could do to stop them. His food, his sleeping bag, even his snowshoes were on the sled. A man couldn't live very long on the lonely tundra without them.

In that reeling instant of terror he seemed doomed. His mind cleared, and instinctively he cried out at the top of his lungs. "Gee! Gee! Gee, Mutt!"

He held his breath. For a terrible instant nothing happened. But suddenly the big lead dog swung to the right. He waited until the whole team had turned. Then he screamed again "Gee! Gee, Mutt!" Once more the lead dog turned.

They were coming back now. Steve got to his feet and stumbled to meet them, waving his arms. He tripped over a snowdrift and sprawled before the onrushing team. That was all he could remember for a long time.

When he opened his eyes finally it seemed that a miracle had happened. Mutt, towering over him, was licking his face.

58

He threw his arms around the big dog, buried his face in the heavy fur, and let the tears come. Even a man could cry in Alaska if there was no one there to see his tears.

From that day on his uncle paid him daily visits to watch his progress and to drop sandwiches and food from Aunt Bess. In the first of these packages he found a note.

"I have seen Sam," wrote his uncle. "He's doing fine, thanks to you. If you keep up your good speed, you should reach home in three days. We'll be waiting."

Steve felt a deep inner excitement. Home! In three days! He could drive a dog team now, and he felt sure that he could be of real use to his uncle. They would not find him soft and useless. They would like him.

Near sunset, three days later, as he came down the slope into the small settlement of Unison in the Yukon, his uncle and half the village came out to meet him. They were cheering and waving and smiling. His tall uncle wore a large smile and threw an arm over his shoulder.

"Good boy, Steve," he said warmly. To the people of the village he said, raising his voice, "I'm mighty proud to introduce you to my nephew Steve. He mushed all the way from Nenana in fifteen days, and that's a record for any of us to shoot at."

When they entered the log cabin which was to be his new home, there were gifts from almost everyone in the village—snowshoes, parkas, beaded reindeer pants, a beautiful malemute pup, a carving from a walrus tusk, and bows and arrows.

Steve mumbled his thanks to the smiling villagers who stood before him. They were a strange mixture of old sourdoughs, Eskimos, Indians, and boys and girls.

One young man spoke up. "The Flying Doctor has cared for us and saved many of us from death. We love him as a father, and we are glad to welcome another of his blood."

It was not until later when Aunt Bess and Uncle Jim and Steve were alone that Uncle Jim spoke.

"I want to confess, Steve, that I've been worried about having you here. I wanted you to be happy, but I knew that a soft white boy from civilization would soon be looked upon by these people with contempt."

He smiled and took Steve firmly by the shoulders. "But I see now that I was wrong. I need not have worried. You did what had to be done. You've got the makings of a real Yukon man."

Steve turned quickly away to play with the pup—and to hide the mist of happiness that had come into his eyes.

Yukon Trail   59

Follow-up discussion: page 59

► [literal] What gifts does Steve receive? (snowshoes, parkas, beaded reindeer pants, malemute pup, carving from a walrus tusk, and bows and arrows)

► [interpretive] When the young man welcomes Steve as another of the Flying Doctor's blood, what does the phrase "of his blood" mean? (related to him)

Read aloud in a proud voice what Uncle Jim says to Steve when they are alone.

► [interpretive] What "mist of happiness" is the author speaking about? (tears of joy because Steve has found a home)

[appreciative] Have you ever felt so happy that you had tears in your eyes?

Worktext Objectives

The student will

■ Infer cause-and-effect relationships.

■ Infer unstated supporting details.

Comprehension:
Worktext page 22

SOMETHING EXTRA

Write About It: My new family

Tell the students the following.

▶ Steve's dream has finally come true in being part of a family. He is excited about sharing the good news with some of his friends at the orphanage and wants to write a letter to them.

Direct each student to pretend he is Steve and write a letter that describes his new family and his adventures in the Yukon.

Red braids like carrots sticking out of her head, six pearly white teeth, and orange freckles! No wonder it was love at first sight when Pecos Bill met the lovely Slewfoot Sue. If only she had listened when he warned her not to ride Widow Maker.

Lesson	Reader pages	Worktext pages
19	60-63	23-24

Materials
- Cowboy hat and bandana
- Marshmallows
- Stick for roasting marshmallows
- Vocabulary sentences for display

Background information

Cowboys—Back when the West was still being tamed, hundreds of cowboys roamed the plains, drifting from job to job. Cowboys have been made to look dashing and brave, but most of them were just young men who worked long hours far from home and with very little pay. Most of them could not read well and books were rare anyway.

Pecos Bill—Developed from a magazine article written by Edward O'Riley, Pecos Bill is an American folklore hero. He is said to be responsible for the invention of roping, branding, and numerous other cowboy skills.

INTRODUCTION

Vocabulary

Use the prepared sentences to introduce the vocabulary words in context.

Storytelling

Wear a cowboy hat and bandana. Huddle around an imaginary fire, pretending to cook some marshmallows.

▶ Have you ever sat around a campfire roasting marshmallows? If so, when was it and who was with you?

What did you talk about as you sat around the fire?

Explain that cowboys would cheer themselves up and pass the time by making up stories around the campfires. Their favorite story character was Pecos Bill, a rootin', tootin' cowboy who could do anything.

VOCABULARY
LESSON 19

*She told her friends he was the brawniest man in town because he was so strong and muscular. (p. 60)

The engagement was a whirlwind, lasting only five days! (p. 61)

*He flattered the girl during their courtship so that she would marry him. (p. 61)

*Women used to use a bustle, or frame, to shape the back of a dress. (p. 62)

*†The horse was tied to the fence with a lariat. (p. 63)

Correlated Activities
- **Recreational Reading, Activity 2: Design-a-Game**
- **Connections, Activity 3: Amazing Ads**
See "Classroom Management for Grouping" in the Appendix.

COMPREHENSION

The student will

- Develop vocabulary related to cowboy life.
- Identify exaggerations in a tall tale.
- Identify fanciful elements in a tall tale.
- Interpret an idiomatic expression.
- Recognize the humor and fun in a tall tale.
- Identify the conflict in a story plot.

Objectives

Before silent reading: pages 60-63

Motivation

▶ What is Pecos Bill's warning to his wife?

Who learns a valuable lesson?

After silent reading

Overview discussion: pages 60-63

▶ [interpretive] How do you know that this story couldn't really be true? (because there is too much exaggeration)

[interpretive] What parts of the story make it impossible to believe? (Possible answers: Widow Maker goes sixty miles an hour; Slewfoot Sue rides a catfish, grizzly bears, and mountain lions; Slewfoot Sue races quicker than a jackrabbit and bounces into space.)

▶ [interpretive] What is the big problem or conflict between Pecos Bill and Slewfoot Sue? (whether or not Sue can ride Widow Maker)

[critical] Do you think Slewfoot Sue will listen to Pecos Bill's warnings after her experience with Widow Maker? Why or why not? (Answers will vary.)

Pecos Bill Gets a Wife

adapted by Becky Henry
illustrated by Bruce Day

Pecos Bill, that rootin' tootin' cowboy, he figured he had just about everything. Why, he had Scat the cougar. And he had Rat the python. And of course, he had Widow Maker, the biggest, brawniest horse in the West, a horse that only Pecos Bill could ride. So the cowboy was mighty content, figuring there was nothing else in the whole wide world he could ever want.

But one day Pecos Bill was moseying down the river trail on old Widow Maker's back. He was taking it kind of slow and easy, 'bout sixty miles an hour, when all of a sudden something stopped him right in his tracks.

60

Follow-up discussion: page 60

▶ [literal] Why is Pecos Bill mighty content? (He figures there is nothing else he could ever want.)

[interpretive] Why is Pecos Bill the only one who can ride Widow Maker? (Widow Maker is so wild that anyone else might be killed trying to ride him.)

Read aloud the sentences that explain what Pecos Bill has that make him so content.

▶ [literal] How fast is Pecos Bill riding down the river trail? (about sixty miles an hour)

[interpretive] Could someone really ride a horse sixty miles an hour? When the author says that Pecos Bill is taking it kind of slow and easy at about sixty miles an hour, what is she doing? (no; exaggerating)

It was a sight. A sight the likes of what Pecos Bill had never seen before in all his days. Speeding down the middle of the river on the back of a giant catfish was a cowgirl. What a cowgirl! Her hair was as red as the evening sun, all tied up in two braids, looking like two carrots sticking out of her head. Her hat flapped on the ends of its strings.

"Yippee! Yahoo!" she yelled. Her two long bony arms wrapped around the catfish's body. "Yahoo-ee! Yip-yip-yahoo!"

No doubt about it; it was love at first sight. Pecos Bill felt his heart do a double flip and the sweat stand out on his brow. He had to meet this cowgirl!

Even while he watched, the catfish took a wild leap and landed on the bank, gasping for breath. The redheaded cowgirl hopped off, and with one quick toss she flipped the catfish back into the water. Then she turned to face Pecos Bill.

"Howdy, cowboy!" She grinned wide enough to show off all six of her teeth, shining white and pearly. The freckles on her face stood out bold and orange.

Pecos Bill's heart jumped into his throat, and he couldn't speak for gazing at her beauty. So she kept right on talking.

"My name's Slewfoot Sue. I come down the river to find me new critters to ride. I done rode everything this country has to offer. I've rode grizzly bars and mountain lions and wild horses, and now I've rode a catfish too." She grinned again and poured the water out of her boot. "What have you rode, cowboy?"

All Pecos Bill could do was smile.

There was a whirlwind court-ship, and Slewfoot Sue decided she loved this cowboy as much as he loved her. But as crazy as Bill was about Sue, there was one thing he wouldn't let her do.

"Sue," he told her, "I've got to warn you. Everything I have is yours, including Widow Maker. But he's a fiery horse, and he won't let anyone ride him but me. If you try, I might never see you again."

Well, those were the very words Sue needed to hear to make her want to ride Widow Maker more than anything else in the

Follow-up discussion: page 61

▶ [literal] What stops Pecos Bill in his tracks? (the sight of a cowgirl riding a catfish)

[literal] What does the author compare the cowgirl's hair to? (the evening sun and two carrots)

Read aloud the paragraph that describes Slewfoot Sue's hair.

[critical] How would you describe the way Slewfoot Sue looks and acts? (Answers may vary, but elicit that the author's description adds humor to the story.)

▶ [literal] Why does Pecos Bill not want Slewfoot Sue to ride Widow Maker? (Pecos Bill does not want his bride-to-be to get hurt.)

[interpretive] Why does Bill's warn-ing make Slewfoot Sue want to ride Widow Maker more than anything? (possible answers: because she loves adventure; to prove that she can ride anything)

Read aloud like a cowboy the para-graph that tells what Pecos Bill warns Sue about.

▶ [interpretive] Why is Pecos Bill so happy? (because he is marrying the girl he loves)

Read aloud the first thing Slewfoot Sue does after she is married.

[interpretive] How does the author describe Slewfoot Sue racing out to ride Widow Maker? (quicker than a jackrabbit)

▶ [critical] What is a rumor? (Accept any answer, but explain that it is a story that is spread through gossip and is usually untrue.)

Read aloud the rumor about Slewfoot Sue.

[interpretive] Why does the bustle keep Slewfoot Sue bouncing? (It is made from a new bedspring that causes her to bounce high.)

world. Sue didn't mention it again, but that's not to say it left her mind. She could think of hardly anything else.

Their wedding day came, and my, didn't Sue look pretty! She wore a white veil and a long white dress with a bustle the size of a bushel basket. Bustles were quite the style back then, you know, and Sue's was made from a brand new bedspring and the fanciest chicken wire around. There never was a happier man than Pecos Bill on his wedding day.

Well, no sooner had they said "I do" and the preacher pronounced his blessing than Slewfoot Sue hollered "Yahoo!" She raced outside quicker than a jackrabbit and hopped on Widow Maker's back. That was one surprised horse.

And that was one surprised bride. Widow Maker bucked hard, and Slewfoot Sue's second "Yahoo!" faded off into the distance as she disappeared from sight behind the clouds.

They all stood watching—Bill, the preacher, and all the cowboys, their mouths hanging wide open. "We might never see her again," Pecos Bill muttered. "I warned her."

Well, rumor had it that Sue had to duck her head to keep from hitting the moon. But whatever happened, she appeared again that evening, falling right out of the sky. She would have landed with only a few bruises except for the bustle she was wearing.

Instead of landing, Sue bounced.

Sue bounced up until she was out of sight in the sky again!

62

When she came back down, she bounced again.

This could have gone on for days or even weeks, but finally Pecos Bill decided he had had enough. He figured his new bride probably had too. So he pulled out his lariat and waited.

The next time Sue bounced, Bill lassoed her and brought her down. If it hadn't been for his strong muscles, she would have bounced again. But she stayed. She was a little dizzy and bruised, but otherwise she was fine.

From what I hear, Pecos Bill and Slewfoot Sue had a right happy life together as husband and wife. And one thing that made it happy was that never again did Slewfoot Sue ask to ride Widow Maker. She was cured of that forever.

Follow-up discussion: page 63

▶ [literal] How does Pecos Bill save his new bride? (He uses his lariat to lasso her.)

Read aloud the paragraph that tells how Pecos Bill finally stops Slewfoot Sue from bouncing.

▶ [interpretive] Why do you think Pecos Bill and Slewfoot Sue have a happy life together? (She learns her lesson and listens to Pecos Bill's advice by never riding Widow Maker again.)

▶ [critical] How are Pecos Bill and Slewfoot Sue alike? (Answers may vary, but elicit that they are always willing to try anything exciting.)

Worktext Objective

The student will

■ Match words and meanings.

Vocabulary:
Worktext page 23

Pecos Bill Gets a Wife

<table>
<tr><td>

Worktext Objectives

The student will

- Match story characters and dialogue.
- Predict dialogue.

</td></tr>
</table>

COMPREHENSION
Characters and dialogue

Guide a discussion about story characters.

▶ How can we learn about a character? (possible answer: by the character's description, actions, and speech or dialogue)

▶ What a character says tells us about the character.

Story characters have traits that help us predict what they will say and the vocabulary they will use.

Comprehension: Worktext page 24

SOMETHING EXTRA
Tell About It: Spin a yarn

Explain that cowboys tried to outdo each other by exaggerating the abilities of a character in a tall tale. Challenge the students to "spin a yarn" or tall tale. Use a tape player to record the story as it unfolds.

1. Begin the tale with a character name and a phrase about the character.
   Examples:
   Tammy Tumbleweed had such long hair that when she combed it . . .
   Bobby Buckaroo had such long legs that when he walked they stretched across . . .

2. Call on various students to exaggerate the abilities and descriptions of the character until everyone has an opportunity to add something creative.

3. Edit the story tape if necessary before "publishing" the tall tale in book form. Select volunteers to illustrate the book.

Materials
- Vocabulary sentences for display

INTRODUCTION
Vocabulary
Use the prepared sentences to introduce the vocabulary words in context.

Stretching the truth
Read the following tall tale to the students.

Boy, what a day! My cat climbed up a six-hundred-foot tree, and I had to climb up to rescue her. Then I jumped down with a perfect landing. I placed Kitty inside the house and zoomed to my car with lightning speed only to find out that the car would not start! So I jogged fifty miles and made it to school in just ten minutes. As I walked into the classroom, I realized that a tornado had struck. Everything was a mess! I quickly repaired all the tornado damage and picked up all the books and papers with just one minute to spare! Whew! What a morning!

▶ Do you really think this happened? Why or why not?

What parts of this story make it impossible or unbelievable? (possible answers: climbing a six-hundred-foot tree; jogging fifty miles in ten minutes)

▶ What are some things in the story "Pecos Bill Gets a Wife" that make it unbelievable? (possible answers: riding a catfish; bouncing out of sight)

What characteristics do these two stories have in common? (Both contain exaggeration and humor that make them impossible to believe.)

Lesson	Reader pages	Worktext pages
20	64-65	25-26

VOCABULARY
LESSON 20

*†His attempt to save the girl was a great feat of bravery. (p. 64)

*†Two basic parts or elements of a story are the setting and plot. (p. 65)

*†The meeting of Pecos Bill and Slewfoot Sue was an unexpected encounter. (p. 65)

The tall tale was very funny because it had a big dose of humor. (p. 65)

†Cowboys exaggerated stories by spinning humorous tales about their heroes. (p. 65)

Correlated Activities
- **Word Work, Activity 4: Worn Words**
- **Creative Writing, Activity 3: Life and Times in 4th Grade**
See "Classroom Management for Grouping" in the Appendix.

COMPREHENSION

The student will

- Develop an awareness of the author's use of imagery.
- Develop a sense of literary heritage.
- Use comparisons to describe an object.

Before silent reading: pages 64-65

Motivation

▶ Why are these stories called tall tales?

How do you "spin" a tall tale?

After silent reading

Overview discussion: pages 64-65

▶ [literal] What is a "tall tale"? (a story that stretches the truth so much that nobody is expected to believe it)

[interpretive] If you were spinning a tall tale, what basic parts or elements would you need? (possible answers: a bigger-than-life character or hero; exaggeration or impossible feats; humor; colorful descriptions)

[critical] What is the difference between a tall tale and a lie? (Answers may vary, but elicit that everyone who reads a tall tale knows that it could not be true.) [BAT: 4c Honesty]

[interpretive] Why did storytellers invent these tall tale characters? (Heroes had more exciting adventures than real men, and the men wanted something to dream about.)

Tall Tales

illustrated by Bruce Day

The story "Pecos Bill Gets a Wife" is called a tall tale. That's an unusual name for an unusual kind of story. A tall tale stretches the truth so much that nobody is really expected to believe it.

• The History of Tall Tales

In early America a man had to be strong just to survive. As a result, BIG stories grew up about BIG men who could do BIG, impossible things. But these impossible characters lived only in the minds of their storytellers.

The storytellers were almost always men who wished they could perform great feats. Sometimes they worked at hard, dangerous jobs. Sometimes their jobs were dull. The men wanted to have something to dream about. They wanted to know a bigger-than-life lumberjack, railroad man, seaman, or cowboy. So they invented characters like Paul Bunyan, John Henry, Stormalong, and, of course, Pecos Bill.

64

Follow-up discussion: page 64

▶ [interpretive] What does the author mean by the phrase "stretches the truth"? (Answers may vary but should express the idea of exaggeration.)

[interpretive] Why does the author choose to write *BIG* in all uppercase letters? (to emphasize the exaggerated elements of a tall tale)

Read aloud how these big stories grew.

▶ [literal] Where do these tall tale characters live? (only in the minds of their storytellers)

[interpretive] What kinds of men told these stories? (all kinds of men who had dull or dangerous jobs: lumberjacks, sailors, cowboys, railroad workers, etc.)

• **Elements of Tall Tales**

It could have taken a real cow-boy a year to encounter the excitement that Pecos Bill met in one day. That was one reason men liked this tall tale character so much. The more impossible the feats he accomplished, the better they liked him. He was the cowboy that other cowboys dreamed of being.

However, Slewfoot Sue was hardly the kind of girl a cowboy dreamed of meeting! Adding a big dose of humor to a tall tale helped make long, lonely nights on the prairie pass more quickly.

The best tall-tale tellers also used colorful descriptions for spinning their tall tales. They wanted to draw pictures in the other fellow's mind, so they used phrases such as "her hair looked like two carrots sticking out of her head," or "her bustle was the size of a bushel basket."

Find examples of tall-tale elements in the story you just read. If you put them all together, you may be able to write a tall tale of your own!

Literature Lesson: Tall Tales   65

Follow-up discussion: page 65

▶ [appreciative] Do you ever dream about doing something heroic? What do you dream of doing?

Read aloud the paragraph that tells why cowboys liked the tall-tale hero Pecos Bill.

▶ [interpretive] What does the phrase "Adding a big dose of humor to a tall tale" mean? (possible answer: including dialogue, descriptions, and actions that are funny)

[literal] In what way did humor help cowboys on the prairie? (It helped make long, lonely nights pass more quickly.)

▶ [literal] What do the best tall-tale tellers use when spinning their tales? Why? (colorful descriptions to draw pictures in another person's mind)

[literal] What colorful descriptions of Slewfoot Sue does the author use in "Pecos Bill Gets a Wife"? ("her hair looked like two carrots sticking out of her head" and "her bustle was the size of a bushel basket")

[critical] What does the author mean by "spinning" a tall tale? (Answers will vary, but elicit that the storyteller tells the story imaginatively.)

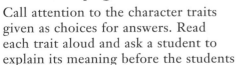

The student will

■ Recognize and identify character traits and motives.

Comprehension:
Worktext page 25

Call attention to the character traits given as choices for answers. Read each trait aloud and ask a student to explain its meaning before the students complete the page independently.

The student will

■ Identify the elements of a tall tale.

LITERATURE
Tall tales

Write the following title for display and read it aloud.

Elements of Tall Tales

Guide the following discussion to review the elements of tall tales.

► Real cowboys liked Pecos Bill because he could do things they couldn't do— he was "bigger than life." Pecos Bill was their hero. One element of tall tales is that the main character is a hero.

Write *Hero* below the title *Elements of Tall Tales*.

► What are some examples of exaggeration in "Pecos Bill Gets a Wife"? (Possible answers: Slewfoot Sue rode a giant catfish; she had to duck her head to keep from hitting the moon.)

► Some of the exaggerations in tall tales are impossible feats or acts. Another element of tall tales is impossible acts.

Write *Impossible acts* as another element of tall tales.

► How did the author describe Slewfoot Sue's hair? (two braids looking like two carrots sticking out of her head)

► The author used a "colorful description" to help you picture Sue's hair.

He could have simply said that she had two braids. Another element of tall tales is colorful description.

Write *Colorful description* as another element of tall tales.

► Is the story of Pecos Bill sad? (no) Is it informative? (no)

► Does the story make you laugh? What word could be used to describe a funny story? (humorous)

Write *Humor* as another element of tall tales.

Literature: Worktext page 26

SOMETHING EXTRA
Write About It: My tall tale

Encourage each student to write a tall tale of his own. Give the following guidelines.

1. Invent a character and give him or her a name.
2. Describe your character.
3. Tell what great impossible feats he or she performs.
4. Be sure to use colorful descriptions.
5. Include humor in your tall tale.

Instruct each student to cut a sheet of paper in half, taping the two pieces together to make a long, narrow sheet of paper.

Tell the students to write their tall tales on the tall sheets.

Kyle hides a computer disk from thieves who have been stealing information from his dad's company. The alarm sounds and the thieves run, but not before they decide to take Kyle along as their "ticket out."

Lesson	Reader pages	Worktext pages
21	66-72	27-28

VOCABULARY

LESSON 21

*Everyone in the room could hear the man's boisterous laugh. (p. 66)

*†A security alarm sounded when the thief broke into the bank. (p. 67)

*Ashley's top priority after school each day was to do her homework. (p. 67)

†In solving the mystery, Steven used clues to find the information leak. (p. 67)

*He could not understand the unintelligible voices. (p. 70)

Materials
• Computer disk labeled "Top Secret"
• Vocabulary sentences for display

Background information
Computer setting—Explain that the setting of this story is the 1980s, when computers operated differently. Although the basic parts, input and output devices, remain the same, programs are now more "user friendly." People using computers can operate a program without knowing an operating or programming language. Earlier, a user had to be very specific when typing in commands. The results could be very confusing to anyone unfamiliar with the language (see reader page 70). Today the mouse is used to tell the computer to run the program. The task is performed without having to type in any information. The computer in this story is old and requires the user to type in simple commands such as "RUN," "PRINT," and "STOP" in order to prompt the computer to perform an operation.

INTRODUCTION

Vocabulary
Use the prepared sentences to introduce the vocabulary words in context.

Top-secret mission
Display a computer disk labeled "Top Secret."

▶ You have been given a top-secret mission. You are to make sure no one steals the information on the disk that I am holding. I cannot tell you what is on the disk, only that it is top secret!

What do you think is on the disk?

Why would someone want to steal it?

Head note
Read aloud the head note on reader page 66.

Correlated Activities
• **Recreational Reading, Activity 3: Frantic Antics**
• **Connections, Activity 4: Recipe Reconstruction**
See "Classroom Management for Grouping" in the Appendix.

COMPREHENSION

The student will

- Recognize the author's techniques in revealing characters through their actions and dialogue.
- Recognize the motives of characters.
- Recognize the character trait of courage.

Before silent reading: pages 66–69

Motivation

▶ What does Kyle discover about the security problem in his father's office?

What happens to Kyle because of his involvement in Project Submarine?

After silent reading

Overview discussion: pages 66–69

▶ [literal] What is the information leak Kyle is able to find for his father? (He discovers the men who are stealing secret information.)

[interpretive] How does Kyle trick the thieves? (He replaces the "Project Submarine" disk with his homework disk.)

▶ [interpretive] Why do the men kidnap Kyle? (They suspect Kyle knows something about the leak and they think they can use him as a hostage to aid their escape.)

[interpretive] Why do the men take Kyle to the warehouse? (possible answers: to hide from the police, to call Wendell, to hide Kyle)

Project Submarine

Paul and Karen Wilt

illustrated by Del Thompson and Noelle Snyder

Kyle Ellis, an average kid with an above average machine, uses current technology to unravel a security problem. Although today Kyle's computer may look strange, outdated, and useless, in the 1980s it was the most recent in computer technology. This trend of computer improvement will even make tomorrow's computers outdate today's!

Kyle Ellis punched the enter button. A bright blue "ERROR" sign flashed at him as the computer started to beep. "Oh, no!" Kyle slumped back in his chair.

"Keep trying," Mr. Javanowitz said. "Ever since your dad set up this homework-checking program, you've always got your homework done in micro-seconds." His boisterous laugh filled the office. Kyle

typed "END PROGRAM" and pulled out the disk.

"Look at this, Kyle," Mr. Javanowitz said. Mr. Javanowitz was Mr. Ellis's partner and an earnest computer fan. He enjoyed Kyle's afternoon visits to the office. Mr. Javanowitz started another program, and a chessboard appeared. "The computer has had

Follow-up discussion: page 66

▶ [literal] What is Kyle Ellis doing at the computer? (checking his homework)

[critical] How can a homework program be helpful? (Answers will vary.)

Read aloud with laughter in your voice what Mr. Javanowitz says about Kyle checking his homework.

me in check all afternoon, but I think I have a way around it."

He punched two keys, and his queen zipped across the screen and landed beside the computer's bishop. The computer hummed for a moment, then moved a knight forward. "CHECKMATE" flashed the screen.

"UGH," Mr. Javanowitz typed onto the screen.

"Well, I'll see you tomorrow," he said, closing the program.

"Good night," Kyle said. He carefully shut down the computer.

The door closed behind Mr. Javanowitz, and Kyle sighed.

Computers could do more things than he had ever imagined. They seemed able to do anything—or at least almost anything. But just yesterday Dad had said they couldn't think up an answer to the security problem at work. With the program Kyle had, he could check his math, but the computer wouldn't just give the answer straight out.

Just then the door from the laboratory opened and a man in a white lab jacket stepped out. He set his toolbox on the office floor and held the door for a repairman. The edge of his slacks caught on the lid of the toolbox and popped it open. A disk lay on the upper shelf. Kyle could see that the other shelves were empty. He looked again. The words "PROJECT SUBMARINE" had been penciled on the label of the disk. Then he noticed the lower label. "High priority. Do not remove from security area."

Kyle's head spun. Dad had just mentioned the security problem at the labs. This was the leak: these men were stealing the secret information.

Quickly and silently Kyle snatched up the disk. He slid it under his chair cushion. His hands felt cold and clammy, but a drip of sweat fell off his forehead as he pretended to adjust the computer.

"Hey," the man in the lab jacket said, reaching for the toolbox. "What happened to the—Kid, did you take a disk from the box?" He leaned over Kyle, frowning and clenching his fist.

Kyle grabbed the homework disk off the desk. "Do you mean this?" he asked. He tried to keep

Project Submarine   67

Follow-up discussion: page 67

▶ [interpretive] What type of security problem does Kyle's dad have at work? (someone is stealing information)

[interpretive] Why does Kyle think at first that the men who come into the office belong there? (One is wearing a white lab jacket and carrying a toolbox; the other man looks like a repairman.)

[interpretive] How does Kyle discover that the men are the thieves? (He sees a disk in the toolbox labeled "Project Submarine" and "High priority" and sees that there are no tools in the box.)

▶ [literal] What does Kyle do once he realizes what the men are doing? (He snatches up the disk and hides it under the chair cushion.) [BAT: 2e Initiative]

Read aloud the conversation between Kyle and the man when the disks get switched.

[interpretive] Why does Kyle give the man his homework disk? (He hopes the man will not notice the switch and will steal the wrong disk.)

Follow-up discussion: page 68

▶ [literal] Why do the thieves have to escape through a window? (the alarm has caused the door to lock)

[interpretive] What does the man mean when he says, "Here's our ticket out of here"? (They will use Kyle as a hostage in case they are caught.)

▶ [interpretive] How does the author let you know that Kyle does not have a comfortable ride in the van? (He has to hold on with all his might.)

[interpretive] How does the author describe the getaway? (as a swerving roller-coaster ride)

Read aloud this section as if you are a sportscaster giving a play-by-play report.

---

his voice steady, but he could hear it rise in his throat.

"Yeah," the man said. He snatched it and stuffed it into his jacket.

The repairman narrowed his eyes. "I don't like the looks of this, Jake," he said.

A loud bell began clanging. "The alarm!" Jake ran for the door.

The bolt shot closed.

"Let's get out of here," the other man said. He pulled on the handle. The door didn't budge. "Come on," he said. He flung the toolbox against the window, shattering the glass. He kicked the broken pieces out of the way. "Here's our ticket out, Jake." He grabbed Kyle by the arm.

Kyle felt himself lifted out the window; then Jake tossed him into a van. He fell backward among a jumble of machines. The other man jumped into the driver's seat next to Jake.

The wheels screeched as the van jerked to life and sped into traffic.

As the van swayed from side to side, Kyle grabbed the seat in front of him and hung on with all his might.

They sped down the highway, passing cars and trucks in a swerving roller-coaster ride. A siren sounded. The driver darted in front of a car and turned into a side street, swinging the back of the van in a wide arc. The ride was a series of stops and starts, jerks and jumbles until they reached an old warehouse.

68

"We'll hide here," said the man who had driven the van. "I'll call Wendell. We'll have to take what we have and go."

Jake dragged Kyle into the warehouse and tied him to a pole. Then he set up a computer.

"The more you find out, the bigger problem you're gonna be, kid," Jake said. "'Cuz what are we gonna do if you find out too much?"

Kyle dropped his eyes to the floor.

Jake laughed and hit his knee. The computer beeped. Kyle peered at it without raising his head. A game flashed onto the screen.

"You're really gonna find out too much this way." Jake piloted his spaceship through asteroids, flying saucers, and enemy rockets, laughing to himself as he shot them down.

Follow-up discussion: page 69

▶ [critical] Who do you think Wendell is? (Accept any answer, but point out that he is probably their boss.)

[interpretive] Why will the men have to take what they have and leave? (The police will be looking for the people who broke into the company and kidnapped Kyle.)

▶ [literal] What does Jake do with Kyle? (ties him to a pole)

Read aloud in a gruff voice what Jake says about Kyle's being a problem.

[interpretive] What does Jake mean when he says that the more Kyle knows, the bigger problem he will be? (Kyle could tell the police what these men are doing.)

▶ [literal] How does Jake use the computer? (to play a spaceship game)

Before silent reading: pages 70-72

Motivation

▶ What will happen to Kyle?

After silent reading

Overview discussion: pages 70-72

▶ [interpretive] How does the author show how upset Jake is? (Possible answer: Jake shrieks, rips the disk from the computer, shoves the disk in Kyle's face, and breaks the disk.)

▶ [literal] What does Kyle do to get loose from the ropes? (He keeps pulling on the ropes until the rope catches on a nail and pops loose.)

[interpretive] How does Kyle use his computer skills to escape? (He uses the disk for the warehouse floor plan to find an emergency exit.)

▶ [interpretive] How do you know that Kyle's dad is concerned about him? (He notified the police when Kyle was kidnapped. He immediately went to the police station to meet Kyle and made certain Kyle had not been harmed.)

[critical] What do you think happens to the thieves? (Answers may vary.)

Follow-up discussion: page 70

▶ [interpretive] What does Harvey mean by "lay low"? (stay in the hideout so no one can recognize or find them)

▶ Read aloud the section where the men find out they have the homework disk.

[critical] Do you think Kyle regrets switching the disks when the men discover that he did? Why or why not? (Answers will vary.)

A car horn honked. Jake ran to the door. A mumble of unintelligible voices reached Kyle's ears. He pulled at the rope on his hands and felt it loosen.

Several men walked toward him, and Kyle held still.

"Well, Harvey, did he say anything else?" Jake asked.

"We'll just have to lay low for a day or two," said Harvey, the man who had driven the van. "Let's check the program we got."

He pulled out Kyle's homework program and stuck it into the machine. "RUN," he typed.

The disk drive hummed, and then the screen lit up with the program:

```
010 RANDOMIZE
020 FOR I = 1 TO 10
030 A = INT(RND(100)*100)
040 B = INT(RND(100)*100)
050 PRINT A; "+" B;
060 INPUT ANSWER
070 IF ANSWER = A+B THEN
    PRINT "GOOD WORK" :
    CORRECT = CORRECT + 1
080 IF ANSWER <> A+B THEN
    PRINT "TRY AGAIN" : WRNG
    = WRNG+1: GOTO 50
090 NEXT 1
```

"What?" Jake shrieked. He ripped the disk out of the computer. "Look; just look at this: 'Homework Program.' I bet that kid . . ." His eyes turned to Kyle.

Kyle's heart raced. "What should I do?" he thought. "I've got to think."

Jake shoved the disk at Kyle's face and broke it into a worthless mess. "We're gonna get that program," he fumed. "Like you said, Harvey, here's our ticket." He tapped Kyle's chest.

"Let's go call the boss and arrange the details," Harvey said.

Kyle heard them lock the door as they walked out. He pulled at the ropes. They seemed to loosen more, but his hand wouldn't fit between them and the pole. As Kyle twisted and turned, the rope caught on a nail. He tugged, and the rope popped loose. Kyle fell forward onto his knees. Wasting no time, he scrambled to his feet and raced to the door.

The men had locked it from the outside. Kyle searched the windows. The lowest one was at least twenty feet from the ground. He paced the floor. "If only computers could figure out a problem like this," he thought to himself.

He stopped in front of the computer. The file of disks lay in a jumble. Kyle stuck one into the slot and typed "RUN." The computer began to list names and addresses. Kyle saw his dad's company name flash by. "Hmm," he murmured.

Kyle stuck in another disk. Quickly he glanced through the files and chose the ones that looked most important. He checked a few more disks, planning to find a safe place to hide them.

Then he ran the program titled "WAREHOUSE." A set of floor plans covered the screen. Kyle reached for the return key. Then two words caught his attention— "EMERGENCY EXIT." Kyle bit his lip. If the emergency exit wasn't blocked, it would be immediately behind him. He pulled out the disk.

The front door rattled. Kyle scooped up the disks and raced for the emergency exit. A big stack of empty boxes blocked his way. Kyle shoved them aside. The emergency exit sign, covered with an inch of dust, lay shattered where it had fallen on the floor. Kyle attacked the door, praying that it would open. The hinges creaked and gave way.

Project Submarine   71

Follow-up discussion: page 71

▶ Read aloud Jake's reaction to finding out that Kyle tricked them.

[interpretive] Why do the men leave? (Possible answer: The men need to discuss what to do with Kyle and come up with a new plan for getting the right disk.)

▶ [literal] Why can't Kyle escape through the door or windows? (The door is locked from the outside, and the windows are too high.)

[interpretive] Why does Kyle look at the disks? (Possible answers: He is curious; he is looking for a solution to his problem.)

Read aloud how Kyle discovers a way to get out of the warehouse. Read with hope in your voice.

[interpretive] How does Kyle demonstrate courage? (Accept any answer, but elicit that he does not just sit and hope for the best; instead he keeps a clear head, gets loose from the rope, saves the stolen disks, and finds a way out.) [BAT: 8d Courage]

Follow-up discussion: page 72

▶ [literal] What does Kyle do once he escapes? (He runs away as fast as he can and looks for someone he can trust.)

Read this section aloud excitedly as if you were reporting a chase.

[interpretive] How does the author let us know it is nighttime now? (The streetlights are just coming on.)

▶ [appreciative] Would you trust the fellow pumping gas? Why or why not?

[interpretive] Why does Kyle run to the police car? (He knows he can trust the police officer.)

[literal] How does the police officer know about Kyle? (His kidnapping was being broadcast on the police radio all afternoon.)

▶ [critical] Why do you think the author chooses not to tell you what happens to the kidnappers? (Accept any answer.)

"Hey, the kid's gone!"

Kyle tore blindly down the alley and then turned down another, expecting someone to grab him at any moment. His lungs felt as if they were bursting. The streetlights were just coming on. The shadows they made seemed to be filled with kidnappers. The streets were deserted. Kyle saw a gas station on the corner ahead.

The fellow pumping gas into a car brushed his long hair out of his eyes and yawned. Kyle watched from the shadows, unable to decide whether or not to trust such a character.

Just then a police car pulled into the station. Kyle broke into a run. "Help!" he yelled.

The police officer jumped out of the car. "What's the problem, Son?" he asked.

Kyle stumbled as he reached him. "I'm Kyle Ellis. I was kidnapped." He held his sides and gasped for air. "I just escaped. Please, help me."

The police officer let out a low whistle. "The radio's been screaming about you and some stolen information all afternoon. Hop in. Let's get you down to the station."

Dad was waiting in the chief's office when they got to the station. "Kyle, are you all right? They called me as soon as the officer radioed in that he had picked you up. Did they hurt you?"

"They tied me to a pole in some old warehouse and tried to scare me. They sure were mad when they found out the disk they had was that homework program you wrote for me."

"How'd they get their hands on that?" Dad looked puzzled.

Kyle grinned. "I switched the disks as soon as I realized that what they had was top security. I hid the real disk under a cushion in your office." He held up the disks. "And here's all of the rest of the stolen disks. I brought them with me!"

Dad put his arm around Kyle's shoulders. "That's quite a save you made there, Son. But how did you find your way out of that warehouse? Surely those men didn't leave you a map."

"I don't suppose they meant to." Kyle laughed. "But when you've got a computer and the right disk, you can find out just about anything."

72

Worktext Objectives

The student will

- Sequence story events.
- Identify plot structure.

Literature:
Worktext page 27

◀ Teaching of this skill was introduced in Lesson 9.

Read aloud the information about plot at the top of the page. Allow the students to complete the page independently after you explain the directions.

COMPREHENSION
Predicting outcomes

▶ When you listen to the weather on the news, what does the forecaster tell you? (Answers may vary but should include telling what he thinks the weather will be.)

▶ The forecaster is predicting the weather. Does he know for certain what the weather will be? (no)

Who is the only one that knows future events? (God)

▶ What does the weather forecaster use to help him make a good "guess" of what the weather will be? (satellite pictures, maps, radar, and computers)

Does the forecaster ever change his mind? (yes)

▶ In "Project Submarine" what helped you predict what would happen? (Answers may vary but should include pictures, the title, and clues in the story.)

Did your predictions change as you continued reading the story?

▶ Predictions may change as new information is gained.

Comprehension: Worktext page 28

SOMETHING EXTRA
Write About It: Be an author

Direct each student to imagine he is the author of "Project Submarine." Tell him to add to the story to tell what happens to the thieves.

Elicit ideas by asking the following questions.

▶ What do the thieves do when they find Kyle gone?

Will they try again to get the secret information?

Will they be captured?

Lesson	Worktext pages
22	220-21

Objectives

The student will

- Divide words into syllables between the consonants in the *VC/CV* pattern (*but•ter, bur•den*).
- Identify consonant digraphs (*ph* as /f/ in *orphan*).
- Recognize that consonant digraphs are treated as one consonant in the *VC/CV* pattern (*or•phan*).

Background information

Syllable Division Rule 1—Divide words into syllables between consonants, even when one of the consonants is written as a consonant digraph.

Consonant digraph—A consonant digraph is a consonant sound that is represented by two consonant letters: *sh* as /sh/ in *ship, ch* as /ch/ in *church, ph* as /f/ in *phone, ck* as /k/ in *back,* and *th* as /th/ in *feather.*

Pony express—Each structural analysis lesson in fourth grade is built around a pony express theme. The newspaper ad featured on worktext page 220 appeared in newspapers in 1860. The first overland mail courier service to connect the eastern states with California needed riders for the fast horses that would carry the mail. William H. Russell resolved to deliver mail from the East to the West in ten days.

Materials

- Overhead marking pen
- Teaching Visual 4: *California Challenge*

WORDS WITH THE *VC/CV* PATTERN

① Introduction: The Beginning of the Pony Express

▶ Historians disagree about who first had the inspiration for the pony express. As you listen to the following account, think about all the ideas that led up to the plan.

Read the following account to the students.

In 1860 there were many important reasons why communication between St. Joseph, Missouri, and California needed to be improved. Gold had been discovered in California, and the northern part of the nation wanted to keep the "free state" of California from being influenced to become a "slave state." California was only five hundred miles from Texas, the nearest slave state, but over two thousand miles of wilderness and high mountains separated it from the closest free state. Not only that, but the present mail route, the Butterfield Overland Mail route, went through the South, where Union communications to California could be cut at any time. A northern mail route between Missouri and California was important to the Union cause.

Benjamin Franklin had organized pony-delivered mail relay service in eastern areas, and the stage coaches already had the idea of changing horses in a relay fashion to keep the passengers moving faster across the country, but now there was a need to use those ideas in a new way. William H. Russell accepted the challenge. Originally, Congress agreed to fund the relay mail project, but slave state senators refused to vote to allocate the money. In spite of this, Russell followed through and backed the pony express himself. So the call went out for pony express riders. Tough, lightweight young men were needed. A newspaper want ad asked for riders at $35 a day. Records show that the riders earned about $100 a month. Eighty young riders were hired for the grueling ride.

Discuss the following.

▶ What were some of the ideas already in place that led to the plan for a pony express route to California? (Benjamin Franklin had a mail relay service in the eastern states, and stagecoaches also used relay horses to keep passengers moving.)

Why was everyone so interested in keeping in touch with California? (Both the free states and the slave states wanted California to join their cause because California had gold.)

▶ How did William Russell find the lightweight, courageous riders he needed? (He found them through newspaper ads.)

Refer to the map on worktext page 221 to show the students the distance between Missouri and California.

▸Read and Think

skinny   expert
orphan

Help Wanted
Wanted: young, skinny, wiry fellows, not over 18. Must be expert riders, willing to risk death daily. Orphans preferred. Wages $35 a week.

▸Compare and Match

Notice the vowel/consonant patterns in the following words. Write a word from the box above to match each set of words below.

VC/CV
a s s u m e
o t t e r
a s s i g n
b u l l y

skinny

VC/CV
b u r d e n
e n g i n e
r a n s o m
o r n a t e

expert

VC/CV
f a r t h e r
d o l p h i n
w o r t h y
a s p h a l t

orphan

© 2000 BJU Press. Reproduction prohibited.

▸Think About It

Look at the words in the ovals. How is the word *orphan* divided? What can you decide about dividing words that have a digraph for one of the consonants?

VC/CV
or • phan

VC/CV
ex • pert

VC/CV
skin • ny

> Divide words between the consonants in the *VC/CV* pattern, even when one is a consonant digraph.

220

---

③ Skill reinforcement:
Visual 4—*California Challenge*

Use the top of the visual to review the simple *VC/CV* rule.

Call attention to the words on the envelopes at the bottom.

▸ Why do you think the *ph* is circled in *orphan?* (It is a consonant digraph.)

▸ Find the digraphs in the other words.

Circle the digraphs as they are named—*th, ph, sh.*

Use the words to reinforce the generalization: Divide words in the *VC/CV* pattern between the consonants, treating a consonant digraph as one consonant.

④ Skill application:
Worktext page 221

Guide the students as they first identify the consonant digraph in each word; then help them divide the words.

SOMETHING EXTRA

Write About It: Help wanted

Instruct each student to write an ad for an unusual job without telling what the job is and then to describe the job in a paragraph. Remind them that each word in an ad costs money.

② Skill development:
Worktext page 220

Read and Think
Read aloud the newspaper ad.

▸ What is the newspaper ad advertising for? (riders for the pony express)

▸ Do you know someone who is about eighteen years old? Can you imagine him answering this ad?

▸ What three words are highlighted in the ad? (skinny, expert, orphans)

▸ Notice the same words in the box. Look for the vowel consonant pattern *VC/CV* in each word. The colors will help you: vowels are green, consonants are red, consonant digraphs are brown.

If necessary, use the background information about consonant digraphs to explain what a consonant digraph is.

Compare and Match
▸ Now look at the three lists of words. Notice the vowel consonant pattern in each word.

Elicit that the words in the first column have two like consonants, in the second column two unlike consonants, and in the third column a consonant and a consonant digraph.

▸ Write each word from the box below the heading that matches it.

Think About It
▸ Now notice the same words. Here the three words are divided into syllables.

Guide a discussion of the patterns in the box. Lead the students to understand the generalization: "Divide words between the consonants in the *VC/VC* pattern, even when one is a consonant digraph."

ENCOUNTERS

Unit Discussion: page 73

▶ What is the title of this unit? (Encounters)

Read aloud the following sentence:

Walking down the wooded path, Tom knew he might have an encounter with an animal.

▶ What do you think an *encounter* is? (Answers may vary, but elicit that it is a meeting between two things that is usually unexpected.)

Do you think an encounter always occurs between two people? (Accept any answer, but explain that it does not necessarily have to be two people.)

Look at the picture. Would you want to have an encounter with this bear?

What will the encounter be in the story "Kit Carson and the Grizzly Bears"? (Kit Carson will encounter some grizzly bears.)

▶ Quickly look through the Table of Contents at the stories listed under *Encounters*. Which encounter do you think you will like best?

Romans 8:28

And we know that all things work together for good to them that love God, to them who are the called according to his purpose.

Life has no chance meetings; rather, each event is scheduled; each encounter is an appointment. "Kit Carson and the Grizzly Bears" and "Johnny and His Mule" feature such appointments between man and beast with successful outcomes. Two humorous encounters are recorded in the limericks, "There Was an Old Man from Pompeii" and "There Was a Young Miner in Yuma." Subtle confrontation takes place in "Roger's Choice" and "Word of Honor" when young men face their own sinful human natures. "On the Road to Damascus" is a choral reading from Scripture that features Paul's miraculous meeting with Christ. The American Civil War and its most famous son, Abraham Lincoln, sweep across the scene in "The Darkest Time" and "Abraham Lincoln Was My Friend," changing forever the memories of those who meet them. Tom learns that no one can be the same after happening upon William Shakespeare in "Hamlet, Augusta Jones, and Me," which is followed by the biographical sketch, "William Shakespeare, Playwright." Prince Janwahr's story is of secret encounters that save a kingdom in "Janwahr's Bridge."

KIT CARSON AND THE GRIZZLY BEARS

In this true account, Kit Carson is quick to volunteer when someone is needed to bring meat into camp. After all, he's a crack shot with his rifle. But when he meets the two grizzlies, his gun is empty.

Lesson	Reader pages	Worktext pages
23	74-77	29-30

Materials
- Coonskin hat or other frontier-type hat
- Vocabulary sentences for display

Background information
Kit Carson—A skillful frontiersman, scout, and guide in the early West, Kit Carson was a true mountain man. When Kit was born in 1809, his family had moved to the western frontier, and Kit was reared in a world of traders, trappers, and Indians. Kit Carson served in the Mexican War and in the American Civil War. Later he became a brevet brigadier general and commanded the men at Fort Garland. On May 23, 1868, Kit Carson died at Fort Lyon in Colorado.

INTRODUCTION

Vocabulary
Use the prepared sentences to introduce the vocabulary words in context.

The Wild West
As you display a frontier-type hat, guide a discussion about the Wild West.
▶ What are some things you think you can't live without today that would not have been around two hundred years ago, especially in the Wild West of the United States?

What kind of clothes did people in the West wear in those days?

How did they get food to eat? Why were there so many hunters and trappers?

Would you like to have lived back then? Why or why not?

Head note
Read aloud the head note on reader page 74.

VOCABULARY
LESSON 23

*†They hoisted the flag to the top of the pole. (p. 74)

†The bear clumsily lumbered toward the cabin. (p. 76)

*†The worn fur on the bear's mangy back stood straight up. (p. 76)

*The brown bears, also called bruins, use their claws as weapons. (p. 77)

The two boys began to tussle until one of them was hurt. (p. 77)

Heritage Studies Connection

Lesson 23 can be linked to the study of the western frontier of the U.S. in the early to mid-1800s.

Correlated Activities
- Vocabulary Box, Activity 1: Word Hunt
- Spelling Practice, Activity 3: Softball Sluggers

See "Classroom Management for Grouping" in the Appendix.

COMPREHENSION

The student will

- Define vocabulary using context clues.
- Identify problems and solutions.
- Note how character actions reveal character traits.

Before silent reading: pages 74-77

Motivation

▶ How does Kit Carson show he is brave?

What problem do the grizzly bears present to Kit?

After silent reading

Overview discussion: pages 74-77

▶ [interpretive] Why is Kit the only one looking for food? (He is the only man who volunteered.) [BAT: 2e Initiative]

▶ [literal] What is Kit doing when the bears attack? (going toward the elk he shot)

[interpretive] How does Kit respond to his dangerous situation? (He climbs a tree and then uses a branch to fight off the bears.)

▶ [critical] How do Kit's actions prove he is brave? (Accept any answer.)

Follow-up discussion: page 74

▶ [interpretive] What is the problem in the camp? (The food is almost gone.)

[interpretive] What needs to be done to get some meat? (Someone has to go hunting.)

[interpretive] How do you know the men are confident that Kit can do the job? (They slap him on the back and say that if anyone can do it, he can.)

▶ [interpretive] What does the author mean by stating that Kit Carson is a crack shot? (He has good aim with a gun.)

Kit Carson and the Grizzly Bears

Becky Henry
illustrated by Preston Gravely Jr.

In the days when the West was wild and untamed, brave men journeyed far to explore this vast wilderness. Kit Carson was one of these brave men. He traveled across the United States, blazing trails, trapping for furs, and fighting Indians. This true story tells of one adventure Kit Carson had in the Wild West.

"Men, we need meat, and we need it soon. With no rain in so long, all the animals have gone looking for a better place to graze. I can't say that I blame them either." The leader of the camp scratched his head and looked around. "Any of you men want to try to catch us some meat?"

"I think I can." The voice belonged to Kit Carson, the twenty-four-year-old crack shot.

"That's the way, Kit!" The other men slapped his back and shook his hand. "If anyone can do it, you can."

Kit hoisted his rifle to his shoulder. "I'm heading out on foot, and I aim to come back with some supper meat."

Kit Carson was one man who usually did what he said he would do. In his soft moccasins, he padded noiselessly through the underbrush for almost a mile. Then his keen eyes spotted a clear imprint in the sand.

74

Read aloud with great confidence what Kit says he will do.

"Elk!" he whispered, running his fingers over the delicate grooves. "And these tracks are pretty fresh. They can't be too far away."

Sure enough, as Kit followed the tracks through the trees, he soon came upon a whole herd of elk grazing on the few plants they could find.

"Only a mile away from camp!" Kit chuckled. "And those men thought there weren't any animals anywhere near here. Well, I'll be bringing supper home pretty soon."

With a snap and a crack of his trusty rifle, Kit brought one big elk down to the ground. He headed toward it with a satisfied smile on his face.

Kit Carson and the Grizzly Bears 75

▶ [literal] What is Kit's first clue that animals are nearby? (fresh tracks)

[interpretive] Why do you think Kit runs his fingers over the delicate grooves? (He is studying the track to see what kind of animal made it.)

▶ [interpretive] Why does Kit chuckle when he sees the herd of elk? (He finds the elk close to camp when the men thought no animals were nearby.)

Read aloud the sentence that tells how Kit kills one of the elk. Read it so we can hear the sound of the gun.

[interpretive] Why does the author use the words *snap* and *crack*? (The author wants us to hear the gunshot by using words that sound like gunshots.)

▶ [interpretive] What character traits describe a man who usually does what he says he will do? (possible answers: honest, dependable) [BATs: 2c Faithfulness; 4c Honesty]

Follow-up discussion: page 76

▶ [literal] What stops Kit from reaching the downed elk? (a roar of two grizzly bears lumbering toward him)

[appreciative] What picture of the two bears does the author create in your mind?

▶ [literal] Why doesn't Kit use his gun to protect himself? (It is empty, and he has no time to reload it.)

But he never got to the downed elk. A roar sounded through the forest, and two grizzly bears lumbered clumsily through the trees. The fur on their mangy backs bristled, and their lips curled back in a snarl, showing long white fangs.

And Kit's gun was empty! There was no time to reload it.

76

Dropping his rifle, he scrambled hastily up a little aspen tree. Even though he climbed as high as he could, his feet were just barely out of the bears' reach. He looked down at the angry bruins trying to swipe at him with their big paws.

Kit tucked his legs under him the best he could. He watched the grizzlies rip some of the bark off the tree, pull at the roots, and tear at the branches, taking an occasional wild swipe at him.

"Well, this can't go on much longer," Kit decided. He couldn't let this situation get the best of him, so he did some thinking. Even though a grizzly was the roughest, toughest animal around, he still had one very tender spot: his nose. Kit pulled out his hunting knife and whacked off a small tree branch. This was his new weapon.

As soon as one bear nose got close enough, Kit was ready. "Well, Mr. Grizzly, I can't say that I'm too sorry to do this to you." Whap! He smacked the bear in the nose. The bear fell down and grabbed his nose with his paws, howling in pain. The other bear came toward Kit. The new weapon hit its mark again. The other bear went down. Kit couldn't help laughing.

"My life may be in danger, but you two bruins are a funny sight to see!"

Another whole hour went by before the grizzlies finally decided that this battle wasn't worth the trouble. With snorts of pain and disgust, they lumbered back into the wilderness.

After Kit was quite convinced that they were gone for good, he climbed down. Making his way with stiff legs to the spot where the elk lay waiting, he discovered that it had been eaten by wolves.

Hours after dark, Kit trudged back into camp. When he told his story, the other men laughed so hard that they cried. They didn't even mind that Kit had come back without any meat for supper.

Kit laughed too. "But I never have been so scared in all my life!"

"Kit Carson," said a friend, "you're a wonder. You're the only man I've ever known who could tussle with grizzly bears without a rifle . . . and win!"

Kit Carson and the Grizzly Bears   77

Follow-up discussion: page 77

▶ [interpretive] How does clear thinking save Kit just in time? (He drops the gun and climbs a tree instead of panicking and trying to run away.)

[appreciative] How would you have reacted?

▶ [literal] How does stopping to think help Kit get out of this situation? (By keeping a clear head, Kit is able to remember the bear's weak spot and thinks to use the branch as a weapon.)

[critical] Do you think it's good to think before you act? Why or why not? (Accept any answer, but point out that God wants us to think before we act.) [BATs: 3b Mind; 3c Emotional control]

Read aloud and discuss II Timothy 1:7.

▶ [literal] Why aren't the men upset about not having anything to eat for supper? (They don't mind because they think Kit's story is funny.)

[literal] What does Kit admit to the men? (that he had never been so scared)

[critical] Is Kit embarrassed about being scared? Why or why not? (No; accept any answer, but elicit that Kit is honest about what really happened.)

[appreciative] As Christians, why are we able to act bravely although we are afraid? (Accept any answer, but elicit that although a person may not feel brave, trusting in the Lord will give him the strength he needs to act bravely.) [BAT: 8d Courage]

Read aloud with amazement what a friend tells Kit.

Worktext Objectives

The student will

■ Infer unstated supporting details.

■ Follow directions.

Comprehension:
Worktext page 29

The student will

■ Note the author's use of descriptive words.

LITERATURE
Descriptive words

Write the word *descriptive* for display.

► Authors use descriptive words to help the reader see a character or action more clearly.

Read aloud the following "plain" sentences without descriptive words. Choose students to add descriptive words to each sentence to give a clearer picture.

► The squirrel came down the tree. (Possible answer: "The curious squirrel scampered to the ground.")

► The rabbit went across the yard. (Possible answer: "The furry brown rabbit hopped quickly across the tall green grass.")

Read each "plain" sentence below. Give the page number in the reader for the students to find the author's descriptive sentence that gives a clearer picture.

► Kit was glad he shot the elk. (page 75—He headed toward it with a satisfied smile on his face.)

► Kit watched the bears try to hit him. (page 77—He looked down at the angry bruins trying to swipe at him with their big paws.)

Literature: Worktext page 30

Read the directions for each section. Guide the students as they complete the page.

LIMERICKS

> These two five-line poems tell silly tales about a man from Pompeii and a miner from Yuma.

Materials
- Picture of a volcano
- A copy of Appendix page A36 for each student
- Vocabulary sentences for display

Background information
Limericks—A limerick is a poem form with five lines. Lines 1, 2, and 5 rhyme, and lines 3 and 4 rhyme. The rhythm also follows a certain pattern: lines 1, 2, and 5 have three strong beats each, and lines 3 and 4 have two strong beats each. The weaker beats can vary in number, but it is best if the rhythm is smoothly anapestic (two weak beats followed by a strong beat). Some limericks make a point. The point may be serious or witty, but the tone is always light. Other limericks are meant only to entertain.

INTRODUCTION
Vocabulary
Use the prepared sentences to introduce the vocabulary words in context.

Pompeii and Yuma
Show a picture of a volcano.

▶ Today one of the poems we will read takes us to Pompeii. Do you know where Pompeii is? (Italy)

Write the word *Pompeii* for display as you say it.

▶ Pompeii was a city near the volcano Mt. Vesuvius.

What happens when a volcano erupts? (Surrounding areas are covered with ash and lava.)

Do you know what happened to Pompeii? (It was covered by lava and ruined.)

▶ In the second poem we will travel to Yuma. Do you know where Yuma is? (in the desert of Arizona)

Yuma is located on the Colorado River. If you were a miner in Yuma near the Colorado River, what do you think you might be looking for? (gold)

VOCABULARY
LESSON 24

†The mountain erupted, spewing ash and lava. (p. 78)

'†The soldiers fired their guns when they encountered the enemy. (p. 79)

†Like a cat, the puma snarled and leaped from its perch on the rock. (p. 79)

Correlated Activities
- **Recreational Reading, Activity 4: Touchable Ta**
- **Creative Writing, Activity 4: Roll-a-Sentence**
See "Classroom Management for Grouping" in the Append

COMPREHENSION

The student will
- Recognize limerick form.
- Identify rhyming words.
- Recognize the poet's use of humor.

Before listening
► As I read this poem to you, listen for the words that rhyme.

Listening: page 78
Read aloud the limerick "There Was an Old Man from Pompeii."

After listening

Discussion: page 78

Explain that this is a limerick, a special form of poetry. Explain that a limerick is five lines of poetry in which the first, second, and fifth lines rhyme and the third and fourth lines rhyme.

► [literal] What words rhyme in this limerick? (Pompeii, day, say; erupted, interrupted)

[interpretive] What is the old man from Pompeii very knowledgeable about? (volcanoes)

[literal] What happens when the volcano erupts? (The old man forgets what he wants to say.)

[critical] What makes this poem funny? (Accept any answer, but explain that we laugh when an expert on volcanoes is surprised by one and that a mountain erupting definitely would be an interruption.)

Allow several students to read aloud the limerick in a light-hearted manner.

THERE WAS AN OLD MAN FROM POMPEII

Eileen Berry and Dawn Watkins
illustrated by Jim Hargis and Sam Laterza

There was an old man from Pompeii
Who gave talks on volcanoes each day.
When the mountain erupted
He got interrupted,
And forgot what he wanted to say.

78

THERE WAS A YOUNG MINER IN YUMA

Unattributed
illustrated by Jim Hargis and Sam Laterza

There was a young miner in Yuma
Who once encountered a puma,
And later they found
Just a spot on the ground
And a puma in a very good huma.

Limericks　　79

Before listening

▶ As I read aloud this limerick, find the rhyming word that is not a real word but is made up.

Listening: page 79

Read aloud the limerick "There Was a Young Miner in Yuma."

After listening

Discussion: page 79

▶ [literal] What words rhyme in this limerick? (Yuma, puma, huma; ground, found)

▶ [interpretive] Which of the rhyming words is made up? (huma)

[interpretive] *Huma* is a funny spelling of what word? (humor)

[interpretive] Why does the poet change the spelling? (to make a rhyme for *Yuma* and *puma*)

▶ [critical] What is the "spot on the ground"? (Accept any answer, but elicit that it is what is left of the miner after the puma eats him.)

[critical] Why is the "puma in a very good huma"? (Possible answer: He had the miner for lunch.)

Allow several students to read aloud this limerick.

▶ [interpretive] After reading these two limericks, do you think the mood or tone of most limericks is serious or light? (light)

LITERATURE
Limerick form

▶ Look at the two limericks in the reader. Which lines rhyme? (Lines 1, 2, and 5 rhyme; lines 3 and 4 rhyme.)

▶ All limericks follow this same rhyming pattern.

Distribute a copy of Appendix page A36 to each student.

▶ Notice that lines 1 and 2 are incomplete and that line 5 is missing.

Listen as I read aloud the incomplete limerick. As I read, think of words and phrases to complete the limerick. Remember that lines 1, 2, and 5 must rhyme.

After you read the limerick, allow the students to share their ideas for completing lines 1 and 2 and for writing line 5. (Possible answers: the outback, backpack, Then decided to carry a knapsack; WalMart, food cart, Then decided that shopping's an art.) Then allow each student to write in the missing words and phrases to complete the limerick in his own way.

Allow the students to illustrate their limericks.

SOMETHING EXTRA
Write It: My own limerick

Encourage each student to write and illustrate his own limerick. Remind the students that lines 1, 2, and 5 rhyme and lines 3 and 4 rhyme in a limerick. Refer them to the limericks on reader pages 78-79 and the limerick they completed on the Appendix page. Display the limericks with the illustrations.

Materials
- Pair of athletic shoes
- A Bible for the teacher and each student

Lesson	Worktext pages
25	222-23

Background information
Moral—Often an author uses his story to teach the readers an important lesson. This lesson is called the *moral* of the story.

MORAL OF THE STORY

The student will
- Define the term *moral*.
- Determine the moral of a story.

Objectives

1 Introduction

Display the pair of athletic shoes.

▶ Have you ever been in a race?

Did you win?

How did you win?

▶ Can you think of one of Aesop's fables that talks about two animals that raced one another? ("The Tortoise and the Hare")

Review the basic events of the story with the students: The tortoise and the hare decided to race. The fast hare was sure he would beat the slow tortoise. The race started, and the hare ran very fast, but it took many breaks to rest. The tortoise, though it was slow, kept going even when it was tired. In the end the tortoise won the race.

▶ What does this fable teach us? ("Slow and steady wins the race.")

2 Skill Development: Parables

▶ While Jesus was here on earth, He told stories that teach lessons. We can read these stories in the Bible. What are these stories called? (parables)

Sometimes we use different words to talk about the lesson a story teaches. We may call it a lesson or a truth. Can you think of another word we might use for the lesson a story teaches? (Accept any answer, but suggest the word *moral* if no one thinks of it.)

Let's look at a moral or a lesson in one of Christ's parables.

Direct the students to turn to Matthew 18:23-35 in their Bibles and read along silently as you read the passage aloud.

▶ What did the master do, at first, when the servant asked him to be patient with him? (He showed the servant mercy and forgiveness; he released him from paying his debt.)

What did the forgiven servant do when someone asked him for forgiveness and mercy? (He refused to forgive him and show mercy.)

What lesson is Christ teaching in this story? (God has forgiven us and shown us mercy; therefore, we are to forgive others even as God has forgiven us.)

3 Skill development: Worktext pages 222-23

Call attention to the story on page 222 and explain that it is a fable.

► What is a fable? (possible answers: a story in which the main characters are animals; a story that has a moral or lesson)

Read the fable "The Frog That Popped" to the students.

Use the following questions to discuss the story and its moral as you guide the students in answering the questions on page 223.

► Why do you think Father Frog puffed himself out bigger than he should have? (He was proud of how big he was and didn't think anyone could be bigger than he was.)

► What do you think Father Frog could have done differently? (Answers will vary.)

► The moral of a story is the lesson the author wants us to learn from the story.

► What lesson did you learn from this story? What is the moral of the story? (Possible answers: We should be content with the way God has made us; we should be content with the situation God has put us in.) [BAT: 7d Contentment]

▶**Find the Answers!**
Read the story on page 222 to find the answers to the questions. Write your answers in complete sentences.

PROVERBS 16:18
Pride goeth before destruction, and an haughty spirit before a fall.

1. What did the little frog see in the pasture?
_____ *He saw a very big ox.*

2. Why was Father Frog angry when he heard about the ox?
_____ *Father was angry because the ox was bigger than he was.*

3. What did Father Frog do to try to show that he was big also?
_____ *He puffed himself out.*

4. What was the consequence of Father Frog's actions?
_____ *He popped.*

5. What is the moral of the story? _____ *It is important to be content with the way God made you and not try to be like someone else.*

6. What could Father Frog have done differently?
_____ *Answers will vary.*

The **moral** of the story is the lesson the author wants the reader to learn from the story.

Reading 4: Skill Station Day, Lesson 25
Literature: determining the moral of the story

223

SOMETHING EXTRA

Write It: Teach the lesson

Direct each student to write a short story with a moral about the harm caused by pride. Allow another person to read the story and tell what the moral is.

Even though Roger is tempted, he knows stealing is not the way to provide food for his hungry little sister. But what can he do? If only Mr. Bradley could afford to hire Roger at his store. Then Roger has an idea.

Lesson	Reader pages	Worktext pages
26	80-85	31-32

Materials

- A small piece of candy for each student
- Vocabulary sentences for display

Background information

Verses—Verses that may be useful in addressing the problems of broken home and material need that are raised by this story include Psalm 27:1, Psalm 34:17, and Psalm 37:3-4.

INTRODUCTION

Vocabulary

Use the prepared sentences to introduce the vocabulary words in context.

Making money

▶ Who provides your meals?

Do you sometimes earn money to buy the things you enjoy eating, such as soda and candy?

What can you do to earn money?

As each student answers, give him a piece of candy.

▶ How could you provide food for yourself if the person who normally provides your food was not able to do so?

In this story Roger has to make a choice about how he will provide food for his sister and himself.

VOCABULARY

LESSON 26

†The old worn dress was still good, clean, and decent. (p. 81)

†A sigh of frustration let his boss know he could not finish the job. (p. 81)

*The makeshift meals were a poor substitute for mom's cooking. (p. 82)

*†Her lips shook in a quivery smile. (p. 85)

Correlated Activities

- **Word Work, Activity 5: Dictionary Challenge**
- **Connections, Activity 1: Fact or Fiction Destinations**

See "Classroom Management for Grouping" in the Appendix.

COMPREHENSION

Objectives

The student will

- Demonstrate understanding of the author's message: It is never right to be dishonest.
- Identify problems and solutions.
- Recognize the changing of a character in the course of action.
- Infer character motives.
- Evaluate character responses.
- Read orally with varied voice inflection to portray emotion.

Before silent reading: pages 80-85

Motivation

▶ What is Roger's home like?

What choices does Roger have to make?

After silent reading

Overview discussion: pages 80-85

▶ [interpretive] Why is Roger making wrong choices? (He is trying to get food for his sister and himself and thinks that the only way to get it is to steal; he thinks the Lord is not hearing his prayers.)

[critical] Why doesn't Roger ask his mother for money to buy food? (Answers will vary, but elicit that the family is poor.)

[interpretive] What helps Roger finally make a good choice? (He realizes that it is not right to steal for any reason and thinks of another way to solve the problem; he listens to the Lord and confesses his sin of stealing.) [BATs: 4c Honesty; 4d Victory]

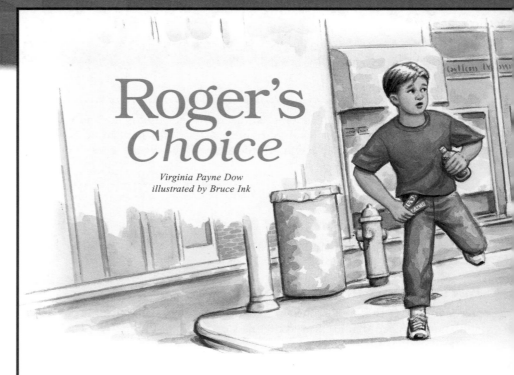

Roger's Choice

Virginia Payne Dow
illustrated by Bruce Ink

Roger felt the two candy bars under his shirt. Slowly he walked to the counter to pay for his root beer. He jingled the change in his hand and tried to whistle a little tune. His throat was dry, and the cheery notes seemed to stick.

"That all you want?" Mr. Bradley asked. He had a big jolly face. When he smiled, his dimples looked like big holes in his cheeks.

"Yes, sir; that's it."

"Can't get over how much you've grown, Roger. Two feet at least, huh?" Mr. Bradley's big hand ruffled Roger's hair before it took the change. He counted it and dropped it into the cash register. Mopping his forehead with a big white handkerchief, Mr. Bradley turned back toward Roger.

"Say hello to that little sister of yours for me, Roger."

"Yes, sir. See you around, Mr. Bradley." Roger went to the front

80

Follow-up discussion: page 80

▶ [interpretive] Why is it difficult for Roger to whistle? (Answers will vary, but elicit that Roger is nervous about stealing the candy.)

Read aloud the clues the author gives to let you know Roger is stealing the candy.

▶ [critical] Does Mr. Bradley know Roger is stealing the candy? How do you know? (Answers will vary but should include that Mr. Bradley does not mention anything about it.)

[critical] Do you think Mr. Bradley's kindness makes Roger feel bad? Why or why not? (Accept any answer.)

of the store and used the bottle opener. Tipping the bottle upside down, he let the cold, fizzy liquid run down his throat.

Roger stopped outside to bend over and tie his sneaker and then ran down the street. As soon as he rounded the corner, he took the two candy bars from under his shirt. They were beginning to melt. Then he ran the three blocks to his home.

"Wendy." Roger's whisper brought a quick scamper of little feet down the hall. Wendy was still in her long, thin nightgown. Her hair was tangled and dirty.

"Hi, Roger. Did you bring me some candy?" Wendy ran forward and clung to Roger's hand. She took her candy bar and smiled up at him.

"Yeah, kiddo. Where's Mom?"

"Sleepin' still," Wendy said, her mouth full of the melting chocolate.

"Listen, Wendy. I want you to comb your hair and get some decent clothes on. We're going for a walk," Roger said quietly. He went to the bare room that he called his own and flung himself down onto the thin mattress. He punched the flat foam pillow in frustration.

It had been two days since his mother had been out of bed. And it wasn't the first time she had stayed in bed for so long either. After Roger's dad had left, his mother had cried a lot. She stopped taking Roger and Wendy to Sunday school. Lots of times she stayed in bed for two, three—maybe even four days at a time.

Roger's Choice   81

Follow-up discussion: page 81

▶ [literal] Whom is the candy for? (Wendy, Roger's sister)

[interpretive] Why does Roger think he needs to steal the candy for Wendy? (He has no money to buy it, and Wendy is hungry.)

Read aloud how Roger feels after coming home and talking with Wendy.

▶ [literal] Where is Wendy and Roger's mom? (in bed)

[interpretive] How does the author let you know that their mom is sad? (She stays in bed, cries a lot, and has stopped taking Roger and Wendy to Sunday school.)

▶ [literal] How does the author describe Wendy as she comes down the hall? (She scampers down the hall in a long, thin nightgown. Her hair is tangled and dirty.)

[interpretive] What descriptions let you know the family is poor? (Roger's bare room, thin mattress, and flat foam pillow; Wendy's thin nightgown; no money for food)

▶ [literal] Whom does Roger want to show him what to do? (the Lord)

Read aloud with despair how Roger feels about his prayers.

[critical] Why does Roger feel this way? (Answers will vary, but elicit that he feels guilty about what he has done and needs to confess his sins.) [BAT: 6d Clear conscience]

▶ [interpretive] How can you tell that Roger is frustrated? (He raises his voice at Wendy and gives her arm a jerk.) [BAT: 6c Spirit-filled]

Read aloud the conversation between Wendy and Roger. Help us to hear the frustration in Roger's voice.

▶ [interpretive] Why does Roger think stealing is the only way for him to get food? (He knows no one will hire an eleven-year-old boy.)

[critical] What are some ways that Roger could make the right choice? (Answers will vary, but elicit that he could do odd jobs for people, such as cutting grass and raking leaves. Also suggest that he should tell an adult about his situation.) [BAT: 2e Work]

▶ [literal] What does Roger decide to do as he walks down the street? (go back to steal more candy)

[critical] Is Roger making a good choice to solve his problem? Why or why not? (No; answers will vary but should express that it is never right to do wrong.)

Roger was sick of the makeshift meals he and Wendy were forced to eat. When everything in the apartment had been eaten, he had used the last of the money in his bank. There wasn't much there, and Wendy needed more than a few candy bars from Mr. Bradley's store.

He wanted the Lord to show him what to do. But, somehow, whenever Roger prayed these days, he felt as if his prayers didn't go very far. The Lord didn't seem to even hear.

"Ready, Roger!" Wendy came to the open doorway in a faded skirt and a bright red T-shirt. Her hair was twisted into a ponytail. She looked terrible, but Roger didn't feel like worrying about his sister's appearance.

"Okay, Wendy, out the door!" Roger jumped from the mattress.

"Where we goin'?" Wendy asked as they left the front steps. She had to skip every three steps to keep up with Roger.

"Oh, I don't know," he answered without looking at her.

"I want something to eat."

"Well, there's no money."

82

"So?"

"Wendy, you just can't get food without money!" Roger raised his voice and gave her arm a little jerk.

"Ouch!"

"Look, I'm sorry. Just don't talk for a few minutes. I'm thinking about how to get something to eat." Roger knew he couldn't get a job. No one hired an eleven-year-old boy.

They walked slowly down the street. It was hot. Really hot. They weren't far from Mr. Bradley's store when Roger decided to go back for some more candy. He turned into the parking lot, pulling Wendy behind him.

"Listen, Wendy, I want you to wait outside for me. You sit down

on this sidewalk—and no noise!" He showed her where to sit and walked into the store.

Roger decided that he would just wait near the candy until he could be sure that no one was looking. He couldn't stop the thumping of his heart. It seemed to be pounding right out of his chest and ears. The worst part about taking the candy was that Wendy would know. She wasn't too young to know that there was a way to get things without money. She would know that her big brother was a thief.

Roger didn't want Wendy to know, but he also didn't want her to be hungry. When he was sure that no one was paying any attention to him, he sucked in his breath and reached for a big chocolate bar. Without even looking around, he quickly slid it under his shirt.

"Roger."

Roger jumped and whirled around. Wendy was standing there, calmly eating a popcorn ball.

"Where did you get that? Why aren't you back where I told you to sit? Nobody told you to come in!" Roger angrily shoved Wendy backward. He had thought for sure he'd been caught. He could see his mother's face with tears in her eyes as she came to pick him up at the police station. Way in the back of his mind, he could hear his Sunday school teacher telling him how God hated stealing.

Tears sprang into Wendy's eyes, and Roger immediately felt sorry. He hadn't meant to yell.

"Mr. Bradley gave it to me," Wendy sniffed. "He told me to come inside out of the hot sun. He gave me some lemonade too."

Roger looked across the store. Several customers were waiting at Mr. Bradley's cash register. He looked pretty hot and tired. Twice while Roger was watching, he wiped his forehead and neck with a big, white handkerchief.

"Listen, kiddo, you go back and tell Mr. Bradley thank you, and I'll be right with you," Roger said gently. As soon as she turned around, he pulled the chocolate bar out from under his shirt and put it carefully back on the shelf.

Roger's Choice 83

Follow-up discussion: page 83

▶ [interpretive] What is Roger's biggest worry as he plans to steal the candy? (that Wendy will know he is a thief)

[critical] Why does Roger not want Wendy to know he is stealing? (Answers will vary, but elicit that people who sin usually don't want other people to know.)

▶ [literal] How does Roger react when Wendy walks up and startles him? (He jumps and becomes very angry.)

Read aloud with a guilty voice Roger's response when Wendy startles him.

[interpretive] Why is Roger angry with Wendy? (He thinks he has been caught.)

[interpretive] Whom else does Roger not want to find out he is stealing? Why? (Possible answers: his mom, Mr. Bradley; he doesn't want to disappoint his mom or get into trouble for stealing.)

▶ [interpretive] How does Mr. Bradley show kindness to Wendy? (He gives her something to eat and tells her to come in out of the heat.) [BATs: 5b Giving; 5e Friendliness]

[critical] Why does Roger decide to put the candy bar back? (Accept any answer, but elicit that he sees Mr. Bradley's kindness and is convicted of his sin.) [BAT: 4d Victory]

Roger's Choice

Follow-up discussion: page 84

▶ [interpretive] What plan does the Lord give Roger? (to work for Mr. Bradley)

[interpretive] Even though Mr. Bradley does not make enough money to hire Roger, does he need help? How do you know? (Yes; he is very busy and sweating from so much work.)

[interpretive] Is Roger's solution to work for food good for both of them? Why or why not? (Yes; it solves Mr. Bradley's need for help and his inability to pay a worker, and it solves Roger's need for food.)

Read aloud the conversation between Mr. Bradley and Roger, showing Roger's persistence and Mr. Bradley's concern.

He looked back at Mr. Bradley, punching buttons on the cash register. His big, jolly face was sweaty. Suddenly it seemed that the Lord gave Roger an idea. He walked over to the cash register and picked up a paper bag. He reached over and started putting groceries into it.

"Need a hand, Mr. Bradley?"

Mr. Bradley frowned and began to shake his head. "Roger, I can't hire you. I don't make enough to have help. I've told you that before."

"Not even for a package of hot dogs? And maybe some bread and peanut butter?" Roger asked. He continued placing groceries in the paper bag.

A slow smile spread across Mr. Bradley's face. He mopped his forehead again and nodded.

84

"Okay, boy. You got yourself a deal."

Roger felt like singing—almost. Just as the Lord had told him to start helping Mr. Bradley, he knew that the Lord was telling him something else now. He felt his whole face get hot, but he knew what he had to do. He watched the last customer in line pay for his groceries and walk out the door.

"Mr. Bradley." Roger felt his voice squeak a little. "Mr. Bradley, please forgive me—I've stolen some candy bars, but I want to pay for them now. I'll work for them. I'm really sorry—the Lord hasn't listened to my prayers ever since I did it. Wendy was so hungry, Mr. Bradley, but it was wrong." Embarrassed, Roger realized that tears were streaming down his cheeks.

Mr. Bradley wasn't smiling. "It's a serious thing, stealing is," he said, looking down. "It costs me a lot of money." He mopped his forehead again, slowly this time. "But I forgive you, Roger," he said. "I know you know the Lord. And He can give you the strength never to steal again."

Roger stood smiling a quivery smile while Wendy watched with big eyes. Mr. Bradley finally broke the silence. "Well, boy, if you're going to earn your keep around here, you'd better get working. Here." He handed Roger the broom. "This floor hasn't been swept in a month of Sundays. Those candy bars can be part of your pay."

"Oh, thank you, Mr. Bradley!" Roger beamed at Wendy and began to sweep the floor with all his might. "Wendy, you sit tight and watch big brother. When I'm done, I'll take you home, and we'll have the best supper ever. I bet Mom'll smell it cookin' and get up and help eat it!"

Wendy looked up at Roger. She had sticky popcorn all over her face, but her eyes were shining.

As Roger swept, he watched the pile of dust gathering in the center of the floor and smiled. That dirt was like his sins—out in the open, not swept under the rug. He felt ten feet tall. He knew he had made the right decision.

Roger's Choice   85

Follow-up discussion: page 85

▶ [interpretive] **What else is the Lord telling Roger to do?** (confess to Mr. Bradley about stealing the candy bars) [BAT: 4c Honesty]

Read aloud Roger's confession to show his embarrassment and repentance for what he has done.

[literal] How does Mr. Bradley respond when Roger asks for forgiveness? (He recognizes that it is a very serious matter but forgives Roger.) [BAT: 6e Forgiveness]

[critical] **Is it hard for Roger to ask Mr. Bradley to forgive him for stealing?** (Answers will vary, but elicit that while it always takes courage to do what is right, we can trust the Lord for His strength.) [BAT: 8d Courage]

▶ [interpretive] **How do you know Roger is excited as he sweeps the floor?** (He beams and sweeps with all his might.)

[critical] **What is the reason for Roger's joy?** (Answers will vary, but point out that Roger is no longer carrying the guilt of unconfessed sin and has made the right choice.) [BAT: 6d Clear conscience]

[interpretive] **What does Roger compare his sin to? Why?** (He compares his sin to dirt that is out in the open and not swept under the rug. Elicit that he is free from the guilt of his sin because he confesses it and is no longer hiding it.)

Read aloud with joy the paragraph telling why Roger feels ten feet tall. [BAT: 4d Victory]

Worktext Objectives

The student will

■ Evaluate character responses.

■ Infer unstated supporting details.

Comprehension: Worktext page 31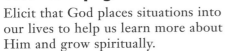

Elicit that God places situations into our lives to help us learn more about Him and grow spiritually.

▶ Everyone makes decisions throughout the day.

The first choice you made today was whether you would get up at the right time. Did you make a right or wrong choice?

What other choices have you made today? Were they right or wrong?

Guide students through the completion of the page.

Comprehension: Worktext page 32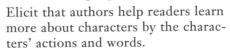

Elicit that authors help readers learn more about characters by the characters' actions and words.

Discuss the first question and possible answers before the students complete the page independently.

SOMETHING EXTRA

Write About It: Solutions

Direct the students to read I Corinthians 10:13. Remind them that all trials should be solved God's way. Instruct each student to write several ways that he could have helped Roger in his situation. Challenge him to think of people around him that he could help (e.g., an elderly person who is a shut-in, a child in an orphanage who would enjoy having a friend and family to visit).

Materials
● Teaching Visual 5: *Dangerous Trails*

Lesson	Worktext pages
27	224-25

COMPOUND WORDS

1 Introduction: Along the Trails

▶ Today well-maintained highways cross the United States. Hotels and restaurants are scattered along the roads for the comfort of travelers. But in 1860, the riders of the pony express rode through little more than wild country. Listen to find out what the trails were like.

Read the following account to the students.

Right from the start, the pony express route posed obstacles for both horse and rider. It all started easily enough for Jim Randall. On the evening of April 3, 1860, at the San Francisco Pony Express Office, he placed a *mochila* over his saddle, jumped on, and galloped away. (A *mochila* was a specially made leather covering that fit over a saddle. A *mochila* had four pouches in which mail was carried.) Crowds cheered for Jim Randall. But his ride was only to the wharf where he boarded a steamer for a placid boat ride to Sacramento. The other eastbound riders had their work cut out for them, though. A two-day rain had churned the trails into mud, and up to thirty-foot snowdrifts threatened to block the path over the Sierra Nevada Mountains. Once these obstacles were overcome, there were still the dangers of darkness, the desert, and ambush to face before the eastbound riders safely delivered their *mochila* of mail.

While eastbound riders were racing from California toward the halfway point in Wyoming, another team of riders began in St. Joseph, Missouri, relaying their *mochila* of mail westward. Johnny Frey, the first westbound rider, took a quiet ferryboat ride from St. Joseph across the Missouri River, but then the ride began in earnest. As with the eastbound riders, obstacles threatened to doom the express to failure. Miles of mud, flooded creeks, wolves, buffalo stampedes, ambush, and horses unaccustomed to the wilderness slowed the riders' progress. But in the end, both teams of riders delivered their mail to the halfway point in Wyoming.

The first express run was a success. In less than ten days, mail from California reached the East and letters from the East were opened in California. In spite of all risks and dangers, the pony express accomplished its two purposes. It affirmed that there was a usable year-round route over the Rocky Mountains, and it helped to keep California in the Union.

Discuss the following.

▶ Name some dangers that threatened to stop the pony express. (possible answers: ambush, bad weather, wolves, buffalo stampedes)

Why did the pony express persist in spite of all the obstacles? (to prove there was a year-round route to California and to keep California part of the Union)

▶ Would you be willing to risk danger to help preserve the United States?

Objectives

The student will

■ Divide compound words into syllables between the base words (*base•ball*, *bas•ket•ball*).

■ Identify primary and secondary accents in compound words.

■ Place the primary accent mark on or within the first base word of a compound word (*base´•ball*).

■ Place the secondary accent mark on or within the second base word of a compound word (*bas´•ket•ball´*).

Background information

Syllable Division Rule 2—Divide compound words into syllables between the base words.

Accent Rule 1—In compound words the primary accent falls on or within the first base word.

In compound words the secondary accent falls on or within the second base word.

2 Skill development:
Visual 5—Dangerous Trails

▶ Westbound mail passed through places with colorful names like Wild-cat Mountain, Lodgepole Valley, Courthouse Rock, and Hangtown Gulch. How do you think these places got their unusual names?

▶ *Wildcat*, *Lodgepole*, *Courthouse*, and *Hangtown* are compound words. Notice that one word of each compound word is pronounced with a stronger emphasis or accent than the other word.

Read the four compound words aloud again, emphasizing the first base word.

▶ Where are compound words divided into syllables? (between the two base words)

▶ Which base word has the stronger accent? (the first one)

▶ This stronger accent is the primary accent. A softer accent is placed on the other base word. This is the secondary accent.

Use the visual to show the two accent marks in each of the four compound words as you read them again.

Read aloud the last three names.

▶ How are the compound words in these names different? (They have more than two syllables.)

Point out that one of the base words in each compound word has two syllables.

Direct the students to whisper the three compound words as you read them aloud.

▶ Does the primary accent still fall within the first base word? (yes)

▶ Does the secondary accent still fall within the second word? (yes)

Lead the students to understand the accent generalization for compound words: In compound words, the primary accent falls on or within the first base word and the secondary accent falls on or within the second base word.

Horsemen in the Badlands

▶ Find and Circle
Circle the compound words in these sentences.

1. The (westbound) rider mounted the (buckskin) pony.

2. (Sagebrush) and (greasewood) shrubs dotted the drifting sand.

3. Although threatened by (rattlesnakes), the pony and rider pressed on.

4. Even a heavy (thunderstorm) did not stop their progress.

> **Compound words** are two words in one.

▶ Divide and Mark
Write the compound words from the sentences above. Divide the words into syllables. Then show the primary and secondary accents.

1. _____west′•bound′_____   4. _____grease′•wood′_____

2. _____buck′•skin′_____   5. _____rat′•tle•snakes′_____

3. _____sage′•brush′_____   6. _____thun′•der•storm′_____

▶ Think and Write
Use the words above to answer the questions.

1. What word describes a horse or pony that is colored much like a deer?

2. What is the name of a low bush that smells like a spice?

3. Which word is used to show the direction the rider was heading?

> **Compound words** are divided between their two base words.

> In a compound word the primary accent is on or within the first base word. A secondary accent is on or within the second base word.

224

3 Skill development:
Worktext page 224

Guide the students in completing the page. Review syllable division as they mark the words.

4 Skill application:
Worktext page 225

Allow the students to complete the page independently.

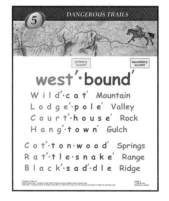

DANGEROUS TRAILS

5

primary accent   secondary accent

west′•bound′

W i l d′•c a t′ Mountain
L o d g e′•p o l e′ Valley
C o u r t′•h o u s e′ Rock
H a n g′•t o w n′ Gulch

C o t′•t o n•w o o d′ Springs
R a t′•t l e•s n a k e′ Range
B l a c k′•s a d′•d l e Ridge

> Using two readers and three choruses, this choral reading presents the dramatic conversion of Paul on the road to Damascus.

Lesson	Reader pages	Worktext pages
28	86-89	33-34

VOCABULARY

LESSON 28

*The earthquake brought havock to the city. (p. 87)

The police were haling the troublemakers out of the ballpark. (p. 87)

*†Jews meet at synagogues to worship God. (p. 87)

Materials
- Blindfold
- Vocabulary sentences for display

Background information

Choral reading—The Greeks developed the art of drama. Their plays, or choral readings, were merely long speeches read aloud or recited before an audience. The lead actors stood before the audience and recited their lines, occasionally stepping sideways or forward. A chorus that recited responses stood in the back, stepping back and forth or from side to side in a certain pattern. Various pitched voices were used to make the choral readings sound appealing. Light voices had a naturally high sound or pitch, and dark voices had a naturally low sound or pitch. The medium voices included all the voices between the high and low voices.

This choral reading, "On the Road to Damascus," is taken from the King James Version of the Bible. The word *shew* on page 89 is an old spelling of *show*.

INTRODUCTION

Vocabulary

Use the prepared sentences to introduce the vocabulary words in context.

Suddenly blind

▶ Have you ever wondered what it would be like to be blind?

Provide a blindfold and allow each student to try to walk to an area of the room while wearing the blindfold.

▶ How do you feel when you are wearing the blindfold? (Accept any answer, but elicit that sudden blindness can be frightening.)

How do you think a person who is proud or likes to be in control might feel if he were suddenly blind? (Answers may vary, but elicit that a proud person would be humbled because he is no longer in control.)

▶ Today you will read "On the Road to Damascus." It is a true account from the Bible in the form of a choral reading.

Share the background information about choral reading.

Head note

Read the head note on reader page 87 aloud, explaining that "new creature" refers to a spiritual change in Saul.

▶ When does this story take place? (in the years after Christ's ascension)

▶ What type of persecution do the Christians experience? (prison and death) [BAT: 8d Courage]

Correlated Activities
- **Vocabulary Box, Activity 4: War of the Words**
- **Creative Writing, Activity 5: Story-in-a-Bag**
See "Classroom Management for Grouping" in the Appendix.

COMPREHENSION

Objectives

The student will

- Convey the meaning of Scripture.
- Use volume and pacing to communicate meaning.
- Use tone of voice to convey emotion.
- Demonstrate self-confidence in oral reading.
- Recognize character growth and change.
- Understand God's plan of salvation.

Before silent reading: pages 86-89

Motivation

▶ What kinds of things does Saul do?

What happens to Saul on the road to Damascus?

After silent reading

Overview discussion: pages 86-89

▶ [literal] At the beginning of this choral reading, what is Saul of Tarsus doing? (persecuting and destroying the church, arresting Christians, and threatening the disciples)

[interpretive] What actions of Saul let you know that his hatred of the church changes? (Possible answers: He obeys the Lord's command to go to the city and wait; he gets baptized; he preaches Christ.) [BAT: 2a Obedience]

[interpretive] Why does Saul's hatred of the church change? (He accepts Christ as his Savior.) [BAT: 1b Repentance and faith]

[critical] Why does the Lord allow Saul to persecute the church but then save him? (Answers may vary, but elicit that persecution of the church scatters Christians and spreads the gospel, that God is merciful, and that Saul's salvation is a great testimony for us today.) [BATs: 5c Evangelism

and missions; 7a Grace; Bible Promise: B. Guiltless by the Blood]

▶ [appreciative] Have you ever realized you are a sinner and accepted Christ as your Savior? How do you know you are saved? (Answers may vary, but discuss the plan of salvation.) [BATs: 1a Understanding Jesus Christ; 1b Repentance and faith; Bible Promises: A. Liberty from Sin; D. Identified in Christ]

ON THE ROAD TO DAMASCUS

A choral reading from Acts 8:1-3 and 9:1-20.

arranged by Ron Shields
illustrated by Del Thompson and Roger Bruckner

Readers		**Chorus One:**	light voices
Reader One:	Saul	**Chorus Two:**	medium voices
Reader Two:	Ananias	**Chorus Three:**	dark voices

86

Follow-up discussion: page 86

▶ [critical] What makes a choral reading different from a play? (Answers may vary, but elicit that a play has much more natural physical movement and dialogue than a choral reading.)

In the years after Christ's ascension, the early church suffered persecution from unbelievers. Many of Christ's followers were thrown into prison, and some of them died for their faith. One man became especially well known as a hater and persecutor of the church—Saul of Tarsus. But when Saul met the Lord on the road to Damascus, he became a new creature.

All: And at that time there was a great persecution against the church which was at Jerusalem. . . .

Reader One: As for Saul,

Chorus Two: he made havock of the church,

Choruses One and Two: entering into every house, and haling men and women

All: committed them to prison. . . .

Reader One: And Saul,

All: yet breathing out threatenings and slaughter against the disciples of the Lord,

Choruses One and Two: went unto the high priest, and desired of him letters to Damascus to the synagogues, that if he found any of this way,

Chorus Two: whether they were men or women,

All: he might bring them bound unto Jerusalem.

Reader One: And as he journeyed, he came near Damascus:

Chorus One: and suddenly

Chorus Two: there shined round about him a light from heaven:

Choruses One and Two: And he fell to the earth,

All: and heard a voice saying unto him,

Chorus Three: Saul, Saul, why persecutest thou me?

Choruses One and Two: And he said,

Reader One: Who art thou, Lord?

Choruses One and Two: And the Lord said,

Chorus Three: I am Jesus whom thou persecutest: it is hard for thee to kick against the pricks.

On the Road to Damascus   87

Follow-up discussion: page 87

▶ [interpretive] What phrase tells you that Saul asks permission from the high priest? ("went unto the high priest, and desired of him letters")

[interpretive] Saul is looking for "any of this way." What does "any of this way" mean? (Christians or believers of Jesus Christ)

[interpretive] What does Saul want permission to do? (bring Christian men and women from Damascus to Jerusalem and put them in prison.)

[critical] Why does Saul want to persecute Christians? (Answers should include that he is not a believer in Jesus Christ at this time.) [BAT: 1a Understanding Jesus Christ]

[critical] Do Christians today face persecution? Explain. (Yes; Possible answers: sometimes Christians are mocked, shunned, imprisoned, or put to death for their faith in Christ.)

[appreciative] How would you feel if you were persecuted like the Christians of Saul's time? [BATs: 6c Spirit filled; 8d Courage; Bible Promise: H. God as Father]

▶ [interpretive] Why does Saul fall to the ground on the road to Damascus? (Possible answer: The bright light he sees and the voice that he hears frighten him.)

[critical] Jesus says Saul has been persecuting Him. How has Saul persecuted Jesus? (Answers may vary, but elicit that Saul has been persecuting Christians who believe in Jesus and so is persecuting Jesus also.)

Read aloud the sentences telling of Saul's experience on the road to Damascus.

On the Road to Damascus

Follow-up discussion: page 88

Read the italicized paragraph to the students.

▶ [interpretive] What does Saul understand the Lord to be saying by "it is hard for thee to kick against the pricks"? (Saul is being stubborn in not believing in and following Jesus.)

[literal] How does Saul react when Jesus says Saul is persecuting Him and is stubborn not to follow Him? (Saul is trembling and astonished.)

[interpretive] Is Saul now willing to follow the Lord? How do you know? (Yes; Saul asks the Lord what the Lord wants him to do, obeys the Lord's command, and fasts and prays.) [BATs: 2a Obedience; 6b Prayer]

Read aloud the Lord's command to Saul.

▶ [literal] Why are the men who are traveling with Saul speechless? (They hear a voice but do not see a man speaking.)

▶ [literal] How do you know Saul is blind? (His eyes are opened and he sees no man, he is led by the hand to Damascus, and he is without sight for three days.)

▶ [interpretive] What is a vision? (God letting people see events in their minds. Explain that this only occurred before the Bible was completed.)

[literal] What does the Lord command Ananias in a vision to do? (go to Judas's house on the street called Straight and ask for Saul of Tarsus)

[literal] What does Saul see in a vision? (Ananias coming in and putting his hand on him so that Saul receives his sight)

▶ [interpretive] How does Ananias feel about going to Saul? Why? (Answers may vary but should express that he is fearful because he has heard of the evil Saul has done to Christians.)

Saul understood immediately what the Lord meant. He had seen the pricks used to prod cattle pulling carts. If the cattle were stubborn and kicked backward, they hurt their legs on the pricks until they started forward again.

Choruses One and Two: And he trembling and astonished said,

Reader One: Lord, what wilt thou have me to do?

Choruses One and Two: And the Lord said unto him,

Chorus Three: Arise, and go into the city, and it shall be told thee what thou must do.

Choruses One and Two: And the men which journeyed with him stood speechless, hearing a voice, but seeing no man.

Reader One: And Saul arose from the earth; and when his eyes were opened, he saw no man:

Choruses One and Two: but they led him by the hand, and brought him into Damascus.

Reader One: And he was three days without sight, and neither did eat nor drink.

Choruses One and Two: And there was a certain disciple at Damascus, named Ananias; and

to him said the Lord in a vision,

Chorus Three: Ananias.

Choruses One and Two: And he said,

Reader Two: Behold, I am here, Lord.

Choruses One and Two: And the Lord said unto him,

Chorus Three: Arise, and go into the street which is called Straight, and inquire in the house of Judas for one called Saul of Tarsus: for, behold, he prayeth. And hath seen in a vision a man named Ananias coming in, and putting his hand on him, that he might receive his sight.

Choruses One and Two: Then Ananias answered,

Reader Two: Lord, I have heard by many of this man, how much evil he hath done to thy saints at Jerusalem: And here he hath authority from the chief priests to bind all that call on thy name.

88

Read aloud Ananias's response to the Lord, showing fear in your voice.

[critical] How should Ananias feel about the Lord's command for him to go to Saul? (Accept any answer, but elicit that he should trust in the Lord and not be afraid.) [BATs: 8a Faith in God's promises; 8d Courage; Bible Promise: H. God as Father]

[appreciative] How would you feel if you were in Ananias's place?

Choruses One and Two: But the Lord said unto him,

Chorus Three: Go thy way: for he is a chosen vessel unto me, to bear my name before the Gentiles, and kings, and the children of Israel: For I will shew him how great things he must suffer for my name's sake.

Choruses One and Two: And Ananias went his way, and entered into the house; and putting his hands on him said,

Reader Two: Brother Saul, the Lord, even Jesus, that appeared unto thee in the way as thou camest, hath sent me, that thou mightest receive thy sight, and be filled with the Holy Ghost.

Reader One: And immediately there fell from his eyes as it had been scales: and he received sight forthwith, and arose, and was baptized. And when he had received meat, he was strengthened.

Choruses One and Two: Then was Saul certain days with the disciples which were at Damascus.

Reader One: And straightway he preached Christ in the synagogues,

All: that he is the Son of God.

On the Road to Damascus   89

Follow-up discussion: page 89

► [literal] How does Ananias obey the Lord's command? (He goes to Saul and puts his hands on him so that Saul receives his sight and is filled with the Holy Ghost.) [BAT: 2a Obedience]

► [interpretive] What three things show that Saul has accepted the Lord as his Savior? (He is filled with the Holy Ghost, he is baptized, and he preaches about the Lord.) [BATs: 2a Obedience; 5c Evangelism and missions]

► [critical] In this choral reading, what two kinds of blindness is Saul healed from? (Answers may vary, but elicit that he is healed from physical blindness and spiritual blindness; before Saul accepted Christ as His Savior, he was spiritually blind—he didn't understand Scripture and spiritual truths.)

Assign the choral readers' parts to the students. Remind the students that they are not to say the reader names before they say the reader lines. Direct the students to read aloud "On the Road to Damascus," modeling natural voice inflection, volume, and pacing.

Worktext Objective

The student will

■ Identify facts and details.

Comprehension:
Worktext page 33

The student will

■ Discriminate between fiction and nonfiction.

LITERATURE
Fiction and nonfiction

Write the words *fiction* and *nonfiction* for display.

Instruct students to turn to "An Emergency" on page 36 in their readers.

▶ Is there true information about llamas in this story? (yes)

Give some examples of real facts given in the story. (Possible answers: Male llamas have fangs to bite with; llamas spit from their stomachs; llamas spit at their attackers.)

Even though it contains some facts and true information, "An Emergency" is fiction.

Fiction is a story that has made-up characters, events, or details. Fiction may contain real facts or be entirely fanciful. Fiction is written to give the reader pleasure.

Discuss parts of "An Emergency" that are probably made up, such as all the llamas getting loose from the pasture, a llama going into the outlet store, and the manager thinking the llama was a baby giraffe.

Instruct the students to turn to "Lama Glama" on page 46.

▶ Is there true information about llamas in this article? (yes)

Are there any parts that are probably made up? (no)

Since "Lama Glama" is factual, it is nonfiction.

Nonfiction writing gives facts and details about real people, places, and things. Most nonfiction provides the reader with facts in an interesting way.

Literature: Worktext page 34

Guide the students through the completion of the page.

Lesson	Worktext pages
29	226-27

Materials

- College dictionary and student dictionary (general dictionaries)
- A Bible
- Bible dictionary, biographical dictionary, and geographical dictionary (optional)
- 3"×5" card for each student
- Teaching Visual 6: *More Than Definitions*

SPECIAL DICTIONARIES

① Introduction

Display the Bible dictionary and Bible. Open the Bible to Esther 8.

▶ In the book of Esther, King Ahasuerus is getting ready to send letters all over the kingdom to rescue Esther's people, the Jews, from a wicked plan for their destruction.

Read aloud Esther 8:8.

▶ What does the word *seal* mean? (Accept any answer.)

Read aloud the definitions for the word *seal* in the Bible dictionary. (This word is also in the *Christian Student Dictionary* if you do not have a Bible dictionary.)

▶ A Bible dictionary is a special dictionary to help the reader understand words in the Bible.

Read some interesting words and definitions from the Bible dictionary to the students.

② Skill development: Visual 6—*More Than Definitions*

▶ What is a dictionary? (an alphabetical listing of words and their meanings)

Display the college and student dictionaries as you explain that these are general dictionaries.

▶ Look at the dictionary entry for the word *Phoebe* on the visual.

Read aloud the definition and the verse reference for the word *Phoebe*.

▶ What kind of dictionary would you find this word in? (a Bible dictionary)

Which other entry on the visual might also be in a Bible dictionary? (phylacteries)

Read aloud the definition and verse reference for the word *phylacteries*.

Look up the verses for these two Bible dictionary entries and read them aloud.

▶ Look at the dictionary entry for the word *Stradivari*. If you were to read an entire book about the violin maker Antonio Stradivari, what would such a book be called? (a biography)

The word *biography* and the word *biographical* refer to life. What name would you give to a dictionary about people's lives? (a biographical dictionary)

Both a general dictionary and a biographical dictionary might include the entry *Stradivari*. Which kind of dictionary would you expect to include more information about Stradivari—a general dictionary or a biographical dictionary? (a biographical dictionary)

(continued on top of next page)

The student will

■ Recognize the dictionary as a valuable source of information.

■ Identify a biographical dictionary.

■ Identify a geographical dictionary.

■ Identify a Bible dictionary.

■ Note some special features of a dictionary.

Objectives

Background information

General dictionary

A general dictionary is an alphabetical listing of words giving pronunciation, meanings, and other information about words. It may also include geographical and biographical entries or have a special section for them. BJU Press publishes the *Christian Student Dictionary*, a general student dictionary that eliminates objectionable features and adds a biblical perspective.

Special dictionaries

A *geographical dictionary* is an alphabetical listing of places giving pronunciation, location, and other significant information. It may also include other visual representations of geographical information, such as maps and weather charts.

A *biographical dictionary* is an alphabetical listing of names giving pronunciation and significant information about each individual.

A *Bible dictionary* is an alphabetical listing of biblical terms, Bible lands, and people.

Although you may not have access to any of the special dictionaries discussed in this lesson, you can use the visual and the worktext pages to introduce the students to these dictionaries.

If special dictionaries are available, the entries may differ somewhat with the samples shown on the visual and worktext page 226.

Notice the entries for Stradivari and William Sunday. What information is given in a biographical entry? (pronunciation, years of birth and death, birthplace, why he is famous)

Why is *Billy* in parentheses? (It is his nickname.)

► Why would the entries *St. Paul* and *Syrian Desert* both appear in a geographical dictionary? (because they are names of places, or geographic names)

What information is given in a geographical entry? (pronunciation, location, population, and unusual facts)

Display the biographical, geographical, and Bible dictionaries as you elicit that these are special dictionaries. Elicit that a special dictionary provides more information for a specific word than a general dictionary does.

③ Skill application:
Worktext pages 226-27

Use questions such as the following to discuss the three special dictionaries pictured on worktext page 226.

► Who was an Egyptian servant of Abraham? (Hagar)

Where in the Bible is a dagger mentioned? (Judges 3:22)

What kind of dictionary has this information? (a Bible dictionary)

► What was the name of the law that Lincoln signed to free the slaves in 1863? (the Emancipation Proclamation)

What different type of jobs did Lincoln have? (possible answers: clerk, store owner, surveyor, post office worker, state government official, president)

What kind of dictionary has this information? (a biographical dictionary)

► Where is Mount Mezenc? (South France)

Which state is nicknamed the Gopher state? (Minnesota)

Dictionaries, Dictionaries

► Compare Them
Notice the different kinds of entries in these three dictionaries.

Bible Dictionary

Habakkuk/Hagar

haft / hăft / A handle, as of a dagger (Judg. 3:22)

Hagab / hă´ • găb / One of the Temple servants whose descendants returned from Babylon under Zerubbabel (Ezra 2:46), before 536 B.C.

Hagaba / hăg´ • ă • bä / One of the Temple servants whose descendants returned from the captivity with Zerubbabel (Neh. 7:48), before 536 B.C.

Hagabah / hăg´ • ă • bä / Another form of the preceding (Ezra 2:45).

Hagar / hā´ • gär / A native of Egypt, servant of Abraham (Gen. 21:9-10), and handmaid of Sarah (16:1).

Taken from *Unger's Bible Dictionary* by Merrill F. Unger, Moody Press, copyright 1966. Used by permission.

Biographical Dictionary

Lincoln/Link

Lincoln / lĭng´ • kən /, Abraham. 1809-1865. Born in Kentucky. Spent about one year in school. Taught himself many things by reading books over and over. Worked as a clerk and later owned his own store. Worked as a surveyor and ran a post office. Served in the Illinois state legislature. Wanted to keep slavery out of the new territories. Became U.S. president in 1860. Announced the Emancipation Proclamation in 1863. Shot by John Wilkes Booth April 15, 1865.

Lindbergh / lĭnd´ • bərg /, Charles. 1902-1974. Born in Detroit, Michigan. Left University of Wisconsin after two years of study. Performed daredevil stunts as a pilot. Trained as a pilot in U.S. Army. Made first solo nonstop flight across the Atlantic Ocean in May 1927. His monoplane was called the *Spirit of St. Louis*. Nicknamed "Lone Eagle" and "Lucky Lindy." Died of cancer in 1974.

Geographical Dictionary

Mezenc/Mira Bay

Mezenc, Mount / mā • zăngk / Volcanic peak in South France. 5,755 ft.

Michigan / mĭsh´ • ĭ • gən / Located in the midwest United States. Nicknamed Wolverine State. Largest city is Detroit. Capital city is Lansing. Economic strengths are transportation equipment, machinery, and fabricated metal products.

Minnesota / mĭn´ • ĭ • sō´ • tə / Located in the midwest United States. Nicknamed the Gopher State. Largest city is Minneapolis. Capital city is St. Paul. Economic strengths are machinery; finance, insurance, and real estate; community, social, and personal services.

226

What kind of dictionary has this kind of information? (a geographical dictionary)

Give help as needed as the students answer the questions on page 227.

④ Skill practice:
Dictionary Hunt (optional)

Give each student a 3" ✕ 5" card. Instruct the student to write on his card a question about an interesting detail found in one of the special dictionaries. Students should write on the back of the card the entry and the special dictionary used. Let them trade cards and use the special dictionaries to find answers to each other's questions.

THE DARKEST TIME

North against South, state against state, brother against brother—it was a conflict that tore apart families, friends, and a nation. This article is an overview of the American Civil War.

Lesson	Reader pages	Worktext pages
30	90-91	35-36

Materials

- Various pictures of Abraham Lincoln and the American Civil War (or the picture on reader page 90)
- Items used during the American Civil War (optional)
- Teaching Visual 5: *Dangerous Trails*
- Vocabulary sentences for display

Background information

The American Civil War—The northern states, the North, and the southern states, the South, had many differences in lifestyles and beliefs that resulted in disagreements. The agricultural economy of the South with large plantations required much manual labor to operate efficiently, and slaves provided cheap labor. Although only one-fourth of Southerners owned slaves, many were in favor of slavery. On the other hand, the industrialized economy of the North with mostly factories and shops did not have much need for slaves. Disagreements between the North and South intensified with the expansion westward. Congress decided whether a territory would be a slave state or free state. The acquisition of a new state meant more power economically and politically. Consequently, slavery and the right of states to decide about it separated the North and the South. As Americans became more and more divided about sectional differences and economic and political power, war seemed to be the only way to settle the disagreements. As a result of the War Between the States, or the American Civil War, the states were reunited, national government control over state government was established, and slavery was abolished.

INTRODUCTION

Vocabulary

Use the prepared sentences to introduce the vocabulary words in context.

American Civil War

Show the pictures and items from the American Civil War.

Share the background information.

▶ Who fought in the American Civil War?

Did some of your ancestors fight in the war?

▶ Today you are going to read about the people who lived during the American Civil War and how the Lord led our country through the war.

VOCABULARY

LESSON 30

†The boys' argument over who owned the ball was a conflict that could not be solved. (p. 90)

†Her constant anger caused her to have years of bitterness. (p. 90)

†His gloomy attitude gave him a bleak outlook on life. (p. 91)

They worked long and hard on the farm and their toil paid off. (p. 91)

Heritage Studies Connection

Lesson 30 can be linked to the study of the American Civil War.

Correlated Activities

- Word Work, Activity 1: Comic Connection
- Spelling Practice, Activity 4: Secret Code Spelling

See "Classroom Management for Grouping" in the Appendix.

COMPREHENSION

Objectives

The student will

■ Appreciate the relevance of a story title.
■ Develop a sense of history.
■ Infer the author's purpose.
■ Read for information.

Before silent reading: pages 90-91

Motivation

▶ What does the title describe?

Who was president of the United States during this darkest time?

How do the author and the country feel about the president?

After silent reading

Overview discussion: pages 90-91

▶ [interpretive] What does the author say is the darkest time in our nation's history? (The War Between the States or the American Civil War)

[critical] Is "The Darkest Time" a good title for this selection? Why or why not? (Yes; elicit that the selection tells about a time when brother fought against brother, friend against friend, and citizen against citizen, and that such a time can well be described as sad and gloomy, or dark.)

▶ [literal] Whom did the Lord give to our country to lead it through the war? (Abraham Lincoln) [Bible Promise: I. God as Master]

[interpretive] What did Abraham Lincoln want to see happen to our country? (He wanted to see it become one strong nation again.)

[literal] What kept Abraham Lincoln from seeing the country become one strong nation again? (He was shot and killed.)

The Darkest Time

Becky Henry

In the year 1861, when Abraham Lincoln was president, our country began the most terrible war of its history. Every other war that we have ever entered has been against another country. But this time, states that were part of the same country fought against each other. This terrible conflict was called the War Between the States, or the American Civil War.

Problems began because the people of the North and the people of the South lived in different ways. They believed different things, and each side thought the other was wrong. They tried to take care of their differences in peaceful ways, but the problems were too serious. To some people, war seemed to be the only solution.

No other war in United States history has created such bitterness. Sometimes even brothers sincerely believed differently from each other and fought on opposite sides of the same battle. The War

90

▶ [interpretive] Has the whole country always remembered Abraham Lincoln as one of the greatest presidents? Why or why not? (No; most of the North liked him because he was on their side, but most of the South didn't like him because he was fighting against them. Today, many people in the North and the South remember him as a great president.)

▶ [interpretive] How does the author want you to remember the president? (as a great president who led the nation through its darkest time to become a better nation)

Follow-up discussion: pages 90-91

▶ [literal] What caused the war? (The North and South had different lifestyles and beliefs, each side thinking the other was wrong.)

▶ [critical] Was it right for families and friends to fight against each other? (Accept any answer.)

Read aloud the paragraph describing why the war created bitterness.

[appreciative] How would you feel if you went to war against your family because of your beliefs?

(Follow-up discussion continues at the top of the next page.)

Between the States tore apart families and friends. It was one of the darkest times in our nation's history.

Abraham Lincoln was the man the Lord gave us to lead our country through that bleak time. He had patience, compassion, a gentle sense of humor, and a real love for his country. After years of toil and heartache, he led the nation to the end of the war. How thankful Mr. Lincoln was then! But only five days later the president was shot and killed. He did not live to see his beloved states become one strong nation again.

When President Lincoln died, many people in the North and some people in the South grieved over his death. Today people in both the North and the South remember him as one of the greatest presidents this country has ever had. He guided our nation through its darkest time, and in the end he brought it to a better light.

▶ [interpretive] What characteristics did Abraham Lincoln have to help him lead the country? (patience, compassion, a gentle sense of humor, a real love for his country)

▶ [interpretive] How do you know Abraham Lincoln cared about the people in both the North and the South? (He had years of toil and heartache, he thought of the states as beloved, and he wanted the states to become one strong nation again.)

[interpretive] What does the author mean when she says that Abraham Lincoln brought the country to a "better light"? (He improved relationships in the country.)

[critical] Why does the author use the words "better light"? (Answers may vary, but elicit that the author is contrasting it with the words "darkest time.")

Read aloud the sentence in which the author compares the darkest time to the better light.

▶ [appreciative] What would our country be like today if Abraham Lincoln had not brought the states back together?

Worktext Objectives

The student will

- Divide compound words into syllables.
- Identify the accented syllable of compound words.
- Identify facts and opinions.

Structural Analysis:
Worktext page 35

◀ Complete teaching of this skill was presented in Lesson 27.

Use Teaching Visual 5, *Dangerous Trails*, to review dividing two- and three-syllable compound words.

Choose a student to read the information at the top of the page.

Instruct the students to complete the page independently.

Comprehension:
Worktext page 36

Use the sentences and illustrations at the top of the page to discuss the difference between fact and opinion.

Point out the words on the magnifying glass on the right. Explain that these words will help identify statements that are opinions rather than facts.

Read the instructions together. Remind the students to circle the word that indicates that the sentence is an opinion. Direct the students to complete the page independently.

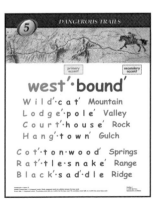

DANGEROUS TRAILS

5

primary accent   secondary accent

west'·bound'

W i l d'·c a t' Mountain
L o d g e'·p o l e' Valley
C o u r t'·h o u s e' Rock
H a n g'·t o w n' Gulch

C o t'·t o n·w o o d' Springs
R a t'·t l e·s n a k e' Range
B l a c k'·s a d'·d l e Ridge

SOMETHING EXTRA

Write About It: A letter to remember

Instruct each student to write a letter, pretending to be a soldier, friend, parent, child, brother, sister, or slave living during the American Civil War. Direct him to write the letter to the president, a friend, or a family member, writing as if he were from the North or the South. Encourage him to include research information, daily events, and feelings about the war in the letter. Display the letter for others to read.

ABRAHAM LINCOLN WAS MY FRIEND

An excited Billy Brown travels from Springfield, Illinois, to see his former neighbor, Abraham Lincoln. They have a grand time, laughing and swapping stories. Billy returns to Illinois and begins saving up new tales for when the war is over and Mr. Lincoln comes home—tales he will never get to tell.

Lesson	Reader pages	Worktext pages
31	92-95	37-38

Materials
- Pictures of Abraham Lincoln and the American Civil War used in the previous lesson
- Map of the United States during the 1860s
- Vocabulary sentences prepared for display

Background information
Abraham Lincoln—Moving frequently during his childhood, Abraham Lincoln grew up with little formal education. To educate himself, he walked many miles to borrow books. He worked various jobs, from that of a handyman to that of a lawyer. He entered and lost many political races. His Senate campaign statement was, "A house divided against itself cannot stand. I believe this government cannot endure permanently half slave and half free." Despite his many failures, he also achieved great success in his political career, and the greatest of these was being elected president of the United States in 1861. He married Mary Todd, and they had four children. Only one child, Robert Todd Lincoln, lived to adulthood. Lincoln was shot while attending a perfomance at Ford's Theater just six days after the Civil War ended.

INTRODUCTION
Vocabulary
Use the prepared sentences to introduce the vocabulary words in context.

Your friend the president
▶ Every president of the United States was your age at one time. Can you imagine if the person sitting next to you or you yourself became the president some day?

What would it be like to have a president as your friend?

The story you will read today is about the sixteenth president of the United States, Abraham Lincoln, and his friend.

Display the pictures and briefly discuss the background information with the pictures.

Head note
Read the head note on page 92 aloud.

▶ Why does Billy wish he could do something for Abraham Lincoln? (He is Abe's friend and would probably like to repay Abe for his kindness toward others.)

How far does Billy travel to see his friend Abe? (from Springfield, Illinois, to Washington, D.C.)

Use the map to show the long distance Billy travels.

▶ What does his traveling such a long distance to visit Abe near a dangerous battlefield tell you about Billy? (He is a true friend.)

VOCABULARY
LESSON 31

†The stoop of the house is a nice place to sit and watch the sunset. (p. 93)

*†Her adventure story was a funny yarn to tell and hear. (p. 93)

I have never seen anything more tired looking than his drawn face. (p. 93)

*†Assuming the party was unimportant, he reckoned it did not matter whether he went. (p. 95)

*†A welcome party was arranged as a reception for their guest's arrival. (p. 95)

Correlated Activities
- **Vocabulary Box, Activity 3: Glossary Day**
- **Recreational Reading, Activity 2: Design-a-Game**
See "Classroom Management for Grouping" in the Appendix.

Objectives

COMPREHENSION

The student will

- Demonstrate an understanding of the author's use of colloquial language.
- Determine emotional responses of characters.
- Infer character traits from dialogue.
- Interpret meanings of idioms.
- Recognize the use of fiction to illuminate historical fact.

Before silent reading: pages 92-94

Motivation

▶ How does Billy Brown try to help Mr. Lincoln?

Why does Abe think Billy is a true friend?

After silent reading

Overview discussion: pages 92-94

▶ [interpretive] How do you know that Abe Lincoln is glad to see Billy? (possible answers: his face lights up; he sees Billy right away without an appointment; he invites Billy to dinner; he talks with Billy a long time.)

▶ [literal] What does Billy do for Abe Lincoln on the back stoop? (He spins every yarn, or tells every story, from their hometown from the last three-and-a-half years and makes him laugh.)

[literal] Why is Billy especially glad to see Abe Lincoln laughing at his yarns? (Billy notices that Lincoln is thinner than ever with his face drawn and gray.)

▶ [interpretive] Why is Abe Lincoln surprised that Billy has come only to visit and not to ask for anything, complain, or give advice? (He assumes that Billy must want something because he has traveled far, and most people come to ask for something, complain, or give advice.)

[literal] What does the president do that shows how happy he is that Billy has come only to visit? (He grabs Billy's hand and shakes it a lot, cries, and says what good Billy has done for him.) [BAT: 5a Love]

[critical] Why is the president crying? (Answers will vary, but elicit that he is homesick and under a lot of emotional stress because of the war, and he realizes that Billy is a true friend.)

Abraham Lincoln
Was My Friend

by Keith W. Jennison
illustrated by Mary Ann Lumm

Billy Brown and Abraham Lincoln were neighbors in Springfield, Illinois. When Mr. Lincoln became the president of the United States and went to Washington, Billy stayed behind. Each day he eagerly read the newspaper for news of his good friend Abe. He read about the war and learned that some people blamed Mr. Lincoln because it lasted so long. He read that each day the president saw dozens of people and that he helped them whenever he could. Billy often wished he could do something for his old friend.

In 1864 Billy Brown made a trip to Washington to see the president. Billy tells of his visit with the president when Mr. Lincoln was staying at a home very near a battlefield.

I footed it up to the Soldiers' Home where Mr. Lincoln was living then, right among the sick soldiers in their tents. There was lots of people settin' around in a little room waiting for him. A door opened, and out came little John Nicolay. I went up to him and said, "How'd you do, John? Where's Mr. Lincoln?"

"Have you an appointment with Mr. Lincoln?" he says.

"No sir, I ain't, and it ain't necessary. You just trot along,

Excerpted from The Humorous Mr. Lincoln: A Profile in Wit, Courage, and Compassion, *by Keith W. Jennison*
Copyright © 1988 Reprinted with permission of the publisher
The Countryman Press /W. W. Norton & Company, Inc.

92

Follow-up discussion: pages 92-93

▶ [critical] If you were to read aloud a section of this page, how would you portray the way the narrator, Billy, talks? (Answers may vary, but elicit that the narrator talks in a colloquial, or conversational, style almost as if he is telling the reader a yarn.)

Read aloud the first paragraph as if Billy is telling the reader a yarn.

[interpretive] What does Billy mean by the expression "footed it up"? (walked)

(The follow-up discussion is continued on the top of the next page.)

Johnnie, and tell him Billy Brown's here, and see what he says."

In about two minutes, the door popped open and out came Abe Lincoln, his face all lit up. He saw me first thing and shook my hand fit to kill. "Billy," he says, "come right in. You're going to stay to supper with Mary and me."

He had a right smart lot of people to see, but as soon as he was through, we went out on the back stoop and talked and talked and talked. I told him about everybody in Springfield—the weddings, the births, the funerals, and the buildings. I guess there wasn't a yarn I'd heard in the last three-and-a-half years that I didn't spin for him. Laugh— you'd ought to have heard him laugh! It just did my heart good, for I could see what they'd been doing to him. He always was a thin man, but he was thinner than ever now, and his face was drawn and gray. It was enough to make you cry.

Abraham Lincoln Was My Friend 93

▶ [interpretive] Why does John Nicolay ask Billy if he has an appointment? (There are many people waiting to see the president, and he does not know that Billy is Lincoln's friend.)

Read aloud Billy's response to John Nicolay's question.

▶ [interpretive] Abe Lincoln's face is all lit up as he comes out to meet Billy. What does the expression "all lit up" mean? (that he has a smile on his face)

[literal] How does Abe Lincoln shake Billy's hand? (fit to kill)

[interpretive] What does the expression "fit to kill" mean? (very hard, very enthusiastically)

Allow a student to demonstrate the president's handshake.

▶ [interpretive] How do you know the president enjoys talking with Billy? (He laughs.)

Read aloud the sentences that let you know Billy cares deeply for Abe Lincoln.

Follow-up discussion: page 94

▶ [literal] What reasons does Billy give for coming to see Abe Lincoln? (Billy says he was "kind of lonesome" and afraid he would "forget some of those yarns" if he did not see him soon.)

[critical] Why does Abe Lincoln ask a second time why Billy came to visit? (Accept any answer, but elicit that Abe Lincoln cannot believe what he hears and thinks Billy must have another reason.)

Read aloud Billy's response to Lincoln's repeated questions.

[critical] What does Billy's response tell you about the kind of person Billy is? (Answers may vary but should express that his response shows Billy is loving and determined. He is a true friend.) [BATs: 5a Love; 2d Determination; 5e Friendliness]

▶ [interpretive] For what is the president homesick? (Springfield and all his friends there)

Read aloud Lincoln's sad words about the war and being homesick.

[critical] What do Lincoln's words about the war and being homesick tell you about the kind of person Abe Lincoln is? (Answers may vary but should express that his words show he feels compassion toward the men who will die and their mothers, yet he is dedicated to saving the Union—the United States.) [BATs: 5a Compassion; 2d Dedication]

Well, we had supper, and then we talked some more. About ten o'clock, I started to leave.

"Billy," he says, "what did you come for?"

"I came to see you, Abe."

"But you haven't asked me for anything, Billy. What do you want me to do for you?"

"Nothing, Abe. I just wanted to see you. I felt kind of lonesome 'cause it had been so long since I'd seen you. And I was afraid I'd forget some of those yarns if I didn't see you soon."

Well, sir, you should have seen his face when he looked at me.

"Billy Brown," he says slow-like, "do you mean to tell me that you came all the way from Springfield, Illinois, just to visit with me? You don't have any com-

94

plaints in your pocket or advice up your sleeve?"

"Yes, sir," I says. "That's about it. Why, I'd go to Europe to see you if I couldn't do it no other way, Abe."

Well, sir, I was never so astonished in all my life. He just grabbed my hand and shook it nearly off, and the tears just poured down his face.

"Billy," he says, "you'll never know just what good you've done me. I'm homesick, Billy, just plumb homesick, and it seems as if this war will never be over. Many a night I can see the boys dying on the fields, and I can hear their mothers crying for them at home. And I can't help it, Billy; I have to send them down there. We've got to save the Union, Billy. We've got to."

Billy Brown returned to Springfield. After a while the war ended, and the nation rejoiced. Billy never saw his friend Abe Lincoln again. Billy tells how he got the news of Mr. Lincoln's death.

I tell you, it was a great day out here when we heard Lee surrendered. Somehow the only thing I could think of was how glad Mr. Lincoln would be. Me and Ma reckoned he'd come right out and make us a visit and get rested, so we began right off making plans about the reception we'd give him. A brass band, parades, speeches, fireworks, everything! Seems as if I couldn't think of anything else. I was coming out to open the store one morning, and all the way down I was thinking how I'd decorate the windows and how I'd tie a flag onto that old chair; then I saw Hiram Jones coming toward me. He looked so old and all bent over that I didn't know what happened.

"Hiram," I said. "What's the matter? Be you sick?"

"Billy," he says, and he could hardly say it. "Billy, they've killed Mr. Lincoln."

Well, I just turned cold all over, and then I flared up.

"Hiram Jones, you're lying. You're crazy! How dare you tell me that? It ain't so!"

"Don't, Billy," he says. "Don't go on so. I ain't lying. It's so. He'll never come back, Billy. He's dead." And he fell to sobbing out loud right there in the street.

Somehow all I could think about was all those yarns I'd saved up—now I'd never get to tell them to him. I'd never get to see him resting out in the old rocking chair and see that smile on his face.

But Ma stopped me from that selfish foolishness. "Don't look like that, Billy," she says. "He saved the Union. That was his job. He saved the Union, Billy."

And I knew it was true. He had done what he had been sent to do.

Abraham Lincoln Was My Friend   95

Motivation

Read the italicized paragraph at the top of page 95 aloud.

▶ How do Billy and his wife react to the news of Mr. Lincoln's death?

After silent reading

Overview discussion: page 95

▶ [interpretive] How do you know that Billy and Ma are excited for Abe Lincoln to come home? (Answers may vary but should express that Billy cannot think of anything but Abe's homecoming, and Billy and Ma are planning a huge party involving the whole town.)

▶ [literal] How does Billy react when Hiram Jones tells him about Lincoln's death? (He gets upset and accuses Hiram of lying.)

[critical] Is Billy's reaction right? Why or why not? (No; answers may vary, but elicit that Billy should not accuse Hiram of lying simply because he hates to hear of Abe's death and that he is thinking selfishly.) [BATs: 3c Emotional control; 5b Unselfishness]

Read aloud the dialogue between Hiram and Billy as if you were the characters.

▶ [interpretive] What does Billy mean by saying Abe Lincoln "had done what he had been sent to do"? (The Lord sent Abe Lincoln to save the Union.)

▶ [appreciative] Does this story help you to understand Abraham Lincoln's life better? How? (Answers may vary, but elicit that the story helps you imagine the time period and see Abraham Lincoln as a real person with real feelings.)

The student will

- Interpret words in a nonliteral way.
- Interpret dialect.
- Infer facts and details.
- Matching words and meanings.

COMPREHENSION
Interpreting dialect

Write the word *dialect* for display.

Elicit that a dialect is a variation of a language used by a particular group of people.

▶ Dialects can include differences in the way the words are pronounced (or said) or in the words themselves.

In *The Adventures of Tom Sawyer*, Mark Twain uses dialect to add humor and portray the setting of his book.

Read the following sentences to demonstrate dialect.

▶ "I whisht I knowed. It's awful solemn like, ain't it?"
"Yes, I reckon that's so."
"I'll try, but don't you be afeared."

▶ Would you say things this way? (probably not)

In different parts of the United States, people say things in different ways. In the North, people say, "I drove him to the store," and in the South, one might say, "I carried him to the store." Both expressions mean the same thing.

If there are students in your class that use different dialects or expressions, allow them to give examples.

Explain that Billy, the narrator in "Abraham Lincoln Was My Friend," also used examples of dialect. Use the following examples from the story, asking students what is meant by each one.

▶ Mr. Lincoln had a right smart lot of people to see. (He had a great number of people to see.)

▶ Out came Abe Lincoln, his face all lit up. (He showed happiness on his face.)

Comprehension: Worktext pages 37-38

SOMETHING EXTRA
Write About It: Spin a yarn

Instruct the students to think about the following question.

▶ If you had a good friend who moved away a year ago, what yarns would you spin for him?

Discuss important or humorous events about school, friends, and family. Direct each student to write down his favorite yarn, using a colloquial or conversational style. Allow him to read his yarn aloud for others.

Materials

- Teaching Visual 7: *Cracking Glossary Codes*
- The coded word *jorvvdub* for display
- Twenty-two cards for the following words: *admonish, ambulance, antenna, approval, aquarium, author, banister, breadboard, broncobuster, cable, caiman, calm, cast, centipede, check, clerk, cog, collide, compass, confirm, contempt, contribute*

Lesson	Worktext pages
32	228-29

The student will

- Recognize the glossary as a valuable source of information.
- Recognize the parts of a glossary.
- Identify a pronunciation key.
- Use a pronunciation key.

Objectives

GLOSSARY

① Introduction

▶ During times of war the enemies try to keep their messages secret. How can a country keep its messages from being read by its enemies? (Possible answers: Hide the messages somewhere or write them in code.)

If one country intercepts a coded message from another country, it tries to crack the code to learn the enemy's plans. Look at the coded word I've written. This word names a place to find information. Do you know what it is?

Let me tell you how the code works; then let's see if you can read it. Each letter represents the letter that appears three places before it in the alphabet. For example, the first letter is *j*. What letter comes three letters before *j* in the alphabet? (g)

Let's figure out the rest of the letters to name a place that has information. (glossary)

② Skill development: Visual 7—Cracking Glossary Codes

▶ Finding out what the glossary has to say about words is a little like decoding a message. Where would you find a glossary? (Many books include a glossary in the back.)

A lot of information is listed in a glossary. What is its purpose? (possible answer: to give understanding about unfamiliar words)

Read aloud each term—*entry word, pronunciation, part of speech, definition*—on the magnifying glasses on the visual and review its purpose. Point out each part in the colored entry for *abound* and then ask volunteers to find examples of each term in the two uncolored entries.

Call attention to the guidewords above the entries.

▶ What are guidewords? (Guidewords are the first and last entry words on a glossary or dictionary page. They are printed at the top of each page to make it easier to locate words.)

Aquamarine is a guideword for this sample glossary page. Why isn't the entry for *aquamarine* shown? (The sample shows only part of the glossary page, the top part. *Aquamarine* is the last entry word on the page, so it is not shown.)

The pronunciations truly look like a code. Are they like the entry words? (no)

Point to the pronunciation key.

▶ You can use the pronunciation key and the pronunciation in an entry to help you crack the code to pronounce an unfamiliar word.

Ask volunteers to use the pronunciation key to crack the code to read each listed pronunciation next to the pronunciation key. Write the word as each pronunciation is read. (adobe, audition, barter, garret, neglect, plot, venture)

Background information

Parts of a glossary

The *entry word* is the word that is defined in a glossary entry. It is in bold print and is divided into syllables. Entry words are arranged alphabetically in the glossary.

The *pronunciation* shows how to pronounce the entry word. It also shows which syllable is accented.

The *part of speech* tells how to use the entry word in a sentence.

The *definition* is the meaning of the entry word.

The *guidewords* are found at the top of the glossary page. Guidewords are the first and last entry words on that page.

The *pronunciation key* is a listing of the sounds and respellings used in pronunciations.

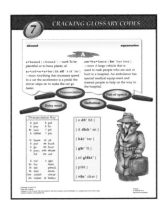

3 Skill application:
Guidewords activity

Review the term *guidewords*.

Distribute the prepared word cards to the students. Write each of the following pairs of guidewords, one pair at a time, for display. The students should hold up the words that would appear on a glossary page with the guidewords you have written.

abandoned—ammunition (admonish, ambulance)

amphibious—azure (antenna, approval, aquarium, author)

balk—barren (banister)

bound—camomile (breadboard, broncobuster, cable, caiman, calm)

canopy—cobblestone (cast, centipede, check, clerk)

cockpit—corral (cog, collide, compass, confirm, contempt, contribute)

One-on-one—Write the pairs of guidewords on a sheet of paper and ask the student to write the words next to the guidewords with which each word would appear in a glossary.

4 Skill application:
Worktext page 228

Guide the students in completing the page together. Explain that the sample glossary shown is only the left-hand column of a page, and therefore only one guideword appears.

5 Skill practice:
Worktext page 229

Finding the Codes

▸**Use the Codes**
Use this glossary section to complete the page.

bay

bay | bā | —*noun* A reddish brown horse.

ba·zaar | bə zär´ | —*noun* A market made up of a street lined with shops and stalls.

bill | bĭl | —*noun* The hard, projecting mouth parts on the head of a bird.

birch | bûrch | —*noun* A tree with smooth bark that peels off easily. There are several kinds of birch trees.

birth·stone | bûrth´ stōn | —*noun* A jewel associated with a certain month, worn by people born in that month.

birthstone

bit | bĭt | —*noun* A shaped piece of metal that is part of a horse's bridle. The bit goes into the horse's mouth and is used to help control the animal.

bluff | blŭf | —*noun* A steep cliff, hill, or riverbank.

bog | bôg | or | bŏg | —*noun* A soft, wet area of land; marsh; swamp.

bois·ter·ous | boi´ stər əs | or | boi´ strəs | —*adjective* Overactive and noisy.

bored | bôrd | or | bōrd | —*adjective* Made weary by lack of interest.

bot·tle·neck | bŏt´ l něk | —*noun* A narrow or blocked section of a river or stream.

bound | bound | —*verb* To run by leaping.

ă	pat	ĕ	pet
ā	pay	ē	be
âr	care	ĭ	pit
ä	father	ī	pie
îr	fierce	oi	oil
ŏ	pot	o͞o	book
ō	go	o͞o	boot
ô	paw,	yo͞o	abuse
	for	ou	out
ŭ	cut	ə	ago,
ûr	fur		item,
th	the		pencil,
th	thin		atom,
hw	which		circus
zh	vision	ər	butter

228

1. Find and circle the pronunciation key.

2. Which entry words are adjectives?
   ___*boisterous and bored*___
   _____

3. What is the definition of the word with the pronunciation | blŭf |?
   ___*A steep cliff, hill, or riverbank.*___
   _____

4. Write two words that have only one syllable.
   ___*Answers will vary.*___
   _____

5. Which two-syllable word is accented on the second syllable?
   ___*bazaar*___

6. Which entry word has an *e* with the sound of *e* in *pet*?
   ___*bottleneck*___

7. What part of speech is *bound*?
   ___*verb*___

8. Write the pronunciation for *birthstone*.
   ___*/bûrth´ stōn/*___

JOHNNY AND HIS MULE

Lesson	Reader pages	Worktext pages
33	96-99	39
34	100-103	40-41
35	104-7	42-44

Materials
- Physical map of the United States
- Picture of the Great Smoky Mountains
- Picture of a mule
- Vocabulary sentences prepared for display

Background information

The Great Smoky Mountains—The Great Smoky Mountains are part of the Appalachian Mountain system. They form a border between Tennessee and North Carolina and were named Smoky because the thickly forested mountains create a humid atmosphere that looks like a smoky mist. In 1930 most of the Great Smoky Mountains were established as the Great Smoky Mountains National Park.

Mules—The mule is an offspring of a male donkey and female horse. The mix creates an animal suitable in size and strength for difficult work. In the 1900s mules were used mostly on farms and as pack animals. However, technology has decreased the need for mules to do hard labor.

INTRODUCTION

Vocabulary

Use the prepared sentences to introduce the vocabulary words in context.

A mule and a mountain

Display the picture of a mule.

▶ Have you ever seen a mule?

   If you owned a mule, would you play with him or would he help you with work? How?

Share some of the background information about mules.

▶ Today we will begin reading a story about a boy named Johnny and his mule who live in the Great Smoky Mountains.

Show the picture of the Great Smoky Mountains.

Display the map of the United States and point out the Great Smoky Mountains.

Correlated Activities
- **Vocabulary Box, Activity 2: Study Buddies**
- **Creative Writing, Activity 1: Runaway Writings**
See "Classroom Management for Grouping" in the Appendix.

VOCABULARY

LESSON 33

*†The children had to bustle along in order to reach school on time. (p. 96)

†Peter was so upset that he stammered the words as he told the story. (p. 98)

*He decided to swap his toy car for his brother's giant cookie. (p. 98)

*†No matter how hard I pulled on the cow's rope, the balker would not move. (p. 98)

LESSON 34

†She is a jolly person who is always smiling and laughing. (p. 100)

†The coach looked on wretchedly as his team was losing. (p. 100)

†That plank of wood is just the size we need. (p. 101)

The dog sat down on his haunches and refused to move. (p. 102)

†She was grieved for a long time that her pet ran away. (p. 103)

LESSON 35

*†That flowering bush in the front yard looks like a rhododendron. (p. 104)

Tyler walked dolefully along with his head hung low and tears in his eyes. (p. 105)

*He was tolling the rabbit into the cage with a carrot. (p. 106)

Tea can be made from the roots of a sassafras tree. (p. 106)

*The farmer's field is not full of hay; it is sorghum. (p. 107)

COMPREHENSION

The student will

- Note elements of setting.
- Evaluate character responses.
- Predict outcomes.
- Draw inferences from picture interpretation and text.

Before silent reading: pages 96-99

Motivation

► What is special about Johnny and the place where he lives and goes to school?

What unusual tale does Johnny tell one day at school?

After silent reading

Overview discussion: pages 96-99

► [interpretive] What clues do you read and see that let you know this story takes place a long time ago? (walking a long distance over mountains to school, one room schoolhouse, clothing, hairstyles)

► [interpretive] How do you know that Johnny thinks it is important to be at school on time? (Possible answers: He gets up very early to walk the long distance to school; he is always in line and in his seat ready to go.) [BAT: 2b Promptness]

► [interpretive] Why are the teacher and schoolchildren worried about Johnny? (He has never been late before.)

[literal] What is Johnny's excuse for being late? (He bid five cents on a mule to get the bidding started at an auction, he ended up getting the mule, and it took him two hours to get to school because the mule balked.) [BAT: 2d Perseverance]

Ellis Credle   illustrated by Stephanie True

Johnny and

A Good Excuse

Away up in the Great Smoky Mountains there is a town called Horny Hollow. It is not a very large town, and the great mountains standing all around make it seem very small indeed. There are no more than twenty dwellings there, a courthouse, several stores, a church, and a schoolhouse.

To this little schoolhouse came all the children in the town and a little mountain boy named Johnny. Johnny lived far back in the hills, a long, long way from town.

He had to get up very early, when the cocks were crowing for the sunrise, to get to school on time. But in spite of the long walk over the mountains, he was never late for school.

The town children might bustle into the schoolyard as the last bell

96

[critical] Should Johnny's teacher have believed his excuse right away? Why or why not? (Answers will vary, but elicit that Johnny's dependability influences her belief.) [BAT: 2c Faithfulness]

► [interpretive] What does the phrase "the thought of his mule lay heavy on his mind" mean? (Johnny thinks of the mule all the time and is worried about what to do with it.)

His Mule

was ringing; they might catch the end of the line as it was marching into the building; they might even tiptoe fearfully into the room after classes had started—but never Johnny! He was always in his place as the line marched in and always in his proper seat when classes began. In the fall, in the winter, and in the spring, it was al- ways the same. Johnny was always on time.

But one day, toward the end of the school year, Johnny was late! The last bell rang—Johnny was not there! Nine o'clock came—and still no Johnny. Ten o'clock rolled around, half past ten, and not a sign of Johnny.

It was so very late now, the teacher and the children began to

Johnny and His Mule   97

**Follow-up discussion:
pages 96-97**

▶ [literal] Describe the town the schoolhouse is in. (possible answers: small; Great Smoky Mountains all around it; only twenty houses and a few other buildings)

▶ [literal] What time does Johnny get up in the morning? (when the cocks are crowing for the sunrise)

[appreciative] What would it be like to get up while it is still dark and walk to school over mountains every school day?

▶ [interpretive] How does the author compare the other schoolchildren to Johnny? (The other schoolchildren might be late sometimes, but Johnny is always on time.)

Read aloud the paragraph comparing the other schoolchildren to Johnny. Read to show how special Johnny is to always be on time.

▶ [critical] Does Johnny like school? Why do you think so? (Answers may vary.)

▶ [interpretive] How does the author let you know the teacher and children are surprised Johnny is late? (The author uses exclamation marks and describes the time passing by.)

▶ [interpretive] What is the "shuffle-shuffle" noise the teacher and children hear outside the door? (Johnny walking up to the door)

[interpretive] What does the phrase "Johnny creaked guiltily into the room" mean? (He enters cautiously, knowing he is not supposed to be late, and perhaps his footsteps make creaking noises on the wooden floor.)

[interpretive] Why does Johnny stammer and look like he might cry when he answers his teacher? (He may be embarrassed to be late and frustrated with his balking mule.)

Read aloud Miss Mary and Johnny's conversation. Use Miss Mary's concerned voice and Johnny's shaky voice.

▶ [critical] Was it wise for Johnny to stop at the auction on his way to school and bid on the mule? Why or why not? (Answers may vary.)

[literal] Why did Johnny bid on the mule? (He bid to get the sale started and thought someone would bid higher because mules cost a lot of money.) [BAT: 2b Helpfulness]

[critical] Do you think Johnny was happy to get the mule at first? Why or why not? (Accept any answer.)

wonder what had happened. Perhaps Johnny was sick, or perhaps he had fallen over the steep mountainside on the way to school. But a half hour later, at eleven o'clock, there was a shuffle-shuffle outside the door. It opened slowly, and Johnny creaked guiltily into the room.

"Why, Johnny!" cried the teacher. "It's eleven o'clock! Why are you so late?"

"I just couldn't help it, Miss Mary!" stammered Johnny, and he looked as though he might cry at any moment.

"But tell me, what happened?" urged Miss Mary.

"I got into town early this morning, Miss Mary," began Johnny, "in plenty of time for school, but I stopped for a minute in the town square to watch the auction."

Everybody knew about the auction. It was held every Friday, and the mountaineers called it "Trade Day." They came in from all the surrounding hills and ranges bringing anything they had on hand that they wanted to swap or sell. Handmade chairs, baskets,

98

turkeys, jackknives, horses, preserves, feather pillows, anything and everything went on sale in the town square on Friday.

"And so," continued Johnny, "while I was standing there, an old mule was put up to be sold. The auctioneer began shouting, 'What am I offered for this mule? What am I bid? What am I bid?'

"Nobody would begin the bidding, and so, just to get the sale started, I hollered out, 'I bid five cents!' I thought sure somebody would bid higher because mules cost a lot of money. But nobody did, and so they gave me the mule.

"And there I stood, Miss Mary, holding the mule by the halter. I didn't know what to do with him. About the only thing I could think of was to take him along to school with me. So I started toward the schoolhouse leading the mule.

"I soon found out why nobody wanted that mule. After we had gone about a block, he stopped stock still. I tried every way to get him to go along, but he wouldn't budge an inch. He was a balker! Lots of other people tried to make him go, but no sir! That mule wouldn't go until he felt like it. After a while, all by himself, he took a notion to start. He walked another block and then he balked again. Miss Mary, I tell you the truth, it took me two hours to get that critter four blocks to the schoolhouse! That's why I'm late, it really is!"

"Why Johnny!" exclaimed Miss Mary. "I never heard such a tale!"

"If you don't believe it, Miss Mary, just look out the window," replied Johnny.

The teacher gazed through the window and so did all the pupils. There, tied to a tree, was a mule. His head hung down and his large ears flopped sadly. There was no doubt about it, Johnny's tale was true.

Lessons began again and the day wore on. Johnny did not pay much attention to his lessons. The thought of his mule lay heavy on his mind. What could he do with him?

Johnny and His Mule 99

Follow-up discussion: page 99

▶ [literal] What is Miss Mary's reaction to Johnny's excuse? (She says she has never heard such a tale.)

[literal] What proof does Johnny have that he is telling the truth? (the mule tied to a tree outside)

Read aloud the paragraph describing the teacher and children looking out the window at the mule.

▶ [interpretive] Why does Johnny worry about the mule for the rest of the day? (He doesn't know what to do with it.) [BAT: 3c Emotional control]

Looking ahead

▶ What do you think Johnny will do with the mule?

Worktext Objectives

The student will

■ Recognize facts and details.
■ Infer unstated supporting details.

Comprehension:
Worktext page 39

COMPREHENSION

The student will

- Identify problems and solutions.
- Determine sequence of events.
- Interpret actions of characters.
- Recognize dialect as part of the setting.

 Use the prepared sentences to introduce vocabulary words in context.

Before silent reading: pages 100–103

Motivation

▶ How do the children and teacher help Johnny with the mule?

What does Miss Mary suggest to help cheer up Johnny?

After silent reading

Overview discussion: pages 100–103

▶ [literal] What solutions do Johnny and his friends try to get the mule going that do not work? (Johnny pulls the rope; Matthey and Nancy Belle help pull; all the children help pull; the teacher helps pull; Nancy Belle twists the mule's ear; they try pushing the mule with a plank.) [BAT: 2b Teamwork]

[literal] What solution finally makes the mule go? (holding out a piece of corn to the mule and walking along)

[interpretive] Why does corn make the mule move? (The mule follows food because he is hungry.)

▶ [critical] Why does the teacher walk home with Johnny and his mule? (Accept any answer, but elicit that she cares about Johnny and wants to help him get his mule home.) [BATs: 2b Helpfulness; 5a Love]

Budging the Balker

When the bell rang for closing time, all the children rushed into the schoolyard and gathered 'round the mule. They were in a jolly mood, laughing and joking and poking fun at Johnny and his animal.

"Such a sad looking critter! What are you going to do with him, Johnny?" asked his little friend Matthey.

Johnny did not feel very happy. "I don't know what to do with him," he said wretchedly. "It took me two hours to get him a few blocks to school; how long will it take me to get him home? I live five miles over the mountain. It will be black night and the owls a-hooting before I get him halfway there!"

Johnny leaned against the tree beside his mule and began to cry.

The children stopped laughing and looked solemnly at each other.

"Hold on there, Johnny, you never can tell about a balking mule," comforted Matthey. "He may be ready to go by now. Maybe he'll start right off!"

Johnny brightened. He untied the mule's rope and tried to lead him forward. But the mule was not ready to go, and he did not start right off. Johnny braced himself and pulled. But the mule was not in the notion.

"Give me a handhold, and I'll help you pull," said Matthey.

"I'll help too," said Nancy Belle. Both children threw their weight against the mule. But he did not budge.

"Make room for us. We'll all pull!" said Hetty and Hank. They grasped the mule's halter and hauled with all their might. But the mule only braced himself and stood in his tracks.

100

[interpretive] Why does the teacher suggest singing a song? (She does not want Johnny to worry and thinks singing will help him forget that his father might be angry about the mule.)

Follow-up discussion: page 100

▶ [critical] Are the children trying to be cruel when they joke and poke fun at Johnny and his mule? (Answers may vary, but elicit that the children probably do not fully understand Johnny's problem, but when they do, they stop joking and try to help.) [BAT: 5a Kindness]

Read aloud Johnny's sad words about his problem.

[interpretive] How do you know Matthey's words help Johnny stop crying? (because Johnny "brightened," or acted happier, after Matthey's words)

Read aloud Matthey's comforting words.

▶ [interpretive] What words describe the balking mule after each try to get the mule to go? (He "was not in the notion," "did not budge," and "braced himself and stood in his tracks.")

While the children were pulling and straining and puffing and blowing, the teacher came out of the schoolhouse. "Let me get a hold. I'll pull too!" she said. But one more made no difference to the mule. His mind was made up.

"My father once had a balking mule," piped up Nancy Belle, "and he used to get him to go by twisting his ear."

"Twisting his ear?" echoed Hezekiah. "Whoever heard of making a mule go by twisting his ear?"

"Well it's true," insisted the little girl. "That made him go."

"It wouldn't hurt to try it," said the teacher. "Go ahead.

Nancy Belle, you are the one who knows how. You twist his ear."

Nancy Belle grasped the long droopy ear and twisted.

The mule stood pat.

"Twist again! Twist harder!" said the children, and Nancy twisted, but it was no good. The mule did not care to move, and twisting his ear did not make him change his mind. He only rolled his eyes and wiggled his ear to make sure it was all in a piece.

"My uncle once had a balking mule," offered Hetty, "and he used to get behind him with a plank and push him."

"That's right," added Hank. "They used to push the mule a

Johnny and His Mule 101

Follow-up discussion: page 101

▶ [literal] What solution does Nancy Belle suggest? (twisting the mule's ear)

Read aloud the paragraph describing the mule's response when Nancy Belle twists his ear. As you read, show the children's hope that twisting will work and their frustration when the mule does not move.

[interpretive] What does the sentence "The mule stood pat" mean? (It stood still and didn't move.)

[appreciative] Have you ever tried to get an animal to do something, but the animal was stubborn like this mule? What solutions did you try?

Follow-up discussion: page 102

▶ [interpretive] How do you know the children and Miss Mary think the plank idea is a good one? (Miss Mary says, "Maybe that's just what this mule needs," and the children hustle to find a plank.)

[interpretive] How do you know the children work hard to move the mule with the plank? (They huff and puff, and they have to stop for breath.)

[interpretive] Does the plank solve the problem? How do you know? (No; the mule stands pat, or still.)

[literal] When the plank does not work, what is Nancy Belle's next suggestion? (The mule might be hungry and follow a piece of corn held in front of him.)

[interpretive] How does the author let you know that the children can hardly wait to see if the corn idea will work? (They hold their breath.)

Read aloud the last paragraph to show the children's hope that the plan will work and their excitement when the plan does work.

few steps forward, and after that he would go all by himself."

"Maybe that's just what this mule needs," said Miss Mary. "Where can we find a plank?"

The children hustled around, and underneath the edge of the schoolhouse they found a long plank. They put it behind the mule's haunches and pushed. They huffed and puffed, but the mule stood pat! They stopped for breath.

"Maybe the mule's hungry," spoke up Nancy Belle. "If we got a

piece of corn and held it out to him, maybe he'd follow after it."

Johnny ran to the nearest house and brought back an ear of corn. He held it out to the mule. Yes, the mule was hungry. He stretched his neck toward the corn.

The children held their breath. The mule took one step forward. Johnny backed away, holding the corn just out of reach. The mule took another step forward, then another, and another. A loud shout rose from the children.

102

"Hurrah! Hurrah! He's going!" they yelled.

The teacher held the mule's halter while Johnny danced ahead with the corn. Through the town they went, clip-clop, clip-clop. Over the mountain trail they started as fast as they could go. But still Johnny did not seem very happy.

"A balking mule is no good to anybody," he grieved. "I'm afraid my Pappy will be cross when he sees this critter. Like as not he'll give me a good licking."

"No use borrowing trouble," said the teacher. "Let's sing a song and forget all about the mule."

Johnny struck up an old mountain song, and along they went singing.

Moon's a-rising on Thunder-head Mountain,
Heigh! Heigh! Step and go lightly!
Hound dog's a-baying and we're a-going hunting,
Heigh! Heigh! Step and go lightly!

Chased a coon into a gum tree,
Heigh! Heigh! Step and go lightly!
Shoot at the coon and hit a froggie,
Heigh! Heigh! Step and go lightly!

Thought I had a possum in a tree there,
Heigh! Heigh! Step and go lightly!
Shook that tree and down came a he-bear!
Heigh! Heigh! Step and go lightly!

Mr. Bear, please don't ketch me, sir!
Heigh! Heigh! Step and go lightly!
Ketch that fellow behind the tree, sir!
Heigh! Heigh! Step and go lightly!

Moon's going down, my song is ended,
Heigh! Heigh! Step and go lightly!
Mighty good thing, for I'm pretty nigh winded!
Heigh! Heigh! Step and go lightly!

Johnny and His Mule   103

Worktext Objectives

The student will

- Identify facts and details.
- Suggest solutions to problem situations.

Comprehension:
Worktext page 40

Direct the students to read the story taken from Numbers 22 on the worktext page and answer the questions.

Comprehension:
Worktext page 41

Ask a student to read the verse at the top of the page.

▶ When do you start being responsible for your actions? (as a child)

▶ What guides you in making right decisions? (Answers will vary but should include following biblical principles.)

Tell the students to read each paragraph and write what they would do if faced with each problem.

Discuss the students' answers as time allows.

Follow-up discussion: page 103

▶ [literal] How do Johnny and the teacher lead the mule towards Johnny's home? (The teacher holds the mule's halter, and Johnny holds the corn in front of the mule. They go through the town and over the mountain trail.)

[critical] Could Johnny take the mule home without someone else's help? Why or why not? (Answers may vary but should express that it would be more difficult to control the mule alone.)

▶ Read aloud Johnny's reason for not being happy even though the mule is moving now.

[interpretive] What does Johnny mean by "a good licking"? (Explain that in the story's setting this phrase means a spanking.)

Read aloud the teacher's response to Johnny's words.

[interpretive] What does the teacher mean by "No use borrowing trouble"? (Johnny does not know how his father will react to the mule, so he should not worry.) [BATs: 3c Emotional control; 7d Contentment]

[interpretive] Does Johnny take the teacher's advice? How do you know? (Yes; he starts singing a mountain song.)

[appreciative] Do you ever sing to make yourself happy when you are sad?

▶ [critical] Would Johnny sing that song and would the characters talk the way they do if they lived today in a big city? Why or why not? (No; answers may vary but should express that the song and expressions the characters use sound like they would be used in a little mountain town a long time ago.)

Looking ahead

▶ Will the mule be of any use to Johnny's pappy?

COMPREHENSION

The student will

- Evaluate emotional responses of characters.
- Develop an awareness of imagery.
- Develop an awareness of mood.
- Identify cause-and-effect relationships.

 Use the prepared sentences to introduce vocabulary words in context.

Before silent reading: pages 104-5

Motivation

▶ How does Aunt Betsy's reaction to the mule make Johnny feel?

After silent reading

Overview discussion: pages 104-5

▶ [literal] On the way home, why does Johnny decide Pappy might like to have the mule? (Pappy needs an animal to help him plow potatoes.)

▶ [interpretive] Why does the teacher start talking about the beautiful mountains? (Johnny starts worrying about the balking mule again, and she is trying to keep him from worrying.)

[literal] The teacher's idea to keep Johnny from worrying works until what happens? (It works until they talk with Aunt Betsy and she says, "I don't know what you'll do with a balker.")

▶ [interpretive] Why do Aunt Betsy's words upset Johnny? (He thinks his father will feel the same way about the mule.)

[critical] Should Johnny feel dismayed, or upset, because of Aunt Betsy's words? Why or why not? (Answers may vary, but elicit that Johnny does not know how his pappy will react.)

Cause for Concern

After that Johnny felt better. "You never can tell," he said cheerfully, "maybe Pappy'll be pleased to have a mule. He needs some kind of critter to help him plow his potatoes. He has to do it now all by himself with an old hand plow."

"Why yes, of course," agreed the teacher. "It's likely he'll be glad to get him."

"If only he wasn't a balker," said Johnny, wrinkling his forehead again. "Hardly anybody would want a balker."

"Oh don't think about it," the teacher tried to cheer him up. "It's too beautiful on the mountains to get a head full of worry."

"Yes, it is pretty on the mountains." Johnny looked all around and forgot to worry about the mule. The air was full of the nice smell of pine and balsam and the pink rhododendron was blooming everywhere.

But the mule did not care for anything except the ear of corn that was always just out of reach. He kept his eyes upon it and went clop-clopping along.

104

[interpretive] Why does Johnny think he will get a licking for sure? (He thinks the mule will eat so much they will lose their home.)

Follow-up discussion: page 104

▶ [interpretive] How does Miss Mary feel about the place where Johnny lives? (She thinks it is beautiful.)

Read aloud the paragraph describing the mountains.

[appreciative] Have you ever seen a beautiful place that made you feel happy? Why did the place make you feel happy? (Accept any answer, but elicit that the Lord made us able to appreciate His beautiful creation.)

Johnny and the teacher felt cheerful until they came opposite Aunt Betsy's house.

Aunt Betsy was sitting on the porch busily spinning some yarn to weave into a bedspread.

"My me! What have you got there?" she cried when she saw Johnny and the teacher and the mule.

"It's a mule," Johnny replied. "I bought him at the auction for five cents."

"Five cents!" Aunt Betsy threw back her hands and laughed. Then she grew sober. "But he's not a balker, is he? I never heard of a mule's going that cheap unless he was a balker. "

"Yes'm," Johnny admitted uneasily. "He's a balker, all right."

"Oh, my." Aunt Betsy shook her head dolefully. "I don't know what you'll do with a balker."

After that there was hardly anything the teacher could say to comfort Johnny.

On up the trail trudged Johnny, feeling more dismay every minute. "The worst of it is: a mule has got a terrible appetite," he worried. "Why, that old mule could probably eat us out of house and home in no time. Miss Mary, I'm going to get that licking sure as anything. I wish I didn't have to go home at all."

Johnny and His Mule 105

Follow-up discussion: page 105

▶ [critical] Why does Aunt Betsy laugh when Johnny tells her he bought the mule for five cents? (Answers may vary, but elicit that she could be excited that Johnny has made quite a deal.)

Read aloud the paragraph showing Aunt Betsy's change from a happy to a sober, or serious, attitude.

[interpretive] Does Johnny want to answer Aunt Betsy's question? How do you know? (No; he is uneasy.)

[critical] Why does Aunt Betsy shake her head dolefully when she says, "I don't know what you'll do with a balker"? (Answers may vary, but elicit that she feels sorry for Johnny.)

[appreciative] If you were Aunt Betsy, what would you say to Johnny?

Read aloud the last paragraph, showing Johnny's feeling of dismay after Aunt Betsy's words.

Before silent reading: pages 106-7

Motivation

▶ How do Mammy's and Pappy's reactions to the mule make Johnny feel?

What does Pappy decide to do with the mule?

After silent reading

Overview discussion: pages 106-7

▶ [interpretive] What does Mammy think of the mule at first? (She doesn't like the mule because she doesn't know what to do with a balker.)

[interpretive] What does Pappy think about the mule at first? (You cannot tell what he is thinking because he doesn't say anything.)

[interpretive] How does Pappy's first reaction to the mule make Johnny feel? How do you know? (Uneasy; he worries about whether his pappy is angry about the mule, so he cannot enjoy supper, the fire, or the music.)

▶ [literal] What happens when Johnny gets up enough courage to talk to Pappy about the mule? (Johnny and the teacher are surprised that Pappy is not angry and knows a trick to make the balking mule work hard.)

[literal] In the morning, what does Johnny find out is Pappy's trick to get the mule to work hard? (The mule, hooked to the plow, is following an ear of corn dangling on a stick in front of his nose, thus pulling the plow.)

[interpretive] What does Johnny's pappy say while he is plowing that probably makes Johnny very happy? ("He's a fine, strong mule!" and "I'm much obliged to you!")

But the mule took them there in a hurry.

Mammy and Pappy were waiting in front of the cabin, looking down the road, wondering what kept Johnny so long. When they saw him tolling the mule along, and the teacher holding the rope, their eyes popped open.

"What have you got there?" cried Mammy, laughing.

"It's a mule," replied Johnny nervously. "I bought him at the auction for five cents."

"For five cents! Then there must be something wrong with him," said Mammy.

"Yes'm there is—a little something wrong. He's a balker, I reckon."

"A balking mule!" exclaimed Mammy. "Whatever could we do with a balking mule?"

"I-I don't know ma'am," exclaimed Johnny, glancing uneasily at Pappy.

Pappy did not say anything at all. He just rubbed his chin and looked thoughtfully at the mule.

The sun was setting by this time. It was much too late for the teacher to return to town. She de-

106

cided to spend the night with Johnny and his parents.

Mammy set a chicken on to stew in a big iron pot and later on they had supper, chicken and dumplings, hot biscuits, and nice cold buttermilk. For dessert, there was honey from their own beehive and a pot full of sassafras tea.

It was a fine supper, but Johnny could not enjoy it. What was his Pappy thinking about that old balking mule? What was he going to do with him?

After the meal, everyone sat around the fire, which leaped brightly in the old stone fireplace. Pappy got out his fiddle and played some merry jigs. Mammy sang some old mountain ballads for the teacher.

Johnny sat in the chimney corner. He did not feel very happy because he kept wondering if his Pappy felt angry about the mule. At last he screwed up his courage and asked him.

"Pappy," he said timidly. "That balking mule is going to be sort of a nuisance, I reckon."

"Nuisance!" cried Pappy. "Why, I know how to make that

Follow-up discussion: page 106

▶ [interpretive] When Mammy and Pappy see Johnny coming, the story says that "their eyes popped open." What does that phrase mean? (They are surprised.)

Read aloud the dialogue between Mammy and Johnny. Read to show Mammy's surprise and Johnny's nervousness.

[critical] Why doesn't Pappy say anything? (Answers may vary, but elicit that he is probably thinking of a plan for the mule.)

▶ [interpretive] Later in the evening, do they sit around a small, dim fire? How do you know? (No; the story says that the fire "leaped brightly.")

[appreciative] Would you like being in the room with Johnny's family and his teacher at this time? Why?

▶ [interpretive] How does Johnny get Pappy to say something about the mule? (Johnny makes a comment that the mule is going to be a nuisance, and Pappy responds to his comment.)

old mule do all my plowing and hauling and turning of my sorghum mill!" He winked at Miss Mary. "Yes siree! I know a little trick that will make a balking mule work harder than a hornet!"

"What's that?" cried Johnny and Miss Mary in a breath.

"Wait until the morning," laughed Pappy. "Look out the window when you first wake up and you'll find out!"

The teacher went to bed in the spare room, and Johnny climbed the ladder to his little room in the loft.

In the morning, he woke up early and looked out the window. There, pulling a plow briskly through the potato patch, was the balking mule. Hanging on to the handles of the plow was Pappy. He looked up and caught sight of Johnny.

"He's a fine, strong mule!" cried Pappy. "I'm much obliged to you!"

But the mule did not look up, nor to the right, nor to the left. He was gazing greedily straight ahead at the ear of corn that dangled on the end of a stick in front of his nose.

Johnny and His Mule   107

Follow-up discussion: page 107

▶ [interpretive] When Johnny wakes up early in the morning, how do you think he feels when he looks out the window and sees the mule plowing? (happy)

Allow a student to demonstrate Johnny's reaction as he looks out the window.

▶ [interpretive] How does Pappy think of the trick to make the mule plow? (Answers may vary, but he probably saw that the mule would follow the corn when Johnny and the teacher arrived, so he thought of dangling an ear of corn in front of the mule to make it plow.)

[critical] How do you think Johnny feels about his mule now? (Answers may vary, but he probably is happy.)

Read aloud what Pappy says to Johnny as Johnny looks out the window.

The student will

■ Determine cause-and-effect relationships.

■ Recall facts and details.

■ Infer unstated supporting details.

COMPREHENSION
Cause-and-effect relationships

Give several examples of cause and effect that may have occurred in your classroom in the last few days (e.g., cause—it started raining during recess; effect—the students had to come inside).

Write the words *cause* and *effect* for display.

▶ Most stories give the reader an effect or result, that is, something that has happened, and leave the reader to figure out the cause or reason for that result.

▶ In "Johnny and His Mule" the children and Miss Mary try to help Johnny get his mule to move. This is the effect, the event or happening. What was the cause? Why did they help Johnny? (Johnny was crying and worried about how to get the balking mule home. The children felt sorry for him and tried to help.)

Call on students to name something that has happened to them—the effect—and to tell why it happened—the cause (e.g., they were late for school because their car broke down).

Write the following sentence for display: *The children tried to help Johnny because he was crying and worried about how to get his balking mule home.*

Read the sentence to the students.

▶ You can test whether you have found the correct cause and effect by making a sentence like the one displayed. By giving the effect, saying the word *because*, and then giving the cause, the sentence and the relationship between the cause and the effect will make sense.

Allow the students to give their cause-and-effect examples as sentences like the one displayed as time permits.

Comprehension: Worktext pages 42-43

Encourage students to check their answers by making a sentence using the word *because* to connect the effect with the cause.

Comprehension: Worktext page 44

Remind students to use complete sentences when writing the answers.

Materials

- Various pictures of people from history (British settlers, mountain people, slaves, lumberjacks, cowboys, etc.)
- Vocabulary sentences prepared for display

INTRODUCTION

Favorite folksongs

Display pictures.

▶ Who are these people?

▶ These people have given us something special—the songs they sang.

▶ Songs that have been passed down from generation to generation are called folksongs. Songs like "Row, Row, Row Your Boat" and "Are You Sleeping?" are folksongs.

▶ What are the names of other folksongs you know?

▶ Today, as you read about American folksongs, try to find out who made up your favorite folksongs.

Lesson	Reader pages	Worktext pages
36	108-11	45-46

VOCABULARY

LESSON 36

Reading the story of Jesus' birth is a Christmas tradition at our house. (p. 108)

†Four cans of soup and two winter coats were our contributions for the poor families. (p. 108)

†It was easy to march slow and then fast to the rhythmic song. (p. 109)

Correlated Activities

- **Recreational Reading Activity 5: Grab It, Read It, Pass It**
- **Connections, Activity 2: Dreamy Domains**

See "Classroom Management for Grouping" in the Appendix.

COMPREHENSION

Objectives

The student will

- Recognize folksongs as part of American literature heritage.
- Associate folksongs with cultural and regional groups.
- Interpret the song "Were You There?"

Before silent reading: pages 108-10

Motivation

▶ Which groups of people contributed to American folksongs?

Why were folksongs created?

After silent reading

Overview discussion: pages 108-10

▶ [interpretive] What does the word *folk* in *folksongs* mean? (common people, not nobility)

[literal] What did folk sing about years ago? (possible answers: everyday things, knights, holidays, romance, death, silly things, work, the Bible, crops, cowboys)

▶ [literal] How did the colonists create the first American folksongs? (by changing British folksong words to fit the new people and events)

[literal] What did people from other countries add to American folksongs? (Countries like Ireland and France brought melodies, and slaves brought a sadder and more tender type of music and spirituals.)

▶ [critical] Why do you think nobody wrote down the tunes or words to these folksongs? (Answers may vary, but elicit that many common people did not know how to read and write, and the songs were traditionally passed down orally.)

LITERATURE LESSON:

American Folksongs

illustrated by Stephanie True

On his way home with his balking mule, Johnny sang a song with his teacher to cheer himself up. Such songs as Johnny's "Heigh! Heigh! Step and Go Lightly" are called folksongs. The tradition of folksongs has been passed down to us from the beginning of American history.

• The History of Folksongs

British common folk who settled in the New World liked to sing the songs from their homeland to cheer themselves up. They sang about knights and nobles, British holidays, and British traditions. But as the colonists began to feel more and more at home in America, they changed the words of their songs to fit new people and new events. Their songs became American in nature instead of British. Thus, American folksongs were born.

Settlers from other countries made their contributions to American folksongs. Melodies from countries like Ireland and France joined with the English tunes. At first, American folksongs were mostly ballads—songs that told stories. They were usually about a broken romance or a tragic death. But as the people from different countries began to live and work together, they made up many songs that told other stories. Some songs, like the one Johnny sang, were silly and didn't mean anything important.

The mountain people developed songs with simple tunes and easy words, like "Go Tell Aunt

108

[critical] Why would passing down a folksong orally and not writing it down cause the folksong to change throughout America? (Elicit that people would change the words to fit their everyday life, and everyday life was different in different parts of the country.)

Follow-up discussion: page 108

▶ [literal] Why did the colonists sing folksongs? (to cheer themselves up)

[critical] Why did the colonists need to be cheered up? (Accept any answer, but elicit that many of them were homesick and poor, and their days were filled with hard labor.)

▶ [literal] At first, what kind of song were most American folksongs? (ballads—songs that told stories)

Read aloud the sentences that tell about the types of stories the songs told.

[critical] Why would people make up silly songs like Johnny's? (Answers may vary, but elicit that silly songs are fun to sing.)

▶ [literal] What type of songs did the mountain people develop? (songs with simple tunes and easy words)

Rhody." This song tells a story, but it leaves out most of the details. It also includes a catchy, rhythmic tune and lines that are repeated often.

When slaves came to America, folksongs changed a little more. Slavery songs added much sadness and tenderness to American folk music. The slaves sang about everything in their lives: the land, the weather, their hard work, even the tools that they used. They sang "Jump Down, Turn Around, Pick a Bale of Cotton" to keep in time with the backbreaking work they had to do.

The slaves, of course, were the ones who developed the Negro spiritual. This type of song became a part of American folk music too. Some Negro spirituals are not accurate about the Bible or about God. Because most slaves could not read, they made some mistakes. The song "Michael, Row the Boat Ashore" does not have a spiritual message, but many slaves thought it did.

Many spirituals, however, are a testimony of the faith and cheerfulness of black Christians in early America. They were locked into slavery on earth, but they were spiritually free by the blood of Christ.

Literature Lesson: American Folksongs   109

Follow-up discussion: page 109

▶ [interpretive] Why were the mountain songs easy to remember? (The songs had lines that were repeated.)

▶ [critical] How would singing a song help slaves with their work? (Answers may vary, but elicit that the slaves would do certain motions to the rhythm of the song and that singing helped them forget the hard labor.)

[literal] What did the slaves sing about? (everything in their lives—the land, the weather, their hard work, the Bible, even the tools that they used)

▶ [critical] Why would the inability of most slaves to read affect the accuracy of the Negro spirituals? (Accept any answer, but point out that details could not be checked in the Bible if the slaves could not read it.)

Read aloud the paragraph telling about the importance of the Negro spirituals.

[literal] What kind of testimony did the slaves give through their spiritual folksongs? (Faith and cheerfulness; they were locked into slavery on earth but spiritually free by the blood of Christ.) [BATs: 1a Understanding Jesus Christ; 1b Repentance and faith; 2f Cheerfulness]

[interpretive] What does "free by the blood of Christ" mean? (The slaves believed that Christ had saved them, that they were free from sin, and that they were going to heaven.)

[appreciative] Do you give a testimony through the music that you sing? How do you know?

Follow-up discussion: page 110

▶ [interpretive] How are Southern folk-songs different from Western folk-songs? (Southern folksongs tell about farms, crops, and hunting; Western songs are about cowboys, cattle-drives, Indian attacks, and buffalo herds.)

Read aloud the sentences that tell why differences occurred in folk-songs.

▶ [literal] Is the source of folk music different today? Why or why not? (No; it is still the music of everyday people doing everyday things.)

[critical] Why is the tradition of passing down folksongs still continued today? (Answers may vary, but discuss that folksongs are part of American literature heritage now.)

[appreciative] What is your favorite type of folksong?

• **Differences in Folksongs**

American folk music differs throughout the country. The lumberjacks in Oregon sang songs different from those sung by the farmers in Georgia and South Carolina. This difference occurred because folksongs were passed down only orally. Nobody wrote down the tunes or the words. The songs were not sold to be recorded or to be printed in music books. Only the common people sang them.

Because the common people did not travel far, their music did not change a great deal. Southern folksongs tend to tell about life on the farms, the crops, and perhaps hunting. Folksongs from the West often tell about cowboys, cattle-drives, Indian attacks, and buffalo herds. But the source of folk music has not changed. It is still the music of everyday people doing everyday things.

110

Were You There?

Freely

Spiritual

1. Were you there when they cru-ci-fied my Lord? Were you there when they cru-ci-fied my Lord? Oh!_____ Some-times it caus-es me to trem-ble, trem-ble, trem-ble. Were you there when they cru-ci-fied my Lord?

2. Were you there when they laid Him in the tomb?
Were you there when they laid Him in the tomb?
Oh! Sometimes it causes me to tremble.
Were you there when they laid Him in the tomb?

3. Were you there when He rose up from the grave?
Were you there when He rose up from the grave?
Oh! Sometimes I feel like shouting glory!
Were you there when He rose up from the grave?

Literature Lesson: American Folksongs   111

Before silent reading: page 111

Motivation

Call attention to the word *Spiritual* in the top right-hand corner of the music.

▶ What does this spiritual tell about?

After silent reading

Overview discussion: page 111

▶ [interpretive] What does the song tell about? (how a person feels about the death, burial, and resurrection of Christ) [BAT: 1a Understanding Jesus Christ]

[critical] Does the songwriter really want an answer to his questions? (no) Why not? (He wants the reader or listener to think about Christ's death, burial, and resurrection.)

[critical] How does the songwriter feel about the death, burial, and resurrection of Christ? (Answers may vary, but the songwriter probably has feelings of sadness, awe, thankfulness, and joy.) [BAT: 7c Thankfulness to God]

Read aloud or sing together "Were You There?" showing how the songwriter feels.

Worktext Objectives

The student will

■ Identify facts and details.
■ Relate types of folksongs to specific groups of people.

Comprehension: Worktext page 45

Background information—It has never been proven whether John Henry really existed, or if this contest ever took place. John Henry worked for the railroad company, driving long spikes into the ground with a heavy sledge-hammer to make holes for explosives.

These explosives would blast away sections of mountains to create tunnels and clear the way for laying track.

Early steam drills were much like the jackhammers used by road construction workers today. Using steam as their source of energy, some were mounted on three legs, while others were attached to the front of their steam-driven engines. Steam drills are still used today for boring holes into rock with more efficiency than men can do with hammers.

Shaker is another name for a supervisor. Share some of the background information as you read the folksong together. Allow the students to complete the sentences independently.

Comprehension: Worktext page 46

Remind the students that the styles and themes of folksongs varied according to the group of people composing and singing them. Before the students complete the page, read the three groups of people given as answer choices and review what each group was like and what they sang about.

SOMETHING EXTRA

Write About It: Fourth grade folksong

Instruct the student to pick a familiar folksong and write new words to go with the tune. Tell the student to use everyday school occurrences for the words. Sing the new song for fun.

Sing It: Working to music

Lead the students in singing the song "Jump Down, Turn Around, Pick a Bale of Cotton" or another rhythmic song while they are doing some kind of work together, such as cleaning up the room or moving desks. Remind the students to work and move with the rhythm of the tune.

David signs his name, giving his word of honor that he has read the book of John in the Bible. After all, he has to go on the camping trip with Mr. Hines and the other guys. What would they do if they knew the truth?

Lesson	Reader pages	Worktext pages
37	112-15	47-48
38	116-20	49-50

Materials
- A name book with meanings
- Vocabulary sentences prepared for display

Background information
Book of John—The apostle John, called "the disciple whom Jesus loved," was guided by the Holy Spirit to write this Gospel. John presents Jesus and the good news of salvation as he advises Christians to abide in the true faith (John 20:30-31).

INTRODUCTION
Vocabulary
Use the prepared sentences to introduce the vocabulary words in context.

A signature
Using the name book, read some names and their meanings. Explain that a person's name generally stays with him all of his life. Discuss things that a person signs his name to and why his signature is needed on those items. Some examples are listed below.

- Checks—By signing a check to be cashed, a person is saying he is the person to whom the check is written. When writing a check to another person, he is saying that the amount on the check is the amount to be paid and is available in the bank account for the person whose name is on the check.

- Assignments, tests, quizzes—By signing his name, a student is saying that this is his work alone.

VOCABULARY
LESSON 37

†His good batting and running made him eligible for the baseball team. (p. 112)

*†He hesitated for a moment before going inside. (p. 115)

†With heavy feet, he trudged off to his room. (p. 115)

LESSON 38

†The alarm in our house is a safeguard against robbers. (p. 117)

The splattered paint dappled the carpet. (p. 117)

†He had a lot of nerve to do such a dangerous stunt. (p. 119)

They knew the tearful boy was truly contrite about his sin. (p. 120)

†The father's hug showed he did not despise his disobedient son. (p. 120)

Correlated Activities
- **Word Work, Activity 2: Blooper Blurbs**
- **Spelling Practice, Activity 5: Pen-a-Pyramid**

See "Classroom Management for Grouping" in the Appendix.

COMPREHENSION

The student will

■ Interpret the significance of the story title.

■ Interpret the motives of characters.

■ Compare a character's actions with his personal convictions.

Before silent reading: pages 112-15

Motivation

▶ Why is a person's name or "word" so important?

What do you think the title "Word of Honor" refers to in the story?

After silent reading

Overview discussion: pages 112-15

▶ [critical] Why do you think David's teacher wants him to read the book of John? (Answers may vary, but discuss the fact that the book of John is easy to understand and clearly presents the gospel of Jesus Christ.)

[appreciative] Have you ever read the book of John?

▶ [interpretive] Why does David keep making excuses for not reading the book of John? (He allows other things to come before his reading; he would rather do other things than read God's Word.) [BAT: 2e Initiative]

▶ [critical] Why do you think a parent needed to sign the permission form as well as the boy? (Accept any answer, but elicit that by having a parent also sign the form, it would help the boy to be more honest and diligent about his reading.)

[appreciative] Have you ever lied and then felt the way David did?

Word of Honor

Eileen Berry
illustrated by Del Thompson

The Signature

When I grow up, I'm going to be just like Mr. Hines, David thought. He watched his Sunday school teacher handing out the permission slips. Mr. Hines attended a faraway college where he was training to be a pastor, so he was never home during the school year. But this summer, he had taught David's fourth-grade boys' Sunday school class. And now, just before the new school year started, he was taking them all on an overnight hike. No parents, no brothers or sisters—just Mr. Hines and the guys.

112

"Now remember, guys." Mr. Hines leaned against the edge of the desk and folded his arms. "It's not just your parents' signature that I need. For you to be eligible for this hike, you have to sign the top line on the form—the line that says you've read the book of John all the way through. Be honest now. Your signature on that line is your word of honor. You've had all summer to read, so I hope you'll be able to sign. I'll need these forms back next week."

Follow-up discussion: page 112

▶ [critical] Why does David admire his Sunday school teacher, Mr. Hines? (Accept any answer.)

▶ [literal] What is Mr. Hines planning for the boys in his Sunday school class? (an overnight hike)

[literal] What must David do if he wants to go on the hike? (He must read the entire book of John and sign a form saying he has done so.) [BAT: 6a Bible study]

[literal] What will David's signature on the paper indicate? (his word of honor that he has read the book of John)

[interpretive] What does "word of honor" mean? (It is a pledge that one is telling the truth.)

Read aloud Mr. Hines's discussion of the signature being the word of honor.

The bell rang and Mr. Hines lifted his hand in a wave. "See you next time."

David stuffed the permission form into his Bible and raced for the door. Mr. Hines caught up with him in three long strides and clapped a friendly hand on his shoulder. "Hey, David," he said. "How's your reading in John coming?"

David gave a slight shrug. He tried to match his steps to Mr. Hines's. "I've still got a ways to go," he said, glancing up.

Mr. Hines's eyes were kind. "Keep plugging," he said. "You'll make it."

David thought about the book of John after supper the next day. He even picked up his Bible and opened it to where his bookmark was in the fifth chapter. But then Aaron called and asked him to come over and play catch. *I'll read tomorrow,* he thought.

Tuesday night his mother asked him to help her in the garden. Wednesday night was church. He spent all day Thursday playing with his brother Ben in their tree fort. And on Friday evening he forgot all about the book of John and read a library book.

Follow-up discussion: page 113

► [critical] Why do you think David stuffs the permission form into his Bible and races for the door? (Possible answer: He knows he has not completed the reading yet and does not want to think about it now.) [BAT: 2c Responsibility]

► [literal] What does Mr. Hines ask David? (how his reading of the book of John is coming)

[interpretive] How does Mr. Hines respond to David's answer that he still has a ways to go in his reading? (He tries to encourage David.) [BAT: 2d Perseverance]

► [literal] How does David use his time during the week? (On Monday he thinks about Bible reading but plays catch instead; on Tuesday he helps Mother in the garden; on Wednesday he goes to church; on Thursday he plays in his tree fort; on Friday he reads a library book.) [BAT: 2e Diligence]

[interpretive] How many chapters has David already read? (four)

Read aloud the excuse David gives himself when his friend calls.

▶ [literal] What does David tell his mother about his reading when he asks her to sign his form? (that he has almost finished it) [BAT: 4c Honesty]

[critical] Why do you think David is not honest? (Accept any answer.)

[appreciative] What is it called when someone is not honest? (Elicit that anything that is not the complete truth is dishonesty and is a sin.) [BAT: 4c Honesty]

▶ [literal] How does David plan to finish his Bible reading? (by reading seventeen chapters in bed on Saturday night)

[critical] How could David have planned better to finish his reading? (Accept any answer, but elicit that if he had set daily goals he would have been able to accomplish his goal and would not be left with seventeen chapters to read the day before the deadline.) [BATs: 2d Goal setting; 2e Diligence]

[literal] What is David's last thought about his Bible reading before he falls asleep? ("Maybe tomorrow")

On Saturday evening, he took his permission slip to his mother. "Mom, will you sign this? It's for the hike," he said.

Mom set her knife down by the heap of potato peelings and wiped her hands. She studied the form for a moment. "Have you read the book of John yet?" she asked. "You haven't signed on the top line."

David shoved his hands deeper into his pockets. "Almost," he said. "I'll sign it as soon as I'm done."

Mom signed her name in tall, even lettering on the bottom line. "Better finish up that reading tonight," she said. "Mr. Hines wants these forms back tomorrow, doesn't he?"

"Yes."

David brushed his teeth and got ready for bed. Then he switched on his bedside lamp and sat up against his pillows with his Bible. *Seventeen chapters to read,* he thought. *Maybe they won't take long.*

David had gotten only to chapter seven when his head sank low onto his chest. His eyelids felt like lead weights pressing down. *Maybe tomorrow,* he thought, halfway between daydreams and sleep.

114

When David awoke the next morning, his lamp had been turned off and his Bible lay open on the bedside table. "John chapter seven," he mumbled sleepily. "There's no way I can make it to the end of the book before Sunday school."

David pulled the permission slip out of his Bible and stared at it for a few moments. He picked up a pen and hesitated. Mr. Hines's voice echoed inside his head. "Your signature on that line is your word of honor."

David glanced out the window. He thought about the new backpack his father had bought him earlier in the summer. If he didn't go on the hike, when would he ever use it? He took a deep breath, trying to ignore the ham-mering of his heart. Then he signed his name on the line.

David ate very little of his pancakes for breakfast. Dad looked at his plate with a raised eyebrow when David stood to leave the table. "You ate hardly enough to keep a bird alive," he said. "Feeling all right?"

David nodded, studying the pattern in the rug.

Mom smiled. "He was up late last night finishing his Bible reading," she said. "Did you get it all done, David?"

David waited only a second before answering. "Yes," he said without looking up.

"Good job," said Dad. David could feel Mom's eyes still watching him as he trudged off to his room.

Follow-up discussion: page 115

▶ [interpretive] Why does David hesitate before signing his name on the permission form and before lying to his father? (because he knows he is sinning but he wants to go on the overnight hike with his Sunday school class) [BAT: 4c Honesty]

[interpretive] Why is David's heart hammering? (because he knows that what he is doing is sin) [BAT: 6d Clear conscience]

Read aloud Dad's description of how David ate his breakfast.

[critical] How do you think David feels when Dad says, "Good job" to him about reading the book of John? (Accept any answer, but elicit that he feels very guilty.) [BAT: 4c Honesty]

Looking ahead

▶ If David goes on the camping trip, do you think he will enjoy himself?

Will someone find out that David has lied?

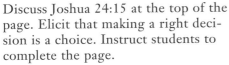

Worktext Objectives

The student will

■ Evaluate character responses and choices.

■ Note how character actions reveal character traits.

Comprehension: Worktext page 47

Discuss Joshua 24:15 at the top of the page. Elicit that making a right decision is a choice. Instruct students to complete the page.

Comprehension: Worktext page 48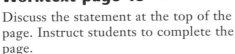

Discuss the statement at the top of the page. Instruct students to complete the page.

Objectives

COMPREHENSION

The student will

- Recognize character growth and change.
- Relate story content to personal experience.
- Evaluate a character's response.
- Identify with a character.
- Relate story content to biblical truth: it is always important to tell the truth.

 Use the prepared sentences to introduce the vocabulary words in context.

Before silent reading: pages 116-20

Motivation

▶ Do you think David will enjoy the overnight camping trip?

What makes a difference in David's attitude toward sin?

After silent reading

Overview discussion: pages 116-20

▶ [interpretive] Why does David feel guilty around Mr. Hines? (because he knows that what he has done is sin)

[literal] What object is a rebuke to David and to all who have sinned? (God's Word, the Bible) [BAT: 8b Faith in the power of the Word of God]

[interpretive] What do you think God uses to speak to David? (the words of Mr. Hines)

[critical] Does David finally acknowledge his sin to God? How do you know? (Accept any answer.)

Follow-up discussion: page 116

▶ [critical] Why does David put his Bible at the bottom when he packs? (Accept any answer, but suggest that it makes him think of his lie.) [BAT: 4c Honesty]

[interpretive] Why does David's stomach feel like someone had used it for a punching bag? (because he knows he has lied, which makes his stomach feel sick)

[appreciative] Have you ever felt sick when someone has talked about God or spiritual things?

The Acknowledgment

Mr. Hines was wearing a tie with golf clubs on it. As David handed the permission slip to him, he stared at the golf clubs rather than looking at Mr. Hines's face.

"I'm glad to see most of you got those permission slips turned in," Mr. Hines told the class. "We'll meet here at the church Friday afternoon at two o'clock." He held up a stack of papers. "This paper I'm handing out now is a list of stuff to bring. Keep it handy while you're packing so you don't forget anything important."

David noticed that the first item on the list was a Bible. All at once, his stomach felt like someone had used it for a punching bag.

David tried to forget about the permission slip for the rest of the week. He concentrated on getting together all the items he would need for the hike. Mom took him shopping for things like insect repellent and flashlight batteries. The stack on the floor beside his backpack grew larger and larger as the week went on.

"Jacket, hat, pocketknife, sleeping bag . . ." He checked off

116

each object on the list as he stashed it in the pack Friday morning. "Bible." He went to his shelf, picked up his Bible, and stood staring down at it. He still hadn't finished the book of John. In fact, he couldn't remember reading the Bible at all this week. Every time Dad had read it after supper, David had gotten that sick feeling in his stomach again. David buried the Bible at the bottom of the pack.

That afternoon the boys gathered in the church parking lot. Mr. Hines looked like a gym teacher with a baseball cap on his head and a whistle around his neck. "The first thing I'm going to do is assign each of you a buddy," he said. "From the minute we get on the bus, you should know where your buddy is at all times."

David and Aaron were assigned to be buddies. "Mr. Hines is the greatest," Aaron said as they boarded the bus to drive into the mountains. "Aren't you glad you got your reading done so you could come?"

Why do people have to keep asking me about my reading? David wondered. He just nodded and said nothing. A moment

---

▶ [interpretive] Why does Mr. Hines assign each boy a buddy? (so no one will be by himself and get lost)

Read aloud the question Aaron asks David that makes David feel guilty.

later, the boys started singing a camp song at the tops of their voices, and Aaron joined in. David turned his face to the window.

When they all got off the bus, Mr. Hines gave each set of buddies a map of the trail they would be hiking. "The trail forks into two different trails at one point," he said, "but we'll go to the right. I've marked the fork we'll take in blue on all the maps. We'll all stay together—the maps are just a safeguard in case someone gets lost."

They set off with Mr. Hines leading the way. "Where He leads I'll follow," Mr. Hines started singing. The boys joined in.

"Follow all the way; where He leads I'll follow, follow Jesus every day."

Sunlight slanted through the branches of the pines and dappled the trail with shadows. The air felt cleaner and cooler as they climbed, and at one point they all stopped to pull jackets or sweatshirts out of their packs.

Near suppertime, they reached the spot Mr. Hines had marked with a star and the word "campsite" on the map. In a few moments, the boys all had assignments. Some were helping Mr. Hines set up tents, some were unpacking food supplies, and some were gathering pieces of wood for a fire.

Follow-up discussion: page 117

▶ [critical] Why do you think David does not join in singing with the other boys? (Accept any answer, but point out that he feels guilty about lying.) [BATs: 4c Honesty; 6d Clear conscience]

[literal] What are the boys singing about on the trail? (following Jesus) [BAT: 2a Obedience]

▶ [literal] Why does Mr. Hines give each set of buddies a map? (as a safeguard in case someone gets lost)

Read aloud the paragraph describing the trail as the boys climb higher.

▶ [critical] Why does David feel uncomfortable around Mr. Hines? (Accept any answer, but point out that he has lied to Mr. Hines) [BATs: 4c Honesty; 6d Clear conscience]

▶ [literal] Why does Mr. Hines say the Bible is the "trail book for life"? (because the Bible helps believers make the right decisions)

▶ [literal] What does Mr. Hines compare each boy's signature or "word of honor" to? (the Bible—God's Word of honor) [BAT: 8b Faith in the power of the Word of God]

[literal] What does the honor of Christ's name rest on? (His ability to keep His word)

[literal] Does God always do what He says? (yes) [BAT: 8a Faith in God's promises]

Read aloud Mr. Hines's explanation of God's Word of honor.

[appreciative] What are some promises God has given to you?

Mr. Hines set lighted matches among the pile of sticks until a steady fire was blazing. David stood with his arms folded across his chest, watching the flames.

Mr. Hines stepped up beside him. "How's it going, David? You've been pretty quiet on this trip. Everything all right?"

David felt like shrinking away from Mr. Hines. What would he say if he knew? David tried to imagine the look on Mr. Hines's face if he found out about the lie on the permission slip. David worked on a design in the dirt with the toe of his shoe, wondering what to say.

Mr. Hines waited a moment, watching him. Then he laid a hand on his shoulder and said, "If you need to talk, you know where to find me." He walked away.

After the hot dogs and marshmallows had all been roasted and eaten, Mr. Hines led them in a few songs. When the stillness closed in after the last notes died, he held up his Bible. David stared at the words "Holy Bible" that glowed on the cover in the firelight.

"This book," Mr. Hines said, "is your trail map for life. Just like the maps I gave you, this book will tell you the right forks to take—the right decisions to make—every day."

David shifted his feet and looked away from Mr. Hines to watch the fire.

"Before you came on this hike, you read the book of John," Mr. Hines went on. "You signed your name on a line, telling me you had finished. You gave your word of honor."

Mr. Hines was quiet for a moment. A stick on the fire cracked with a loud pop and sparks shot up.

"Everything God says in this book is His Word of honor to us," said Mr. Hines. "Every promise He makes, He will keep. The Bible says in Psalm 138 that He has magnified His Word above His name. The honor of His name rests on His ability to keep His word. So you'd better believe if He says something, He'll do it. Let's name some of the promises God gives us in His Word."

David was quiet, listening to the other boys naming promises.

118

God never leaves or forsakes. God saves. God hears and answers prayer. When all was quiet again, Mr. Hines said, "I'd like to read one more of God's promises. It's in I John 1:9. 'If we confess our sins, He is faithful and just to forgive us our sins, and to cleanse us from all unrighteousness.' Let's pray."

David hardly heard the prayer over the beating of his heart. *How had Mr. Hines known to read that verse? Does he know I lied?* David wondered. *Did he read that verse just for me?*

"Hey, David, want to get our flashlights and play hide and seek?" asked Aaron as soon as the prayer was finished.

"I'll be there in a minute," David said. The other boys were wandering off toward the tents. Mr. Hines stood by himself, throwing a few more sticks on the fire. David hurried to him before he could lose his nerve.

"Mr. Hines? I'm ready to talk now." With his eyes on the ground, David blurted out the whole story—the lie on the permission slip, the lie to his parents, and the lie he had let all the other boys on the hike believe. "My word of honor isn't good for much," he finished.

Word of Honor   119

Follow-up discussion: page 119

▶ [literal] What promise does Mr. Hines directly point out in the Bible? (God promises to forgive us our sins when we confess them to Him [I John 1:9].) [BAT: 8a Faith in God's promises; Bible Promise: C. Basis for Prayer]

Read aloud the paragraph in which David tells Mr. Hines the truth.

[interpretive] Why does David finally acknowledge his sin to Mr. Hines? (The Holy Spirit convicts him through the reading of Scripture.) [BAT: 8b Faith in the power of the Word of God]

[critical] Do you think it takes courage for David to confess his sin to Mr. Hines? (Accept any answer.)

[interpretive] Why does David come to the conclusion that his word is no good? (because he was dishonest by lying to his parents, to the other boys, and to Mr. Hines by signing his signature, his word that he had read the book of John)

Follow-up discussion: page 120

▶ [critical] Why do you think Mr. Hines does not get angry with David? (Possible answer: Mr. Hines is more concerned with David's sin toward God and his asking for God's forgiveness than with David's sin against him.) [BAT: 6e Forgiveness]

▶ [literal] To whom in the Bible does Mr. Hines compare David? (David, the writer of Psalm 51)

Read aloud the paragraph in which David reads Psalm 51.

[interpretive] What words of the author indicate that David does ask God to forgive him? ("Then he bowed his head.") [BAT: 6b Prayer]

He couldn't bring himself to look up at Mr. Hines's face. *What must he think now? He'll probably never be as friendly to me anymore now that he knows he can't trust me,* David thought.

He heard the rustle of paper and looked up to see Mr. Hines turning the pages of his Bible. "I'm glad you told me this, David," Mr. Hines said. "You did the right thing in coming to me. I'll talk to you about this further. I think you'll want to say something to your parents and to the other guys as well. But first, there's Someone else you need to talk to." He handed David the open Bible.

"Psalm 51," he said, "was written by another David long, long ago. Why don't you sit here and read it and then pray it back to God? Remember—He keeps His Word."

As Mr. Hines walked back toward the tents, David sat by the dying fire and read. " 'For I acknowledge my transgressions: and my sin is ever before me. Against thee, thee only, have I sinned, and done this evil in Thy sight. . . . Create in me a clean heart, O God . . . a broken and a contrite heart, O God, Thou wilt not despise.' "

A leaf blew into the fire, and David watched it shrivel and break apart in the flame. Then he bowed his head.

120

STUDY SKILLS
Locating Bible verses

The student will
- Locate Bible verses and apply biblical principles.
- Recall details.
- Recognize character traits.

Objectives

Direct the students to the contents page at the front of their Bibles. Ask the following questions.

▶ What are the two main sections of the Bible? (Old Testament and New Testament)

What is the first book of the Bible as well as of the Old Testament? (Genesis) Turn to the book of Genesis in your Bible.

Turn back to the contents page. What is the first book of the New Testament? (Matthew) Turn to the first page of the book of Matthew in your Bible.

Which section is larger—the Old Testament or New Testament? (Old Testament)

Turn to the last book in your Bible. What is it? (Revelation)

Point out that the Psalms and Proverbs are near the middle of the Bible.

Continue questioning in a similar way, choosing two books from the Old Testament and two from the New Testament for the students to locate on the contents page and in their Bibles.

▶ In the story "Word of Honor," Mr. Hines reminded the boys that God keeps His promises and the boys named some of God's promises. Let's look up some verses where those promises are given.

Direct the students to find the following verses in their Bibles. Give assistance if necessary. Choose students to read the verses aloud and name God's promises.

Hebrews 13:5—God never leaves us or forsakes us.

John 3:16—God saves.

Matthew 21:22—God hears and answers prayer.

Guide the students in locating Psalm 138:2, the verse Mr. Hines spoke about.

Study Skills: Worktext page 49

Explain the activities on the page. Give the students assistance if necessary as they locate the verses in their Bibles.

Comprehension: Worktext page 50

SOMETHING EXTRA
Write About It: A classroom contract

Before writing a contract for your students, allow the students to brainstorm for ideas for a special trip or a class activity that they would like to do. Guide them in deciding the criteria they will need to meet in order to go on the trip or participate in the activity (e.g., read a specified number of books, write a story, finish all homework on time, maintain good behavior for a specified time).

Design the contract and make a copy for each student. Distribute the contracts, encouraging each student to fulfill the requirements. At the end of the allotted time, allow only those students who have fulfilled the requirements to sign on the line and join in the fun.

Lesson	Worktext pages
39	230-31

Objectives

The student will

- Divide into syllables words ending with a consonant + *le*: divide most words before the consonant, but divide words with *ck* + *le* after the *ck* (sad•dle, ta•ble, tick•le).

- Apply one of three syllable rules to a list of words: divide words with the *VC/CV* pattern between the consonants, divide compound words between the base words, and divide words ending with a consonant + *le* before the consonant or after the *ck*.

Background information

Syllable Division Rule 3—In most words ending with a consonant + *le*, divide into syllables before the consonant.

In words ending with the consonant digraph *ck* + *le*, divide into syllables after the *ck*.

Materials

- Teaching Visual 8: *Eighty Stables*

WORDS ENDING WITH A CONSONANT + *LE*

1 **Introduction: Keepers and Assistants**

▶ Remount stations were where the pony express riders changed horses. But who kept the stations? Listen to find out who lived at remount stations and what kind of work they did.

Read the following account to the students.

About 190 remount stations were stocked with supplies to give support to pony express riders and horses. Each station had a keeper who was in charge. Usually two other men also lived at the station: a blacksmith to shoe the horses and a spare rider in case injury or emergency prevented another rider from completing his assigned route. These men lived at the stations, feeding and caring for the horses from day to day. They also kept the tack—saddles and bridles—in good condition.

Life at remote stations could be slow and quiet, but twice a day the sound of galloping hoof beats or three short blasts from a horn brought the remount station to life. Either of these signals meant that a pony express rider was approaching. One of the men would quickly saddle and bridle a fresh horse and have it waiting when the arriving horse slid to a halt. The keeper would also provide a quick drink and food if the rider needed it.

All the excitement lasted no more than two minutes. After the fresh horse raced away with the rider and mail, the keeper would strip the tack off the weary horse and walk the horse to the stable or corral for rest. Then it was back to the daily chores and routine of keeping the station ready for the next rider.

Discuss the following.

▶ Who lived at remount stations? (usually a keeper, a blacksmith, and a spare rider)

What jobs did these men perform? (possible answers: cared for horses and tack, had fresh horses waiting for riders)

What other chores do you think the men did? (possible answers: cooked, cleaned the station, pumped water from a well, groomed horses, repaired fences)

▶ What kind of injury might prevent a rider from continuing his assigned route? (possible answers: a bad fall, a gunshot wound, a wound from an arrow)

Leather and Buckles

▶**Remember How**

Where should these words be divided?

c o f•f e e s i g•n a l t h u n•d e r

Where should these compound words be divided?

s a f e•g u a r d b l a c k•s m i t h

▶**Something New**

Move one letter in each group of letters to make a word **ending** with **le**. Write each word and divide it into syllables.

1. roublet

_t r o u • b l e_

2. andlce

_c a n • d l e_

3. taclke

_t a c k • l e_

4. itlet

_t i • t l e_

5. peeopl

_p e o • p l e_

bri•dle

buck•le

© 2000 BJU Press. Reproduction prohibited.

> Divide words ending with a consonant + *le* before the consonant + *le*.
> In words ending with the consonant digraph *ck* before the *le*,
> divide the word after the *ck*.

230

---

② Skill development:
Visual 8—*Eighty Stables*

Briefly review rules for dividing words with the *VC/CV* pattern and compound words. Refer to Lessons 22 and 27 for complete teaching of these rules.

▶ There are more rules to help in dividing words into syllables. Let's look at a rule for dividing words ending with the pattern found in words such as *stable*.

▶ What is the rule for dividing most words ending with a consonant + *le?* (Divide the words into syllables before the consonant.)

Lead in reading the first two lists aloud.

▶ Are the vowels in these words long or short vowels? (The first list has short vowels. The second has long vowels.)

▶ If one of these words were new to you, how could you tell whether the vowel is pronounced as a long or short vowel? (Syllables ending with consonants as those in the first list are called closed syllables and have short vowels. Syllables ending with vowels as those in the second list are called open syllables and have long vowels.)

▶ One exception to this rule is the consonant digraph *ck*. Words with the *ck* digraph + *le* are divided after the *ck*.

Lead in reading aloud the words in the last two lists.

▶ Can you think of any other words with the digraph *ck* + *le?* (possible answers: chuckle, speckled, fickle, tackle)

---

③ Skill application:
Worktext page 230

Remember How

▶ Read the first line of words. Which rule tells how to divide this list? (Divide words with the *VC/CV* pattern between the consonants.)

Put in a dot to divide each word into syllables.

▶ Read the next line of words. What type of words are they? (compound words)

Where should compound words be divided? (between the two base words)

Put a dot to divide each word into syllables.

Something New

▶ Look at the first group of letters. One letter can be moved to a different position to form a word ending with a consonant + *le*. What is that word? (trouble)

Write the word then put a dot to divide it into syllables.

Guide the students in completing the page.

④ Skill application:
Worktext page 231

HAMLET, AUGUSTA JONES, AND ME

Lesson	Reader pages	Worktext pages
40	121-23	51-52
41	124-27	53-54
42	128-130	55-56

VOCABULARY

LESSON 40

*She did not like the layout of the room, so I moved things around again. (p. 123)

†Without a word of complaint, the boy meekly obeyed his mother. (p. 123)

†After seeing the huge box Mom wrapped, my prospects for getting a bike seemed great. (p. 123)

LESSON 41

*Having a lot of homework is my loophole for getting out of doing extra chores. (p. 124)

*†John is a responsible boy because he is always on time and learns his lines. (p. 124)

*Debbie's great acting during her audition got her the best part in the play. (p. 124)

*†I lunged forward to catch the falling book. (p. 126)

*The doublet fit the young boy like his dad's suit jacket. (p. 126)

LESSON 42

*†During intermission, everyone can stand and stretch before the play starts again. (p. 128)

The big, heavy costume was too cumbersome to move in. (p. 128)

*†A play that has an unhappy ending is called a tragedy. (p. 129)

Drama with a capital *D* characterizes Mimosa Street after Augusta Jones moves in. Tom thinks maybe the girls will want to be in Augusta's plays, but surely the guys will know better. Then one day after school, the kick ball field is empty.

Materials

- Costumes or articles of clothing that could represent costumes (e.g., variety of shoes, hats, old shirts, new shirts, vintage clothing)
- Vocabulary sentences for display

Background information

Hamlet—In William Shakespeare's play *Hamlet*, Hamlet's father has been murdered by Hamlet's evil uncle, Claudius. Hamlet is asked by his father's ghost to seek vengeance. Hesitant to act, Hamlet appears to be going insane. Polonius, an elderly courtier, thinks that Hamlet is only lovesick over Polonius' daughter, Ophelia. Hamlet decides to hire a group of actors to perform the events that led to his father's murder. The play disturbs Claudius, revealing his guilt of the crime. Hamlet confronts his mother (who married Claudius quickly after his father's murder) and kills the eavesdropping Polonius. Now fearful, Claudius attempts to have Hamlet killed on an expedition, but Hamlet discovers the plot. Hamlet returns home only to discover that Ophelia has killed herself and that Ophelia's brother Laertes is seeking to avenge his father's (Polonius's) death. Claudius arranges the duel. In the end, the sword dipped into poison by Claudius pierces both Laertes and Hamlet. Hamlet's mother drinks the poison meant to ensure Hamlet's death, and before dying, Hamlet is able to pierce Claudius through the heart.

INTRODUCTION

Vocabulary

Use the prepared sentences to introduce the vocabulary words in context.

Performing a play

▶ What are some things that we would need in order to put on a play? (possible answers: costumes, props, a stage, actors)

Show the costumes and discuss how the various items could be used. Encourage the students to suggest the kind of characters that would wear these costumes.

▶ What type of preparation would we need before performing a play? (possible answers: practice what to say and when to say it; make the props; choose the actors)

How would we choose the actors for the play? (Elicit that auditions would be held.)

Who would direct the play and make sure everyone learns his lines? (Elicit that a director makes decisions about the play.)

Correlated Activities
- **Vocabulary Box, Activity 3: Glossary Day**
- **Recreational Reading, Activity 2: Design-a-Game**
See "Classroom Management for Grouping" in the Appendix.

▶ Do you think it takes a lot of work to put on a good play? Why or why not?

In this story we will see how much work and responsibility it takes to put on a play.

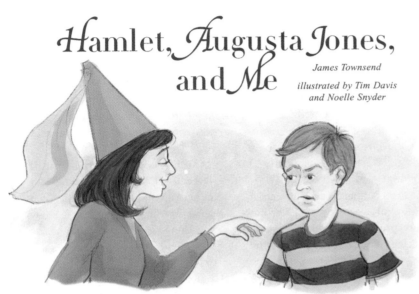

Hamlet, Augusta Jones, and Me

James Townsend

illustrated by Tim Davis and Noelle Snyder

Mimosa Street Drama Club

Since Augusta Jones moved into the house next door to mine, Mimosa Street has changed. I had never met anyone like her, and I don't think Mimosa Street will ever be the same again.

Right off the bat I thought that girl was really strange. It's not that I don't know about girls. I have two sisters. It's just that Augusta is different. When she gets out a box of paper dolls, it's not to play with them but to try out costumes for those plays of hers. She hadn't been here for very long before she had every girl on Mimosa Street acting the part of this princess or that one or, worse yet, some animal or other.

When she first started this play business, she tried to get us boys interested too. But we were too smart to get caught. After all, who wants to be a giant rabbit when we could be playing kick ball in my back yard instead?

At least, that's what we were doing before one of my sisters volunteered our garage for a playhouse. Then the Mimosa Street

Hamlet, Augusta Jones, and Me   121

COMPREHENSION

The student will

- Evaluate emotional responses of characters.
- Recognize first-person point of view.
- Discern motives of a character.
- Identify conflicting points of view.

Before silent reading: pages 121-23

Motivation

▶ What is the Mimosa Street Drama Club?

How did the club get started?

Who is the *Me* in the title, and how does this person feel about the drama club?

After silent reading

Overview discussion: pages 121-23

▶ [literal] Who starts the drama club? (Augusta Jones)

▶ [interpretive] Who is telling the story? (Tom)

▶ [critical] Does Tom have a good reason for not liking the club? Why do you think that? (Answers will vary. He doesn't want to dress up in silly costumes and the club has ruined the kick ball games.)

[interpretive] Why does Tom think Augusta wants the boys to join her club? What do you think is the reason? (To be giant rabbits; answers will vary.)

[critical] Do you think Tom will grow to like the idea of a play? (Answers will vary.)

Follow-up discussion: page 121

▶ [interpretive] What makes Tom think Mimosa Street will never be the same? (Augusta Jones has moved to that street.)

[literal] Why does Augusta Jones seem so strange to Tom? (She doesn't play with paper dolls the way other girls do—she uses paper dolls to try out costumes for her plays.)

[appreciative] Do you think costumes and plays are strange? Why or why not?

[interpretive] How do the rest of the boys feel at first about Augusta Jones and her plays? (They would rather play kick ball than join in one of her plays.)

Read aloud the paragraph that tells how Tom and the other boys feel about Augusta's plays.

Follow-up discussion: page 122

▶ [literal] What does Tom think would be trouble? (having the Mimosa Street Drama Club meet at his house)

[literal] How does Tom's prediction come true? (A princess and something that looks like a frog run through their kick ball game and ruin it.)

[critical] Why do you think Augusta apologizes to the boys and tells them about swords and fighting? (Accept any answer.)

▶ [interpretive] Why does all this talk about fighting persuade the boys to be in Augusta's play? (Possible answer: They think it would be something fun to try.)

Read aloud the paragraph in which Tom tells how Augusta persuades the boys to be in the play.

[critical] Do you think talking sense into the guys is the only reason Tom also signs up? If not, why does he sign up? (Answers will vary, but point out that Tom is probably a little curious about the drama club.)

Drama Club started meeting at our place every day. "Nothing but trouble," I predicted. And sure enough, one day when Barry Horton tried for a home run, a princess and something that looked like a frog dashed across the yard from our house to the garage. We lost the game five to nothing!

Then Augusta came out, apologizing all over the place. The boys were pretty sore until she started talking about swords and fighting battles. It wasn't long before the whole kick ball team was over in the garage signing up for parts.

Fighting! I thought she probably meant setting out to kill a giant rabbit or something. But who would she get to be the rabbit?

Well, I couldn't play kick ball alone. I thought that maybe if I signed up too I could talk some sense into those guys. But I knew one thing: If Augusta thought she was going to get me into a rabbit

122

suit, she would have to think again!

When I reached the door of the garage, Augusta gave me a sticky smile. For a moment I thought she had been waiting for me. Not likely, since Augusta and I didn't get along too well . . . and ruining my kick ball game didn't help any either.

"Hello, Thomas," Augusta said.

Now that's not any way to smooth things over. Thomas! Everybody knows my name's Tom. "Ahem," I said, clearing my throat. "Er, how're things going?"

"Just fine," she replied, pulling me inside. "Look."

I whistled in spite of myself. So this was what they had been doing all week! The garage hadn't been really dirty. Dad didn't use it for storage. But still it was cleaner than I had ever seen it. Just inside the doors was the open space where the car usually parked. Beyond that was the platform that had been brushed clean and made into a stage. Sheets hung from the rafters. They were pulled back at either side and

tied to make curtains for the stage.

"Neat, isn't it?" Augusta beamed. "And take a look at the layout. The paying customers come in the front doors and sit in the open area. The actors are on the stage. They won't even have to enter from the audience. That side door opens onto the stage. We can do our entrances and exits there."

"Paying customers?" I said, a little dazed.

"Sure, why not?" Augusta replied cheerfully, but I wasn't listening. My attention had been caught by a flash of steel. Jonathan Lee was chasing a girl across the stage, waving a sword over his head.

"That's real!" I croaked. "Are you crazy?"

Augusta gave Jonathan a cold look. "That's enough," she called, "or you're out!"

I watched in amazement as Jonathan meekly returned the sword to a big trunk near the side door. The prospects of getting the boys back to the game seemed smaller and smaller.

Hamlet, Augusta Jones, and Me   123

Follow-up discussion: page 123

Follow-up discussion: page 123

▶ [critical] What does the author mean by saying that "Augusta gave me a sticky smile"? (Accept any reasonable answer.)

[critical] Do you think Augusta knows that Tom doesn't like to be called Thomas? Why does she call him that? (Answers will vary.)

▶ [interpretive] Why does Tom whistle? (He thinks the garage looks pretty nice.)

Read aloud with pride Augusta's description of her playhouse.

▶ [interpretive] What really impresses Tom about Augusta's handling of his friends? (They do what she says.) [BAT: 2b Teamwork]

Looking ahead

▶ Do you think Tom can get his friends back to playing kick ball?

Will Tom change his mind about Augusta and her plays?

Worktext Objectives

The student will

■ Predict outcomes.
■ Use the glossary to build vocabulary.

Comprehension:
Worktext page 51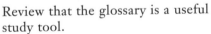

Use the information at the top of the page to discuss how to have real joy.

Remind students to use complete sentences as they finish the page.

Study Skills:
Worktext page 52

Review that the glossary is a useful study tool.

Instruct the students to use the glossary entries at the top of the page to answer the questions.

COMPREHENSION

The student will

- Develop an awareness of a change in a character.
- Discern the motives of characters.
- Notice the author's use of foreshadowing.
- Recognize character traits of leadership and responsibility.

 Use the prepared sentences to introduce the vocabulary words in context.

Before silent reading: pages 124-27

Motivation

▶ Will Augusta be able to talk Tom into being in the play?

After silent reading

Overview discussion: pages 124-27

▶ [interpretive] Who has the leading role in the play? (Tom. Point out that since the play is named *Hamlet* and Tom is playing the character Hamlet, he must be the main character.)

[critical] What do you think changes Tom's mind about plays? (Answers will vary, but elicit that he enjoys the story when he reads the script.)

▶ [interpretive] How do you think Augusta gets the actors to learn their lines and come to practices? (Possible answers: She takes charge of the group; she tells them that they will not be in the play if they do not behave.)

[critical] Do you think Augusta makes a good director? Why or why not? (Accept any answer, but elicit that she is responsible, organized, and in control.) [BATs: 2a Authority; 2c Responsibility; 2d Goal setting]

Auditions

"Have you got permission for all this?" I demanded triumphantly, seeing a loophole.

"Why of course, Thomas," Augusta replied haughtily. "I am a responsible person."

I winced.

"The swords and costumes are from my attic. No, they aren't real. My mother used to run a small theater, and she's delighted that I want to follow in her footsteps. Good stuff, you know. *Hamlet, Macbeth,* all those," she said with an airy wave of her hand. "Oh, and of course both your parents and mine gave permission to charge a slight fee. Twenty-five cents. We'll make a fortune!"

"Oh," I said weakly.

"Come on," she said. "We're auditioning for parts already."

She pushed me up to the stage where my sister Eva was listening to Benny reading—or rather, trying to read. What was coming out didn't resemble anything I had ever heard before.

"Try again," Eva said encouragingly. "You can do it."

124

" 'But look, the morn, in . . . russet mantle clad, walks o'er the dew of yoon . . . yon high eastward hill. Break we our watch up.' . . . What watch?" Benny stopped, puzzled. "Why would anyone want to break a watch?"

"Never mind," Augusta said. "Isn't it beautiful? The morning walks over the dew of the hills— just beautiful!"

"But Augusta," Eva protested, "it may be pretty, but nobody knows what anybody else is talking about. How can we put on a play when we don't understand each other?"

"It's just the language," Augusta said thoughtfully. "Why don't I rewrite it so we can understand it?"

"Whew," Benny said. "Anything would be better than this!"

"Okay, okay." Augusta stepped onto the stage. "Listen up, everybody. Come back tomorrow at four o'clock, and we'll audition for parts then."

There was a lot of bike traffic on Mimosa Street after school the next day. By four o'clock

---

Follow-up discussion: page 124

▶ [literal] What question does Tom ask Augusta, hoping the answer will cause her plans to be ruined? ("Have you got permission for all this?")

[interpretive] How does Augusta respond to Tom's question? (She says she is responsible.) [BAT: 2c Responsibility]

Choose two students to read aloud the conversation between Augusta and Tom, or allow one student to portray the motives of the characters as he reads the conversation.

▶ [interpretive] Why is Benny struggling with his lines? (He doesn't understand what he is saying.)

[interpretive] Why are the lines so difficult to understand? (Elicit that it is poetry and that they do not know the meaning of many of the words.)

[literal] What is Augusta's suggestion to help each actor understand the others? (She says she will rewrite it.)

▶ [interpretive] What is the author hinting at when he says that there is a lot of bike traffic on Mimosa Street? (There are many children wanting to try out for parts.)

there must have been twenty kids in our back yard. How the word got passed around, I'll never know. Every kid there wanted either a crown or a sword. I knew even Augusta didn't have that many, so I wandered out to watch the fun. Augusta was moving about quickly, giving out copies of the play and organizing the kids into groups. I picked up a copy and sat down on the edge of the stage.

"Hmmm," I thought as I flipped through the pages. "Typewritten and photocopied! Wonder who Augusta got to do that?" I settled down to read.

"Thomas! Thomas, hurry up!" Augusta thumped me on the head. "I've called you three times already. Come on!"

I glanced around. Most of the kids had been given scripts and sent home. Only a few were still reading. I stretched and got up, holding the script.

"Hey, Augusta," I said. "This is a great story. Who wrote it anyway?"

"Some man named William Shakespeare," she replied. "I think I'll test you for the part of Hamlet."

"Did he write any others?" I asked, following her to the center of the stage.

Hamlet, Augusta Jones, and Me   125

Follow-up discussion: page 125

▶ [interpretive] What does Tom think would be fun to watch as the kids gather in the yard? (Since there are not enough swords for everyone, Tom wants to see how Augusta will handle all the kids who are arguing over the crowns and swords.)

▶ [interpretive] Why does Tom think Augusta asked someone else to type and photocopy the play? (He doesn't think she could type and make the copies all by herself.)

[critical] Do you think Augusta prepared the copies herself? Why do you think that? (Answers may vary.)

▶ [literal] What begins to interest Tom? (the rewritten play)

[interpretive] Why is Tom interested in the play now? (He likes the story about Hamlet.)

[appreciative] Have you ever heard of Shakespeare or seen one of his plays?

Read aloud the sentences that show Tom's interest in the play.

Follow-up discussion: page 126

▶ [interpretive] How do you know the actors are getting tired of practicing? (The sounds coming from them are complaints now instead of their lines.)

[literal] How does Augusta change the actors' complaining to joy? (She lets them try on the costumes for the first time.)

Read aloud about the excitement of the cast members as they run toward the costume trunk.

▶ [interpretive] Does Augusta think ahead about problems they might have with the costumes? How do you know? (Yes; she has a supply of pins and twine ready to fix the oversized costumes.)

[interpretive] How does the author let you know that Augusta is not happy with the costumes? (It is the first time Tom has ever seen Augusta without a cheerful face.)

"Sure, lots of them. Now turn to page two and read where it says 'Hamlet.'"

"I'd rather be the ghost."

"No, silly, that part is perfect for Benny."

"Why?"

"Because Benny can make more noises than any boy I have ever heard," Augusta said patiently. "Now read!"

I read.

Two weeks later we were still practicing. We had shouted and whispered and murmured. We had lunged and dodged and thrust. Finally the mutters that arose from the cast had nothing to do with the parts.

"Are we ready yet?"

"When do we get our swords?"

"I'm tired!"

"Well," Augusta said, "you know, practice makes perfect, but I guess we can get out the costumes."

With a shriek of joy the cast raced for the trunk. Augusta was the first there, but she really had to move fast.

Silks and velvet, iron and steel! What a rainbow of colors came from that old trunk! Squeals of delight came from the girls as yards of material slid over their heads and trailed on the floor.

"Here. I knew they'd be too big," Augusta said, opening a box full of twine and pins. "This should help."

When everyone had been pinned and tied as much as possible, Augusta lined us up along the platform and looked us over. I think that's the first time I had ever seen Augusta without a cheerful face. I looked slowly down the line of kids. Eva's dress was all bunched around her waist, and her coronet had slipped over one ear. Benny's hose had settled around his ankles in deep folds, and Jonathan Lee's doublet reached to his knees. The rest of them didn't look much better. Personally, I thought my costume looked fine.

"I guess we could make our own costumes," Augusta said hesitantly.

"Oh, no!"

"I like mine!"

"Mine is perfect," Eva called, spinning around and making her

126

veil fan out behind her. "Let's put the play on tonight."

"Not tonight," Augusta said. "We need a dress rehearsal."

"Aw, Augusta, we've practiced enough," Benny pleaded.

"Yes, let's do it," the others said as they gathered around her. "We know our parts. And we can go around the neighborhood, telling everyone to come tonight."

"Well," Augusta said doubtfully. "I guess we can use tonight as a trial performance."

How much of a trial it was going to be we didn't know. Otherwise, I'd have been in the audience, not on the stage.

Hamlet, Augusta Jones, and Me   127

Follow-up discussion: page 127

▶ [critical] Why does the cast want to put on the play right away? (Possible answers: They are tired of practicing; they are too excited to wait.)

[appreciative] Have you ever been so excited about doing something or going somewhere that you just couldn't wait? Tell us about it. [BAT: 6c Patience]

▶ [interpretive] Why does Augusta want to have a dress rehearsal before putting on the play? (She is organized and wants the final performance to go well.)

[appreciative] Have you ever been in a play that had a dress rehearsal? Why do you think a dress rehearsal is helpful?

[interpretive] How does Augusta compromise between what she wants and what her cast wants? (She decides to have a trial performance.) [BAT: 3c Flexibility]

[critical] Do you think Augusta is wise in not having the dress rehearsal? Why or why not? (Answers will vary, but elicit that it is better to practice before the play to find out what can go wrong than to not practice and find out during the performance.)

[interpretive] How does the author let you know in advance that the trial performance will be a terrible experience? (Tom says that if he had known how much trouble it was going to be, he wouldn't have wanted to be in the play.)

Read aloud this foreshadowing about the performance the way you think Tom would say it.

Looking ahead

▶ Why would Tom rather be in the audience than in the play after all the hard work he put into it?

Worktext Objectives

The student will

- Identify character traits.
- Make inferences.
- Apply punctuation.

Comprehension: Worktext page 53

Discuss that a play part is sometimes assigned according to the actor's personality.

Guide students through the first two parts.

Instruct the students to use people *a–d* for parts 1–4 and people *e–h* for parts 5–8.

Comprehension: Worktext page 54

Review that paying attention to the "signals" of punctuation helps the reader to better understand the meaning of the author.

Instruct the students to complete the page.

COMPREHENSION

Objectives

The student will

- Evaluate the emotional responses of characters.
- Recognize character growth and change.
- Relate story content to personal experience.
- Interpret a cliché.

Use the prepared sentences to introduce the vocabulary words in context.

Before silent reading: pages 128-30

Motivation

▶ What trouble will there be during the trial performance?

Will Tom and Augusta resolve their differences?

After silent reading

Overview discussion: pages 128-30

▶ [interpretive] How do you think a dress rehearsal could have helped the actors do a better job? (Possible answer: They would have known how the big costumes would get in the way and could have done some of the scenes differently.)

▶ [interpretive] Why does the audience love the play even though the actors have so many problems? (The audience thinks the play is funny and enjoys it.)

[interpretive] Do you think Augusta is pleased with the performance? Why or why not? (At first she isn't, but after she hears the audience's clapping, the happy light comes back into her eyes and she is pleased.)

The Performance

The first thing that went wrong happened in the first act. Benny was playing the ghost of the dead king, Hamlet's father. He was doing a fine job, too, until he reached the front of the stage. He wouldn't have had any problem if his sagging hose hadn't unrolled over his shoe. Benny grabbed for my arm and missed. He pitched headlong into the first row, right where we had put the little kids so they could see. Well, they could see all right. They scattered everywhere, screaming and yelling.

Augusta called a brief intermission to calm things down. Then with a "the-show-must-go-on" expression, she motioned us back on stage.

From then on things went from bad to worse. The problem was the costumes. Terrific as they were, they definitely were too big. Since we didn't know what to expect from the cumbersome outfits, we had a hard time moving around. I wasn't doing too badly because I had double-pinned everything and

Follow-up discussion: page 128

▶ [literal] What happens in the first scene that is the start of the problems? (Benny trips over his sagging hose and falls into the first row of children.)

Read aloud this scene including Benny, making us laugh as you read.

[critical] How do you think Augusta feels about this scene? Does Augusta think this is funny? (Answers will vary, but elicit that she is not happy.)

[appreciative] Have you ever worked hard at something that did not turn out well? How did you respond to the situation? [BATs: 3c Self-control; 7d Contentment]

▶ [interpretive] What does the author mean when he says that Augusta has a "the-show-must-go-on" expression? (She is determined to finish the play no matter what.)

[literal] What word does the author use that best describes the oversized costumes? (cumbersome)

even put square knots in the twine. But being Hamlet, I was on the receiving end of some clumsy sword thrusts that kept me dodging. It's hard to look brave when you duck instead of facing the other person. By the end of the second act (Augusta had shortened the play a lot), the audience was roaring with laughter.

"This is a tragedy," Augusta moaned as the curtain closed. "Why are they laughing?"

"They won't laugh in the next act," Eva promised. "Nobody laughs at a drowning person."

"I certainly hope not," Augusta murmured.

But she was wrong. The girl who played Ophelia had been having trouble all night. She was a thin girl anyway, and that dress had been made for a very healthy woman. When "Ophelia" had been on stage with me, the dress had kept slipping. Pins or not, I didn't think it could last much longer, and I was right.

"Ophelia" must have been expecting the same thing, because when she felt the dress slip, she caught it at her waist. Quickly looping one end of the twine around it, she continued her speech. She didn't miss a word, but

Hamlet, Augusta Jones, and Me 129

Follow-up discussion: page 129

▶ [literal] By the end of the second act, what is the audience doing? (roaring with laughter)

[interpretive] What is Augusta referring to when she says, "this is a tragedy"? (Elicit that this is a play on words, but Augusta is referring to the type of play it is supposed to be. Explain that a tragedy is a type of play that is supposed to be sad.)

Pretend you are Augusta and read aloud what she moans that lets the reader know she isn't happy with the audience's laughter.

▶ [literal] What makes Eva so sure that the audience won't laugh in the next act? (Nobody laughs at a drowning person.)

[interpretive] What proves Eva wrong? (The dress slips on the girl playing Ophelia and she catches it at her waist.)

[interpretive] Does "Ophelia" react with a "the-show-must-go-on" attitude? How? (Yes; She continues with her lines even though her dress is now tied at her waist.)

[critical] Do you think the audience is enjoying the play, even though they are laughing during a play that is supposed to be a tragedy? (Answers will vary, but they probably are.)

[appreciative] Do you think you would like the play better this way or as a tragedy? Why?

Hamlet, Augusta Jones, and Me

Follow-up discussion: page 130

▶ [critical] Is "Ophelia's" dress problem the only thing that makes Augusta walk out the door? Why do you think that? (Answers will vary.)

[literal] What stops Tom from going after Augusta? (Benny hisses, "You're on!")

[interpretive] What does Benny mean when he hisses at Tom, "You're on!"? (It is Tom's turn to say his lines on stage.)

▶ [critical] Why do you think Tom thinks the last scene is the best? (Answers will vary, but elicit that since he is the main character in this scene, he gets to have a sword fight and a lot of action.)

Read aloud Tom's description of the best part of the play.

▶ [interpretive] Why does Tom go out to Augusta and encourage her to come in and take a bow? (Possible answer: He cares about her and wants her to be happy again.) [BATs: 5a Kindness, Thoughtfulness]

[interpretive] Why is the play such a big success? (The mix-ups make it humorous and enjoyable.)

[appreciative] Would you like to see or be in a play like Augusta's? Why or why not?

▶ [critical] What lessons do Tom and Augusta learn through all that happens with the play? (Answers will vary, but elicit that Augusta learns that things may not always turn out the way you want and Tom learns that you have to get to know a person before you judge him.) [BAT: 5e Friendliness]

[critical] Do you think you will find Tom on stage during *Romeo and Juliet*? Why or why not? (Accept any answer.)

the sight of all that rich material wadded at the waist of a T-shirt was too much for Augusta. She walked out the back door. I started to go after her, but Benny hissed, "Hamlet! You're on!"

The last scene was where the wicked King, the Queen, Laertes, and finally Hamlet all die. It was the best part of the play, if I do say so myself. The audience loved it. We were used to the clothes by then, and I didn't have to dodge so much . . . although Laertes got tangled up in the Queen's trailing skirts and almost didn't manage to kill me. For a moment I was tempted to rewrite Augusta's play and finish him off so I could live and become the new king. But Augusta was feeling so bad already that I couldn't. I just leaned on my sword and waited until he got to his feet again.

Well, surprisingly enough, the play was a success. Everyone clapped and clapped. While the others were taking their bows, I

slipped outside. Augusta was sitting on the porch steps. She was looking surprised to hear all the clapping and whistling going on.

"Come on," I said, pulling her to her feet. "They loved us. You have to take a bow too."

"They liked it?" she said in an unbelieving voice.

"Not liked—loved."

After a few bows, that happy light was back in Augusta's eyes. When the curtain went down for the last time, she turned to the cast. "Thank you all for doing such a good job. And forgive me for not believing in you."

Well, I've still never met anyone like that Augusta Jones. But you know, I guess she isn't so strange after all. You just have to get to know her. When we left, she was sitting on the trunk, murmuring something about *Romeo and Juliet.* I wouldn't mind doing another play, but *Romeo and Juliet?* Not me. Augusta will just have to find herself another boy. Absolutely no. Never. Not me.

130

The student will

■ Predict outcomes.

■ Write and illustrate a description of a play.

■ Recall facts and details.

■ Infer unstated supporting details.

Comprehension:
Worktext page 55

Call attention to the picture at the top of the page. Discuss the probability of the children's performing another play and the willingness of the actors to try again.

Guide students through the completion of the page.

Comprehension:
Worktext page 56

Remind students they may use their readers as they complete this page.

SOMETHING EXTRA

Act It Out: Fairy tale fun

Gather several familiar fairy tales for the students to look at. Divide the students into four groups, assigning each group a fairy tale to act out. Select a student in each group to act as the director to assign parts and direct rehearsals. Allow time for the groups to practice and have a dress rehearsal before performing their plays for parents and other students.

Hamlet, Augusta Jones, and Me

Lesson	Worktext pages
43	232-33

The student will

■ Determine whether statements are fact or opinion.

Background information

Fact—A fact is a statement that is true. The five senses and reference materials are some sources for determining whether a statement is a fact.

Opinion—An opinion is a statement that tells what a person thinks about a subject. Opinions often include words such as *everyone/no one*, *always/never*, *more/most*, *better/best*, and *worse/worst*.

Materials

• Two kinds of candy, such as M&M's and Smarties

FACT OR OPINION

① Introduction

Display the two types of candy.

▶ How many of you think M&M's taste good? How many of you think Smarties taste good?

Which one tastes better? Does everyone agree? (no)

▶ What colors are the M&M's? What colors are the Smarties? How do you know what colors they are? (by the sense of sight) Does everyone agree? (yes)

▶ "Some Smarties are pink." Is that statement a fact or an opinion? (Elicit that it is a fact because it is something that we know is true by sight.)

▶ "M&M's taste better than Smarties." Is that statement a fact or an opinion? (Elicit that it is an opinion because it is what a person thinks about the taste of M&M's. Point out that the word *better* was used in the statement.)

② Skill development

Use the background information about *opinion* to discuss some key words often used in opinion statements.

Use the background information about *fact* to discuss some sources for determining facts.

▶ What are the five senses? (sight, hearing, smell, taste, touch)

▶ What are some reference materials? (dictionary, encyclopedia, atlas)

Read the following statements aloud. Choose students to tell whether the statements are facts or opinions. Allow the students to identify the keyword in each opinion and the sources that could be used to determine the facts.

Some cars are red. (fact; sight)

Red cars are prettier than blue cars. (opinion; *prettier*)

An airplane can travel faster than a train can. (fact; sight and encyclopedia)

Dogs are better than cats. (opinion; *better*)

A purebred dog is a dog whose mother and father are the same breed. (fact; dictionary or encyclopedia)

Hounds are bred to be hunters. (fact; dictionary or encyclopedia)

Hound dogs are the best kind of dog to have. (opinion; *best*)

Fact or Opinion?

Decisions, Decisions!

"Grocery shopping is harder than I thought it was going to be," Marcos sighed.

He picked up a box of cereal and read the information on the side. "Forty percent fiber. Fruit 'n Bran contains seven major vitamins."

"Let's get this one," his sister, Julieanna, pleaded.

"No, wait, this one is better!" She held up a box of Marshmallow Puffs. "This is the best cereal in the store. It's yummy!"

"Well," Marcos said doubtfully. "I guess it'll be all right. Let's look for some milk."

Julieanna hurried to the dairy case and came back with a half gallon of milk.

"This one is low-fat," she said. "It has only two percent butterfat."

Marcos checked his list. "Yes, that's what Mother wrote down. She likes to use lowfat milk."

"Now," he continued, "Mother said to get a fresh pumpkin. They're on sale."

At the fresh food counter, Julieanna reached for a plump pumpkin. "This one is the prettiest."

She pulled it out from the bottom of the stack. The pumpkins trembled, then began to roll. They tumbled off the counter and bounced across the floor.

"Oh no," Julieanna groaned. "That's the dumbest thing I've ever done!"

"Don't worry," Marcos said. "Here comes the manager, and he doesn't look very angry."

© 2000 BJU Press. Reproduction prohibited.

▶ **Choose One**

Circle *F* if the statement is a fact or *O* if the statement is an opinion.

Ⓕ O   "Fruit 'n Bran has forty percent fiber."

F Ⓞ   "Marshmallow Puffs tastes better than Fruit 'n Bran."

F Ⓞ   "This is the best cereal in the store."

Ⓕ O   "This milk has only two percent butterfat."

Ⓕ O   "This store advertised fresh pumpkins for sale."

F Ⓞ   "This is the prettiest pumpkin in the pile."

F Ⓞ   "That's the dumbest thing I've ever done."

F Ⓞ   "The manager doesn't look very angry."

232

A **fact** is a statement that is true. An **opinion** is a statement that tells what a person thinks about a subject.

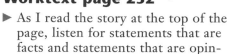

③ Skill application:
Worktext page 232

▶ As I read the story at the top of the page, listen for statements that are facts and statements that are opinions.

Guide the students as they read each statement below the story and decide whether it is a fact or an opinion.

④ Skill practice:
Worktext page 233

SOMETHING EXTRA

Write It: Fact or opinion

Direct the student to make two columns on his paper and label one *Facts* and the other *Opinions*. Instruct him to write some facts and opinions that he finds in the story "Hamlet, Augusta Jones, and Me" (Reader 4, pages 121-30).

Lesson	Reader pages	Worktext pages
44	131-33	57-59

This biographical sketch highlights the boyhood of William Shakespeare in Stratford-on-Avon. It also points out his later accomplishments as a master writer of plays.

VOCABULARY

LESSON 44

*†John wanted to be a playwright, so he practiced writing plays. (p. 131)

*† When I saw the beautiful sunset, I was inspired to write a poem about it. (p. 132)

†A guild chapel is a meeting place for people with similar jobs. (p. 132)

*†The business prospered and grew because of the owner's wise handling of his money. (p. 133)

Heritage Studies Connection

Lesson 44 can be linked to the study of sixteenth-century England.

Materials

• A cape, hat, or any type of old-looking costume piece
• Vocabulary sentences for display

Background information

William Shakespeare—William Shakespeare was born on April 23, 1564. In 1582, he married Anne Hathaway. Within the first three years of marriage, they had a daughter and a set of twins. Because we have no information about Shakespeare's life between 1585 and 1592, this time is often referred to as the Hidden Years. Following this period, Shakespeare began establishing himself as a writer in London. He worked for the largest and most famous acting company, the Lord Chamberlain's Men. They began acting for the royal court after James I came to the throne, and they changed their name to The King's Men. Shakespeare wrote many plays performed by this company. Shortly after his death at age fifty-two, his friends gathered all his works and published them in Shakespeare's first folio.

INTRODUCTION

Vocabulary

Use the prepared sentences to introduce the vocabulary words in context.

To be, or not to be

Put on the costume piece. With a bold voice and a far-off look, read aloud the first line of Hamlet's soliloquy:

▶ "To be, or not to be: that is the question."

Use the following to lead the students in a discussion about the origin of this saying and to explain the connection with the story they previously read.

▶ Have you ever heard this saying before? (Accept any answer.)

What do you think the speaker is talking about? (Accept any answer.)

▶ Think about the story "Hamlet, Augusta Jones, and Me."

What play does Augusta Jones direct, and who does she say wrote the play? (Allow students to look back in the story if they need help recalling the answers—*Hamlet*, William Shakespeare)

The saying I just read is from Shakespeare's play *Hamlet*. Shakespeare is also responsible for many other famous sayings.

Correlated Activities

• **Spelling Practice, Activity 1: Spell Check**
• **Creative Writing, Activity 3: Life and Times in 4th Grade**
See "Classroom Management for Grouping" in the Appendix.

Objectives

William Shakespeare, Playwright

Beki Gorham   illustrated by Bob Martin

Have you ever sat down at a crowded table and had to ask for more "elbow room"? Have you ever told anyone that you had "caught a cold"? Or have you ever heard that someone was "full of the milk of human kindness"?

If you have, you were using or hearing language written down over four hundred years ago by a man named William Shakespeare. William was born in Stratford-on-Avon, England, a little over a hundred miles from the big city of London. It was a small town on the Avon River, full of houses and shops and bordered by meadows, orchards, and rolling fields. Merchants and sailors visited this town, so William could sit and listen to the stories they told about shipwrecks and people in faraway places. It was a fine place to grow up.

William Shakespeare, Playwright   131

COMPREHENSION

The student will
- Perceive time relationships.
- Infer unstated facts and details.
- Recall story details.

Before silent reading: pages 131-33

Motivation
▶ What do you think influenced William Shakespeare to write his famous plays?

After silent reading

Overview discussion: pages 131-33
▶ [critical] What events influenced William Shakespeare to write his famous plays? (possible answers: listening to stories that merchants and sailors told about faraway places; his schooling; having to earn a living; moving to London; watching the plays at the guild chapel)

▶ [interpretive] What makes you think that William Shakespeare was responsible and had close ties with his family? (He felt that he needed to leave school to earn money for his family.)

▶ [critical] Do you think that William Shakespeare could have thought that his plays would become so popular? Why or why not? (Accept any answer.)

Follow-up discussion: page 131
▶ [critical] What do you think "full of the milk of human kindness" means? (Answers will vary, but elicit that it refers to a person who is very kind.)

[appreciative] Have you ever used any of Shakespeare's sayings before?

▶ [literal] In what country was William Shakespeare born? (England)

[interpretive] Why do you think the town William Shakespeare was born in was called Stratford-on-Avon? (because the town was on the Avon River)

[appreciative] After reading the description, would you have liked to live in Stratford-on-Avon over four hundred years ago? Why or why not?

Follow-up discussion: page 132

▶ [literal] What activity at school might have inspired William to write? (reading plays)

[appreciative] Has something you studied or read about at school ever inspired you to write? Tell us about it.

▶ [literal] Why don't we know a lot about William Shakespeare's childhood? (Not much has been written about his childhood.)

[literal] How might William have helped his father? (by working in his father's glovemaking shop)

Read aloud what we can imagine William Shakespeare's early childhood to have been like.

▶ [critical] What do you think was William's favorite thing to do? (Answers will vary, but elicit that he might have liked to see the plays at the guild chapel.)

[appreciative] Do you have something that could be called a guild chapel where you live? Where in your community do people go to see plays?

▶ [literal] Why did William Shakespeare leave school? (to earn a living because his father was in debt)

William attended the Stratford grammar school with the other boys. Every morning at six o'clock he was in his seat, ready to study Latin and literature. All day long, till five or six at night, the boys sat up straight on wooden benches. Perhaps it was here that William read the plays that inspired him to write. At any rate, he was a good student.

William's father, John Shakespeare, was mayor of Stratford and owner of one of its small businesses. William had a sharp sense of humor, which may have come from his father, who was said to have been a cheerful and clever man. Perhaps William also helped in his father's glovemaking shop, along with some of his brothers and sisters.

Little is written of William's early childhood, so we can only imagine what it would have been like to live in Stratford-on-Avon in the 1500s. In the spring and fall a boy could visit the fair in town, or he could go to see a play in the guild chapel. When he grew tired of the town, he could run off to play with friends in the

woods and fields outside the city. Perhaps he could fish in the Avon River or sail toy boats made of leaf and bark in a shallow stream. He could make forts in the Forest of Arden, which edged the sunny fields. Surely William must have been fun to be with. His rich imagination could have provided hours of games and adventures for his companions.

When William was about thirteen, John Shakespeare had business misfortunes and went into debt. So William left school to earn a living. Later he married

132

The Taming of the Shrew by William Shakespeare
(Bob Jones University Classic Players)

and then went to London. There he began to act and to write plays.

His plays became popular, and William Shakespeare prospered. He wrote comedies and tragedies, poetry, and tales of kings. *The Comedy of Errors* might have been his first play, written around 1591. Others of his comedies, or funny plays, are *The Taming of the Shrew, All's Well That Ends Well, Twelfth Night,* and *The Tempest.* The tragedies, or plays that end sadly, include *Romeo and Juliet, Julius Caesar, Hamlet,* and *Macbeth.*

Today, William Shakespeare's plays are produced all over the world, and millions of students study his work in high school and college. Hundreds of magazine articles and books have been written about him. He is probably the most famous writer in the world.

So the next time you hear the name William Shakespeare, or you find yourself "catching a cold," don't forget the little boy who lived in Stratford-on-Avon, who went to school and played with his friends just as you do today.

William Shakespeare, Playwright   133

Follow-up discussion: page 133

▶ [literal] Once in London, what kind of plays did William Shakespeare begin writing? (comedies, tragedies, poetry, and tales of kings)

[interpretive] Would an audience laugh or cry at a play that is a comedy? (laugh)

[critical] What makes a play that is a tragedy sad? (Answers will vary, but explain that in a tragedy something bad happens and some of the main characters die in the end.)

▶ [critical] Why do you think William Shakespeare's plays became so popular? (Accept any answer.)

[literal] What evidence makes the author say that William Shakespeare is probably the most famous writer in the world? (His plays are produced all over the world, and hundreds of magazine articles are written about him.)

Worktext Objective

The student will

▪ Find the main idea of a paragraph.

◄ Complete teaching of this skill was presented in Lesson 12.

Comprehension:
Worktext page 57

STUDY SKILLS

Teaching of main idea and supporting details was presented in Lesson 12.

Outlining main ideas and supporting details

Prepare the following outline frame for display.

    I.
        A.
        B.
        C.
    II.
        A.
        B.
        C.

Elicit that the format displayed is used for writing an outline.

▶ Outlines have two important uses.

  1. An outline is used to organize information.

  2. An outline is a summary of written information.

▶ The first step in outlining is to find the main ideas of the paragraphs. These main ideas are called main topics in an outline.

Direct attention to the first paragraph on page 132 of the reader.

▶ As I read the paragraph aloud, find out what the paragraph is about.

  What is the paragraph about? (William attending school)

Call attention to Roman numeral *I* in the outline format displayed.

▶ Let's write the main idea of the paragraph after Roman numeral *I*.

Write *William as a student* after the *I*.

▶ *William as a student* is the main topic in the outline of this paragraph.

▶ The next step in outlining is to find the supporting details and important facts about the main topic. These details are called subtopics in an outline.

▶ Look at the paragraph again. What are some details given about William as a student? (possible answers: studied Latin and literature, sat on wooden benches all day, was a good student)

After students give details, call attention to the uppercase letters below the main topic and write a supporting detail after each letter.

Read the supporting details aloud, pointing out that they are subtopics in the outline.

You may complete the outline format, conducting a similar discussion with the second paragraph on page 132.

The completed outline should be similar to the following.

    I.   *William as a student*
         A. *Studied Latin and literature*
         B. *Sat on wooden benches all day*
         C. *Was a good student*
    II. *William's father*
         A. *Was mayor of Stratford*
         B. *Owned a glovemaking shop*
         C. *Was a cheerful, clever man*

Study Skills:
Worktext pages 58-59

After discussing outlining main ideas and supporting details, guide students as they finish the pages.

SOMETHING EXTRA

Write About It:
Long lost letter

Allow each student to do further investigating into the life of William Shakespeare, using books and encyclopedias. Challenge the students to gather enough information about Shakespeare, the time period, and the place where Shakespeare lived to write a letter as if they were Shakespeare, describing some portion of his life (or what it might have been like). Encourage the students to share their letters with each other and their families.

Materials

- A note card with the following words written on it: *computer, screen, monitor, keyboard, type, mouse, power button, disk, CD, mouse pad, programs*
- Sewing pattern and pattern directions
- Vocabulary sentences for display

Lesson	Reader pages	Worktext page
45	134-35	60

INTRODUCTION

Vocabulary

Use the prepared sentences to introduce the vocabulary words in context.

Mystery description

▶ Some things are hard to describe with just words.

Give one student the note card with computer-related words written on it. Whisper to him that he may not use these words as he tries to describe a computer to the rest of the group.

▶ You will try to guess the object that he will describe. He will not be able to use certain words in his description, so you will have to listen well.

Allow the student a few minutes to attempt his description and for the other students to guess. If the students do not guess correctly after a few minutes, allow him to tell them he was describing a computer.

▶ Why was it difficult to describe the computer? (Accept any answer.)

▶ What might help a person to understand or describe a computer? (Accept any answer, but elicit that it would have been helpful to use a labeled picture while describing a computer.)

Display the sewing pattern and pattern directions.

▶ What makes it easier to follow the directions in this pattern? (Elicit that the drawings make it easier to follow the directions.)

▶ Today we will learn how a diagram is helpful in understanding or explaining things that are not familiar to us.

VOCABULARY

LESSON 45

†Dad and I went to the theater to see the play. (p. 135)

†The judge's chamber is a room behind the courtroom. (p. 135)

†The audience clapped loudly as Sarah finished her performance. (p. 135)

†At the concert, four tiers of balconies were filled with people. (p. 135)

†Large, painted pictures of scenery were used to create a garden for the play. (p. 135)

Correlated Activities

- **Word Work, Activity 4: Worn Words**
- **Connections, Activity 3: Amazing Ads**

See "Classroom Management for Grouping" in the Appendix.

COMPREHENSION

The student will
- Recognize a diagram.
- Note the purpose for diagrams.
- Read for information.

Before silent reading:
pages 134-35

Motivation
▶ Why is the drawing on the page useful?

After silent reading

Overview discussion:
pages 134-35

▶ [interpretive] How can a diagram be useful? (Because some things are hard to explain with just words, a diagram helps one to understand better when learning about an unfamiliar object or subject.)

Follow-up discussion: page 134

▶ [literal] What is a diagram? (a drawing of an object you want to explain)

[critical] Name some things that would be difficult to explain without a diagram. (Accept any answer.)

[interpretive] How are the important parts of the drawing set apart from the rest of the drawing? (The important parts of the drawing are labeled.)

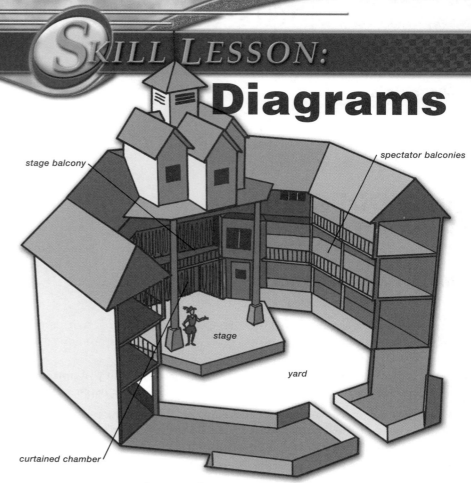

SKILL LESSON:
Diagrams

stage balcony

spectator balconies

stage

yard

curtained chamber

Cutaway diagram of the Globe Theater

Some things are hard to explain with just words. How would someone explain the parts of a car to a friend who had never seen one? A diagram comes in handy then. A diagram is a drawing of the object you want to explain. It labels the important parts of the drawing.

• Reading a Diagram

The stage where William Shakespeare's plays were performed wasn't like the one Augusta Jones used in the story "Hamlet, Augusta Jones, and Me." Many of Shakespeare's plays were performed in a theater in London called the Globe Theater. Notice the labeled parts of the Globe Theater in the diagram as you read the following paragraph.

In the Globe Theater there was no curtain for the stage. Performers would show that a scene was changing by simply leaving the stage and going behind the curtained chamber. The stage balcony could represent the deck of a ship, a prison window, or the balcony where Juliet waited for Romeo. The stage itself reached right into the first rows of the outside audience, the poorer people who sat in the yard. The yard was the area in front of the stage that was always exposed to weather. The rich people could sit in three tiers of covered spectator balconies where they would be protected from the rain.

• Uses for Diagrams

If you had read the above description without a diagram, it might have been hard to picture the Globe Theater. But the diagram helped you to understand much better.

Suppose you were reading instructions about how to make a costume for a play or build a piece of scenery. One diagram or a series of diagrams could help you then.

Remember how useful a diagram can be the next time you have to explain something to a friend. It may make all the difference between confusion and understanding!

▶ [literal] Where were many of Shakespeare's plays performed? (in London at the Globe Theater)

[critical] Why do you suppose the theater was named the Globe Theater? (Accept any answer, but suggest that it was named the Globe Theater because it was round.)

[critical] Why was there no curtain for the stage? (Accept any answer.)

▶ [literal] What are some of the advantages to having a stage balcony? (It could represent the deck of a ship, a prison window, or the balcony where Juliet waited for Romeo.)

[literal] What advantage would people have sitting in one of the tiers? (They would be protected from the rain.)

▶ [interpretive] Why are some parts of the Globe Theater diagram labeled? (to show where they are located and to help you understand the description)

Instruct the students to point on the diagram to the part of the Globe Theater where the poorer people sat. (the yard)

Instruct the students to point to the place where the actors went after they left the stage. (the curtained chamber)

▶ [appreciative] Have you ever used a diagram? What did you need it for?

[critical] How will a diagram make all the difference between confusion and understanding? (Answers will vary, but elicit that there will be less confusion if the object is pictured and labeled rather than just described.)

Worktext Objective

The student will

■ Read a diagram for information.

Study Skills:
Worktext page 60

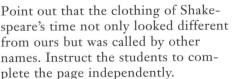

Point out that the clothing of Shakespeare's time not only looked different from ours but was called by other names. Instruct the students to complete the page independently.

SOMETHING EXTRA

Write It: Diagram your description

Instruct each student to draw a diagram of something familiar, such as an airplane, musical instrument, or bicycle. Remind the student to make the diagram simple and to label the important parts. Instruct the student to write a brief description about the object. Display the diagrams and descriptions.

Make It: Origami

Guide a project that requires the use of a diagram. Provide several books on origami—Japanese paper folding. Have available different colored sheets of paper. Pick several simple origami projects and allow the student to make the figures, using the diagrams as guides.

JANWAHR'S BRIDGE

> Blind Janwahr has never felt like the royal prince he is by birth until the day of the southern invasion. His knowledge of the secret bridge and Danzee, the kingdom's secret friend, saves his sister and the entire kingdom.

Lesson	Reader pages	Worktext pages
46	136-41	61
47	142-47	62
48	148-52	63-64

Materials
- A paper crown
- Vocabulary sentences for display

Background information
Sea dragons—Despite the elusiveness of creatures that we call dragons, dragon stories abound in folklore and mythology. Both Eastern and Western cultures often mentioned dragons in their literature. Dragons represented power, wisdom, or ferocity. "Janwahr's Bridge" includes a sea dragon.

INTRODUCTION

Vocabulary
Use the prepared sentences to introduce the vocabulary words in context.

Feeling royal
Place the crown on a student's head.

▶ How do you think it feels to be a royal prince or princess?

What characteristics do you think a royal prince might have?

VOCABULARY

LESSON 46

The king asked his yeoman to bring him his royal robe. (p. 137)

*†When the queen saw the servant napping, her opinion was confirmed that he was lazy. (p. 137)

*†My grandmother says the columns on our front porch make it look like a portico. (p. 137)

*†The steep, rocky cliff was a treacherous place to climb. (p. 139)

LESSON 47

*†The surrounded castle was under siege by the attackers. (p. 143)

*†A group of men was sent as a delegation to stop the battle. (p. 143)

*†The king asked the old philosophers, who were his wisest men, to think of a plan. (p. 143)

LESSON 48

Sturdy straps or martingales prevented the horse from throwing back its head. (p. 150)

The knights carefully put the swords back into their scabbards. (p. 150)

*†They looked at the magnificent animal in awe, amazed by its size and beauty. (p. 152)

He clambered up the steep hill. (p. 152)

Correlated Activities
- **Vocabulary Box, Activity 1: Word Hunt**
- **Recreational Reading, Activity 3: Frantic Antics**

See "Classroom Management for Grouping" in the Appendix.

COMPREHENSION

The student will

- Infer attitude from the actions of the characters.
- Demonstrate enjoyment of fantasy.
- Recognize the author's use of imagery.
- Distinguish between realistic fiction and fanciful fiction.

Before silent reading: pages 136-41

Motivation

▶ What is unique about Janwahr?

Janwahr has a secret. What is it?

After silent reading

Overview discussion: pages 136-41

▶ [interpretive] How does Janwahr feel about being a prince? (His blindness causes him to have a lack of confidence in himself; he does not think he is worthy to be a prince.)

[appreciative] Do you feel sorry for Janwahr? Why or why not?

▶ [literal] Whom does Janwahr talk to and play with down by the water? (Danzee, a huge beast)

[critical] Why do you think Janwahr keeps Danzee a secret from everyone? (Accept any answer, but elicit that he is probably afraid people will not believe him and he enjoys the friendship he alone has with Danzee.)

JANWAHR'S BRIDGE

Dawn L. Watkins
illustrated by Del Thompson and John Bjerk

Silver Horn

Janwahr, the youngest son of King Rolday, was blind. He sat in his tower room and pulled at the leather strap of his boot as if the boot could be on any more securely than it already was. He always did everything twice, just to be sure.

In the courtyard below, his brothers, Taytan and Nadar, called for their horses to be saddled. Servants ran across the cobblestones to the stables.

"I wonder if Gemla is going riding this morning," he thought. Gemla, his sister, whom everyone called beautiful, would let him ride behind her sometimes, but only when Taytan and Nadar were not there to scold about his getting hurt.

He tugged the strap of his other boot a second time.

"Bandeen," he called.

"I am here, Prince Janwahr," a servant about the prince's age answered.

136

Follow-up discussion: page 136

▶ [literal] Who is Janwahr and what is special about him? (He is the youngest son of King Rolday, and he is blind.)

[interpretive] What unusual thing does Janwahr do? Why does he do it? (He always does everything twice; because he is blind, he worries that he cannot do things right.)

▶ [literal] Who are Janwahr's brothers and sister? (His brothers are Taytan and Nadar, and his sister is Gemla.)

Read aloud Janwahr's thoughts about riding a horse.

[critical] What do you think Janwahr's brothers are like? (Answers may vary, but suggest that since they are older they look out for their little brother. They also try to protect him because of his blindness.)

It was true that the palace servants addressed him as Prince Janwahr; the stablemen and yeomen always said "Your Highness" when they spoke to him. But in all his nine years he had never felt like a prince.

" 'Janwahr' would do," he told his servant.

"I know you do not want me to use your title, sir, but I should not call my master by his name only—it is disrespectful."

Janwahr nodded. "Shall we go?"

The prince put out his arm for Bandeen. The servant took it.

"To the river as always, Your Highness?"

"Yes, to the river."

As Bandeen stepped forward, Janwahr felt confirmed in his belief—a blind boy could never truly be a prince.

Janwahr and Bandeen walked out onto a gray marble portico. The prince felt the smooth sun on his cheeks and neck.

Janwahr's Bridge 137

Follow-up discussion: page 137

▶ [literal] How old is Prince Janwahr? (nine years old)

[interpretivel] Why would it be disrespectful for Bandeen to call his master Janwahr rather than Prince Janwahr? (Janwahr has a very high position in the kingdom, and using a title is a sign of respect.) [BAT: 2a Authority]

Read aloud Janwahr's views about himself as a prince.

[critical] Does Janwahr have a good reason not to feel like a prince? Why or why not? (Answers may vary, but elicit that he thinks that being blind makes him less worthy to be a prince.)

▶ [interpretive] How does the author tell us that Janwahr knows the sun is shining? (The author says that Janwahr can feel it on his cheeks and neck.)

▶ [interpretive] Why does Bandeen hesitate to tell Janwahr that the sky is blue? (Bandeen does not want Janwahr to feel bad since he cannot see the color blue.) [BAT: 5a Compassion]

[interpretive] How does Janwahr distinguish between colors? (He compares colors to things he can feel or hear.)

Read aloud how Janwahr describes blue and red.

[critical] Do you think Janwahr gives good descriptions of blue and red? (Accept any answer.)

▶ [literal] How does the author describe Janwahr's favorite spot by the water? (There is a hollow between the two roots and the armrests Janwahr uses. The upper branches reach far out over the river and keep the spot cool.)

"Is the sky clear?" he asked.

"As blue as . . ." the servant began.

There was silence.

"The sky is cloudless, Prince Janwahr."

"It is all right to say blue, Bandeen. I think of blue as the way the air feels on a calm summer evening."

"How is red to you, sir?" the servant asked.

"Like my brother Nadar when our sister outshoots him on the archery fields."

Bandeen and the prince laughed together and then went down the jade steps.

At the river, Janwahr sat under his favorite wildalia tree. He had sat there so often that he had worn a comfortable hollow between two big roots. The roots now stuck up so far that they made armrests for the prince. The upper branches of the huge old wildalia reached far out over the river and kept it as cool as early morning around the roots all day.

138

"Come back for me at noon," said Janwahr, and the servant left him, as always, without a word.

Where Janwahr sat was at the narrowest point in the river. Bandeen had told him once that it was two palace lengths to the other bank. Janwahr could not imagine how high and rough the ridges were behind him, but Bandeen had said they were treacherous. He leaned back against the tree, smelling the river flowers and the damp earth. The julas sang above him, and the water sloshed against the bank just below him. When he was sure Bandeen had gone, Janwahr whistled—a high, swift whistle— and listened. Some way off he heard a rush and swirl of water. He smiled widely. Then there was a sound like milk being poured into a tall glass, and Janwahr knew that his companion was coming.

"Good morning, Danzee," he called out.

A rolling roar answered him.

"You are such a noisy fellow in the morning. We could never have you about the palace."

Janwahr heard splashing right at his feet, and he knew Danzee had reached the bank and was tossing the water off his great head.

The prince reached forward, and Danzee laid his head on the bank. Janwahr patted the broad expanse familiarly. He ran his hand over the rough scales, each of which was bigger than his hand.

"I never get used to how big your nose is. Just the tip of it is bigger than I am!"

Danzee gurgled deep in his throat in response.

Janwahr came forward on his hands and knees, climbing right up Danzee's massive nose until he came to the giant curved horn.

The horn was always cold and smooth like the silver cups in the palace. Janwahr was sure the great horn was solid silver. He looped one arm halfway around the horn, pulling himself onto it, straddling the base as he would a horse. He adjusted his position on the inside of the sweeping curve.

"Let's go, Danzee!"

Janwahr's Bridge   139

Follow-up discussion: page 139

▶ [critical] What do you think julas are? (Accept any answer, but elicit that they may be some kind of bird.)

▶ [interpretive] Why is the spot by the river Janwahr's favorite place to be? (because of his friend, Danzee)

[interpretive] What sound does the author use to describe Danzee's coming up out of the water? (She compares the sound to milk being poured into a tall glass.)

Read aloud what happens when Janwahr whistles.

▶ [interpretive] What distinguishes this story as fanciful fiction instead of realistic fiction? (the huge beast, Danzee)

[interpretive] What special thing does Janwahr know about Danzee even though Janwahr is blind? (that Danzee has a great horn of solid silver)

Read aloud the paragraph that describes Danzee's horn.

▶ [critical] Do you think Janwahr is brave? Why or why not? (Answers may vary, but elicit that even though he is blind, he is brave enough to ride a huge beast.) [BAT: 8d Courage]

[interpretive] What does the author compare Janwahr to as Danzee swings him? (a blade of grass)

[literal] Why does Janwahr wish his brothers could see him ride Danzee? (then they would let him ride a horse)

Read aloud the author's description of "roundabout" as if you were riding on the huge beast.

[appreciative] Would you like the "roundabout" ride?

▶ [literal] What fun thing does Janwahr do for Danzee as Danzee rests? (He sings him a song.)

▶ [literal] What are some descriptive verbs the author uses to shows Danzee's actions? (swayed, glided, gurgled, stirred, snorted, nudged)

The huge beast lifted his head. Up and up went Janwahr through the air, through the leaves of the wildalia, into the strong sunlight. Then Danzee swayed his head from side to side, gently swinging the prince about like a blade of grass.

Janwahr thought, "Someday I will bring Nadar and Taytan here to see me ride. Then they will let me on the horses."

The prince laughed aloud with delight.

"Now roundabout!"

Danzee swung his head in a wild circle, first clockwise, then counterclockwise, then clockwise again, and again, and again.

"Well done, Danzee," said the prince, patting the vast cheek as soundly as he could. "Good boy."

Danzee glided to the shore and lowered his head as softly as the snow comes down. He blew gusts of wind from his nostrils as he waited for the boy to get off.

"All tired out, are you? Then you rest, and I will sing a song I made up for you." In clear tenor, Janwahr picked up a merry tune:

The banks are steep,
The water's deep,
But I shall never have a fear-O.
For I can fly
Like the julas shy
When Danzee Boy is near-O.

Danzee gurgled and blew out one big gust.

"Well, let's see you do better, then," said the prince, and gave the beast a tap on his nose.

Danzee dozed awhile, and Janwahr tried to make up another verse for his song. He could not come up with a rhyme for *silver;* so by and by he gave up the effort.

"Wake up, Danzee, you old snoozer. Do you want your back scratched?"

Danzee stirred himself lazily.

"Hurry along. It takes some time, you know," Janwahr said.

Danzee snorted and nudged the prince.

140

The boy pulled a sturdy, forked branch from beside the tree and held it firmly out over the bank.

Danzee ducked his head under the branch and began to swim forward, close to the bank. Janwahr pointed the branch downward until he felt it touch the back of the beast. Danzee swam on, arching his great length to come under the prongs of the branch.

For ten minutes he passed by, until at last he slapped the tip of his tail in the water to let Janwahr know he could stop holding the branch.

"You get longer every day, Danzee!"

Janwahr's Bridge   141

Follow-up discussion: page 141

▶ [interpretive] What does the length of time Janwahr scratches Danzee's back suggest about Danzee? (He is very long.)

[critical] How do you think Janwahr feels toward Danzee? (Accept any answer, but elicit that he enjoys being with him and likes him as we would like a pet.)

[literal] How does Janwahr know to let go of the branch? (Danzee slaps the tip of his tail in the water.)

Read aloud what Janwahr says to Danzee.

Looking ahead

▶ Will anyone find out about Danzee?

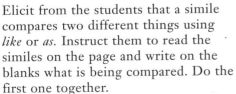

Worktext Objective

The student will

■ Understand similes.

Literature:
Worktext page 61

Elicit from the students that a simile compares two different things using *like* or *as*. Instruct them to read the similes on the page and write on the blanks what is being compared. Do the first one together.

COMPREHENSION

Objectives

The student will

- Identify fanciful elements in a story.
- Differentiate between realistic fiction and fanciful fiction.
- Identify actions and traits of the characters in the story.
- Identify conflicting points of view.

Before silent reading: pages 142-47

Use the prepared sentences to introduce the vocabulary words in context.

Motivation

▶ From the title of this chapter, what do you think is going to happen in the kingdom?

How will Janwahr play a part in this invasion?

After silent reading

Overview discussion: pages 142-47

▶ [literal] What big event is happening in the kingdom? (Janwahr's kingdom is being attacked.)

[interpretive] How many different plans for responding to the invasion are discussed? (Four—all three brothers and the sister have their own plan.)

[literal] What reason does the southern king have for attacking Janwahr's kingdom? (He wants to marry Gemla.)

[critical] Were you surprised that King Rolday chose Janwahr's plan over his older brothers' plans? Why or why not? (Accept any answer.)

[interpretive] What friend has a special part in this plan? (Danzee)

Invasion

The beast had made a mighty circle; his head was nearly to the bank again. He roared his gratitude.

"Someday I'll bring my sister here to see you. You'll like her. She is beautiful, they say. And she will know how to appreciate so fine a creature as you. The gift I bring you today," said the prince, "is the North Star. My father's sailors say they use it to steer their ships. You may have it."

Danzee slapped the water with the end of his tail and roared.

"You like that gift, do you?" said Janwahr. "Do you like it better than the summer breeze I gave you yesterday?"

Janwahr could feel Danzee's head very near.

"You had better go now, before Bandeen comes. I'll see you tomorrow, my friend."

Danzee put his nose against Janwahr and then swam slowly backwards, submerging himself as he went. He left so quietly that the prince was often not sure he was gone.

142

On this day, Danzee had hardly disappeared before the prince heard Bandeen calling.

"Prince Janwahr!"

Janwahr stood up and turned toward the sound.

"Your Highness!" Bandeen called.

"What is it? Why are you early?"

Bandeen came thrashing through the tanglebriars, forsaking the safer but longer path. He arrived before the prince, breathless and scratched.

"What is it, Bandeen?" Janwahr reached out to take his servant by the shoulders.

Follow-up discussion: page 142

▶ [critical] Why do you think Janwahr prefers to have his sister see Danzee rather than his brothers? (Possible answer: She understands Janwahr and will appreciate Danzee's beauty.)

Read aloud Janwahr's explanation of the person he would like Danzee to meet.

▶ [critical] Are Janwahr's gifts to Danzee real or imagined? (Answers may vary, but elicit that the gifts themselves are real but cannot be given to anyone.)

▶ [interpretive] How does Danzee say good-bye to Janwahr? (He puts his nose against Janwahr before swimming away.)

▶ [interpretive] Why does Bandeen take the short and dangerous path through the forest? (He has very urgent news to tell Janwahr.)

Read aloud in a troubled voice the paragraphs showing how Bandeen returns.

"An invasion," he said between pants. "The kingdom to the south!"

"Are we under siege right now?" Janwahr felt his heart leaping.

"No," the servant puffed.

"What then?"

"A messenger delivered a declaration of war this morning. The southern king begins his march tomorrow!"

"Why?"

"For your sister, Your Highness."

"Gemla! Come, take me home. Quickly!"

At the palace, an argument was going on in the court. "Give me five hundred horsemen, Father," Nadar said. "I can meet the invaders in the third valley."

"No, no," said Taytan, the eldest. "We must send a delegation to discuss the matter."

"Stop it, all of you," said Gemla in her quiet voice. "I will marry the southern king to spare our father all this trouble." She turned away to the window.

"Five hundred men, and I will hold them in the valley," Nadar began again.

"You only know how to settle things by taking sword in hand!" Taytan glared at Nadar.

"And you would send old philosophers and the aged of our court into the very teeth of war!"

"Silence!" King Rolday stood up, and the hall went silent.

Janwahr still stood at the west door with Bandeen.

"Hear what I say," said the king. "Your solutions are not real solutions at all. First, I ask you, Gemla, do you love this king?"

"I love the rats in the grain more," said she without raising her voice.

Janwahr's Bridge 143

Follow-up discussion: page 143

▶ [interpretive] What does Janwahr mean when he says, "Are we under siege right now?" (He is asking if the enemy soldiers have already started fighting them.)

Choose two students to read aloud the conversation between Bandeen and Janwahr or allow one student to read aloud the conversation, using a different voice for each character.

▶ [interpretive] How does Janwahr show his concern for his sister? (He requests to be taken home immediately.) [BAT: 5a Love]

▶ [interpretive] What is the disagreement between Nadar and Taytan about a plan? (Nadar wants to fight and Taytan wants to talk.)

[literal] What is Gemla's plan? (She will marry the southern king to avoid a battle.) [BATs: 2b Servanthood; 5b Unselfishness]

[literal] What does the king think of the three different plans? (The solutions are not real solutions.)

▶ [literal] What does the princess say she loves more than the southern king? (the rats in the grain)

[interpretive] What does Gemla mean by saying she loves the rats more than the southern king? (She does not love the king at all; she despises him.)

Janwahr's Bridge

Follow-up discussion: page 144

▶ [interpretive] Why does Gemla blush when talking to her father? (because she realizes that her father knows that she likes a different king)

[interpretive] Why does King Rolday forbid Gemla to marry the southern king for any reason? (because he is very wicked) [BAT: 4c Fairness]

▶ [critical] Is King Rolday a wise or foolish king? Why do you think so? (Answers may vary, but elicit that he is wise because he gives sound advice to his sons and daughter.)

Read aloud King Rolday's reply to Taytan explaining why it is too late for negotiations.

"As I thought. The king of Wehdona is more to your liking, is he not?"

She blushed in answer.

"So no more foolish talk from you then. You will not marry so wicked a man as the southern king for any reason. Now, Nadar, do you know the size of the invading army?"

"No, sir," he replied.

"Then how can you say five hundred of my horsemen will hold them? In years past I have known this king to go to war with two thousand soldiers. He may have as many now."

Nadar studied the toe of his boot.

"And you, Taytan, what is there to negotiate? War has been declared already. It is too late for talking."

No one there, not the princes, nor the counselors, nor the captains, made any answer to the king.

Janwahr listened, every nerve tight. He would die to save Gemla, but what could he do? He could not ride; he could not hold a bow. He strained forward, hoping to hear comfort from his father.

144

But before the king could speak, one of his outriders appeared at the north door, winded and pale. He bowed low and waited.

"Speak, man," said the king.

"Your Majesty," he said, "the southern army is in the second valley!"

Astonishment gripped the hearers.

"Say on," said the king.

"If they march on at the rate they are coming, they will be here at dusk."

"How many men?" said the king.

"About a thousand, sir."

The king's mouth was set and grim. He scanned the room as if searching for an answer.

Janwahr felt his heart throbbing against his ribs. He wanted someone to think of a way to save Gemla. But no one spoke.

"Call up a thousand horsemen," said the king.

Nadar paced toward the door.

"Wait!" cried Janwahr.

All eyes turned to him. The king was amazed.

"Janwahr. What is it?" he asked.

Janwahr's Bridge   145

Follow-up discussion: page 145

▶ [literal] What news does the outrider bring now? (The southern king's forces are in the second valley and much closer now.)

▶ [critical] Although Janwahr lacks confidence, do you think he is braver than he realizes? Why or why not? (Answers will vary, but elicit that no one in the room has a good idea, and Janwahr speaks up because he thinks his plan might work.) [BAT: 8d Courage]

Read aloud how Janwahr speaks up to everyone and the reactions of the others.

[appreciative] What would you be thinking right now if you were one of Janwahr's brothers?

▶ [critical] Why does everyone expect the king to dismiss Janwahr's plan? (Answers may vary, but elicit that the others do not take Janwahr seriously because of his age and blindness.)

[literal] What is Janwahr's plan? (to use a secret bridge that comes out of the water)

Read aloud in a confident voice what Janwahr's plan is.

▶ [critical] Why does King Rolday order his people to obey Janwahr? (Answers may vary, but elicit that the people will believe in Janwahr only if the king is confident in his plan.)

Read aloud King Rolday's surprising answer to everyone.

▶ [interpretive] Why does Gemla ask "Where is the bridge?" (It is not there yet because Janwahr has to call the "bridge" with a whistle.)

"I have a plan, sir."

The king saw the desire in the boy.

"Quickly, Son."

"Let Nadar take the horsemen to the ridges above the river at the narrow place and stay out of sight. I will get Gemla to the other side. When the southern army comes to the river, let Nadar and the men sweep down and trap them against the river. The ridges will be too steep and the pass too narrow for them to escape. Then let Taytan and the counselors talk."

Everyone waited for the king to dismiss the plan.

"How will you get Gemla across quickly enough? Our best rowers cannot steer across that current in one whole day."

"I know a bridge, my father."

"What bridge? There are no bridges."

"A bridge that comes out of the water."

"And what is to stop the southern king from sending his men across that bridge?"

"It is a secret bridge, sir."

King Rolday weighed the risks. He wanted to believe his son for many reasons.

Then to the surprise of all he said, "We will do as Janwahr suggests. Obey him."

Janwahr could hardly breathe in the silence that followed.

"Please bring up the horsemen, Nadar," he said.

Nadar glanced at the king, who nodded once. Nadar left immediately.

"Sir," said the youngest prince, "Bandeen and I will take Gemla to safety. Taytan and what counselors you choose should come behind the horsemen. Yes?"

"As you say, Son," the king replied. "But I will come with you. I want to see this miraculous bridge that even I did not know existed in my kingdom."

Before long, the king, Princess Gemla, the king's guards, Bandeen, and Janwahr stood at the bank by the wildalia tree.

"Where is the bridge?" Gemla asked, a quiver in her voice.

Janwahr gave a high whistle and then another.

146

Near the other shore a huge blue sea dragon's head broke the surface, roaring. The king and the princess gasped in wonder. Bandeen and the guards fell back.

The dragon lifted its head high out of the river and shook the shining water off in all directions. Its horn glistened in the sun.

"That horn must be solid silver," said Gemla under her breath, holding Janwahr's arm.

"Is it silver?" Janwahr said. "I thought it was."

Danzee swam forward.

"It's coming here," said Bandeen, running behind the wildalia.

Janwahr smiled. "Danzee won't hurt you."

When the shining monster neared the shore, even the king stepped back. Two of his guards advanced and crossed their swords in front of him. The great beast put his head beside the roots of the tree and waited.

Follow-up discussion: page 147

▶ [literal] What color is Danzee? (blue)

[critical] How do you think the people feel when they see Danzee come up out of the water? Why do you think so? (Answers may vary, but elicit that they are surprised and shocked; they gasp in wonder and fall back.)

Read aloud with great emotion what Gemla says under her breath.

[appreciative] Would you be afraid of Danzee?

Read aloud the sentence that tells us Danzee is harmless.

Looking ahead

▶ Will Janwahr's plan work to save Gemla and the kingdom?

Worktext Objectives

The student will

■ Match words and definitions.
■ Recall facts and details.

Comprehension:
Worktext page 62

Encourage the student to use his glossary as needed to find the correct definition of each word at the top of the page.

COMPREHENSION

Objective

The student will

■ Recognize character growth and change.

Trapped

"Danzee, this is my father, the king, and my sister, Princess Gemla. We need your help." Janwahr heard Danzee gurgle. "Can you stretch from one bank to the other?"

Danzee swirled himself around. He arched himself in several dozen places and made the water toss out beside him for yards and yards.

Then, from far across the river, a slap of his tail sounded.

"He's ready," said Janwahr.

Gemla, still holding her brother's arm, hesitated.

"It's all right," the prince said. "Danzee will help us. I would go with you, but I must wait here for the invaders."

Use the prepared sentences to introduce the vocabulary words in context.

Before silent reading: pages 148-52

Motivation

▶ How does Danzee help with the invasion of the southern king's army?

Will Janwahr ever feel like a real prince?

After silent reading

Overview discussion: pages 148-52

▶ [interpretive] How does Danzee defeat the southern king? (He carries Gemla to safety and then comes back to grab the southern king and swing him in the air, causing the king to surrender.)

▶ [critical] Do you think the relationship between Janwahr and his father has changed? Why do you think so? (Accept any answer, but elicit that their relationship is stronger now; his father believed in Janwahr's plan over his brothers' strategies, King Rolday developed a new confidence in Janwahr due to his clever plan, and they worked together to defeat the enemy.)

Follow-up discussion: page 148

▶ [interpretive] How does Janwahr know Danzee has stretched himself across the river? (He hears Danzee's tail hit the water.)

▶ [critical] Why do you think Gemla hesitates to walk across the river on the sea dragon? (Answers may vary.)

Read aloud Janwahr's reassuring words to his sister.

At last Gemla stepped forward, and at the king's command four guards took her across the dragon bridge to the other side.

"Is he beautiful?" Janwahr asked his father as Gemla was crossing.

"Worthy of a prince," said the king.

Janwahr said nothing.

"Thank you, Danzee," said the king. And Danzee dropped beneath the surface, flashed the tip of his tail once, and was gone.

Janwahr's Bridge   149

Follow-up discussion: page 149

► [interpretive] How do we know that Gemla trusts her brother Janwahr? (She is willing to cross the dragon bridge.)

► [critical] Why do you think Janwahr asks his father if Danzee is beautiful? (Answers may vary, but elicit that because he is blind, Janwahr has painted a picture of Danzee in his mind that is beautiful, and he wants to know if Danzee truly is beautiful.)

Read aloud the king's answer to Janwahr's question about Danzee.

► [critical] Why doesn't Janwahr say anything after his father's answer? (Accept any answer, but point out that Janwahr feels unworthy to be a prince and his father has just reminded him of his worthiness to be a prince when he says that Danzee is worthy of a prince.)

Follow-up discussion: page 150

► [literal] How much time has passed before hoofbeats and trumpets are heard? (a few hours)

► [interpretive] Is Janwahr beginning to doubt his plan? How do you know? (Yes; Janwahr says, "If my plan fails," which could mean he considers it a possibility.)

Read aloud why King Rolday says a king must not doubt a plan once it is under way.

[interpretive] What does Janwahr's father encourage him to do? (to believe in himself to gain the soldiers' trust)

[critical] Why does it feel good to Janwahr to stand by his father while they wait? (Accept any answer, but elicit that King Rolday's statement about choosing the best plan shows his confidence in Janwahr.) [BAT: 2b Teamwork]

► [interpretive] How does the southern king feel about himself and his army? (He is confident they will win against King Rolday's weak, feeble army.)

Read aloud in a confident manner what the southern king says to King Rolday.

After some hours Janwahr could hear hoofbeats and trumpets and shouts.

"Can you see them yet?"

"Not yet," said King Rolday.

"If my plan fails—" the prince began.

"Never doubt your plan once it's under way. Choose the best plan and stay with it. A king must believe in himself if he would have his men's trust."

Janwahr remained silent. It was good to stand here by the river with his father. He straightened and clasped his hands loosely behind his back.

At length the king said, "They are here."

The whole pass between the ridges was suddenly filled with riders on huge battle horses. The armor and swords shone out in the setting sun. On and on they came, leather creaking and metal clinking. The horses tossed their heads, rattling their martingales and chest plates. They drew up before King Rolday and Prince Janwahr.

The southern king leaned forward in his saddle, throwing back his black hood. "Where's your feeble army, Rolday?"

All along the ridges above and in the pass, Rolday's soldiers appeared silently, gray and solemn against the dusk. King Rolday pointed.

The southern king looked back and started. His men tensed in their saddles and put their hands to their scabbards.

150

The southern king swung back around. "A stupid trap! You do not have me—I have you!"

And with that he sprang from his horse and drew a dagger against Rolday's throat. He leaned toward Rolday's ear. "Call them down, or I kill you!"

Janwahr whistled high and long and loud. Just behind them the river burst open with a great rush and a horrible roar. The silver horn gleamed as the water streamed off the giant creature.

Danzee saw the armies and raised himself a hundred feet out of the water, shaking his head and screaming.

The southern king staggered back.

"Help us, Danzee!" Janwahr called.

The great head swooped down. Danzee caught up the evil king by his tunic and held him there.

"Your men surrender, or I give you to my friend here—for his supper!"

Follow-up discussion: page 151

▶ [critical] Why does the southern king say, "You do not have me—I have you!" (Answers will vary, but elicit that although the southern king has now seen Rolday's army he is still confident that his own army will win.)

Read aloud what the southern king does to King Rolday next.

▶ [literal] Who takes action now and what does he do? (Janwahr whistles for Danzee's help.)

[critical] Do you think the southern king is surprised to be hanging from the mouth of a sea dragon? Why or why not? (Accept any answer.)

Read aloud very confidently Janwahr's words to the southern king.

Follow-up discussion: page 152

▶ [critical] Why would the southern king refuse to speak after hearing Janwahr's words? (Accept any answer.)

[critical] Why is Janwahr's next command to Danzee a smart decision? (Answers may vary, but elicit that the "roundabout" shows Danzee's power, which is just what the king needs to encourage him to surrender.)

Read aloud in a desperate voice what the southern king calls out.

▶ [interpretive] How do King Rolday and the whole kingdom feel about Prince Janwahr now? How does the author let us know? (They are proud of him; Bandeen is overcome with wonder, and King Rolday puts the emphasis on *Prince* in his title now.) [BAT: 5a Thankfulness]

Read aloud what King Rolday says to his son. Say it like a proud father would.

[interpretive] How does Janwahr show that he has gained self-confidence and feels like a prince now? (He straightens his tunic—*once*.)

The two armies stood frozen in horror and awe. But the southern king refused to speak.

"Roundabout," called out Janwahr.

Danzee took the southern king in four giant circles, skimming the water with him on the downward moves, raking him through the wildalia on the upward.

"Enough," the king called. "We surrender!"

"Well done, Danzee! Drop him," called the prince.

In mid-arch, Danzee opened his jaws and the king flew out and down into the water.

As he clambered about in the water, Taytan and the counselors came forward through the invading armies. The southern king dragged himself onto the bank.

"Shall we discuss the terms of surrender?" said Rolday to the dripping king.

Bandeen, overcome with the wonder of it all, ran forward to his master. "Well done, Janwahr!"

"Prince Janwahr," said King Rolday.

Janwahr smiled broadly and straightened his tunic—once.

152

LITERATURE
Fantasy

Read the following passage from "Janwahr's Bridge."

> Janwahr gave a high whistle and then another. Near the other shore a huge blue sea dragon's head broke the surface, roaring. The king and the princess gasped in wonder. Bandeen and the guards fell back.

▶ Is this story fiction or nonfiction? How do you know? (fiction; because sea dragons do not exist)

"Janwahr's Bridge" is fanciful fiction. The author and reader pretend something unbelievable is true—that a sea dragon is friends with Janwahr.

Allow the students to name other stories they have read that are fanciful.

Write the word *fantasy* for display. Point out that "Janwahr's Bridge" is a type of fanciful fiction called fantasy. Guide the following discussion about the elements of fantasy.

▶ Fantasy stories have characters and/or events that could not occur in real life. Although a fantasy story has an element that obviously could not exist in real life, it creates a believable environment by providing many details about the people, setting, and "real life" themes and motives.

▶ What identifies "Janwahr's Bridge" as a fantasy story? (the dragon)

Is the rest of the story believeable? Why or why not? (Yes; other than the dragon, the events could have occurred sometime in history.)

Do the characters in the story act like real people? (Yes—they exhibit human emotions and actions.)

What "real life" problem does Janwahr have? (He feels as if he cannot truly be a prince because of his blindness.)

Point out that though the kingdoms are set to battle, the real conflict of the story is Janwahr's battle with himself.

▶ What "real life" attributes does Janwahr show when he tells the king his plan? (courage, resourcefulness)

Literature: Worktext page 63

Instruct the student to read the story. Discuss the elements of fantasy in the story. Tell the student to complete the fantasy story and then to draw a picture to illustrate his story. Allow the students to read their completed stories aloud.

Vocabulary: Worktext page 64

SOMETHING EXTRA
Write It: My own ending

Guide the student to imagine he is the author of this sea-dragon story. Instruct him to write a different ending to this fantasy, beginning at the time when Janwahr stands side by side with his father, waiting for the southern army to appear.

Lesson	Worktext pages
49	234-35

Objectives

The student will

- Divide words with affixes into syllables between the base word and the affixes (re•view•ing).
- Recognize that the suffix *-ed* is in a separate syllable after base words that end with /d/ and /t/ (land•ed, test•ed).
- Recognize that the suffix *-es* is a separate syllable after base words that end with *ch, sh, s, x,* or *z* (lunch•es).
- Place the primary accent mark on or within the base word of a word with an affix (un•lock´•ing).
- Place the primary accent mark on the first syllable of a two-syllable word (bas´•ket) or on the second syllable when that syllable contains two vowels (col•lapse´).

Background information

Syllable Division Rule 4—In words with prefixes, divide into syllables between the prefix and the base word. In words with suffixes, sometimes divide into syllables between the base word and the suffix.
If the base word ends with /d/ or /t/, the suffix *-ed* is in a separate syllable.
If the base word ends with *ch, sh, s, x,* or *z,* the suffix *-es* is a separate syllable.

Accent Rule 2—In words with affixes, the accent usually falls on or within the base word.

Accent Rule 3—In two-syllable words without affixes, the accent usually falls on the first syllable.
In two-syllable words without affixes, the accent falls on the second syllable when that syllable contains two vowels.

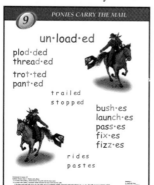

Materials

- Teaching Visuals 9 and 10: *Ponies Carry the Mail* and *End of a Hard Ride*

WORDS WITH AND WORDS WITHOUT AFFIXES

① Introduction: Two Types

▶ At its peak the pony express was delivering mail overland with the help of about eighty courageous and determined men and over four hundred fast horses. The riders had to be honest, dependable, and lightweight—but what about the horses? What did they have to be like?

Read the following account to the students.

For the eastern half of the trail, the pony express chose horses bred for speed and endurance. The land in Kansas, Nebraska, and Wyoming was flatter than land farther west, so swift racing or cavalry horses were best suited to this part of the trail. Many of these were thoroughbreds and Morgan horses whose lengthy strides could quickly eat up long prairie miles.

For the middle and western sections of the pony express trail, pintos and mustangs were purchased. Though not as fast as thoroughbreds or Morgan horses, mustangs that had tough hooves and that were used to desert conditions could scramble over rocky obstacles more quickly than the sleek racing horses of the East. While running the western section of the express trail, the little mustangs seemed to be able to run endlessly under very harsh conditions.

Both types of horses had qualities that made them valuable. They were very different, yet one type was not better than the other. Both types were needed to accomplish the task of the pony express and to make it a success.

Discuss the following.

▶ What type of horse did the pony express need? (Swift racehorses were best for flat prairie lands, and tough mustangs were best for dry or rocky land.)

▶ How were the pony express horses like a team? (Possible answer: Their different abilities and talents were combined to work for a particular goal.)

② Skill development: Visual 9—*Ponies Carry the Mail*

▶ Signals alerted pony express station keepers that an approaching rider needed another horse. At the blast of the rider's horn or at the sound of his horse's hoof beats, the keeper knew just what to do.

There are signals in words, telling where one syllable stops and another begins.

Call attention to the word *unloaded* at the top of the visual.

▶ What in this word signals how to divide it into syllables? (a prefix and a suffix)

Prefixes and suffixes are signals. A word with a prefix or suffix is usually divided into syllables between the base word and the prefix or the suffix.

▶ The suffix *-ed* has its own special signal. Read the next four words, noticing the ending consonants of the base words. What are those consonants? (*d* and *t*) How many syllables does each word have? (two)

▶ Read the next two words. Even though *trailed* and *stopped* have the suffix *-ed,* how many syllables does each word have? (one)

▶ The suffix *-ed* is in a separate syllable only when the base word ends with /d/ or /t/.

Use a similar procedure to teach the signal that if a base word ends with *ch, sh, s, x,* or *z,* the suffix *-es* is a separate syllable.

Alert to Signals

▶Identify It

Read each word. Write any signal letters. Divide the word if it has more than one syllable. Then write the number of syllables.

	Signal	Syllables		Signal	Syllables
p a i n t•e d	t	2	h i d e s		1
s t o r m e d		1	s w i s h•e s	sh	2
w a l k e d		1	s h a m e s		1
b a n d•e d	d	2	c o a x•e s	x	2

▶Accent It

Place an accent mark over each accented syllable.

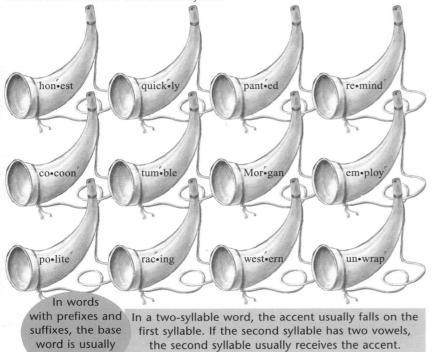

hon•est quick•ly pant•ed re•mind

co•coon´ tum•ble Mor´•gan em•ploy´

po•lite´ rac•ing west•ern un•wrap´

In words with prefixes and suffixes, the base word is usually accented.

In a two-syllable word, the accent usually falls on the first syllable. If the second syllable has two vowels, the second syllable usually receives the accent.

234

④ Skill development: Worktext page 234

Guide the completion of the page.

Identify It

▶ Some of these words have signals that tell when the suffix is in a separate syllable. Do you recognize the signals? The first word is *painted*. Is there a signal? (Yes, the *t* is a signal.) How many syllables does *painted* have? (2)

Accent It

▶ These words have already been divided into syllables. Which syllable is accented in the word *honest*? (the first syllable)

⑤ Skill application: Worktext page 235

(10) END OF A HARD RIDE

dis•mount´•ed

un•sad´•dle
cur´•ry•ing

bron´•co

stir´•rup   bri´•dle
gal´•lop   mar´•shal

can´•ter   mus´•tang
am´•bush   ket´•tle
prob´•lem   splen´•dor

fron•tier´

en•joy´   bal•loon´
trom•bone´   col•lapse´

③ Skill development: Visual 10—*End of a Hard Ride*

▶ It's the end of a hard ride for this pony. The rider has dismounted. Now the keeper will unsaddle it and begin currying it, or grooming and cleaning it.

▶ Look closely at the divided word *dismounted*. What is its base word? (mount)

Which syllable is accented? (the base word)

▶ In words with prefixes or suffixes, the accent usually falls on or within the base word.

Draw attention to the next two divided words.

▶ Some base words have two syllables, as do *saddle* and *curry*. Do you remember the rule for dividing words between consonants?

If needed, briefly review Syllable Division Rule 1, dividing words with the *VC/CV* pattern, introduced in Lesson 22.

▶ *Bronco* is an example of a word without a suffix or prefix. Which syllable is accented? (the first syllable)

Two-syllable words are usually accented on the first syllable. Read the lists of two-syllable words next to *bronco*. Are they all accented on the first syllable? (yes)

Notice how many vowels are in the second syllable of each of these words. How many are there? (one)

▶ Two-syllable words usually are accented on the first syllable, but look at *frontier*. It is a two-syllable word that is accented on the second syllable. Why?

Read the lists of two-syllable words next to *frontier*. Each has an accent on the second syllable.

Compare these lists with the lists above. Can you find the signal that tells when the accent falls on the second syllable? (The accent is on the second syllable of a two-syllable word when the second syllable has two vowels.)

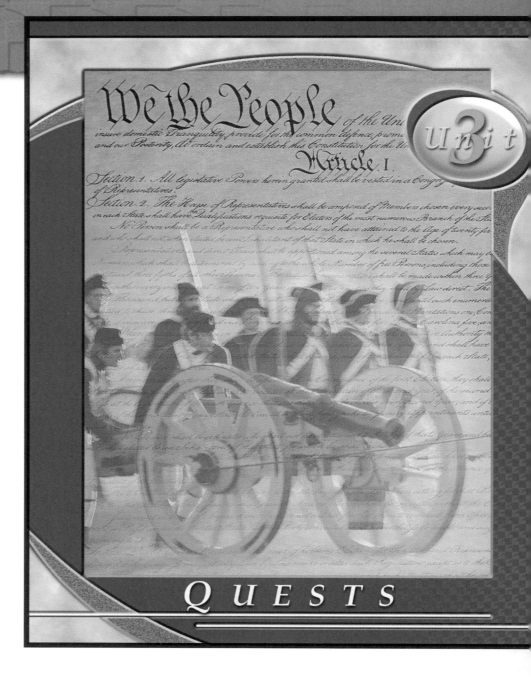

Unit discussion: page 153

▶ What is the title of the unit? ("Quests")

Read aloud the following sentence:
Soldiers who fought in the War for Independence were on a quest for freedom.

▶ What is the meaning of the word *quest*? (The word *quest* means a search.)

▶ What are these soldiers searching for? (Elicit that they are searching for freedom or individual rights.)

Some people search for answers to important issues. Many individuals search for specific places they would like to visit. Others may be on a quest for tangible things such as animals, collectibles, and so forth. One person might be searching for a good friend, while another could be searching for God.

▶ What have you searched for? Did you find it?

Colossians 3:23

And whatsoever ye do, do it heartily, as to the Lord, and not unto men.

The steps of a search weave into a good story. Paul is searching for the Phantom in "Pony Penning Day," and the huntsman pursues the elusive white bird in "The Snow-White Robin." Many seek to understand God and His wise ways as does the young Philistine boy in "Jakko's Answer," who searches for the true God. "Cherry Time," a Japanese form of poetry called haiku, precedes "The Cherry Trees," a story in which Charis searches for the answers to her grandmother's death. The quest for peace and freedom is highlighted in "World War II," and it is seen through the eyes of Zoli in "When the War Is Over." A whole group of Tibetan lamas seeks to know the God who loves in "John 3:16—A True Story."

PONY PENNING DAY

> Paul has one goal on his first ride to round up the wild ponies on Assateague Island: to find the Phantom. When he does, she is not alone. Can her spindly foal make the swim across the channel?

Lesson	Reader pages	Worktext pages
50	154-59	65
51	160-63	66-67
52	164-67	68-70

Materials
- Ear of corn, small amount of sugar, a carrot
- Map of Virginia
- Vocabulary sentences for display
- Teaching Visuals 4 and 8, *California Challenge* and *Eighty Stables*

Background information
Scow—A *scow* is a sailing vessel with a flat bottom and square ends, often used for moving freight.

INTRODUCTION

Vocabulary
Use the prepared sentences to introduce the vocabulary words in context.

A special day
Display the ear of corn, a carrot, and sugar.

▶ What do you think these items have in common?

What type of animal would eat these kinds of food? (possible answers: horse, pony)

Locate the island of Chincoteague on the map of Virginia.

▶ Have any of you ever heard of Chincoteague?

Read the story title on reader page 154 aloud.

▶ What do you think will happen on this special day?

Head note
Read the head note on reader page 154 aloud.

▶ What dream do Maureen and Paul have? (to have a horse of their own)

Have you ever wanted a horse of your own?

Correlated Activities
- **Vocabulary Box, Activity 3: Glossary Day**
- **Spelling Practice, Activity 2: Spelling Makes Cents**

See "Classroom Management for Grouping" in the Appendix.

VOCABULARY

LESSON 50

*†They used a stout wagon to carry the heavy loads of bricks. (p. 154)

*She cleaned and set up the dining room until it looked prim for the guests. (p. 157)

*She almost couldn't see the men on the horses as the cavalcade raced past her house. (p. 157)

LESSON 51

*He got on the horse warily because he knew the horse might buck him off. (p. 160)

*†The horse collided with the fence because it did not jump high enough. (p. 161)

*†Their mounts finished the race faster than any other horses in history. (p. 162)

LESSON 52

*She knew her brother was afeared as the dog chased him, because she was scared too. (p. 164)

*†The whole town was looking for the fugitive horse that ran away last night. (p. 165)

*†By using the boat's tow rope, he could pull the small boat to shore. (p. 167)

*†He felt sorrow when his dog ran away but felt ecstasy when the dog came home on its own three weeks later. (p. 167)

COMPREHENSION

Objectives

The student will

- Recognize the author's use of imagery to create setting.
- Relate story content to biblical truth: Obey those in authority.
- Recognize the author's use of suspense to maintain the interest of the reader.

Before silent reading: pages 154-59

Motivation

▶ How do Paul and Maureen plan to make their dream come true?

Why is this Pony Penning Day special?

After silent reading

Overview discussion: pages 154-59

▶ [literal] What big event is taking place on Chincoteague Island? (Pony Penning Day)

[interpretive] What is Paul and Maureen's plan for this Pony Penning Day? (They plan to capture the Phantom.)

▶ [interpretive] Why is this Pony Penning Day different for Paul? (He is old enough to go with the roundup men to Assateague.)

[critical] How does Paul feel about being on the chase? (Answers will vary.)

Pony Penning Day

taken from Misty of Chincoteague
Marguerite Henry

illustrated by Preston Gravely Jr.

In the book Misty of Chincoteague, *two children named Paul and Maureen want very much to have a horse of their own. The following story, taken from that book, tells how Paul and Maureen try to make that dream come true.*

The Straggler

Pony Penning Day always comes on the last Thursday in July. For weeks before, every member of the Volunteer Fire Department is busy getting the grounds in readiness, and the boys are allowed to help.

"I'll do your chores at home, Paul," offered Maureen, "so's you can see that the pony pens are good and stout."

Paul spent long days at the pony penning grounds. The pens for the wild ponies must be made safe. Once the Phantom was captured, she must not escape. Nothing else mattered.

154

Follow-up discussion: page 154

▶ [interpretive] How do you know Pony Penning Day is a special day? (Possible answers: It takes place once every year in July; people prepare for weeks before the event.)

[literal] How do Paul and the men prepare for Pony Penning Day? (by making the grounds ready and making sure the pens are strong)

[literal] In what way is Maureen able to help Paul with the preparations for the big day? (She does his chores at home so that Paul can make sure the pens are safe.)

Read aloud Maureen's offer to help Paul with kindness in your voice.

▶ [literal] What is the one thing that matters to Paul as he works? (The pens must be ready and safe so that the Phantom cannot escape.)

Paul and Maureen Beebe lived on their grandfather's pony ranch on the island of Chincoteague, just off the Virginia shore. Across a narrow channel lay another island, Assateague, which was the home of the wild herds. They were said to be the descendants of a bunch of Spanish horses off a Spanish galleon which had been shipwrecked there several hundred years ago. Once every July the men of Chincoteague crossed the channel to Assateague and rounded up wild ponies. They swam them across the channel to Chincoteague to be sold on Pony Penning Day.

Paul and Maureen had gentled many a wild colt. But just as the colt was learning that they were his friends, Grandpa Beebe would sell it and the children would never see him again. They had earned a hundred dollars to buy a horse of their own—and the horse they wanted was the Phantom. This was the mysterious wild mare about whom so many stories were told. None of the roundup men had ever been able to capture her. But this year Paul was old enough to go with the men and he was determined to get her.

"When I do," he said, "I'll tie a rope around her neck to show she's already sold. To us."

The night before the roundup, Paul and Maureen made last-minute plans in Phantom's stall. "First thing in the morning," Paul told Maureen, "you lay a clean bed of dried sea grass. Then fill the manger with plenty of marsh grass to make Phantom feel at home."

"Oh, I will, Paul. And I've got some ear corn and some 'lasses to coax her appetite, and Grandma gave me a bunch of tiny new carrots and some rutabagas, and I've been saving up sugar until I have a little sackful."

It was dark and still when Paul awoke the next morning. He lay quiet a moment, trying to gather his wits. Suddenly he shot out of bed.

Today was Pony Penning Day! He dressed quickly and thudded

Pony Penning Day   155

▶ [literal] Where do Paul and Maureen live? (with their grandparents on the island of Chincoteague)

[interpretive] What is important about the location of their home? (It is across the channel from Assateague where the wild herds of ponies live.)

[literal] How do people think the wild herds came to live on Assateague? (The ponies are said to be descendants of Spanish horses off a Spanish galleon that was shipwrecked there several hundred years ago.)

▶ [interpretive] How have Paul and Maureen earned money? (They have gentled or trained wild colts for their grandfather to sell.)

[literal] What are Paul and Maureen planning to buy with the money they have earned? (their own horse, the Phantom)

[appreciative] Have you ever saved money for something that you really wanted? What was it?

▶ [interpretive] Why do Paul and Maureen want the Phantom so much? (Elicit that it is the horse that everyone has been talking about but no one has ever been able to catch. It is mysterious.)

Read aloud the paragraph that explains why Paul and Maureen want the Phantom.

▶ [interpretive] How do you know Paul and Maureen believe that they will get the Phantom this time, even though no one has ever been able to catch it before? (Paul says he will tie a rope around the wild horse to show it is theirs; they have built a stall for the Phantom, and Maureen has food ready.)

▶ [literal] What special treatment does Grandma give Paul this morning? (She cooks him a special breakfast.)

[interpretive] What phrase shows that Paul thinks the breakfast of fried ham and coffee is special? ("as if he were man-grown")

[interpretive] What do you think *man-grown* means? (He is grown up—not a boy anymore.)

[critical] Why do you think Grandma is treating Paul as if he were man-grown? (Answers will vary, but elicit that he is old enough to go with the roundup men, so his grandma is treating him as a grownup.)

▶ [critical] Do you think Grandpa gives Paul good advice? Why or why not? (Accept any answer, but elicit that the Bible tells us to obey those in authority.) [BAT: 2a Authority]

Read aloud Grandpa's words to Paul.

barefoot down to the kitchen where Grandma stood over the stove, frying ham and making coffee for him as if he were man-grown!

After a hurried breakfast, he ran out the door. He mounted Watch Eyes, a dependable pony that Grandpa had never been able to sell because of his white eyes. Locking his bare feet around the pony's sides, he jogged out of the yard.

Maureen came running to see him off.

"Whatever happens," Paul called back over his shoulder, "you be at Old Dominion Point at ten o'clock on a fresh pony."

"I'll be there, Paul!"

"And you, Paul!" yelled Grandpa. "Obey yer leader. No matter what!"

Day was breaking. A light golden mist came up out of the sea. It touched the prim white houses and the white picket fences with an unearthly light. Paul loped along slowly to save his mount's strength. All along the road, men were turning out of their gates.

"Where do you reckon you'll do most good, Bub?" taunted a lean sapling of a man. He guffawed loudly, then winked at the rest of the group.

Paul's hand tightened on the reins. "Reckon I'll do most good where the leader tells me to go," he said, blushing hotly.

The day promised to be sultry. The marsh grass that usually billowed and waved stood motionless. The water of Assateague Channel glared like quicksilver.

Now the cavalcade was thundering over a small bridge that linked Chincoteague Island to little Piney Island. At the far end of the bridge a scow with a rail fence around it stood at anchor.

In spite of light talk, the faces of the men were drawn tight with excitement as they led their mounts onto the scow. The horses felt the excitement, too. Their nostrils quivered, and their ears swiveled this way and that, listening to the throb of the motor. Now the scow began to nose its way across the narrow channel. Paul watched the White Hills of Assateague loom near. He watched the old lighthouse grow sharp and sharper against the sky. In a few minutes the ride was over. The gangway was being lowered. The horses were clattering down, each man taking his own.

All eyes were on Wyle Maddox, the leader.

"Split in three bunches," Wyle clipped out the directions loud and sharp. "North, south, and east. Me and Kim and the Beebe boy will head east, Wimbrow and Quillen goes north, and Harvey and Rodgers south. We'll all meet at Tom's Point."

Paul touched his bare heels into Watch Eye's side. They were off! The boy's eyes were fastened on Wyle Maddox. He and Kim Horsepepper were following their leader like the wake of a ship.

Pony Penning Day   157

**Follow-up discussion:
page 157**

▶ [interpretive] Why do you think the man teases Paul? (Possible answer: He thinks Paul is too young and inexperienced to be much help.)

[interpretive] What words does the author use to tell you that the man is making fun of Paul? What do they mean? (*taunted*—teased; *guffawed*—laughed)

Read aloud Paul's answer to the man the way you think he would say it.

[interpretive] How does Paul feel about the man's question? What makes you think so? (Embarrassed or angry; possible answer: he blushes hotly and tightens his hand on the reigns.)

▶ [interpretive] Why does the author compare the men and their horses to thunder? (to help you to "hear" the horses as they cross the bridge)

▶ [literal] How does the author describe Paul and Kim as they follow Wyle Maddox? (like the wake of a ship)

[critical] What is the wake of a ship? (Accept any answer, but explain that it is the churning of the water behind a ship.)

[critical] Do you think the author makes a good comparison? Why or why not? (Answers will vary, but elicit that they are following right behind Wyle Maddox just like a ship's wake is right behind the ship.)

Read aloud the author's description of Paul after Wyle Maddox gives his orders.

▶ [interpretive] Why is it difficult to travel on this island? (There are no paths to follow.)

[literal] How does the author say they move through these woods? (thrash through underbrush, jump trees, and wade brackish pools and streams)

[interpretive] What does the author mean when she writes that there are "only openings to skin through"? (The openings are very small to pass through.)

▶ [literal] What startles Wyle Maddox's horse? (the band of wild ponies they are looking for)

Read aloud how the woods come alive so that we can hear the sound of the chase as you read.

▶ [literal] What task does Wyle Maddox order Paul to do? (to go after the straggler)

[interpretive] How does Paul feel about this task? (He is angry that he has to go and feels as if they are not treating him like one of the men.)

[interpretive] What helps Paul decide to obey Wyle Maddox's order? (He remembers his grandfather's advice.)

As they rode on, Paul could feel the soft sand give way to hard meadowland, then to pine-laden trails. There were no paths to follow, only openings to skin through—openings that led to water holes or to grazing grounds. The three horses thrashed through underbrush, jumped fallen trees, waded brackish pools and narrow, winding streams.

Suddenly Paul saw Wyle Maddox's horse rear into the air. He heard him neigh loudly as a band of wild ponies darted into an open grazing stretch some twenty yards ahead, then vanished among the black tree trunks.

The woods came alive with thundering hoofs and frantic horse calls. Through bush and briar and bog and hard marshland the wild ponies flew. Behind them galloped the three riders, whooping at the top of their lungs. For whole seconds at a time the wild band would be swallowed up by the forest gloom. Then it would reappear far ahead—nothing but a flash of flying tails and manes.

Suddenly Wyle Maddox was waving Paul to ride close. "A straggler!" he shouted, pointing off to the left. "He went that-a-way! Git him!" And with a burst of speed Wyle Maddox and Kim Horsepepper were after the band.

Paul was alone. His face reddened with anger. They wanted to be rid of him. That's what they wanted. Sent after a straggler! He was not interested in rounding up a straggler that couldn't keep up with the herd! He wanted the Phantom. Then Grandpa's words flashed across his mind, "You, Paul, obey yer leader. No matter what!"

He wheeled his pony and headed blindly in the direction Wyle had indicated. He rode deeper into the pine thicket, trying to avoid snapping twigs, yet watching ahead for the slightest motion of leaf or bush. He'd show the men, if it took him all day! His

158

thin shirt clung to him damply and his body was wet with sweat. A cobweb veiled itself across his face. With one hand he tried to wipe it off, but suddenly he was almost unseated. Watch Eyes was dancing on his hind legs, his nose high in the air. Paul stared into the sun-dappled forest until his eyes burned in his head. At last, far away and deep in the shadow of the pines, he saw a blur of motion. With the distance that lay between them, it might have been anything. A deer. Or even a squirrel. Whatever it was, he was after it!

Pony Penning Day 159

Follow-up discussion: page 159

▶ [interpretive] What causes Paul to almost fall off his pony? (Possible answer: He is holding on with only one hand when Watch Eyes rears up on his hind legs.)

▶ [interpretive] What does it mean to stare "until his eyes burn in his head"? (He looks hard and long to try to see what caused Watch Eyes's excitement.)

[interpretive] What does a sun-dappled forest look like? (Answers may vary, but elicit that the sun is coming through the trees and leaving shadows of the leaves on the ground.)

▶ [interpretive] Why do you think Paul is so determined to capture the straggler? (Possible answers: He wants to show the men he is able to do the job; he wants to please his grandfather.)

Read aloud the sentence that shows Paul's determination to find the straggler.

Looking ahead

▶ Will Paul find the straggler?

Worktext Objectives

The student will

- Read a map.
- Use a map scale.
- Follow directions.

Study Skills:
Worktext page 65

Review with the students how to use a map scale and a ruler to measure distance on a map. Practice measuring distance together if necessary. Instruct students to complete the page independently.

COMPREHENSION

Objectives

The student will

- Recognize the author's use of imagery to convey emotion.
- Determine the origin of the chapter title.
- Read orally to convey emotion.

Use the prepared sentences to introduce the vocabulary words in context.

Before silent reading: pages 160-63

Motivation

▶ Will Paul be able to find the straggler?

What or who is Misty?

After silent reading

Overview discussion: pages 160-63

▶ [interpretive] What horse does the straggler turn out to be? (the Phantom)

▶ [literal] How is Paul able to find the rest of the roundup men? (The Phantom hears the Pied Piper, the lead horse, and goes in that direction, which is towards Tom's Point and the other roundup men.)

[interpretive] How do the men react when they discover that they sent Paul after the Phantom? (They are surprised and amazed.)

[interpretive] How does bringing in the straggler affect Paul's reputation with the other men? (They accept him as one of them.)

▶ [literal] Who is Misty? (the Phantom's colt)

Misty

Watch Eyes plunged on. There was a kind of glory in pursuit that made Paul and the horse one. They were trailing nothing but swaying bushes. They were giving chase to a mirage. Always it moved on and on, showing itself only in quivering leaves or moving shadows.

What was that? In the clump of myrtle bushes just ahead? Paul reined in. He could scarcely breathe for the wild beating of his heart. Here it was again! A silver flash. It looked like mist with the sun on it. And just beyond the mist, he caught sight of a long tail of copper and silver.

He gazed awestruck. "It could be the Phantom's tail," he breathed. "It is! It is! It is! And the silver flash—it's not mist at all, but a brand-new colt!" he murmured.

He glanced about him helplessly. If only he could think! How could he drive the Phantom and her colt to Tom's Point?

Warily he approached the myrtle thicket. Just then the colt let out a high, frightened whinny. In that little second Paul knew that he wanted more than anything in the world to keep the mother and the colt together. Shivers of joy raced up and down

160

Follow-up discussion: page 160

▶ [literal]] What does the author say they are chasing? (a mirage)

[critical] What is a mirage? (Accept any answer, but explain that it is something that looks real but isn't.)

▶ [literal] What does Paul see that makes him awestruck? (a long tail of silver and copper that could be the Phantom's tail)

[interpretive] What has Paul been describing as mist? (the Phantom's brand-new colt)

[critical] How do you think Paul feels when he realizes that he is chasing the Phantom and her colt? (Answers may vary but should express that he is overwhelmed with excitement and joy.)

Read aloud with excitement and awe Paul's comments about what he sees.

▶ [literal] Now that Paul has the Phantom, what is his new desire? (to keep the Phantom and her colt together)

his spine. His breath came faster. He made a firm resolution. "I'll buy you both!" he promised.

But how far had he come? Was it ten miles to Tom's Point or two? Would it be best to drive them down the beach? Or through the woods? As if in answer a loud bugle rang through the woods. It was the Pied Piper, the pinto stallion in command of the herd. And unmistakably his voice came from the direction of Tom's Point.

The Phantom pricked her ears. She wheeled around and almost collided with Watch Eyes in her haste to find the band. She wanted the Pied Piper for protection. Behind her trotted the foal, all shining and clean with its newness.

Paul laughed weakly. He was not driving the Phantom after all! She and her colt were leading him. They were leading him to Tom's Point!

Tom's Point was a protected piece of land where the marsh was hard and the grass especially sweet. About seventy wild ponies, exhausted by their morning's run, stood browsing quietly, as if they were in a corral. Only occasionally they looked up at their captors. The good meadow and

Pony Penning Day   161

► [literal] What are some of the questions racing through Paul's mind? (How far has he come? Is it ten miles to Tom's Point or two? Is it better to drive them down the beach or through the woods?)

[interpretive] How are Paul's questions answered? (He hears the Pied Piper, the stallion that heads the herd of horses, and its voice is coming from the direction of Tom's Point.)

[interpretive] What does the author compare the Pied Piper's voice to? (a loud bugle)

[interpretive] Who else hears the Pied Piper? (the Phantom)

[interpretive] How does the Phantom react? Why? (She turns around and hurries to find the lead horse for protection.)

[interpretive] Why is Paul glad the Phantom and her colt hear the Pied Piper? (He knows that the Pied Piper is at Tom's Point, and the Phantom is leading him there.)

Read aloud the paragraph that describes Paul's realization that it would be easy to get the Phantom to Tom's Point. Show amazement in your voice.

[critical] What might have happened if the Phantom and her colt had not heard the Pied Piper? (Answers will vary, but elicit that it might have taken Paul longer to find Tom's Point, and he could have lost the Phantom and her colt.)

► [critical] Why do you think the roundup men chose Tom's Point as the meeting place? (Answers may vary, but elicit that it is a safe place for the ponies to graze.)

[literal] At Tom's Point, is the herd of restless wild ponies anxious to escape? Why or why not? (No; the ponies are tired from the morning run and are grazing peacefully in the good meadow.)

► [literal] How does the author describe
the scene of the roundup men and the
ponies? (like the lull in the midst of a
storm.)

[interpretive] What does the author
call these horses? (peaceful prisoners)

► [interpretive] What stops the laughing
and quiet talk of the men watching the
horses? (the sight of Paul bringing in
the Phantom and her colt)

[critical] As the shouts of wonder and
admiration go up from the crowd of
men, how do you think Paul feels?
(possible answers: proud, happy, excited)

Read aloud the comments among the
men as they gaze in disbelief at the
spindling youngster.

► [literal] As Paul looks out across the
water, what does he see? (two lines of
boats forming a pony-way and people
and horses waiting on the shores of
Chincoteague)

[literal] What is Paul thinking as he
sees these sights? (Maureen is out
there somewhere, and soon she will
carry on.)

[interpretive] What does Paul's
thought mean that soon Maureen will
carry on? (Possible answer: she will
purchase the Phantom and the colt
and take care of them in the pony
pens.)

► [critical] How do you think Paul comes
up with the name Misty for the colt?
(Accept any answer, but note that the
colt looked like mist to Paul during the
chase.)

their own weariness kept them
peaceful prisoners.

At a watchful distance the
roundup men rested their mounts
and relaxed. It was like the lull in
the midst of a storm. All was quiet
on the surface. Yet there was an
undercurrent of tension. You could
tell it in the narrowed eyes of the
men, their subdued voices and
their too easy laughter.

Suddenly the laughter stilled.
Mouths gaped in disbelief. Eyes
rounded. For a few seconds no one
spoke at all. Then a shout that was
half wonder and half admiration
went up from the men. Paul Beebe
was bringing in *the Phantom and a
colt!*

The roundup men were swarm-
ing around Paul, buzzing with
questions. "Beats all!" he heard
someone say. "For two years we
been trying to round up the
Phantom and along comes a spindling youngster to show us up."

" 'Twas the little colt that hin-
dered her."

" 'Course it was."

"It's the newest colt in the
bunch; may not stand the swim."

"If we lose only one colt, it'll
still be a good day's work."

The men accepted Paul as one
of them now—a real roundup
man. They were clapping him on
the shoulder and trying to get him
to talk. "Ain't they a shaggy-
lookin' bunch?" Kim Horsepepper
asked.

"Except for Misty," Paul said,
pointing toward the Phantom's
colt. "Her coat is silky." The mere
thought of touching it sent shivers
through him. "Misty," he thought
to himself wonderingly. "Why,
I've named her!"

He looked out across the
water. Two lines of boats were
forming a pony-way across the
channel. He saw the cluster of
people and the mounts waiting on
the shores of Chincoteague and he
knew that somewhere among them
was Maureen. It was like a relay
race. Soon she would carry on.

162

"Could I swim my mount across the channel alongside the Phantom?" Paul asked Wyle Maddox anxiously.

Wyle shook his head. "Watch Eyes is all tuckered out," he said. "Besides, there's a tradition in the way things is handled on Pony Penning Day. There's mounted men for the roundup and there's boatmen to herd 'em across the channel," he explained.

"Tide's out!" he called in clipped tones. "Current is slack. Time for the ponies to be swimmed across. Let's go!"

Suddenly the beach was wild with commotion. From three sides the roundup men came rushing at the ponies, their hoarse cries whipping the animals into action. They plunged into the water, the stallions leading, the mares following, neighing encouragement to their colts.

"They're off!" shouted Wyle Maddox, and everyone felt the relief and triumph in his words.

Pony Penning Day   163

▶ [critical] Why does Paul want to swim his mount beside the Phantom? (Answers may vary, but elicit that he wants to make sure the colt can make the swim.)

Read aloud Wyle Maddox's explanation as to why Paul can't ride his mount across the channel.

▶ [critical] Why do you think the roundup men feel "relief and triumph" as the ponies begin to swim to the island? (Accept any answer, but point out that the roundup men have finished their job and probably feel very good that they finally have their herd of ponies.)

Looking ahead

▶ Will the colt be able to make the swim?

▶ Will all that Maureen and Paul have hoped for come true?

Worktext Objectives

The student will

■ Discern meaning of a word from context.

■ Apply Syllable Division Rules 1 and 3—VC/CV pattern and words ending with a consonant + le.

Vocabulary:
Worktext page 66

Direct students to complete the page.

Structural analysis:
Worktext page 67

Complete teaching of Syllable Division Rules 1 and 3 was presented in Lessons 22 and 39.

Use Teaching Visuals 4 and 8, *California Challenge* and *Eighty Stables*, to review the rules.

Read the directions and direct students to complete the page.

COMPREHENSION

Objectives

The student will

- Recognize the author's use of similes.
- Recognize the character trait of courage.
- Read orally to convey the characters' emotions.

 Use the prepared sentences to introduce the vocabulary words in context.

Before silent reading: pages 164-67

Motivation

▶ What kind of trouble will Paul face?

Will the triumph be what Paul and Maureen would like?

After silent reading

Overview discussion: pages 164-67

▶ [literal] What trouble does Paul run into? (The colt can't swim to the island, and the Phantom goes back after her colt.)

▶ [critical] What is the triumph? (Accept any answer, but elicit that Paul's bringing the Phantom and her colt home would be the crowning triumph.)

Trouble and Triumph

On the shores of Chincoteague the people pressed forward, their faces strained to stiffness, as they watched Assateague Beach.

"Here they come!" The cry broke out from every throat.

Maureen, wedged between Grandpa Beebe on one side and a volunteer fireman on the other, stood on her mount's back. Her arms paddled the air as if she were swimming and struggling with the wild ponies.

Suddenly a fisherman, looking through binoculars, began shouting in a hoarse voice, "A new-borned colt is afeared to swim. Wait! A wild pony is breaking out from the mob! Swimming around the mob! Escaping!"

An awed murmur stirred the crowds. Maureen dug her toes in

164

Follow-up discussion: page 164

▶ [interpretive] How do you think the people on Chincoteague Island are feeling as they watch the ponies set off into the water? (possible answers: excited, anxious, worried)

[literal] What is Maureen doing as the ponies begin swimming? (She is standing on her mount's back, paddling in the air as if she were swimming and struggling with the ponies.)

Read aloud what the man with the binoculars says as he might shout the news.

her mount's back. She strained her eyes to see the fugitive, but all she could make out was a milling mass of dark blobs on the water.

The fisherman leaned far out over the water. "It's the Phantom!" he screamed.

The people took up the cry, echoing it over and over. "It's the Phantom! She's escaped again!"

Maureen felt tears on her cheek, and impatiently brushed them away.

The fisherman was waving for quiet. "It's the Phantom's colt that won't swim!" he called out in a voice so hoarse it cracked. "The Phantom got separated from a bran'-fire new colt. She's gone back to get it!"

The people whooped and hollered at the news. "The Phantom's got a colt," they sang out. "The Phantom's got a new colt!"

Again the fisherman was waving for silence.

"She's reached her colt!" he crowed. "But the roundup men are closing in on her! They're making her shove the colt in the water. Look at her! She's makin' it swim!"

Grandpa Beebe cupped his hands around his mouth. "Can the little feller make it?" he boomed.

The crowd stilled, waiting for the hoarse voice. For long seconds no answer came. The fisherman remained as fixed as the piling he stood on. Wave after wave of fear swept over Maureen. She felt as if she were drowning. And just when she could stand the silence no longer, the fisherman began reporting in short, nervous sentences.

"They're half-ways across. Wait a minute! The colt! It's bein' sucked down in a whirlpool. I can't see it now. My soul and body! A boy's jumped off the scow. He's swimming out to help the colt."

The onlookers did not need the fisherman with the binoculars any more. They could see for themselves. A boy swimming against the current. A boy holding a colt's head above the swirling water.

Pony Penning Day   165

Follow-up discussion: page 165

▶ [literal] What does Maureen see as she strains her eyes? (only "a milling mass of dark blobs on the water")

[interpretive] What makes tears come to Maureen's cheeks? (She hears people yelling that the Phantom has escaped again.)

[interpretive] Why would Maureen cry about the Phantom's escaping? (She and Paul have been hoping to capture the Phantom and buy her.)

▶ [literal] What news does the fisherman shout? ("It's the Phantom's colt that won't swim!")

[interpretive] Why do the people whoop, holler, and sing out that the Phantom has a new colt? (They are excited about the news.)

[interpretive] What is the crowd silently waiting for? (to hear from the fisherman whether or not the Phantom's colt can make the swim)

[literal] As the crowd waits in suspense, how does Maureen feel? (as if she is drowning in fear)

Just as Maureen can stand it no longer, the fisherman reports. Read aloud his short, nervous sentences.

[critical] Do you think Paul shows courage by swimming out to the colt? Why or why not? (Accept any answer.) [BAT: 8d Courage]

[appreciative] Would you jump in the water to help the colt?

▶ [interpretive] Who is pictured on the
page? (Maureen and Grandpa)

[interpretive] Why is Grandpa standing on the horse's back? (Answers
may vary, but elicit that he is cheering for Paul and the colt.)

166

Maureen gulped great lungfuls of air. "It's Paul!" she screamed. "It's Paul!"

On all sides the shouts went up. "Why, it's Paul!"

Grandpa leaped up on his mount's back as nimbly as a boy. He stood with his arms upraised, his fists clenched.

"God help ye, Paul!" his words carried out over the water.

"Yer almost home!"

Grandpa's voice was as strong as a tow rope. Paul was swimming steadily toward it, holding the small silver face of the colt above the water. He was almost there. He was there!

Maureen slid down from her mount, clutching a handful of mane. "You made it, Paul! You made it!" she cried.

The air was wild with whinnies and snorts as the ponies touched the hard sand, then scrambled up the shore, their wet bodies gleaming in the sun. Paul half-carried the little colt up the steep bank; then suddenly it found its own legs. Shouts between triumph and relief escaped every throat as the little filly tottered up the bank.

For a brief second Paul's and Maureen's eyes met above the crowds. It was as if they and the mare and her foal were the only creatures on the island. They were unaware of the great jostling and fighting as the stallions sorted out their own mares and colts. They were unaware of everything but a sharp ecstasy. Soon the Phantom and her colt would belong to them. Never to be sold.

Dodging horses and people, Grandpa Beebe made his way over to Paul.

"Paul, boy," he said, his voice unsteady, "I swimmed the hull way with you. Yer the most wonderful and the craziest young'un in the world. Now git home right smart quick," he added, trying to sound stern. "Yer about done up, and Grandma's expectin' ye. Maureen and I'll see to it that the Phantom and her colt reach the pony pens."

Follow-up discussion: page 167

▶ [interpretive] What does Maureen do when she realizes that it is Paul helping the colt? (She screams out, "It's Paul!")

▶ [critical] Why does the author choose to compare Grandpa's voice to a tow rope? (Answers will vary, but elicit that a tow rope is used to pull boats ashore. Grandpa's strong voice is helping to pull Paul ashore as it encourages Paul.)

Read aloud the words of encouragement that Grandpa yells.

▶ [critical] What do you think Paul and Maureen are thinking as their eyes meet? (Answers will vary, but elicit that they are excited to think that the Phantom and her colt will soon belong to them.)

▶ [critical] What does Grandpa mean by saying that he "swimmed the hull way with" Paul? (Answers may vary, but point out that Grandpa felt as if he were actually helping Paul.)

[interpretive] Is Grandpa proud of Paul? How do you know? (He says that Paul is the most wonderful and the craziest young'un in the world.)

Worktext Objective

The student will

■ Determine cause-and-effect relationships.

Comprehension: Worktext page 68

Read the definitions of *cause* and *effect* at the bottom of the page. Instruct students to complete the page independently.

The student will

- Read a schedule.
- Infer unstated supporting details.
- Identify facts and details.
- Follow directions.

STUDY SKILLS
Reading a schedule

Display a copy of a daily school schedule, including several starting times and events or tasks. Ask questions such as the following about the schedule displayed.

▶ What time do you have reading?

 What do you do before reading?

 When do you have math?

Guide the following discussion.

▶ What is the purpose of a schedule? (possible answers: to plan events or tasks; to remind you of tasks you must complete; to help you be on time for events)

▶ Look at the schedule again. What do you notice about the times and events? (They are listed in chronological order—the order in which they will happen.)

 Are the times listed the starting times or ending times? (starting times)

Study Skills: Worktext page 69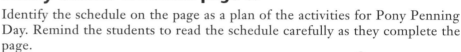

Identify the schedule on the page as a plan of the activities for Pony Penning Day. Remind the students to read the schedule carefully as they complete the page.

Comprehension: Worktext page 70

SOMETHING EXTRA
Write It: An interview

Direct each student to write an interview that he might have with Paul about his experience on Pony Penning Day. The interviewer should ask about the events that took place on the island and whether or not Paul thought he really would capture the Phantom. Allow the student to conduct the interview with another student, using the interview he has written.

Find It: Pony Penning Day

Allow the student to research Pony Penning Day. Encourage the student to send a letter to the Chincoteague, Virginia, Chamber of Commerce requesting more information about the Pony Penning Day celebration that still takes place every year on the island.

Materials

- Teaching Visual 11—*Getting the Information*

CHARTS

1 Introduction: Teaching Visual 11—*Getting the Information*

▶ Do you like ponies?

Let's find out about some of the different kinds of ponies and how they are alike and different.

Cover the chart at the bottom of the visual and read aloud the paragraph "Ponies" at the top of the visual.

▶ What information about the ponies is given in the paragraph? (their size, where they come from, and their color)

Which kind of pony came from Sweden? (the Gotland)

Which other pony averages the same height as the Gotland? (the Chincoteague)

What color are New Forest ponies? (solid colors)

Even though you found these answers in the paragraph, there is a way to arrange the same information so that it is more convenient to read and use.

2 Skill development: Teaching Visual 11—*Getting the Information*

Uncover the chart on the visual. Point out the title of the chart and the heading for the information charted in each column.

▶ Use this chart to answer these questions. See if it is easier to answer these questions reading the chart rather than the paragraph.

Which kind of pony is a solid color? (New Forest Pony)

Which breeds originated in the United States? (Chincoteague and Pony of the Americas)

Which breed is the tallest? (New Forest Pony)

How tall is the average New Forest Pony? (14.2 hands)

Discuss that horses are measured in hands, and give the students the following information.

One hand equals four inches. Horses are measured not from the top of their heads but from the place where the base of their neck joins the back. This point on the back is called the *withers*.

Refer to the withers in the picture on worktext page 237.

▶ Is it easier to read the paragraph or the chart to compare the ponies?

Lesson	Worktext pages
53	236-237

Objectives

The student will

- Recognize charts as a format for comparing information efficiently.
- Read and interpret information on a chart.

Background information

Charts—Charts are used to organize information in an orderly, easy-to-read fashion. Charts help us to compare likenesses and differences of several things, all at one time. Charts or tables usually have titles and headings or categories. Sometimes they include illustrations.

3 **Skill application:**
Worktext page 236

▶ This chart compares the islands of Chincoteague and Assateague. Instead of listing information in the boxes below each island name, the box is checked with an *X* if the information applies to that island.

▶ Where are wild ponies found? In the information column, look for the phrase "Inhabited by wild ponies."

Which island has wild ponies? (both islands—Chincoteague and Assateague) How do you know? (There is an *X* in the box below each island name.)

Write the island names in the answer blank.

▶ On which island is the roundup held? Use the chart to find out. (Assateague)

Continue the activity and discussion until the page is completed.

4 **Skill practice:**
Worktext page 237

After giving instructions for the page, lead an examination of the chart and explain any unfamiliar terms.

draft horse: a horse that is used to pull or drag heavy loads

saddle horse: a horse that is primarily used for pleasure riding

harness horse: a horse that has been trained to pull a coach, cart, or wagon

Allow the students to complete the page independently.

SOMETHING EXTRA

Write It: A chart

Direct each student to research three or more breeds of an animal, such as dogs, cats, or birds, and then to construct a chart to compare the information easily.

Two Islands

Islands Near the East Coast

Characteristics	Chincoteague Island	Assateague Island
Barrier island	X	X
Inhabited by people	X	
Inhabited by wild ponies	X	X
Abundant wildlife		X
Auction site	X	
Roundup site		X
Part of Virginia	X	X
Part of Maryland		X

▶**Read a Chart**
Use the information from the chart to answer the questions.

1. On which islands are wild ponies found?

   Chincoteague

   Assateague

2. On which island is the roundup held?

   Assateague

3. On which island is the auction held?

   Chincoteague

4. Which island belongs partly to Virginia and partly to Maryland?

   Assateague

236

5-7-5—syllables that count in this traditional Japanese poetry style.

Lesson	Reader page
54	168

Materials

- A bucket
- Vocabulary sentence for display
- The following haiku for display:
    Maine Moose
    The Maine moose managed
    To give two muffled bellows.
    The awed marksman missed.

Background information

Haiku—Haiku is a Japanese poetic form consisting of three lines. Haiku has no rhyme. The structure of the poem lies in the number of syllables in each line: five in the first, seven in the second, and five in the third. Haiku usually makes a striking comparison between two unlike objects, employing an image from nature. Some haiku draw a surprising conclusion in the third line from observations in the first and second.

INTRODUCTION

Vocabulary

Use the prepared sentence to introduce the vocabulary word in context.

A bucket full

Show the bucket.

▶ What kinds of things could you put in the bucket?

Have you ever picked fruit or vegetables?

What kinds of fruit could you pick from a tree and put in the bucket?

VOCABULARY

LESSON 54

†The branches of our birch trees were drooping, burdened with snow.

Correlated Activities

- **Creative Writing, Activity 4: Roll-a-Sentence**
- **Connections, Activity 4: Recipe Reconstruction**

See "Classroom Management for Grouping" in the Appendix

COMPREHENSION

The student will

- Interpret the concise language of haiku.
- Recognize the author's use of imagery.

Before listening

► As I read the poem, listen to find out what the speaker of the poem is looking at.

Listening: page 168

Read aloud the poem on page 168.

After listening

Discussion: lines 1-3

Explain that this poem is written in a Japanese poetic form called *haiku*.

► [interpretive] What kind of burden are the cherry limbs bearing? (ripe cherries)

[interpretive] What season of the year is being described and why? (late spring or early summer; because the cherries are ripe on the trees)

► [literal] To what unusual thing does the author compare the cherry limbs? (a battleground)

[literal] What two enemies are fighting one another on this "battleground"? (man and bird)

[interpretive] About what are the two enemies fighting? (They both want to eat the cherries.)

[interpretive] What equipment does each side use in this battle? (Man uses a bucket; bird uses its beak.)

[critical] Who do you think will win? (Accept any answer.)

Cherry TIME

Haiku
Wendy M. Harris

Burdened cherry limbs
Battleground of man and bird
Bucket against beak.

168

LITERATURE

Alliteration

Call attention to the poem "Cherry Time."

▶ What beginning consonant letter is repeated most often? (b)

What words begin with the consonant letter b? (burdened, battleground, bird, bucket, beak)

What does the sound of b—/b/—in this poem make you think of? (possible answer: the sound of cherries dropping in a bucket)

Write the word *alliteration* for display.

Explain that alliteration is the repetition of beginning consonant sounds, such as the sound of b—/b/—in "Cherry Time."

Display the poem "Maine Moose."

▶ What beginning consonant letter is repeated most often? (m)

What words begin with the consonant letter *m?* (Maine, moose, managed, muffled, marksman, missed)

What does the alliteration—the sound of *m*—in this poem make you think of? (possible answer: the noise the moose makes)

Explain that a haiku does not have to have alliteration, but that using alliteration makes it more interesting.

COMPOSITION

Haiku

Guide the following discussion about the elements of haiku, using "Cherry Time" and "Maine Moose."

▶ How are the words *snow, sky, squirrel, daffodil,* and *caterpillar* related? (Accept any answer, but elicit that they are all things in nature.)

What "nature" words can you find in "Cherry Time" and "Maine Moose"? (cherry limbs, bird, beak, man; moose, marksman)

What are both poems about? (nature)

Explain that the first rule for writing something in haiku poetry is that it is about nature.

▶ How many lines does "Cherry Time" have? (three)

How many lines does "Maine Moose" have? (three)

Explain that the second rule for writing haiku poetry is that it has three lines.

Clap the syllables in the first line of the poem "Cherry Time" together as you read it aloud.

▶ How many syllables are there? (five)

Do the same with the first line of "Maine Moose." (five)

Repeat the same procedure with the second and third lines of "Cherry Time" and "Maine Moose." (seven; five)

Explain that the third rule for writing haiku poetry is that the first and third lines have five syllables and the second line has seven syllables.

▶ Write your own haiku. Remember the three rules. You may want to try to use alliteration as you write.

Lesson	Reader pages	Worktext pages
55	169-75	71-72

Charis learns about grace, God's little gifts of strength, as she watches the cherry trees survive the heavy snowfall. Can God's grace help her survive now that Grandma is gone?

VOCABULARY

LESSON 55

†I built a clubhouse on the strongest bough of the tree. (p. 172)

†When the fragile vase fell, it broke into many pieces. (p. 172)

†The raindrops were prickling my arms, so I put on a jacket. (p. 174)

†The tall man was stooping down to talk with the little boy. (p. 174)

Materials
- A flashlight
- Vocabulary sentences prepared for display

INTRODUCTION

Vocabulary

Use the prepared sentences to introduce the vocabulary words in context.

Light of the world

Display the flashlight.

▶ What does a flashlight do? (shines light to allow you to see in the dark)

We can use the characteristic of a flashlight—its ability to shine light—to help explain an important characteristic of God.

How is the flashlight's ability to shine light similar to a characteristic of God? (Answers may vary, but elicit that just as the light of the flashlight helps us see where we should go, God's light helps us see where we should go in our lives; just as a flashlight may be our only light in the dark, God is our only hope in this dark, sinful world.)

▶ In the story you will read today, a girl named Charis goes through a difficult struggle. Her father uses a comparison to explain other important characteristics of God to help her through this difficult time in her life.

Correlated Activities
- **Vocabulary Box, Activity 1: Word Hunt**
- **Recreational Reading, Activity 5: Grab It, Read It, Pass It**
See "Classroom Management for Grouping" in the Appendix.

The Cherry TREES

Eileen M. Berry
illustrated by Del Thompson and Steve Mitchell

I remember the day I found out about Grandma. The bus had brought me home from school early because of the snowstorm, and Dad was sitting at the kitchen table holding Mom's hand. Dad never came home this early in the day. I knew that something had happened.

"Sit down, Charis," Mom said. She poured me a cup of hot cocoa, and when she brought it to me she stayed behind me with her hands on my shoulders.

"Sweetheart," Dad said, "we have some sad news for you." He looked down at the coffee cup in his big, rough hands. "Your grandma died today." For a moment he just sat without speaking. Then he looked up at me, and the crinkles around his eyes were back. "But the good news is, Grandma is with Jesus now."

Grandma had been in the hospital for a long time, but before that she had lived at our house. Mom and Dad told me about the things she had said in her hospital bed right before she died. Then they talked about funeral arrangements. Nothing could be

The Cherry Trees   169

COMPREHENSION

The student will

- Identify emotional responses of characters.
- Make comparisons.
- Relate story content to biblical truths: God gives grace to the needy; God is sovereign.

Before silent reading: pages 169-75

Motivation

► How do Charis and her family respond to unwanted news?

After silent reading

Overview discussion: pages 169-75

► [critical] How can Dad think Grandma's death is both sad and good news? (Answers may vary, but elicit that the news is sad because they will miss Grandma but good because Grandma is in heaven now.) [BAT: 1a Understanding Jesus Christ]

► [critical] Why does Charis say to Dad, "Why did God let us keep the trees but not Grandma? I prayed we could keep both"? (Accept any answer, but point out that she is confused and she would rather have kept Grandma, not the trees.) [BAT: 6b Prayer]

[literal] How does Dad compare Grandma to the cherry trees to help Charis understand death and life? (With heavy burdens or a lot of pain Grandma grew weak like the fragile cherry twig; often God takes away burdens by death, like Grandma, or by healing, like the cherry trees.)

[interpretive] How does God help people who feel sad about losing loved ones? (He gives grace.)

[literal] How does Dad describe what grace is? (little gifts of strength, just enough for each day)

Follow-up discussion: page 169

► [interpretive] Who is telling this story? (Charis)

► [critical] Why does Charis's mom stay behind her with her hands on Charis's shoulders? (Answers may vary, but suggest that she knows Charis will need comforting after she hears the sad news.)

[interpretive] How does the author show that it is hard for Dad to tell Charis the news? (Possible answer: He calls her sweetheart, looks down at his cup, and sits without speaking.)

[interpretive] What does the author mean when she says, "the crinkles around his eyes were back"? (Dad is smiling again; his eyes squint and form wrinkles.)

Read aloud the paragraph with Dad telling Charis of Grandma's death. Show sadness about the death and happiness about Grandma's being with Jesus.

[critical] Why is Grandma able to be with Jesus now? (She must have accepted Christ as her Savior while she was alive.) [BAT: 1a Understanding Jesus Christ]

Follow-up discussion: page 170

▶ [literal] What two things does Charis see as she looks out the window? (snow falling and the reflection of the candle flame)

▶ [interpretive] What does Dad mean when he says, "if this storm keeps up, we could lose some of those trees"? (The heavy snow may break the branches, killing the trees.)

Read aloud Charis's thoughts about the snow and God. Show her sadness and anger as you read.

[critical] Is Charis right to be angry with God? Why or why not? (Answers may vary, but guide the student to the conclusion that it is wrong for Charis to be angry with God. God has a reason for everything and does everything for good.) [Bible Promise: I. God as Master]

▶ [critical] Does Mom have the same attitude that Charis has? How do you know? (Answers may vary; elicit that Mom's words and actions show she is sad, but not angry with God.)

Read aloud what Mom says about the cherry trees.

▶ [critical] How does Mom show her love for Charis? (When Charis starts to cry, Mom holds her.) [BAT: 5a Love]

[appreciative] How does your mom or dad comfort you when you are sad?

done until the storm was over, Dad said. I just sat and drank my cocoa and listened.

I didn't eat much for supper. Darkness came early, and I brought a chair to the kitchen window and sat where I could look out. In the dim light I could just see the snow falling on the cherry trees outside. Behind me on the table, a candle flame danced, making a bright spot of fire in the pane.

"If this storm keeps up," Dad said, "we could lose some of those trees."

I turned around. "Why?"

He leaned close to me, peering out the window over my head. "Their limbs aren't strong enough to hold the heavy snow," he said. "Much more of this, and the branches will crack beneath the weight."

I watched the snow, wondering how something so lovely and soft could be so deadly at the same time. Everything dies, I thought. And God just lets it happen.

"Remember how your grandma loved those cherry trees in the spring, Charis?" Mom said. "With all the white blossoms on them? If we do lose them, I'm glad she's not here to see it."

And then I tried to ask Mom why God would let the trees die, but I started to cry. Mom put her arms around me. She kept holding me even when the sobs made me

170

jerk and tremble. When I was finally able to be silent, we just watched the snow together.

The next morning when I got up, the sun was shining on a clean, white world. I ran straight to the kitchen. Mom turned from the stove where she was frying eggs and smiled at me. "No school for you today," she said.

I looked out at the cherry trees. Just before I'd gone to bed the night before, I had prayed that God would not let the snow break the trees. And now here they were, all standing tall. Each branch was coated with a layer of snow like thick frosting on dark cakes. But not many branches had fallen—only a few of the smaller ones.

Dad was busy on the phone for most of the morning, calling my aunts and uncles and making plans for Grandma's funeral. I helped Mom sort through some of Grandma's things in the room where she had stayed. In the afternoon I went outside and built a snowman under the cherry trees. I used some of the fallen twigs for the snowman's arms. And I made him a smile with pieces of gravel from the drive.

The Cherry Trees   171

Follow-up discussion: page 171

▶ [critical] Why did Charis pray that God would not let the snow break the trees? (Accept any answer.) [BAT: 6b Prayer]

Read aloud the sentence describing what Charis sees when she looks out the window.

▶ [literal] What does Charis do while she is home from school? (She helps Mom sort through Grandma's things and makes a snowman.)

[critical] How do you think Charis feels as she helps her mom sort through Grandma's things? (Answers may vary, but elicit that she probably feels sad.)

[interpretive] How does the author let you know Charis is feeling happier while she builds her snowman? (Charis makes him a smile.)

Follow-up discussion: page 172

▶ [interpretive] How do you know Charis is feeling happy when her dad comes out to look at her snowman? (Charis and Dad smile at the snowman.)

[interpretive] How does the author let you know Charis is nervous about asking her Dad why God spared the trees but not Grandma? (Charis takes a deep breath, and her voice sounds rushed.)

[interpretive] How do you know that Charis feels sad again? (She stares at the snowman but does not smile.)

Read aloud Charis's question, sounding nervous.

▶ [critical] Why does Dad use a cherry twig to answer Charis's question instead of just telling her that Grandma was weak? (Answers may vary, but elicit that seeing something fragile helps Charis understand what *fragile* means.)

Read aloud Dad's answer to Charis's question. Read to show the seriousness of the answer.

[literal] What does Dad say is the way God releases us from suffering? (God takes the burden away.) [Bible Promise: H. God as Father]

Dad came out after a while to see my snowman. "Good work, Charis," he said. He put an arm around my shoulders while we smiled back at my smiling white man. Dad reached over our heads and touched a cherry bough. "The Lord spared our trees," he said.

"Dad?" I shivered and took a deep breath. My voice came out

172

sounding rushed. "Why did God let us keep the trees but not Grandma? I prayed we could keep both." I couldn't look up at him. I just kept staring at my snowman, but I was no longer smiling.

"I don't know, Charis," Dad said. "But I do know that God did what He knew was best."

He thought for a moment. Then he broke another twig off the cherry tree and handed it to me. "See how small that is—how fragile?"

I turned the little twig over in my mittened hands.

"We're like that sometimes," Dad said. "When we've had heavy burdens to bear, or when we've been in a lot of pain, we can grow pretty weak and frail. Grandma was like that."

I nodded, knowing what he meant. Right before she had gone to the hospital, Grandma could not even stand up without help.

"And sometimes when that happens," Dad said, "God decides it's time to release us from the suffering altogether. He takes the burden away."

"You mean dying?" I asked.

"Sometimes it's dying. And sometimes—like with the trees—God heals. Either way, He knows how much we can handle, and He knows when we've had enough."

"But how does He choose—dying or living, I mean?"

A whisper of wind stirred the cherry boughs above us, and a little dusting of snow sprinkled down. I looked up at Dad, and he smiled at me. "He chooses," he said, "because He *knows* what is right. That's why He's God."

The Cherry Trees   173

Follow-up discussion: page 173

▶ [interpretive] How does God take away our burdens? (sometimes by death and sometimes by healing)

[interpretive] Does Charis understand at this point how God chooses to take away burdens? How do you know? (No; she asks Dad how God chooses dying or living.)

Read aloud the last paragraph that gives Dad's answer about how God chooses dying or living.

[critical] Why does Dad smile at Charis before he answers? (Answers may vary, but elicit that he loves Charis and is comforting her about God's ability to always know what is right.) [Bible Promise: I. God as Master]

The Cherry Trees

Follow-up discussion: page 174

▶ [interpretive] Why is it hard for Charis to smile like Dad is smiling? (She remembers how it was when her grandma was alive and thinks about how much she misses her.)

[interpretive] What makes Charis start to cry? (She misses Grandma and wonders how God will take away her pain of missing Grandma.)

Read aloud Charis's questions to Dad, showing her sadness.

[literal] What does Dad write in the snow? ("Charis")

[critical] Why does Dad write Charis's name in the snow? (Answers may vary, but elicit that her name is the answer to her question because *Charis* means "grace.") [BAT: 7a Grace]

[interpretive] How do you know that Charis still does not understand God's grace? (She asks what grace is exactly.)

I wanted to be able to smile too. But as I looked at Dad, I suddenly remembered the photograph of Grandma on the desk in my room, and the rocking chair by my bed where she had sat and read to me. The photograph was all I had of her, and the chair was empty now.

"What about the people who get left with the pain?" I asked. I felt tears prickling in my eyes. "What if God doesn't take it away?"

Instead of answering, Dad took the twig from my hand. Stooping down in the snow, he used the twig as a pencil to write my name. *Charis*. "Do you remember what your name means?" he asked.

Of course I remembered. Dad had told me many times that he had named me after a Greek word in the Bible. "Grace," I said.

"That's right. And that's your answer. For the people who get left with the pain, God gives His grace."

"What is grace exactly?" I wiped my mitten across my eyes.

174

Dad looked far away for a moment, thinking. Then he looked back at me. "It's like little gifts of strength," he said. "Not all at once, just enough for each day. It means becoming like these tree branches when they're able to bend under the snow but not break. Do you understand?"

I looked at my name in the snow for a long time. Then I looked at him. And I suddenly found I could smile. "I think so."

Dad gave me a hug. Then he took my hand—just like he used to when I was very little—and led me back toward the farmhouse. "I guess we can thank God for leaving us the trees," I said.

He gave my hand a squeeze. "We sure can, Sweetheart. There'll be blossoms again in the spring."

I thought for a moment. "And cherry pies," I added.

I looked up at Dad in time to see his eyes crinkle when he grinned. "That's my Charis," he said.

The Cherry Trees   175

Follow-up discussion: page 175

▶ [interpretive] Why does Dad compare God's grace to the tree branch's ability to bend under heavy snow and not break? (Dad is helping Charis to see or understand that God's grace is the help and strength He gives us as we need it.)

Read aloud Dad's description of God's grace.

Read aloud the paragraph that tells you Charis finally understands the meaning of God's grace.

▶ [critical] Why does Dad hug Charis and take her hand like he used to when she was very little? (Answers may vary but should express that Dad is comforting and showing his love for Charis.) [BAT: 5a Love]

▶ [interpretive] What does Dad say that lets you know Charis is back to feeling like her old self before Grandma's death? ("That's my Charis.")

[critical] Do you think Charis is feeling God's grace now? Why or why not? (Answers may vary, but elicit that she is able to be happy again as a result of God's grace.)

[appreciative] Have you ever felt God's grace during a difficult or painful time in your life?

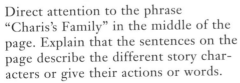

Worktext Objective

The student will

■ Match story characters with their actions and dialogue.

▶ Read the sentences and write in each box the name of the character that fits with the two sentences connected to each box.

Comprehension:
Worktext page 71

Direct attention to the phrase "Charis's Family" in the middle of the page. Explain that the sentences on the page describe the different story characters or give their actions or words.

▶ Who are the four characters mentioned in the story? (Charis, Mom, Dad, Grandma)

The Cherry Trees

The student will

■ Recognize first-person point of view.

LITERATURE
First-person point of view

Call attention to the story "The Cherry Trees."

▶ Look at page 169 in your reader. Who are the characters in the story? (Mom, Dad, Charis, Grandma)

Is one of the characters telling the story? (yes)

▶ Who is telling the story? (Charis)

How do you know? (She uses words like *I*, *me*, *my*, and *our* as she tells the story to the reader.)

▶ When we read a story that is told by one of the story characters, we say the story is told in the first-person point of view. It is a first-person story.

Write the pronouns *I*, *me*, *my*, *we*, *our*, and *us* for display. Choose students to read the pronouns aloud.

▶ These pronouns help us to determine that a story is a first-person story.

Literature: **Worktext page 72**

Use the information at the top of the page to review first-person point of view. Read the directions and guide the students in completing the page.

Materials

- Teaching Visuals 8, 9, 10, and 12: *Eighty Stables, Ponies Carry the Mail, End of a Hard Ride*, and *A Special Mailbag*

Lesson	Worktext pages
56	238-39

WORDS WITH SCHWA SYLLABLES

1 Introduction: Keeping the Mail

▶ Pony express riders carried little to protect themselves from all the danger they faced; yet the mail was lost only once in the eighteen months the express operated. How could this be? Listen to learn about certain plans that helped keep the mail safe.

Read the following to the students.

Mail security was a major concern for the Overland Pony Express Company. For this reason Mr. Russell had special locked mailbags designed to keep the mail as safe as possible. Four leather pouches for holding mail were attached to the corners of a leather saddle cover. Keys to the locked pouches were kept only in Salt Lake City, San Francisco, and St. Louis. No one in between these cities was allowed access to the mail.

The leather saddle cover with its four pouches was called a *mochila*. Mochilas helped keep the mail with the horse and rider. Two openings in each mochila fit over the saddle horn and cantle, anchoring it in place. As long as a rider stayed in the saddle, the mochila could not be removed. Even if a rider were separated from the horse, the mochila would stay in place while the pony ran on alone to the next station.

Even though mochilas were designed to stay in place, they were not tied down; so they were very easy to remove. At a remount station, riders could quickly pull the mochila off the saddle and toss it across the saddle of the next waiting horse. These special mailbags were also light so that they would not slow the horse down. A pony express horse's saddle, bridle, and mochila weighed only about thirteen pounds. Because of mochilas, no time was wasted transferring the mail. They were an ideal way to carry and protect the mail.

Discuss the following.

▶ Name some security features designed for the pony express mail delivery. (possible answers: locked mochilas, keys for the mochilas kept in only three cities, lightweight mochilas, mochila held in place over saddle)

▶ How could a lightweight mochila help keep the mail safe? (Possible answer: The less weight a horse carried, the easier it would be for it to outrun dangers.)

▶ What do you think the horses would do if the rider was lost? (Answers will vary. The horses didn't necessarily realize that they were carrying the mail but would respond to satisfy physical needs. Most domestic horses left to themselves will return or go to where they know they will receive food and water.)

2 Skill review: Teaching Visuals 8, 9, and 10— *Eighty Stables, Ponies Carry the Mail,* and *End of a Hard Ride*

Use Teaching Visuals 8, 9, and 10 to lead a brief review of Syllable Rule 3 for words ending with a consonant + *le* and Syllable Division Rule 4 and Accent Rule 2 for words with affixes. These rules were presented in Lessons 39 and 49.

Objectives

The student will

- Recognize that schwa syllables have various spellings, such as *a-* (again), *con-* (content), *-le* (little), *-er* (never), *-ain* (captain), *-ous* (famous), and *-tion* (nation).
- Recognize that the accent never falls on a syllable with a schwa sound.
- Identify the accented syllable in words with a schwa sound.

Background information

Accent Rule 4—The accent never falls on a syllable with a schwa sound.

In words with schwa ending /shən/, the accent usually falls on the syllable that precedes the ending.

(3) **Skill development:**
Visual 12—*A Special Mailbag*

▶ Look at the word *mochila* and its pronunciation. The green letter in the pronunciation is called *schwa*. What vowel letter represents the schwa sound in the word *mochila*? (a)

Look at the words below *mochila*. The green letters represent the schwa sound in these words. Is schwa spelled *a* in all the words? (no)

What other spellings for schwa do you see in this list? (e, i, o, u, ai, ou)

▶ Notice the mark above one syllable in each word. What is that mark called? (an accent mark)

Read the list while tapping your pencil below each syllable on the visual, emphasizing the accented syllable.

▶ Which syllable has the schwa—one that is accented or one that is not accented? (Schwa is always in an unaccented syllable.)

▶ Look at the next list of words. Read the sample word with me: *desperation*.

Which syllable in *desperation* contains the schwa? (the last syllable, *tion*)

The schwa ending *-tion* is found in many words.

Choose students to read the columns of words.

▶ Is the schwa ending *-tion* accented? (no)

There is an accent pattern for words ending with *-tion*. Can you discover the pattern? (The accent falls on the syllable that precedes the *-tion* ending.)

Mochilas and Saddles

▶**Find It**
Underline the schwa syllables in each of the words below.

gal´•<u>lop</u>	trou´•<u>ble</u>
col•lapse´	cus´•<u>tom</u>
sten´•<u>cil</u>	<u>a</u>•bide´
bal´•<u>ance</u>	junc´•<u>tion</u>

mō•chē´•lə

▶**Identify It**
Write the schwa vowels in the blanks.
Add the accent mark to the correct syllable.

_a_ roy´•al•ty		_a_ pa•trol´	
_i_ jus´•ti•fy		_u_ faith´•ful	
_o_ fal´•con		_e_ cy´•press	
_e_ dag´•ger		_ou_ ner´•vous	
_u_ Ve´•nus		_ai_ foun´•tain	

lĕth´•ər

stûr´•əp

> **Schwa** is a vowel sound like a soft "uh." It is in many syllables. Schwa never occurs in an accented syllable.

▶**Review the Rules**
Rewrite each word. Divide it into syllables and add the accent mark.

1. washcloth   *wash´•cloth*
2. unlocking   *un•lock´•ing*
3. ramble   *ram´•ble*
4. basket   *bas´•ket*

238

---

(4) **Skill application:**
Worktext page 238

Find It
▶ Listen to each word as it is read and identify the syllable that contains the schwa by underlining it.

Identify It
Choose students to read each word and to identify its schwa vowel before the students complete the activity.

Review the Rules
Guide the students in dividing each word into syllables and adding the accent mark. Discuss the rules used for each word.

washcloth—Divide compound words between the two base words; the accent falls on the first base word.

unlocking—Divide words between the base word and affixes; the accent falls on the base word.

ramble—Divide before the consonant + *le*; the accent never falls on a schwa syllable.

basket—Divide between consonants (*VC/CV*); the accent falls on the first syllable.

(5) **Skill application:**
Worktext page 239

JAKKO'S ANSWER

Jakko leaves Samson at the central pillars of the temple and hurries home as the blind prisoner has instructed him. Why doesn't Samson's loving, all-powerful God release him from his suffering and the torments of the Philistines? When the ground begins to shake and the great roof of the temple falls, Jakko understands.

Lesson	Reader pages	Worktext pages
57	176-79	73
58	180-82	74

Materials
- A strong, short metal chain
- Vocabulary sentences for display

INTRODUCTION
Vocabulary
Use the prepared sentences to introduce the vocabulary words in context.

A test of strength
Allow the students to take turns testing their strength by attempting to pull the chain apart.

▶ Were you able to pull the chain apart?

Why weren't you able to do it?

What would you need in order to accomplish this? (more physical strength)

Explain that some difficult tasks take inward strength rather than physical strength.

▶ Sometimes there are tasks that we have to do that seem impossible, but God can give us inward strength to overcome our weakness and complete the task.

Can you think of a time when you needed inward strength? (possible answers: witnessing to an unsaved person, telling the truth, obeying parents)

What can we do to receive the strength we need from the Lord? (possible answers: pray, read the Word of God, seek wise counsel)

The story you will begin reading today will show you how both physical and inward strength can be used for God's glory.

Head note
Read the head note on reader page 176 aloud.

VOCABULARY

LESSON 57

*†On Grandpa's farm we used a millstone to grind the grain. (p. 177)

The man was considered a fiend because of his wicked cruelty to animals. (p. 177)

*†The principal did not tolerate the boy's rude manners. (p. 177)

LESSON 58

†The lumberjack's hands had become calloused from his years of swinging an ax. (p. 180)

†Dad threaded his way between the people in the crowd. (p. 180)

The explosion of the car avenged the criminal on his enemies. (p. 181)

†The girl tightly clutched the coins her mother gave her. (p. 181)

Correlated Activities
- **Vocabulary Box, Activity 2: Study Buddies**
- **Word Work, Activity 3: The Title Match**

See "Classroom Management for Grouping" in the Appendix.

COMPREHENSION

The student will

- Recognize the use of fiction to illuminate facts.
- Recognize the author's technique of revealing the characters through conversation and thoughts.
- Recognize the genre of biblical fiction.

Before silent reading: pages 176-79

Motivation

▶ What kind of jobs does a temple boy have?

What important thing does Samson tell Jakko?

After silent reading

Overview discussion: pages 176-79

▶ [interpretive] "Jakko's Answer" is called *biblical fiction* because some parts of the story are from the Bible. What parts are true Bible facts? (possible answers: Samson's capture, the Philistines' cruel treatment, Samson's disobedience, the great feast)

▶ [literal] What are some of Jakko's duties as a temple boy? (possible answers: sweeping, polishing silver, working in the kitchen, waving palm branches over the food, helping at the temple rites)

▶ [interpretive] Think about the title of the story. What do you think is the question that Jakko needs an answer for? (Is there a God greater than Dagon?)

▶ [critical] How does Samson's friendship affect Jakko's life? (Answers will vary, but elicit that because of Samson Jakko learns about Israel's God.) [BAT: 5c Evangelism and missions]

Jakko's Answer

Mary Elmhurst and Jeri Massi
illustrated by Steve Mitchell

This is a fictional story based on Judges 13-16. Its central character is only briefly mentioned in Scripture, but in this story he is given a name.

A Temple Boy

"Did you grind the corn yet, Jakko?"

"Almost," Jakko said, hurrying to the bag of corn in the corner.

"Almost?" His mother looked stern. "You mean you haven't even started yet! Lazy boy!"

"I'm sorry. I—"

"Don't do it now. You have to get up to the temple within the hour for the sacrifice. Change your clothes."

Jakko hurriedly found his working tunic.

176

Follow-up discussion: page 176

▶ [interpretive] How do you know Jakko's mother is losing patience with him? (She gives him a stern look and says he is lazy.)

[interpretive] How do you know Jakko's mother thinks his job as a temple boy is important? (She excuses him from grinding corn so he won't be late for the temple sacrifice.)

Read aloud with a stern voice what Jakko's mother says to him about grinding the corn.

"I suppose you and that blind man were blabbing again," his mother said. "If the priests found . . . Ah me, how am I supposed to keep track of you all the time? But mark my words, someday that Samson is going to snatch you up and give you a good lesson!"

Jakko couldn't help smiling. "Oh, Mother, he's chained."

"Chains! Hah!" She snapped her fingers. "He picked up the gates of the city of Gaza one time and carried them away on his shoulders. And he killed a thousand men once with some old bone he picked up off the ground. Chains won't hold him if he gets mad."

"Mother, poor Samson never gets mad at me. He's my friend. Besides, he's really not that strong. I've watched him turning the millstone, and sometimes he can barely move it."

"Mark my words, boy, if the priests find you making friends with that fiend, it will go hard for you—you, a temple boy!"

Jakko already knew that. The priests didn't tolerate very much at all. When Jakko had cried out because of their cruel punishments, the priests had only punished him again.

Temple boy! He hated the very name! When he had been afraid of the huge statues of Dagon, the priests had pushed him into the temple and made him stay through all the long, horrible ceremonies.

"Today," Jakko said softly, "Samson told me about the time he caught three hundred foxes."

His mother was interested. "What did he do with them?"

"He put burning wood between their tails and let them loose, two by two, to go wherever they wanted." He laughed.

"Ah!" She suddenly shook her head. "It was no doubt a trick of his to burn our crops. Isn't that so?"

"Well, yes," Jakko admitted. "They ran into the cornfields."

"Enough!" she said. "Not another word about Samson! Get to the temple! You'll get a whipping if you're late to help with the sacrifices."

Follow-up discussion: page 177

▶ [interpretive] What makes Jakko's mother think Samson is dangerous? (He picked up the gates of the city of Gaza and carried them away on his shoulders, and he killed a thousand men with a bone.)

▶ [literal] What relationship does Jakko have with Samson? (They are friends.)

[critical] Why would the priests be upset with Jakko if they found him making friends with Samson? (Accept any answer, but suggest that Samson is the enemy of the priests.)

▶ [critical] Why does Jakko speak softly when he begins his story of the foxes? (Answers may vary, but elicit that he does not want to upset his mother again by talking about Samson.)

[interpretive] Does Jakko's mother think the story is funny? Why or why not? (No; their crops were burned as a result of Samson's act.)

Read aloud Jakko and his mother's conversation as he tells her the story of Samson and the foxes.

Follow-up discussion: page 178

▶ [literal] What does Samson tell Jakko about the god Dagon? (Samson tells Jakko that the God of Israel is greater than Dagon.) [Bible Promise: I. God as Master]

[interpretive] Who is Dagon? (a god that the Philistines worship)

[critical] How does Jakko feel about the possibility of an all-powerful God? (Answers will vary, but elicit that he hopes it is true.)

▶ [critical] How do you think Jakko would feel if he were freed from the temples? (Accept any answer.)

Read aloud with hope the paragraph in which Jakko thinks of freedom from the temples.

▶ [literal] What is Jakko's least favorite job? Why? (helping at the temple rites before the feasts; because of the awful things that happen during the sacrifices such as the priests' cutting themselves)

[critical] Why do you think the priests cut themselves when they pray? (Accept any answer.)

▶ [appreciative] How do you worship God? (possible answer: by praying to Him, singing, praising Him, hearing His Word preached) [BATs: 6a Bible study; 6b Prayer]

Jakko hurried out. But his mind was full. Samson told him many things—and not all of them were funny. He said that Israel's God was greater than Dagon. Jakko wondered if it could be true. He was more afraid of Dagon than he was of the priests. But he knew he had to spend the rest of his life in service to the gods, for he was a temple boy, born and raised in the shadow of the temples.

But if there were another God—an all-powerful God—the thought of being free from the temples made Jakko's throat feel tight.

Jakko soon was busily sweeping floors, polishing silver, and doing other tasks at the great temple of Dagon in preparation for the sacrifice.

Jakko hoped that he would be chosen to work during the feast, waving palm branches over the tables to keep the flies away. Kitchen work always made him hot and tired, and helping at the temple rites before the feasts was even worse. The things that happened during the sacrifices frightened Jakko. The priests cut themselves when they prayed. They did worse things, too, that he couldn't bear to think about.

178

In the middle of the afternoon, Jakko was sent to watch the roasting meat that was slowly turning over the coals in the huge fireplaces. It was kitchen work, but he consoled himself: at least he didn't have to help with the sacrifices.

As the afternoon wore slowly away, Jakko thought about the things that Samson had told him. Was there really a God who was greater than Dagon? If there was, then why was Samson in prison and why were the Philistines having a feast to celebrate his capture? It didn't make sense. How was he to know what to believe?

Jakko suddenly realized he was hungry. It was almost evening, and he hadn't seen a thing that was going on in the temple. The feasting had begun already. Finally, he was told that he could go.

Jakko hurried to the great hall to get something to eat. Mother would expect him to get his dinner there. What he saw made him gasp in wonder. He had never seen so many people in his life. There must have been thousands!

Jakko's Answer   179

Follow-up discussion: page 179

▶ [literal] The feast that Jakko is helping with is to celebrate what? (Samson's capture)

▶ [interpretive] Why is it hard for Jakko to believe that there is a God greater than Dagon? (It is hard for him to believe that a God so great would allow Samson to be captured and allow his enemies to celebrate.)

[critical] If God is in control, why is Samson in prison? (Accept any answer, but elicit that God has a purpose for everything.) [Bible Promise: I. God as Master]

Read aloud the inward struggle Jakko is having as he does his kitchen work.

Looking ahead

▶ What purpose could God have in Samson's capture?

Will Jakko find the answer he needs?

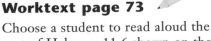

Worktext Objectives

The student will

■ Locate verses in the Bible.

■ Match Bible characters with actions.

Study Skills:
Worktext page 73

Choose a student to read aloud the part of Hebrews 11:6 shown on the page.

Call attention to the other Bible references in Hebrews listed in the box. Instruct the students to look up the verses and then write the name of the character that matches each testimony on the page.

COMPREHENSION

Objectives

The student will

- Demonstrate understanding of characters' perspectives.
- Discern the motives of characters.
- Relate story content to biblical truths: God is holy; God forgives; God is just.

Use the prepared sentences to introduce the vocabulary words in context.

Before silent reading: pages 180-82

Motivation

▶ Will Jakko find the answer to his question?

How will God use all of these people and events to bring glory to Him?

After silent reading

Overview discussion: pages 180-82

▶ [interpretive] Why is Jakko confused about Samson's God? (He does not understand why God has allowed Samson to be treated this way.)

▶ [interpretive] Why isn't Samson angry at God for his present situation? (He understands that his own sin has brought this upon himself.)

[critical] Do all bad things that happen to Christians mean they are being punished? How do you know? (No; sometimes bad things happen for a reason, e.g., the life of Joseph.) [Bible Promise: I. God as Master]

[critical] How do you know God has forgiven Samson? (Accept any answer, but point out that Samson has repented and asked for forgiveness, and God has promised to always forgive; and point out the fact that God hears and answers Samson's prayer for strength.) [BATs: 6b Prayer; 6e Forgiveness]

[interpretive] How does God use this bad situation to bring glory to Him? (Samson defeats Israel's enemies.)

▶ [interpretive] What is the answer to Jakko's question? (God is greater than Dagon.)

Follow-up discussion: page 180

▶ [literal] What does Jakko see when he first enters the temple? (men and women dressed splendidly, laughing and making fun of Samson)

[interpretive] How does the author let you know that Jakko is not happy with this sight? (His heart sinks.)

▶ [critical] Why do you think Samson hesitates so long before answering Jakko's questions? (Accept any answer.)

[literal] How does God sometimes show love for His people? (He punishes them when they disobey to drive them back to Himself.) [BAT: 2a Obedience; Bible Promise: H. God as Father]

Read aloud the conversation between Jakko and Samson to show how they feel among all the wicked Philistines.

The Answer

Jakko heard shouts of laughter from a group of splendidly dressed men and women and edged toward them. What he saw made his heart sink! There was Samson—he had been brought from the prison house—and everyone was making fun of him. Priests, soldiers, and even that beautiful lady they called Delilah. After a few moments Jakko heard one of the priests calling.

"Here, boy, lead him over there so the people on the roof can see him too." Jakko timidly edged forward through the laughing, pushing people and took Samson's arm.

"Samson, just go with me. I'll show you the way."

"Jakko, my boy." Samson's calloused hands touched Jakko's shoulders. "I forgot. You are a temple boy. Poor lad."

Jakko's eyes filled with tears. Somehow Samson understood what there was to fear and hate in the temples.

"Where are you taking me?" Samson whispered.

"To the middle of the hall. Where the pillars are." As they threaded their way through the crowd, Jakko decided that he had to ask. "Samson?"

"Yes, boy?"

"Samson, please don't be angry, but I must know. If your God is so powerful, why are you here in Dagon's temple with everyone laughing at you? And why did your God let them put your eyes out?"

Samson sighed and hesitated so long that Jakko was afraid he wouldn't answer. Finally he said, "Jakko, God is not just powerful; He is holy. He will not let His people do wrong without being punished. I disobeyed Him. I joined myself to the Philistines, even though I knew their wickedness."

Unseeing, he raised a hand and gestured around him at the people and priests. In the harsh light from the torches Jakko thought they looked twice as cruel. "And because of that, I am now suffering. Oh, how I am suffering!"

"But you told me that God loves you and all His people."

"He does. He does. And so He punishes us—not like the priests

180

punish you by being cruel. God drives us back to Himself. I was very far from Him, Jakko. He has had to drive me back very hard indeed to return me to Himself. Can you understand that?"

"Yes."

"I demanded in my heart to live among the pagan Philistines and be a part of them. And now I am. Now I know how evil I was." Howling and laughter rose around them again.

"And yet your God will accept you?" Jakko asked.

"Yes. And I have repented for my wrongdoing. Soon I will be with Him; all my blindness will be past." His big, rough hands patted Jakko's head. "God listens to those who truly ask His for-giveness. Someday He will send His Messiah who will be able to make us right with God."

By now the two had reached the center of the great feasting hall. Jakko shrank back from the eyes of all the people. They were looking, laughing.

"Are we in the middle of the hall?" Samson asked him.

"Yes." The words stuck in Jakko's throat. "I'm sorry, Samson."

But Samson wasn't listening.

"O Lord God, remember me, I pray Thee, and strengthen me, I pray Thee, only this once, O God, that I may be at once avenged of the Philistines for my two eyes." Then Samson clutched Jakko's shoulder.

Follow-up discussion: page 181

▶ [interpretive] **Why does Jakko ask the question "And yet your God will accept you?"** (He is surprised that Samson's God forgives even after Samson deliberately sinned against Him.) [BAT: 6e Forgiveness]

[critical] **How is the true God different from Dagon?** (Accept any answer, but elicit that God is merciful and forgiving.)

▶ [interpretive] **What does Samson mean when he says that he will soon be with God and his blindness will be past?** (He is going to die and go to heaven to be with the Lord.)

[critical] **Has God sent the Messiah Samson was talking about? Who is it?** (yes; Jesus Christ)

▶ [critical] **How does Christ make us right with God?** (Answers may vary, but elicit that Christ paid the debt for our sins when He died on the cross.) [Bible Promise: E. Christ as Sacrifice]

Read aloud what God does for those who ask.

▶ [critical] **Do you think Jakko knows what Samson is going to do?** (Accept any answer.)

Read aloud with a mighty voice Samson's request to God. [BAT: 6b Prayer]

Follow-up discussion: page 182

▶ [interpretive] How does Samson show he cares about Jakko? (possible answers: tells him about God, tells him that God loves him, commands him to go home so he doesn't get hurt) [BAT: 5a Kindness]

▶ [critical] What kind of look does Samson have on his face that frightens Jakko? (Accept any answer.)

[interpretive] How do you know Jakko believes what Samson says? (He does exactly what Samson tells him to do.)

▶ [interpretive] How are the walls of the temple brought down? (God gives Samson the strength to bring down the pillars that support the roof.)

▶ [critical] Do you think Jakko now believes that God is greater than Dagon? Why do you think that? (Accept any answer.)

Read aloud the answer to Jakko's question.

"Jakko, take me to the pillars that support the roof, and then go home quickly. God is going to give me strength as He did in the past. I will show that He is alive and that He is the only true God. Always remember what I have told you about Him. And remember that He loves you too."

The look on Samson's face frightened Jakko; he dared not disobey. After leading Samson to one of the pillars, he hurried to the entrance of the hall and fled down the steps toward the road leading home. Then he paused and turned. What could one old, blind man do in the temple of Dagon? Suddenly he heard Samson's voice, loud above the noise of the festivities.

"Now let me die with the Philistines!"

Die? With the Philistines? Suddenly the great slab walls of the temple shook and then buckled with a terrific roar that knocked Jakko to the ground. The roof of the temple caved in. Jakko hid his head in his arm until the thunderous crash subsided. Then there was nothing but silence. He looked up and saw a cloud of dust rising over the mass of fallen stone where the temple had been.

Jakko had his answer about the God of Israel. Who but a living, all-powerful God could bring such defeat to His enemies? And through just one man—a man who wouldn't have to suffer anymore.

182

COMPREHENSION

Motives

► Why do people do the things they do? We do some things because it is practical or it makes sense to do them.

► Why do you eat? (Answers may vary but should include that we need nourishment.)

Why do you wash your hands before eating? (Answers may vary but should include that it is to remove germs and be clean.)

► Sometimes people do certain things because of their personality or their perspective.

Why do thieves steal? (They are selfish and greedy.)

Why do gentlemen hold open doors for girls and women? (to demonstrate manners and courtesy)

Why does a mother hold the hand of a young child when crossing a street? (A mother loves her child and wants to protect him or her.)

► Christians should look to the Bible to guide their actions. [BATs: 2a Obedience; 6c Spirit-filled]

Why do you obey your parents? (because God commands it; to demonstrate your love for God and others)

Why do you do your best in school? (because God commands it; to honor God)

Write the word *motive* for display.

► The reason a person or character does something is called a *motive*.

Comprehension: Worktext page 74

Read the definition of *motive* at the top of the page. Remind the students to think about the reason or the motive each action was done as they answer the question.

LITERATURE LESSON: BIBLICAL FICTION

Lesson	Reader pages	Worktext pages
59	183-85	75-76

VOCABULARY

LESSON 59

†The pillars that support the porch roof are in need of repair. (p. 183)

†Luke was well-liked at school because of his friendly personality. (p. 183)

*†Long ago many streets were paved with naturally rounded stones called cobblestones. (p. 185)

Column Chart

Characteristics	Jelly-beans	Both	Peanuts
A. salty			
B. sweet			
C. crunchy			
D. many colors			
E. small pieces			
F. gummy			
G. snack food			

Venn Diagram

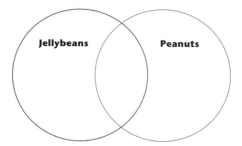

Jellybeans   Peanuts

Materials

- Vocabulary sentences for display
- Small jar of different-colored jellybeans
- Small jar of peanuts
- Several different types of charts and graphs
- Prepared blank column chart (see below)
- Prepared blank Venn diagram chart (see below)
- A Bible for the teacher and each student

INTRODUCTION

Vocabulary

Use the prepared sentences to introduce the vocabulary words in context.

Fact or fiction?

Read aloud Genesis 6:13-7:1 and 7:11-16

▶ Something is wrong in the story I'm going to read to you. Can you tell what it is?

Read aloud the following story to the students.

"Come on, Japheth," one of the townspeople called out, "you're not going to get on that thing with your crazy old father, are you?"

The townspeople had been watching in amazement as the multitude of animals gathered around the huge wooden structure. They had never seen such strange happenings in all their lives.

After the last animal entered through the doorway, Noah and his family followed. Noah looked back sadly at the people who had rejected God. He slowly pulled the great door shut. He went to the highest level of the ark and looked through the window, pressing his forehead against the cold glass, praying to the great Creator God for mercy.

Ask the following questions about the story.

▶ Does the Bible say that the townspeople tried to talk Noah's son out of going on the ark with his father? (no) Do you think this could have happened? (probably)

Why would someone make up a story about the Bible and add things that people said and did that aren't recorded there? (The Bible doesn't give every detail, so some fictional details make the story come alive.)

What is one thing in this fictionalized story of Noah that we know could not be true because of the time period? (There would be no glass in the window.)

▶ What is one detail that is added to this story that contradicts what the Bible says? (It says Noah closed the door. Genesis 7:16 says, "the Lord shut him in.")

Why do you think it is important for us to know that God closed the door? (Possible answers: we know God was in control; it demonstrates that Noah would not be able to reopen it; God might have closed it before the townspeople decided to try to enter the ark when they saw the floods coming.)

▶ Today you will find out how and why people write fictional stories based on events in the Bible.

Correlated Activities

- **Creative Writing, Activity 5: Story-in-a-Bag**
- **Connections, Activity 5: Treasure Hunt**

See "Classroom Management for Grouping" in the Appendix.

LITERATURE LESSON:

Biblical Fiction

"Jakko's Answer" contains many facts that you probably recognized. Yet it is a fictional story. Everything in the story about Samson is true and followed the scriptural account. But the main character of this story is the little boy who led Samson to the pillars in the temple. We don't know what that boy's name really was.

And we don't know what he really learned from Samson's death. But the authors gave him a name and a personality. They wanted you to think about the story of Samson in a new way. They wanted to help you understand what life was really like in Philistia when Samson was there.

Literature Lesson: Biblical Fiction   183

COMPREHENSION

The student will

- Recognize the use of biblical fiction to illuminate biblical facts.
- Distinguish biblical events from historical fiction details.
- Recognize the author's use of details to create setting.
- Recognize the author's use of historical research to plan a story plot.
- Recognize that plot and setting build an understanding of Scripture in biblical fiction.

Objectives

Before silent reading: pages 183-85

Motivation

▶ How can you benefit from reading biblical fiction?

What kind of research must a writer of biblical fiction do?

After silent reading

Overview discussion: pages 183-85

▶ [interpretive] What makes a story biblical fiction? (following the true scriptural account and using historical details from research to add to the plot and setting)

[interpretive] How do the writers of "Jakko's Answer" know what Jakko would do as a temple boy? (They did historical research to find out what temple boys did in Samson's time.)

[literal] What are two important parts of the author's job when writing biblical fiction? (researching to plan the story plot and researching for the details of the setting)

[appreciative] Do you think writing biblical fiction would be difficult? Would you like to try it?

Follow-up discussion: page 183

▶ [interpretive] Why might a person think that "Jakko's Answer" is a true story about a real little boy? (because it contains many true facts about Samson and it follows the scriptural account)

[critical] How could we find out if a story is true biblical fiction? (Answers will vary, but elicit that we can compare the story to the biblical account to make sure the Bible facts in the story are true to the Bible. Point out that the author's interpretation of the biblical account can be good or bad.)

[interpretive] What part of "Jakko's Answer" lets you know that it is biblical fiction and not exactly what is written in Scripture? (The boy who led Samson to the pillars is not named in Scripture, nor does the Bible tell what he learned from Samson.)

Read aloud the sentences that tell why the authors wrote "Jakko's Answer."

▶ [literal] What must be true for biblical fiction to be good? (Every Bible fact mentioned must be told the way the Bible tells it.)

[critical] Why shouldn't an author write whatever he wants in biblical fiction? (Answers may vary, but elicit that the author needs to read and correctly understand the scriptural account and do historical research in order to write accurate biblical fiction.)

[appreciative] What reason could you have for being cautious about reading a story that claims to be biblical fiction? (Accept any answer, but point out that the story might not be true to the Bible, and you would be reading something false.)

▶ [interpretive] Besides checking with the scriptural account, what else should an author do when planning the plot? (historical research)

[literal] What part of the plot in "Jakko's Answer" depends on historical research? (Jakko's job in the temple)

[literal] How might a writer learn about something from the past? (visit a museum or look in books)

Read aloud the paragraph that tells about good biblical fiction.

• **Plot That Builds an Understanding of Scripture**

Good biblical fiction is always true to Scripture. Every Bible fact that the story mentions is told the way the Bible tells it.

Other parts of the plot may depend on historical research. Jakko's job in the temple was a job that some boys had in Philistia in Samson's time. Suppose Jakko had used a tool or a weapon. The writers would have had to visit a museum or look in books to learn about that object. Suppose Jakko had visited the market. The writers would have had to know all about the products available in the markets of Philistia. Authors must do research in planning the story plot.

184

- **Setting That Builds an Understanding of Scripture**

Authors of stories set in Bible times must plan an accurate setting for their stories too. The writers of "Jakko's Answer" might have visited the ruins of a temple. Or they might have studied books with drawings and descriptions of temples. Suppose Jakko had taken a journey. The writers would have had to know about the roads. Were they paved with cobblestones? Were they dusty trails? And what kind of land did Jakko travel on? Did he cross mountains? Did he walk on grassy flat-lands? Research for the details of the setting is a big part of the author's job.

Biblical fiction can be very exciting. It can help you feel as if you were actually there when some biblical event happened. A good story can take you right to the setting and help you live there with the characters. Someday you may decide to write a story like "Jakko's Answer." If you do, you may find that doing the research and writing will help you understand the Bible even better.

Literature Lesson: Biblical Fiction   185

Follow-up discussion: page 185

▶ [literal] What research could an author do to describe an accurate setting for "Jakko's Answer"? (visit the ruins of a temple or study books filled with drawings and descriptions of temples)

[critical] Why does the setting for biblical fiction need to be accurate? (Accept any answer, but elicit that biblical fiction must be as accurate as possible in order for us to learn more about the Bible.) [BAT: 2e Thoroughness]

▶ [critical] Why would researching and writing biblical fiction help you understand the Bible better? (Accept any answer, but elicit that it would cause you to meditate upon Scripture, and researching would teach you more about the setting where the biblical account takes place.)

Read aloud the sentence that tells an important reason for writing biblical fiction.

Worktext Objective

The student will

- Distinguish biblical truth from error.

Study Skills:
Worktext page 75

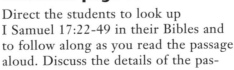

Direct the students to look up I Samuel 17:22-49 in their Bibles and to follow along as you read the passage aloud. Discuss the details of the passage.

Guide the students in reading the two stories on the page. Continue the discussion of accurate biblical fiction as you compare the two stories to Scripture. Complete the page together.

Column Chart

Characteristics	Jelly-beans	Both	Peanuts
A. salty			X
B. sweet	X		
C. crunchy			X
D. many colors	X		
E. small pieces		X	
F. gummy	X		
G. snack food		X	

Venn Diagram

Jellybeans — B, D, F

Both — E, G

Peanuts — A, C

STUDY SKILLS
Venn diagram

The skill of reading charts was presented in Lesson 53.

Display the various charts and briefly discuss their uses.

▶ There are many types of charts.

▶ A common way of charting information is using columns.

Display the jars and the column chart for comparing jellybeans and peanuts.

▶ Let's compare the jellybeans and peanuts and their characteristics on the chart.

Choose students to read the characteristics listed in the left column of the chart and mark the *Jellybeans*, *Peanuts*, or *Both* columns with an *X*.

▶ We used this chart to compare the jellybeans and peanuts. Now let's use that same information and put it in another type of chart.

Display the Venn diagram chart for comparing jellybeans and peanuts.

▶ This type of chart is called a *Venn diagram*. We'll put all the information about the jellybeans in the green circle and all the information about the peanuts in the orange circle.

▶ What do you think we will put in the middle intersecting area? (the characteristics of both jellybeans and peanuts.)

▶ What heading should be written for the intersecting area? (Both)

Write *Both* on the Venn diagram. Allow the students to write the letters of the characteristics on the Venn diagram, using the column chart as a guide.

Study Skills: Worktext page 76

Read aloud the information about nonfiction and fiction at the top of the page. Call attention to the two story titles above the stories and on the Venn diagram. Point out the section labeled *Both* on the Venn diagram. Direct the students to read the two stories and then write the letter of each characteristic in the correct section of the chart. Give help if needed.

SOMETHING EXTRA
Write About It: Biblical fiction

Assign the student to read I Samuel 14:1-15. Instruct him to write the Bible account as if he were Jonathan's armorbearer. Tell the students that an armorbearer was the person chosen by an important officer to bear or carry the armor. The armorbearer could also carry orders for the officer. Remind the student to use true Bible facts in his story. Encourage him to use dialogue in the story.

Elicit ideas by asking the following questions:

▶ How were you dressed?

How did you feel?

What did you do?

Were you afraid?

Did you trust the Lord?

THE SNOW-WHITE ROBIN

A lowly huntsman captures the rare snow-white robin for which the king is searching. In order to get an audience with the king, he agrees to give the castle guard half of the reward the huntsman will request of the king. Imagine the court's amazement when the huntsman asks for fifty lashes as his reward.

Lesson	Reader pages	Worktext pages
60	186-89	77-78
61	190-93	79-80

Materials
- Wrapped birthday gift
- Vocabulary sentences for display

Background information

Folklore—Folklore is any story, belief, custom, or tradition that people pass on from generation to generation. Written records left by the earliest civilizations include examples of folklore.

Folktale—A folktale is a type of folklore. Folktales are fictional stories about animals or humans and are not set in a particular time or place. Folktales were first told by word of mouth, so over time they changed as each person told the tale. "The Snow-White Robin" is a folktale.

INTRODUCTION

Vocabulary

Use the prepared sentences to introduce the vocabulary words in context.

Birthday gifts

Show the wrapped birthday gift to the students. Guide a discussion about the gift.

▶ Do you like to receive gifts? Why?

What do you think is inside this box?

If you could choose anything for a birthday gift, what would you ask for?

Most children would choose a toy or clothing, but sometimes a child may ask for something very unusual. In the story you will begin reading today, a young princess asks for an unusual birthday gift.

VOCABULARY

LESSON 60

The doctor said Grandma's disease was incurable because he was unable to help her get better. (p. 186)

*The mother was admonishing her son as she gently reminded him of his obligation to finish his chores before playing. (p. 186)

*The wealthy parents lavished upon their daughter everything she desired. (p. 187)

*†Amy knew that if she worked hard her goal was attainable. (p. 189)

*†The king held up his scepter to show his power as he declared peace in the kingdom. (p. 189)

LESSON 61

*The messenger heralded the prince's command to all the people. (p. 190)

†The thief tried to extract money from the poor people in the village. (p. 190)

†The guard struck the prisoner, giving him a cuff with his hand. (p. 190)

Instead of staying with her family, the widow secluded herself from everyone. (p. 191)

*The brave soldier would not let anything dissuade him from going on the dangerous mission. (p. 193)

Correlated Activities
- Spelling Practice, Activity 3: Softball Sluggers
- Recreational Reading, Activity 4: Touchable Tales

See "Classroom Management for Grouping" in the Appendix.

The Snow-White Robin

adapted by Karen Wilt
illustrated by Del Thompson and Noelle Snyder

COMPREHENSION

Objectives

The student will

■ Use a chapter title to predict story content.

■ Recognize the author's use of the characters' speech and actions to reveal their traits.

Before silent reading: pages 186-89

Motivation

▶ What does the princess want for her birthday?

How does the guard of the castle perform his duties?

After silent reading

Overview discussion: pages 186-89

▶ [interpretive] How does the evil guard get put in charge of the gate? (Authority gets passed down until he is given responsibility for the gate.)

▶ [interpretive] What do the peasants of the kingdom want? (They want the king to start paying attention to the affairs of the kingdom and get rid of the wicked guard.)

[critical] Does the author give you the impression that the princess and the king are happy or sad? Why or why not? (Accept any answer.)

▶ [literal] Why is this chapter called "The Birthday Gift"? (The princess asks for a snow-white robin for her tenth birthday.)

[interpretive] How do the ministers and counselors suggest the king find a snow-white robin? (ask the people to help find one)

The Birthday Gift

Many years ago a noble and just king ruled a kingdom surrounded by snow-capped mountains and azure blue seas. His people lived simple but happy lives. And the king himself lived a simple life with his queen and his

daughter. As time passed, though, the queen fell ill with an incurable disease. Though doctors from countries far and wide treated her, nothing could be done, and she left the world, admonishing her hus-

186

Follow-up discussion: pages 186-87

▶ [critical] What does it mean to live a simple life? (Answers may vary, but elicit that it is living with very few things.) [BAT: 7d Contentment]

Read aloud the description of the kingdom and the people.

▶ [literal] How many children do the king and queen have? (one daughter)

[interpretive] What tragedy comes into the life of the king? (his wife dies of an incurable disease)

▶ [literal] Before the queen dies, what does she admonish her husband to do? (take care of their beloved daughter)

band to care well for their beloved daughter.

The king sorrowed greatly in his loss. But as his daughter Aurelia grew, her likeness to her dead mother charmed the king, and his heart grew tender. He surrounded her with beautiful gardens and peaceful forests. The palace walls abounded with wonderful paintings. Only the best foods were placed before the royal princess. Everything to make her life happy was lavished upon her.

But as the king spent more time with Aurelia, he spent less time on his throne. He began to turn the rule of the land over to wise counselors and ministers. They in turn allowed some of their own counselors to take charge of smaller matters. These counselors then allowed their secretaries to have some special duties, and so it went, until it came to pass that a single soldier was put in charge of the gate to the castle.

Most of the ministers, counselors, and secretaries acted on all the king's charges wisely. They tried their best to be fair and just.

But this guard of the castle gate was a wicked man. He flattered and praised his superiors until they trusted him completely. He allowed the rich people to pass through the gate without a murmur. But he was rude to the peasants of the kingdom, and he demanded money of them before they could see the king. The simple people could not pay the prices he demanded, so they could not get to the king to tell him of this unjust guard. They hoped that soon the king would start paying attention again to the affairs of the kingdom. Then he would realize how unfair this man was and dismiss him.

Meanwhile, the king breakfasted each morning with Aurelia, walked her to the royal tutors, lunched with her, read the chronicles of the kingdom with her, pondered several hours in his gardens, dined with Aurelia, and then returned to bed.

The wicked guard continued to demand money of the poor, the counselors and ministers continued to rule for the king, the king continued to seclude himself, and Aurelia continued to grow.

The Snow-White Robin   187

Follow-up discussion: page 187

▶ [interpretive] **What causes the king's heart to become so tender?** (watching Aurelia grow up looking much like her mother) [BAT: 5a Love]

▶ [critical] Does the king make a wise decision when he allows counselors, ministers, and secretaries to be in charge of important affairs? Why or why not? (Answers will vary, but elicit that when he is not ruling the people himself, it is difficult to know what is happening in his kingdom.)

Read aloud what happens as a result of the king's spending so much time with Aurelia.

[literal] **Why are the poor people not able to have the wicked gatekeeper removed from his job?** (They do not have the money that the guard demands, so they cannot get past the gate to tell the king about the guard.)

Follow-up discussion:
page 188

▶ [literal] How old is princess Aurelia?
(ten years old)

[interpretive] What does the king
want to do for his daughter? (He
wants to give her a nice birthday present.)

[critical] What does Aurelia mean
when she says, "the things I desire
most cannot be given"? (Answers may
vary, but elicit that she wishes her
mother could be with them.)

Read aloud what unusual gift Aurelia
asks of her father.

On Aurelia's tenth birthday the
king asked, as he did every year,
what present he could give to
please her.

Aurelia's eyes filled with tears
as she looked at her father. "I
have learned that the things I desire most cannot be given."

Her father's eyes clouded.
"Yes, my dear," her father replied.
" 'Tis often so. But surely there is
something I could give to please
you."

"Then, Father," she said, "may I
please have a snow-white robin
to sing for us as we walk in our

188

garden? That would bring me great joy."

The king twirled the end of his beard around his finger. "Well now, I shall try," he said. "But this is a hard request."

"Thank you, dear Father," Aurelia said. She tapped her feet on the walk and scared a royal chipmunk into its nest in the great stone wall.

After the princess had gone to sleep, the king called his royal counselors and ministers. They pondered long and hard over the request. At last they brought a solution to the king.

"Your Highness," the eldest and most respected began, "we have concluded, or come to the end of, an idea that might accomplish the task, or supply the ends of the dilemma on hand."

"Yes, yes," the next said with much nodding of his head. "The request will be attainable, and we think all can be done. Positively, sire. We have no doubts."

The third bowed slowly to the ground without a word.

"Well," the king said, "tell me."

Slowly the third minister raised himself.

"Come now," the king said. "Out with it."

The minister opened his mouth. "The people," he murmured.

"Yes, yes," the second agreed. "If anyone can do it, the people can."

The king stroked his beard, as if this were a completely new thought to him. "The people . . . oh, yes, the people," he said.

"Your Highness," the first continued, "we see that the problem can be solved, completed, finished, ended, et cetera."

The king waved his scepter. "Do it," he said.

Follow-up discussion: page 189

▶ [critical] Why does the king say this is a hard request? (Answers may vary, but elicit that white must be a rare color for a robin.)

[critical] Why do you think the ministers are so slow to tell the plan to the king? (Accept any answer, but elicit that all the ministers are afraid to tell the king that he should think about his people and ask for their help.)

[interpretive] How does the king react to their plan? (He is pleased and accepts it.)

[critical] Why do you think the king had not thought of this plan himself? (Answers may vary; point out that he has been thinking so much about his daughter and himself that he has forgotten all about the people of his kingdom.) [BATs: 2b Servanthood; 2e Work]

Choose a student to read aloud the dialogue between the king and his ministers, encouraging him to make his voice take on the personality of each speaker as he reads; or choose four students to read the parts, portraying the characters' personalities.

Looking ahead

▶ Will a snow-white robin be found for Aurelia?

Worktext Objectives

The student will

- Match words and definitions.
- Write sentences to convey word meaning.
- Use a glossary.
- Label a diagram.

Vocabulary:
Worktext page 77

Study Skills:
Worktext page 78

The Snow-White Robin   Lesson 60 . . . 277

COMPREHENSION

The student will

- Identify the author's use of similes.
- Recognize good and evil elements in the story.
- Read orally to portray character traits.

Use the prepared sentences to introduce the vocabulary words in context.

Before silent reading: pages 190-93

Motivation

▶ Will someone find a snow-white robin?

Will anyone get past the castle guard?

After silent reading

Overview discussion: pages 190-93

▶ [interpretive] Why is finding a white robin so important to the huntsman? (He wants the reward and knows the robin will bring joy to the princess as well.)

[literal] How is the huntsman able to get past the guard to see the king? (He agrees to share half of his reward.)

[critical] Are you surprised by the huntsman's choice of fifty lashes as his reward? Why or why not? (Accept any answer.)

▶ [interpretive] How does the finding of this snow-white robin affect the kingdom? (All the wicked deeds of this guard are brought to the king's attention, the guard is punished, and the king opens his heart to the people once again.) [BATs: 4a Sowing and reaping; 4c Fairness]

A Reward

The proclamation of the king was heralded in every city and town in the kingdom. Whoever could bring the king a snow-white robin would receive the reward of his choice. People flocked to the castle, bringing blue, brown, red, and even pink robins, but no snow-white robin was found.

The castle guard demanded payment to inspect the birds. His eyes squinted into narrow slits to appraise each peasant's wealth so that he could extract the last penny from his purse. Then he turned each one away with a cuff.

But in the village farthest from the castle there lived a poor huntsman. He had often seen a snow-white robin singing in the valleys where he lived. Before the herald could finish the proclamation, the huntsman was off to capture the robin and obtain the reward.

By nightfall he had found the nest, and as the first star lit the sky, the robin slipped from the sky, singing its solemn evening song.

Follow-up discussion: page 190

▶ [literal] How are the people told of the search for the snow-white robin? (The proclamation is heralded in every city and town in the kingdom.)

[literal] What is the reward for finding the robin? (whatever the person chooses)

[literal] What different kinds of robins are brought to the castle? (blue, brown, red, and pink robins)

▶ [literal] What happens when peasants bring their robins to the castle? (The castle guard demands payment to inspect the birds.)

[interpretive] Does the guard charge each person the same amount? (No; he demands from each one as much as he has.)

[interpretive] What does the guard do after the peasants pay him? (He slaps them and turns them away.)

▶ [literal] Where has the poor huntsman seen a snow-white robin? (in the valleys where he lives)

[interpretive] How does the author describe the robin returning to its nest? ("The robin slipped from the sky.")

Read aloud in a hushed voice the paragraph describing the robin.

The huntsman threw his tattered cloak over it and wrapped it in his arms. As the night deepened, he turned toward the city of the king.

Though the cold night wind chilled him, he remembered the king's noble spirit of years ago when the queen had reigned with him. He wondered why the king had secluded himself from his people. But his heart flew like the snow-white robin as he thought of the joy he would provide for the young princess.

By morning he reached the gate of the city. He held his precious bundle carefully, lest someone should steal it and win the prize. At last his eyes, heavy with sleep, beheld the palace. He knocked timidly at the gate.

Grumpily the castle guard opened the iron doors. "Begone," he snarled.

"I have come to see the king," the huntsman said.

The Snow-White Robin   191

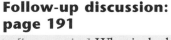

Follow-up discussion: page 191

▶ [interpretive] What is the huntsman thinking about as he travels to the castle? (He is thinking about how his noble king ruled years ago and how things have changed in the kingdom.)

[interpretive] What does the author compare the huntsman's heart to? (the snow-white robin)

Read aloud the simile that the author uses to describe the huntsman's heart. Read in a voice that shows the joy of the huntsman, knowing he will bring joy to the princess.

[interpretive] Why are the huntsman's eyes heavy with sleep? (He has been traveling all night.)

▶ [interpretive] Do you think the
huntsman is afraid of the guard? Why
or why not? (The huntsman is not
afraid; he speaks up to the guard.)
[BAT: 8d Courage]

[interpretive] What happens while
the huntsman and the guard are arguing? (The huntsman's cloak opens
and reveals a snow-white wing.)

[interpretive] What does the author
mean by saying that "the guard's eyes
lit up"? (His eyes get bigger and
brighter when he sees the bird and
realizes that he can get the reward by
taking the bird from the huntsman.)

Choose a student to read aloud the argument between the huntsman and the
guard or two students to read the argument, portraying the huntsman as confident and the guard as mean and angry.

"To see the king costs much
more than one of your station and
means can well afford," the guard
said.

"I will see the king," the huntsman said. "I have brought him
something of great worth."

"Anything brought to the king
must be inspected by me, and of a
certainty, you could not pay the fee
for such a privilege."

The huntsman wrinkled his
brow. "I must see the king. I have
found the gift for the princess." A
corner of his cloak slipped back,
and a snow-white wing fluttered.
The guard's eyes lit up.

192

"Give me that cloak!" he said, reaching for the huntsman.

The huntsman stepped back. "I will see the king," he said.

The guard lowered his eyelids until his eyes became as thin as silk threads. "You may see the king under one condition. Half of your reward must be given to me."

The huntsman nodded. "As you desire," he said.

The king's joy was boundless as he examined the pure white feathers and listened to the sweet morning song of the snow-white robin.

Then the king turned to the huntsman, and his heart gripped him, because he had not seen any of the peasants in many long years. "Whatever you wish shall be your reward," he said.

The huntsman bowed. "I desire only fifty lashes," he said.

The king's mouth opened in dismay. "Fifty lashes?" he asked.

Nothing could dissuade the huntsman from his choice. A strong soldier with a huge whip was summoned.

"Be gentle," the king murmured. "The man seems a loyal subject, though I cannot understand his ways."

As each strike was called, the king shuddered to see the huntsman suffer. "Twenty-two!" the soldier cried out. "Twenty-three! Twenty-four!" But when he reached twenty-five, the huntsman halted him.

"O king," he said, "the guard at your gate demanded half of the reward for the gift I brought you. He justly deserves the other twenty-five lashes."

The king gasped. Then he quickly motioned to the soldier to bring the guard. That wicked man's greediness was soon punished, and the huntsman received honor and riches from the king.

The princess trained the snow-white robin to sing in the palace to cheer her father. And once more the king opened his heart to his people and ruled wisely and justly on his throne.

The Snow-White Robin   193

Follow-up discussion: page 193

▶ [literal] What does the evil guard demand in order for the huntsman to see the king? (The huntsman must give him half of the reward.)

Read aloud what the huntsman requests as his reward.

[interpretive] Is the king surprised at the huntsman's request? (Yes; he tries to get the huntsman to choose a different reward.)

[critical] Is the huntsman a clever man? Why or why not? (Answers may vary, but elicit that his quick thinking allows the king to hear about the cruel treatment of the peasants by the guard at the gate and brings about the punishment of the guard.) [BATs: 2e Initiative; 4a Sowing and reaping]

▶ [interpretive] What does the verse Numbers 32:23 mean—"be sure your sin will find you out"? (God can see all we do and will judge all sin.) [BAT: 4b Purity]

[interpretive] Whose sin is found out and punished? (the evil guard's)

The student will

■ Recall facts and details.

■ Infer unstated supporting details.

■ Draw conclusions.

Comprehension:
Worktext page 79

Allow the students to refer to the story if necessary.

The student will
- Identify good and evil in a story.
- Identify the moral of a story.
- Locate verses in the Bible.

LITERATURE
Good and evil elements

Write *hero* and *villain* for display.

▶ Which of these characters represents good in a story? (hero) evil? (villain)

▶ Who is the hero of "The Snow-White Robin"? (the huntsman)

Write *huntsman* under *hero*.

▶ Who is the villain? (the guard)

Write *guard* under *villain*.

Elicit character traits of the huntsman and guard that help identify them as the hero or villain. Write these traits below each name. (possible answers: wise, loyal, courageous; deceitful, greedy, cruel)

▶ In a well-written story, good overcomes evil. Does that happen in this story? (yes)

▶ What are some of the good things that happen in the story? (The wicked guard is punished; the king is restored to the people; the princess gets her wish; the huntsman is rewarded and honored.)

▶ Some stories teach a lesson. The lesson taught in a story is called the *moral*. What is the moral of this story? (Possible answers: Crime does not pay; "your sin will find you out.")

Literature: Worktext page 80

SOMETHING EXTRA
Write About It: A folktale

Elicit from the students that in "The Snow-White Robin" the huntsman receives riches and honor and the guard receives twenty-five lashes—a just punishment for his wrongdoing. Explain that justice is a common theme in folktales; folktales usually end with punishment for the villain and reward for the hero.

Encourage each student to write a folktale of his own. Direct him to invent a hero and a villain and to choose a moral to be taught.

Materials

• Teaching Visual 13: *Victory Garden*

TIME RELATIONSHIPS AND TIME LINES

Introduction

▶ Let's take a look at one way to record information.

Draw a long horizontal line for display. Intersect the long line with eleven short vertical lines and quickly label them with abbreviations for the months of the year beginning with August and ending with June.

▶ What month did we begin school? Write *school begins* below that month. (Aug. or Sept.)

What month will we take our Christmas vacation? Write *Christmas vacation* below that month. (Dec.)

Continue until several school events have been added to the time line.

▶ What is the month of your birthday? Write your name below that month.

Continue until several birthdays have been recorded on the time line.

Skill development: Visual 13—*Victory Garden*

▶ Now listen as I read another way to record information.

Read the following paragraph.

During World War II food was in short supply. Many patriotic Americans planted gardens. Even in the cities, Victory Gardens appeared in vacant lots. Mom was the chief gardener in our family. She planted the lettuce first, about the first week in May. Seven weeks later the lettuce was ready, and we enjoyed our first lettuce salad. On Memorial Day weekend, May 30, everybody helped plant the rest of the garden. We planted green beans first; then at the top of the garden in a big cleared space Mom planted several hills of cucumbers. And last we planted rows and rows of corn, because my big brother in the navy liked corn and we all missed him so much. We picked our first green beans about eight weeks after they were planted. Cucumbers began to ripen in nine weeks, and we got our first corn in about ten weeks. Our family did what we could by growing food on the home front.

▶ What did you notice as I read the information in this paragraph? (There are many days, weeks, and crops mentioned.)

Is there so much information that it is hard to understand? (Elicit that there are so many crops, days, and weeks given that the ideas are not clear and are difficult to remember.)

How could all this information be presented in a way that is easier to comprehend? (Accept reasonable answers, but elicit that recording the events on a time line would make them easier to understand and remember.)

Call attention to the time line on the visual.

▶ What is alike about this time line and the one we made for school events and birthdays? (Both have a horizontal line with time periods marked.)

Use the background information to explain that the time periods are called *intervals*.

(continued on next page)

Lesson	Worktext pages
62	240-43

The student will

■ Recognize a time line as a concise, visual tool for organizing and recording time-related information.

■ Demonstrate understanding of the term *interval*.

■ Recognize a time line as a way to relate one event to another.

■ Interpret time lines.

Objectives

Background information

Time lines—Detailed, time-related information can be presented in a time line that is concise and easy to read rather than in information-laden paragraphs. The dates on time lines are arranged in chronological order and are placed at different intervals.

Intervals—Time lines can range from recording daily events to recording events that occurred over many centuries. The *intervals*, or periods of time shown, will vary from one time line to another.

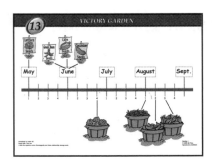

▶ What interval is shown on the school year time line? (months)

▶ What interval is shown on the Victory Garden time line? (weeks)

What is the first recorded event? (planting the lettuce)

When will the family with the Victory Garden get their first produce? (about the last week in June)

What month will the family can or freeze beans? (August)

What month would the family hope to see their sailor on leave (so he can eat his favorite food)? (in August, when corn gets ripe)

3 Skill development:
Worktext page 240

Read the short paragraph above the time line.

▶ What part of World War II does the time line tell about? (1941)

▶ The time line on the page puts some events of the war in sequence. What is the first event on the time line? (the first British commando raid)

Guide the students in answering the questions below the time line.

▶ Which do you think is a better way to give the information on this page—in paragraph form or on a time line? (Use the statement at the bottom of the page to reinforce one purpose of time lines.)

4 Skill application:
Worktext page 241

Direct the students to read the paragraphs silently.

▶ What do the paragraphs record? (the dates and the development of special weapons in World War II)

▶ What interval is shown on this time line? (one-year intervals)

Give help as needed as the students transfer the information in the paragraph to the time line on the page.

▶ Which do you think is a better way to give the information on this page—in paragraphs or on a time line? (Use the statement at the bottom of the page to reinforce another purpose of time lines.)

5 Skill practice:
Worktext pages 242-43

▶ What does this time line record? (space shuttle flights)

▶ What interval is shown on this time line? (two-year intervals, from 1982 to 1998)

Discuss the short paragraph about space shuttles. Direct the students to use the time line to answer the questions on the pages.

SOMETHING EXTRA

Make It: My time line

Instruct each student to make a time line of his activities on a given day in one-hour intervals, or of his life in one-year intervals.

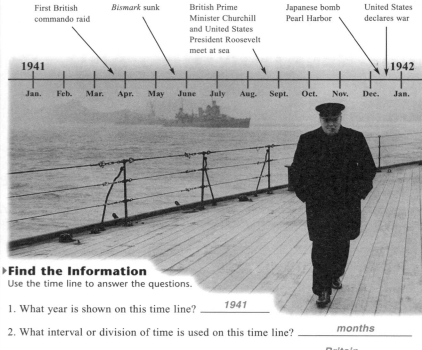

Wartime

World War II began when Germany declared war on Poland. The six-year-long war involved many countries. Read the World War II events shown on the time line.

First British commando raid • *Bismark* sunk • British Prime Minister Churchill and United States President Roosevelt meet at sea • Japanese bomb Pearl Harbor • United States declares war

1941   1942
Jan. Feb. Mar. Apr. May June July Aug. Sept. Oct. Nov. Dec. Jan.

▶**Find the Information**
Use the time line to answer the questions.

1. What year is shown on this time line? _____1941_____

2. What interval or division of time is used on this time line? _____months_____

3. Who entered the war first, Britain or the United States? _____Britain_____

4. When was the ship *Bismark* sunk (month and year)? _____May 1941_____

5. What event happened just before the United States entered the war?
_____The Japanese bombed Pearl Harbor._____

6. When did the United States join the war (month and year)? _____December 1941_____

A **time line** organizes events chronologically. It also helps to show how one event relates to another.

240

WORLD WAR II

> Written with a child's perspective in mind, this article relates the progression and hardship of the war years in Europe. The French resistance movement is highlighted along with the role children played in many of its missions.

Materials
- Tattered or worn clothing
- One or two pieces of fruit
- Vocabulary sentences for display

Background information
World Wars I and II—After World War I, many soldiers in France were unable to find work, and many people faced poverty. In Germany, one man promised economic prosperity and security to the people. He attacked many smaller countries surrounding Germany and initiated World War II. In 1940, France became Germany's next target. In an effort to regain their freedom, resistance groups secretly organized to begin fighting back. France finally regained economic stability several years after the end of World War II.

INTRODUCTION
Vocabulary
Use the prepared sentences to introduce the vocabulary words in context.

Hitler and World War II
Show the fruit and clothing to the students.

▶ Do these items look like they are worth much money?

Simple things like these become very valuable to people during times of war.

Read the following to the students.

Many countries faced poverty after World War I. Soldiers in France were unable to find work and were forced onto street corners, selling fruit and flowers for money. In Germany, a man named Adolf Hitler began telling the Germans that he could make things better if they would do as he said. The German people made Hitler their leader. As Hitler made Germany strong again, he began attacking weaker countries.

▶ How do you think the French people felt about Hitler's actions?

What do you think happened when Germany attacked these other countries?

Today you will read an article about World War II and its effect on European countries, particularly France.

VOCABULARY
LESSON 63

*†Bullets are ammunition for guns. (p. 195)

*†The soldiers entered, or invaded, the country to gain control of it. (p. 195)

†Refugees leave their country to find shelter elsewhere. (p. 196)

†The government started rationing the food, giving out only small amounts to the people. (p. 196)

*†The men secretly smuggled guns and supplies to help their country win the war. (p. 197)

Correlated Activities
- **Vocabulary Box, Activity 4: War of the Words**
- **Connections, Activity 3: Amazing Ads**

See "Classroom Management for Grouping" in the Appendix.

Objectives

COMPREHENSION

The student will

- Demonstrate an understanding of the author's message: The people of France suffered during World War II.
- Draw conclusions from information explicitly stated.

Before silent reading: pages 194-97

Motivation

▶ What did the French people think of Hitler?

How did World War II affect France?

After silent reading

Overview discussion: pages 194-97

▶ [interpretive] How did World War I affect the country of France? (Many people were left in poverty.)

▶ [interpretive] What might have happened if France and England had not gone to war against Germany? (Hitler would have invaded the rest of Europe.)

▶ [interpretive] What kind of life did the people of France have during and after World War II? (During the war, people were forced to flee their homes while facing starvation and death. People did not recover from war for many years until the country became strong again.)

[appreciative] How would you have felt if you had been a French child during World War II? [Bible Promise: H. God as Father]

WORLD WAR II

Jeri Massi
illustrated by Preston Gravely Jr.

In 1933 the country of France was still trying to recover from World War I. Some of the men who had been hurt in that terrible war could not get jobs. They had to stand on the street corners selling flowers or fruit. Food and clothing were expensive. Most people had to work very hard just to keep food on the table.

Meanwhile, across the border from France, a man named Adolf Hitler had become the ruler of Germany. His country was also poor and weak; many people did not have jobs, and food was scarce in many places.

194

Hitler promised his country that he would make Germany great. He turned it into a military nation. He told the people that loyalty to the military leaders would save them from poverty.

Many people believed Hitler and joined his military movement. He even appointed men and women to start clubs for children, called Hitler Youth. The children in the Hitler Youth wore uniforms and learned about military life. They were taught to be physically fit and self-disciplined.

Hitler soon began to take back lands that had belonged to

Follow-up discussion: page 194

▶ [interpretive] In what ways were France and Germany similar after World War I? (They were both weak, poor countries with little food.)

▶ [literal] What did Hitler promise the people of Germany? (to make Germany great and to save them from poverty)

Read aloud how Hitler taught and influenced children.

[critical] Why did so many German people believe in Hitler? (Answers may vary, but elicit that the German people were poor and weak and wanted their lives to improve.)

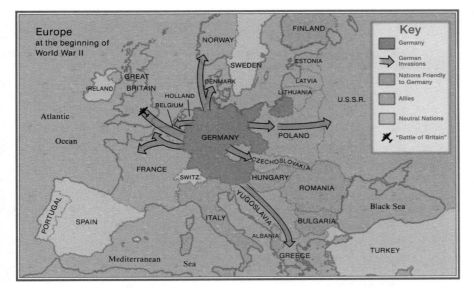

Europe
at the beginning of
World War II

Key
Germany
German Invasions
Nations Friendly to Germany
Allies
Neutral Nations
"Battle of Britain"

FINLAND
NORWAY
SWEDEN
ESTONIA
LATVIA
LITHUANIA
U.S.S.R.
GREAT BRITAIN
IRELAND
Atlantic
Ocean
HOLLAND
BELGIUM
DENMARK
GERMANY
POLAND
FRANCE
SWITZ
CZECHOSLOVAKIA
HUNGARY
ROMANIA
PORTUGAL
SPAIN
ITALY
YUGOSLAVIA
BULGARIA
Black Sea
ALBANIA
TURKEY
Mediterranean
Sea
GREECE

**Follow-up discussion:
page 195**

▶ [literal] What two countries did Germany conquer first? (Czechoslovakia and Poland)

Read aloud the reason France and England decided to fight Germany after all.

▶ [critical] What mistake did France and England make? (Answers may vary, but elicit that because they wanted peace they waited too long to build their own armies.)

[interpretive] How did Hitler move so quickly into a territory and take it over? (He had armored vehicles called panzer units that moved rapidly into enemy territory.)

Germany in the past. He took part of Czechoslovakia. He put soldiers and ammunition along the border between Germany and France. Finally, he invaded Poland. The Polish people fought back and asked for help from the free countries. But at last they were conquered.

Leaders in France and England had not wanted to go to war. They knew that Hitler was making Germany a military nation. But they wanted all the countries of the world to stop making guns and ammunition. However, when Hitler invaded Poland, European leaders knew that they would have to declare war on Germany or else Hitler would invade the rest of Europe too.

By that time it was too late for England and France to get ready for war. Germany was already fully prepared to fight. The Germans had thousands of soldiers, tanks, big guns, and fighter planes. They used armored vehicles that could move quickly into enemy territory and take over. These fast mobile units were called panzer units.

Germany invaded France in 1940. The French people in the north heard that the lightning-fast German panzer units were

World War II   195

Follow-up discussion:
page 196

► [literal] What did the French people do when they heard about the on-coming German army? (The poor people took their belongings with them as they walked to safer places.)

Read aloud what happened to the children of France during this war.

► [interpretive] Why were the French people hungry? (The Germans kept taking their food from them and using it to feed German soldiers.)

[critical] Do you think taking away food was fair to the people of France? Why or why not? (Answers may vary.)

[appreciative] Would your family have received eggs, vegetables, milk, or cheese? Why or why not? (Answers will vary, but elicit that ration coupons for these items were given only to families with young children.)

Read aloud how the Germans started a food rationing process.

coming. Quickly, the French people closest to danger packed their belongings and fled to the south. Many of these people were poor, so they had to walk, carrying whatever they could hold. These homeless people were called war refugees. The German planes traveled deep into France and attacked the refugees. The planes also bombed many of the quiet farms and villages.

The children of the refugees quickly learned what war meant. They faced starvation and death just as their parents did. Many of

196

them became orphans. They had to learn to survive.

France soon surrendered to Germany. Then the Germans took control of the French government. The refugees returned to their homes and tried to rebuild. But the Germans demanded food and valuables from France. Food grown in France was sent to feed German soldiers. Soon the French people did not have enough to eat.

The German-controlled French government started a process called rationing. Even if a French person had enough money to buy what he wanted, he could not buy farm products like eggs, vegetables, milk, and cheese. He needed a ration coupon. Only families with small children were given ration coupons for these items.

The people of France had to live through rationing and the hard German rule. But some French people were determined to be free again. Many secret resistance groups were started in France. The most famous group of all was the *Forces Francais d'Interieur,* or *F.F.I.* for short. This French name means "The Forces of the French Interior." The F.F.I. smuggled guns and ammunition into the country. It also spied on the Germans and reported German war plans to the British army. Sometimes the F.F.I. smuggled prisoners out of Germany.

The Germans suspected any French man or woman of being in the F.F.I. Because of this, many French children volunteered to help in the secret fight against Germany. A child could carry a piece of information in his pocket and walk right past a German soldier without even being noticed. After a while, the Germans realized what was going on. Some children were caught passing information for the F.F.I. They were punished just as if they were adults.

Finally, in 1945, America, Great Britain, and their allies defeated Germany. France was freed, but her government fell apart. The rationing and poverty continued in France for several years until the government became strong again. Only then could the French children return to childhood.

World War II   197

Follow-up discussion: page 197

▶ [interpretive] What did the French do to win back their freedom? (They started secret resistance groups such as the F.F.I. that smuggled guns and prisoners, spied on the Germans, and reported secrets to the British army.)

Read aloud who helped carry messages past the German soldiers.

[literal] What happened to these children if they were caught passing along information for the F.F.I.? (They were punished as adults.) [BAT: 8d Courage]

Read aloud the good news that came in 1945 for France and other countries.

▶ [critical] What does the author mean by saying, "Only then could the French children return to childhood"? (Answers may vary but should express that food rationing and poverty continued and affected children for a long time until the government became strong again; many children were hungry, afraid, sick, injured, starving, without parents, and struggling to survive.) [BATs: 2d Perseverance; 6c Patience]

Worktext Objectives

The student will

■ Read and write captions.
■ Recall facts and details from expository writing.
■ Read a map.

Study Skills: Worktext page 82

Review how to use a map key to gain information from a map.

Instruct students to complete the page.

Comprehension: Worktext page 81

Read the information about a caption at the top of the page. Call attention to the caption below the first picture and choose a student to read it aloud before the students complete the page.

SOMETHING EXTRA

Make It: Family coupons

Encourage each student to make and design "ration coupons" of daily chores, such as making beds, folding clothes, washing dishes, and doing yard work for family members. Have the student distribute the coupons to family members for them to redeem during the week.

Materials
- Teaching Visual 14—*True or False?*

PROPAGANDA

2 Skill development: Visual 14—*True or False?*

▶ Often we not only hear but also read or see messages that are meant to make us think or feel a certain way.

Have you ever seen or read an advertisement that made you want to buy something? Tell us about it.

The writing and advertising technique that uses emotions such as anger or fear to influence or change the opinions of others or to encourage them to believe or to do a certain thing is called *propaganda*. There are several methods of propaganda. Let's look at two of them.

Call attention to the cartoons in the first column on the visual.

▶ Students aren't the only ones who practice name calling. Politicians and even governments use name calling to convince people to think a certain way. Why would a country label people or groups with names? (possible answer: to keep the support of the citizens; to keep them from revolting)

Can you name other situations in which name calling is used? (possible answers: during election campaigns; in commercials)

Call attention to the cartoons in the second column of the visual.

▶ Another type of propaganda is called *bandwagon*. Do you know what it means to "jump on the bandwagon"? (Accept any answer, but elicit that when something becomes very popular and everybody wants to do it, we say that they are jumping on the bandwagon. Use the background information to explain how the propaganda term *bandwagon* originated.)

Why would advertisers want us to "jump on the bandwagon"? (They want us to spend our money to buy their product.)

During World War II in Germany, Hitler had all of his followers wear uniforms and parade down the street with bands playing and flags waving. He did everything he could to make it look as if his ways and beliefs were sweeping the nation, until finally his ways and beliefs really were sweeping the nation. Almost everybody wanted to join and feel that sense of belonging to the Hitler movement, without thinking about how wrong Hitler's beliefs were.

Can you think of other examples of the bandwagon technique? (possible examples: buying only popular-label clothing, the Y2K scare in the late 1990s)

As Christians, should we allow our feelings to be affected by what others, especially unsaved people, think and say? (No; through the power of the Holy Spirit, we should act upon the principles found in God's Word.) [BAT: 3c Emotional control]

Lesson	Worktext pages
64	244-45

The student will
- Identify propaganda.
- Recognize propaganda's impact on the reader.

Background information
Bandwagon—Many years ago, a bandwagon carried the musicians in a parade. Sometimes bystanders, attracted by the activity and noise, would jump on the bandwagon and ride along.

1 Introduction

▶ Would you rather be called *a bookworm* or have it said *that you like to read?*

Would you rather be called *a good student* or *the teacher's pet?*

Allow several students to tell what each of the above phrases or labels makes them feel or think.

▶ Often, the words we use to describe someone show how we feel about them and how we want others to feel about them. What would you think about someone who was always in trouble and was called *the bad kid* by those who knew her?

Do you think *the bad kid* is a fair label?

Would your opinion change at all if you then found out that her parents criticized everything she did, never came to watch any activities she was involved in, and had never told her that they loved her?

▶ Should you try to influence someone's opinion of another by name calling? [BAT: 5a Love]

3 **Skill application:**
Worktext page 244

▶ Why is propaganda used? (to try to change what people think or do)

▶ Read the first cartoon. Is the politician using name calling or bandwagon propaganda? (name calling)

▶ The politician wants you to have a bad opinion of his opponent and a good opinion of himself. What is he trying to get you to do? (He is trying to get you to vote for him.)

Continue discussing each cartoon with the students and answering the questions following it.

4 **Skill practice:**
Worktext page 245

Why Act?

▶**Circle and Write**
Look at the illustrations. Then answer the questions in each box.

What is this?

✓ name calling _____ bandwagon

What does the politician want you to do?

vote for him

What is this?

_____ name calling ✓ bandwagon

What does the company want you to do?

buy their phone

Join the Crowd
Ingall's Ice Palace
7 p.m. to Midnight
Skates free on Tuesdays
Come one, Come all
Meet your friends at Ingall's!
$2.50/person

What is this?

_____ name calling ✓ bandwagon

Why does Ingall's want you to come?

to make money

"We need to force these greedy, evil poachers out of our country."

What is this?

✓ name calling _____ bandwagon

Is the announcer trying to make someone act from love or anger?

anger

244

SOMETHING EXTRA

Find It: Propaganda in print

Label a bulletin board or a large sheet of poster board with the title **"Propaganda."** Divide the surface into two sections labeled with the subtitles *Name Calling* and *Bandwagon*. Provide newspapers and magazines for the students to cut out examples of the bandwagon and name calling techniques to be mounted beneath the correct subtitles.

WHEN THE WAR IS OVER

> Thrown out of his home for choosing to serve God, Zoltán Galambos has no idea how the Lord will use him to preserve the lives of many in war-torn Hungary. As headmaster to orphaned boys, an officer in the reserve army, and ultimately the one who leads his own family across the Austrian border to safety, he demonstrates bravery and dependence upon God.

Lesson	Reader pages	Worktext pages
65	198-205	83
66	206-9	84
67	210-13	85-86

Materials

- Small suitcase or backpack
- Map displaying Hungary and Austria
- Teaching Visuals 9 and 12: *Ponies Carry the Mail* and *A Special Mailbag*
- Vocabulary sentences for display

Heritage Studies Connection

Lessons 65, 66, and 67 can be linked to the study of World War II and the study of Hungary.

Background information

Hungary—When the German military took over Hungary in 1944, the Hungarian people felt the full effects of war and became refugees. Many Hungarians moved west with the troops. Hungarian-German troops were fighting against the Russian troops during this time and finally surrendered in 1945. Russia now occupied the country of Hungary. Altogether, almost 650,000 Hungarians died during the war.

Zoltán Galambos—This story is based on the life of a real person. Zoltán, along with his family, eventually came to the United States and became a junior high and high school chemistry teacher. His four sons all live in the United States as well.

Hungarian names—The following names appear in the story. Zoli /zō´ lē/; Zoltán /zōl´ tän/; Galambos /gä´ läm bŏsh/; Kis néni /kēsh nā´ nē/; Dani /dä´ nē/; Komarom /kō´ mä rōm/; Ilona /ē´ lō nä/; Henrik /hěn´ rēk/; Kalman /käl´ män/.

INTRODUCTION

Vocabulary

Use the prepared sentences to introduce the vocabulary words in context.

Head note

Read aloud the head note on reader page 198. "Zoli" is a nickname for "Zoltán," and both names are used throughout the story.

▶ Why is Zoli thrown out of his home? (for choosing to serve God)

Point out the location of Hungary and Austria on the map.

Small suitcase

Show the small suitcase or backpack to the students and emphasize that all of Zoli's possessions could have fit in a small suitcase like it.

▶ Zoli was so poor that he arrived at the orphanage with only a few books.

Would you be able to fit all of your possessions in one suitcase?

Do possessions really matter? Why or why not?

Correlated Activities

- **Word Work, Activity 5: Dictionary Challenge**
- **Creative Writing, Activity 2: Senses in Setting**

See "Classroom Management for Grouping" in the Appendix.

VOCABULARY

LESSON 65

The headmaster was in charge of all the students in the school. (p. 199)

The nanny cared for the children by washing their clothes and cooking their meals. (p. 200)

The pots and pans made a loud clamor in the kitchen. (p. 201)

†The terrorists were hijacking the airplane. (p. 201)

LESSON 66

The bedroom looked messy with clothes and toys strewn all over. (p. 206)

†As the enemy came closer, the soldiers started retreating from their position. (p. 207)

†Hearing the sad news, the girl's face looked sober. (p. 207)

†The soldiers warned families to evacuate the city and go to a safer place. (p. 207)

The older sister gingerly carried the special glass dish. (p. 209)

LESSON 67

†The strong wind rustled the leaves in the night air. (p. 210)

†To hide from the enemy soldiers, the family quietly crouched behind the big bushes. (p. 212)

†Soldiers put hidden land mines in the ground by burying the explosives in shallow holes. (p. 212)

Objectives

COMPREHENSION

The student will
- Infer the motives of characters.
- Relate the story to World War II.
- Recognize first-person point of view.
- Recognize the author's use of simile and metaphor.
- Demonstrate understanding of the author's message: Be responsible for your own work.

Before silent reading: pages 198-201

Motivation
▶ What are the boys like who live at the orphanage?

What does Zoli think of the boys' daily activities?

After silent reading

Overview discussion: pages 198-201

▶ [interpretive] Do the boys at the orphanage have good habits? Why or why not? (Answers may vary, but elicit that the boys do not use good manners during meals, comb their hair, or tuck in their shirts.)

[critical] Do you think Zoli has an easy job taking care of all these boys? Why or why not? (Accept any answer.)

[appreciative] How would living in an orphanage be different from the way you live?

When the War Is Over

Adapted from Zoli's Legacy: Bequest
Dawn L. Watkins

Zoli Galambos, a young Hungarian, has been thrown out of his home for choosing to serve God. He arrives in the town where he once went to school to become the head of an orphanage.

A Little War of Wills
1937

Mrs. Toth gazed at me through the screen door of the orphanage.

"Yes?"

"Mrs. Toth, I'm Zoltán Galambos."

"Zoltán! I didn't know you. How you've changed! Come in. Please! Bring in your things!"

She swung open the door.

"My husband will be so happy to see you here already."

I set my books down by the threshold. I stepped inside the building that still smelled of fresh-cut lumber. Some of the windowsills were planed smooth but were yet unvarnished. The whole place was airy and clean.

I set down my parcel of books. "My baggage is all in."

198

She tilted her head. "Oh. Well, come along and let me find my husband. He has a thousand things lined up for you."

"Yes," I said.

"Zoltán!" The booming voice caught me just as a big hand closed over mine. Mr. Toth shook my hand vigorously.

Mrs. Toth said, "Let's show him to his quarters first." She leaned sideways toward me. "Once he gets to talking about the orphanage, you'll never get settled."

"Sure," said Toth. "Where are your things? I'll help you carry them up."

Follow-up discussion: page 198

▶ [literal] What year does this story begin? (1937)

[critical] What do you know about this year in relation to World War II? (Accept any answer, but elicit that it is just two years before the beginning of the war.)

▶ [interpretive] What do you think Mrs. Toth means when she says, "I didn't know you. How you've changed!"? (Mrs. Toth knew Zoli when he was younger.)

[critical] Are Mr. and Mrs. Toth happy to see Zoli? Why do you think that? (Accept any answer, but elicit that Mrs. Toth eagerly welcomes him in and Mr. Toth gives him a big handshake.)

[appreciative] Would you like Mr. and Mrs. Toth? Why or why not?

▶ [interpretive] Is the orphanage building old or new? How do you know? (new; the building smells like new lumber, some windowsills are not varnished, and it is airy and clean.)

Read aloud the description of the new orphanage.

[interpretive] From whose point of view or perspective is this story being told? What is this point of view called? (Zoli's; first-person. If necessary, point out the use of first-person pronouns.)

"I've only some books in the hall," I said.

We went into Komárom, and Mrs. Toth bought me a brand-new suit. I asked her whom I could pay back when I got the money, but she only waved her hand at me.

"The Lord provided," she said.

When the boys came from school that day, they had a new headmaster, all turned out in neat suit pants and a clean shirt.

Thirty boys, some as tall as I, rushed past me toward the upstairs. They threw down their schoolbooks by the stairs, yelling to each other and banging into each other.

"They're all yours," said Toth.

The kitchen vibrated with their shouts. Two women hurried to put down kettles on the table and lay out trays of bread. The boys plunged the dippers into the kettles and sloshed the stew into their bowls. The bread disappeared like snow in the April sun.

For a while, the shouting died into a slurping and jostling, and then it swelled again. The boys skidded back their benches. The spoons clanged into empty bowls and a few rattled onto the floor. The boys left in groups, twos and

The orphanage in Komárom, Hungary

threes and fours, and thundered up the stairs. I could hear them overhead, running and shouting.

The women began to take up the bowls and the glasses. I stood in the doorway, still expecting to find a reason for what had just gone on.

"Excuse me."

The women looked up.

When the War Is Over   199

Follow-up discussion: page 199

▶ [interpretive] How do you know that Zoli is poor? (He brings only books with him and Mrs. Toth buys him a brand-new suit.)

▶ [literal] What is Zoli's new job? (He is the headmaster of the orphanage.

[literal] Who lives at the orphanage? (thirty boys and no girls)

▶ [interpretive] Do the boys have good or bad manners? Why do you think that? (Bad manners; they throw down their schoolbooks, yell, bang into each other, slurp the stew, leave their bowls on the table, drop spoons unto the floor, and run back up the stairs.)

[critical] Why do you think Zoli is "still expecting to find a reason for what had just gone on"? (Answers may vary, but elicit that he does not like the boys' manners and does not understand why they would be allowed to act that way.)

Read aloud the description of dinner time, expressing the noises in the kitchen.

▶ [interpretive] What simile does the author use to describe the boys eating bread? (The bread disappeared like snow in the April sun.)

[critical] What does the author mean? (Answers may vary, but point out that the boys were hungry and gobbled up all the bread very quickly, just like sun shining in April would melt the snow quickly.)

▶ [interpretive] Who takes care of all these boys in the orphanage? (Greta and Kis néni)

Read aloud the sentence where Greta describes the wild boys.

[critical] What does Zoli mean when he says that his being young "may come in handy"? (Answers may vary, but elicit that caring for thirty boys will take a lot of energy.)

[interpretive] What kind of worker is Zoli? (A hard worker: he gets up early, asks Kis néni how he can help, and begins making sandwiches.) [BAT: 2e Initiative]

[critical] Why does Zoli say, "the day's got the jump on you"? (Answers may vary, but elicit that the boys have slept late in the morning, and much work has been accomplished while they have been sleeping.)

Read aloud the paragraphs showing how Zoli calls the boys.

"I'm Zoltán Galambos. I think I'm to be in charge here."

"Hello," said the older woman. "Everyone calls me Kis néni. The nanny. This is Greta."

"Let me help you," I said.

Kis néni nodded once and handed me a cloth.

"Is it always so noisy?" I asked.

"Yes," said Greta. "They run wild like pigs."

From the window I could see the boys playing soccer again, and some of the smaller ones wrestling on the sidelines.

"You are young," said Kis néni.

"That may come in handy," I said.

In the morning, before light, I heard tables being moved in the kitchen. I dressed quickly and went down.

"You're here early," I said.

Kis néni yawned and patted her mouth. She stood beside a lantern hanging by the wall. It still swung a little, and the shadows wavered back and forth around her.

An orphanage similar to Zoli's, but housing both boys and girls

"Yes," she said. "But much is to be done."

"What can I do to help?"

I tucked in my shirt and rolled up the sleeves.

"You could make sandwiches," she said. "The stuff is there." She pointed to a worktable by the sink. "And wrap each one in a paper. Here, I'll show you."

The first light began to come in the windows after perhaps the fifteenth sandwich. Upstairs no one had begun to stir.

"I'll call the boys," said Kis néni, "or do you want to?"

I went upstairs and down the hall, throwing doors open as I went and bellowing.

"Up, boys. The day's got the jump on you. Let's go!"

"Who are you?" The voice came from the dim lower bunk in the last room.

"The new headmaster."

The boy rolled out and stood up.

"Any boy not down in fifteen minutes is out of his breakfast."

Toth arrived amid the charge for the tables. Above the clamor of breakfast, he banged the sink with a metal ladle. All heads turned his way.

"Good morning, fellows."

"Good morning." The response was jumbled and feeble.

"This is Zoltán Galambos. He has come to be the headmaster here."

Thirty pairs of eyes looked me over.

He laughed his hearty laugh, too big for the small hour, I thought.

"Don't think you can slip anything by him, boys. He's an old hand at this."

In a while, the racket rose to its old level.

"I have been walking them to the school. But I expect you know where it is, yes?" said Toth to me.

I nodded and surveyed the company I would have.

The walk was not long, but I could see the wisdom of having a sheepdog herd the sheep toward the Gymnásium. The older boys made a sport of hijacking the younger ones for their sandwiches. And the younger ones had to be prodded to keep going toward their own school. Shirttails hung out from waistbands at every angle, and not one head of hair looked sufficiently combed. But the shoes, I noticed, were all shined.

"Mr. Galambos?"

I looked at the boy beside me.

"Hello."

"You don't remember me, but I used to call you Zoli bacsi. A long time ago, up in Farna."

The face joggled something way back in my mind. Uncle Zoli, he called me.

"I'm Dani."

► [critical] Do you think all the boys made it to breakfast in fifteen minutes? Why or why not? (Accept any answer.)

► [literal] What kind of appearance do the boys have as they go to school? (Their shirttails hang out and their hair is not well combed, but their shoes are shined.)

Read aloud what the older boys do to the younger ones on the way to school.

[interpretive] What does the author compare Zoli and the boys to? (a sheepdog herding sheep)

[critical] Do you think this is a good comparison? Why or why not? (Accept any answer, but point out that Zoli feels as if he is chasing the boys and guiding them to school just as a sheepdog would lead sheep to and from a pasture.)

► [interpretive] What is the Gymnásium? (the school; the name used for a school in Hungary)

► [literal] How does Dani know Zoli? (They knew each other when they were in Farna.)

[literal] What did Dani call Zoli when he knew Zoli in Farna? (Dani called him Zoli bacsi, which means "Uncle Zoli.")

Before silent reading: pages 202-5

Motivation

▶ What are some changes that take place at the orphanage after Zoli arrives?

How do these changes affect the boys?

After silent reading

Overview discussion: pages 202-5

▶ [critical] Do you think that Zoli really understands what life is like for the boys? Why or why not? (Answers will vary; remind the students that Zoli was thrown out of his own home and understands their feelings of being alone.)

[interpretive] How does Zoli try to teach the boys responsibility? (He assigns chores for the boys and reads the Bible to them every day.)

▶ [interpretive] What do you think the author means by the chapter title "A Little War of Wills"? (Possible answers: Zoli sees sadness and bitterness in many of the boys' attitudes; there is a "battle" with the boys over Zoli's changes.)

I suddenly remembered this face, smaller and fearful, looking to me for help. Four years before, my friend "Bootblack" and I had helped Toth at an orphanage in another town. I felt a pang at realizing Dani was still an orphan, still waiting to be wanted.

"Why sure," I said. "I hardly knew you. You're so big. What are you now? Nine?"

Zoli at the age he took over the orphanage

"Yes, sir."

He said nothing more, but just as before, he walked beside me, his chin tucked slightly, asking by his posture to stay with me.

I dispatched the older boys to the school lane I knew well. A little way on, I said good-bye to the younger fellows. I felt embarrassed at their ragged collars and their thin pants. A few waved to me, and I, but an older version of them, waved back.

At the orphanage upstairs, Kis néni and Greta were making beds. The hall had been swept as far as the room they were in, the brooms resting against the doorjamb. The two women lifted the mattress together and snapped the sheet under it, and in the same motion, pulled the top of the sheet to the pillow. The washbasins were dry, the pitchers empty. I lifted the towel on the stand. It was dry as well.

"Kis néni," I said, "has everything been going about as usual around here? Last night and today, I mean?"

She straightened up from thumping a pillow into place.

"Pretty much."

"You always make the beds?"

"Sure."

She stared at me for a moment and then went past me and took up the sheets and broom.

"Let me carry that stuff," I said.

202

Follow-up discussion: page 202

▶ [literal] Why does Zoli feel a pang for Dani? (He remembers Dani from another orphanage four years ago and realizes he has not been adopted by a family yet.)

[critical] Why do you think Dani wants to walk with Zoli? (Accept any answer, but elicit that Dani remembers him from earlier in his life, so likes Zoli and feels safe with him.)

[critical] What does Zoli mean when he says, "A few waved to me, and I, but an older version of them, waved back"? (Answers may vary, but elicit that the boys' ragged, thin clothes remind Zoli of his own clothing and of being poor and without a family.)

Read aloud why Zoli feels embarrassed for the boys.

▶ [critical] Why do you think Zoli asks Kis néni, "has everything been going about as usual around here?" (Answers may vary, but elicit that he is wondering if Kis néni and Greta do the boys' work every day and why the boys don't do any of the work at the orphanage.)

That afternoon when the boys came tearing in from school, I met them at the stairs. I stood three steps up, leaning on the rail.

They halted at the bottom and milled in the lobby.

"Good afternoon, gentlemen."

A couple of the smaller boys answered me.

I came down a step.

"I'm glad to see you home."

Still they said nothing.

"I've been just looking around," I said, "seeing how things go around here. And I've noticed a job or two that needs a man, but I haven't the time. I thought I might look over this group here and see if I could find a suitable worker."

"What jobs?" one of the tallest boys said.

"Well, for starters, splitting wood and carrying water."

"Mr. Toth did that," said a boy with wavy black hair.

I ignored the rustle among the troops.

"And shining shoes."

"Ahh," the first boy said.

I sat down on the second stair. "Kis néni does that now, doesn't she? Every night while you sleep.

Well. That's no job for women. They haven't got the arm for it. A man can get a real shine on leather when he wants to."

I slid my foot out and leaned back on the third stair. A few eyes went down to my gleaming shoe and back to me.

"But," I said, "maybe there's no one here to do it but me."

There was no volunteer, but neither were there any deserters.

"And," I said, "men have to learn to look after themselves. Kis néni and Mrs. Greta won't always be around. What I like is independence. Don't you?"

I waited. At last, Dani spoke up.

"I'll do it, sir."

A bigger boy said, "You? It'll take you a week to learn how."

The tallest of them spoke again. "Can't you idiots see what he's doing? He's tricking you into doing his work."

I stood up slowly and glowered down on him. "No, boy, I'm trying to trick you into doing your own work. But if you won't be coaxed, there are other methods."

When the War Is Over   203

Follow-up discussion: page 203

▶ [interpretive] What is Zoli's new plan? (He wants the boys to split wood, carry water, and shine shoes.)

[literal] How does Zoli try to persuade the boys to change their work habits? (Possible answer: he tells them that these particular jobs need a man, that women do not have an arm for shining shoes, that men need to look after themselves, and that Kis néni and Greta will not always be around.)

Read aloud in a sarcastic tone what the tallest boy says about Zoli to the other boys.

[interpretive] What is Zoli trying to get the boys to do? (be responsible for their own work)

Follow-up discussion:
page 204

▶ [literal] What are Zoli's new changes for the boys? (Each boy must make his own bed and carry his own plate to the sink.)

[critical] Do you think Zoli made wise changes at the orphanage? Explain in your answer. (Accept any answer.) [BATs: 2b Teamwork; 2c Responsibility]

[literal] What are the younger boys begging to do? (They want to do the older boys' chores like shining shoes and splitting wood.)

Read aloud what Zoli reads after supper to teach the boys about hard work and obedience.

▶ [literal] What does Zoli realize the boys are not doing after school? (their homework)

Read aloud in a disrespectful voice how Gab answers Zoli's question about homework.

By the end of the next week, there was a new order at the Komárom orphanage. Every boy made his own bed and carried his own plate to the sink after meals. The shining of shoes and the splitting of wood were rotated among the privileged older few. Younger boys watched as though from the sidelines of a soccer game and begged for something important to do.

"Please, Zoli bacsi," they said, "we'll do a good job."

"Well, I don't know," I said. I rubbed the back of my neck. "This sweeping is tricky."

"Show us how," they said.

I drew my hand across my chin as if in deep thought. "I guess we could try it for a week. But if it starts to look shabby in here, I'll have to take the job back myself."

I did not have to take the job back.

Every night after supper, I read from the Bible. At first I chose verses from the Proverbs about the value of hard work and obedience. I watched the faces, some smooth with innocence, some al-ready cloudy with bitterness and rebellion. The tallest boy, Gab, had eyes like stones. His chin jutted out in constant defiance of all the world.

"Now," I said, closing the Bible, "I think we should talk about homework. I haven't seen any being done around here. Surely you all have some."

"No," said Gab, "they don't give orphans homework because they don't have homes to work it in."

The boys looked to me with wide eyes, expecting perhaps a sermon or punishment for Gab. Gab balanced his chair on the two back legs.

"Boys," I said, "when your parents died, God gave you many mothers and fathers in their stead. You have Mrs. Greta and Kis néni and Pastor and Mrs. Toth and me. And as your papa, I'm asking you, where is your homework?"

Gab's chair slammed down. "You are not my father!"

"Suit yourself. But where is your homework?"

His eyes blazed at me.

204

"Get it or I go with you to the Gymnásium tomorrow."

The other boys looked at him cautiously. He finally stood and cast his chair backward and strode out. The others looked again to me, waiting.

"From now on," I said, "you will do your homework and show it to me."

The eyes went down to the tables and plates.

"You have to learn to work. Knowing how to work makes you enjoy your life. Don't you want the pleasure of being able to do many kinds of things?"

"Yes." The replies put all together made but a feeble response.

Gab returned and threw the notebook down in front of me so that it spun to a stop just beside my hand. "Very good. Now I'm going to put a note to the teacher here, asking him to write the assignment out so that I can check on it."

Kis néni smiled over from her chair by the stove and nodded.

"And before you do any chores tonight, I want to see everyone's notebook. And if you don't have a notebook, we'll send a piece of paper to your teacher."

I gave Gab his book, looking at him directly.

"The rest of you can go," I said. "Bring me your notebooks."

They piled out of the kitchen. I had not taken my eyes from Gab.

"Gab, the handwriting in this book is terrible. Now, I know you can do better. I suspect you are the smartest boy in your class. Why do you make an effort to hide it?"

"You think you know all about it, don't you?"

"More than you think," I said.

"What do you care about my handwriting?"

"I care about your handwriting because I care about you. If you have the right heart, you'll have a better hand. Laziness has many witnesses."

He shoved away from the wall he had been leaning on and, looking at me as he might at a growling dog, went out.

Kis néni said, "You're not as young as you look."

Worktext Objective

The student will

- Match characters with dialogue.

Comprehension:
Worktext page 83

Follow-up discussion: page 205

▶ [critical] Why is Gab so angry with Zoli? (Possible answers may include that he might have been in the orphanage a longer time than the other boys and might be bitter about not being adopted; he may remember his father and does not want Zoli to try to take his father's place.)

▶ [interpretive] Why does Zoli want the boys to show him their homework? (Possible answer: Zoli wants the boys to be accountable for their work.)

[critical] Why does Zoli want to teach the boys the importance of working hard in school? (Accept any answer, but elicit that Zoli wants a better future for these boys.)

Read aloud Zoli's explanation of why work is important.

▶ [critical] What does Zoli mean when he says, "Laziness has many witnesses"? (Answers may vary, but elicit that an attitude of laziness can affect every task.)

▶ [critical] Why does Kis néni say to Zoli, "You're not as young as you look"? (Answers may vary, but elicit that she thinks Zoli is very wise in his advice to Gab and in showing Gab that he cares about him.)

Looking ahead

▶ What lies ahead for the boys of the orphanage?

COMPREHENSION

The student will

- Recognize the author's techniques of revealing setting through characters' actions.
- Demonstrate understanding of biblical truths: Trust God to take care of you; God loves you more than anyone else does.

Use the prepared sentences to introduce the vocabulary words in context.

Head note

Read aloud the head note on reader page 206.

▶ How much time has passed in the story now? (seven years)

What changes have taken place in Zoli's life? (He is married, has two sons, and is an officer in the reserve army.)

Before silent reading: pages 206-9

Motivation

▶ What news does Zoli receive?

How does Zoli encourage the boys in the orphanage?

After silent reading

Overview discussion: pages 206-9

▶ [literal] What difficulty is facing Zoli and all the boys in the orphanage? (They need to evacuate the city immediately because Russia is invading Hungary.)

[interpretive] How would you describe the general mood of the boys now? (Answers may vary, but elicit that they are sad and fearful; they realize they may never see Zoli again and that they may be killed.)

[interpretive] What is Zoli's response to the boys' concerns? (Zoli tells them that he loves each of them and that he wants them to put their trust in God as he does.)

▶ [interpretive] How does God take care of Zoli's family and the reserves as they travel? (He gives Zoli wisdom in trading for food for them.) [Bible Promise: H. God as Father]

Seven years later, Zoli is still running the orphanage. He is married now with two sons. Throughout World War II Zoli has been an officer in the reserve army.

Riding Out World War II
April 1944

"A major to see you, sir."

I nodded and stood up. My desk was strewn with papers, by which I was trying to stretch short rations and medicine further than they would go.

The major was Bootblack, my friend from school days.

I saluted the rank and took the hand of my friend.

Zoli and Ilona on their wedding day

Ilona (right) before she was married

206

Bootblack said, "How's Ilona—and Henrik?"

"They're well." I motioned to a chair. "Henrik has a brother since you were here last. Kalman."

He smiled widely and shook my hand again. Then he sat down, and I followed his lead.

He passed his hand over his mouth and then dropped his hands, gripping his knees.

"I am here officially to order you to take the reserves out of Komárom immediately."

Follow-up discussion: page 206

▶ [literal] Who comes to visit Zoli? (Bootblack, an old school friend)

[literal] What news does Bootblack bring with him? (He is officially ordering Zoli to take the army reserves out of Komarom.)

Read aloud Bootblack's official order.

"The war is over then."

He sighed. "The Germans are retreating. The Russians are advancing. They will occupy Hungary within the week."

"Where do we go?"

"Try to get the supply unit west to Austria or Germany. Take what supplies you can. Don't leave anything for the Russians. Burn stuff, if you have to."

"How long do I have to move out?"

"Three days. Advise the citizens to get out as well. But you can't take the time to force them."

He was standing again.

"Can I take Ilona with me?"

"Your privilege, Zoli. Do what you think best there. Move at night as much as you can. The Russian airplanes are always overhead."

*   *   *

Ilona's face was white. She held Kalman asleep in her arms.

"Henrik," I said, "come sit down."

He came and stood by his mother. The boys were there, waiting with sober faces. Gab and eight others had already left to join the army. But twenty-one were still in my charge.

"We have to evacuate the city," I told them. "I have to go with the reserves. But Pastor Toth will be here in the morning to take you with him or find you a place to stay."

Destruction of war in Eastern Europe

When the War Is Over   207

Follow-up discussion: page 207

▶ [interpretive] Why is Bootblack's official news a serious matter? (The Germans are retreating and the Russians are planning to take over Hungary within a week.)

Read aloud with a sense of urgency the conversation between Bootblack and Zoli.

[literal] How will this situation affect the boys in the orphanage? (Gab and eight other boys have already joined the army, but twenty-one boys still at the orphanage will be in Pastor Toth's care.)

Follow-up discussion: page 208

- ▶ [appreciative] What would you feel if you were a child in the orphanage right now?
- [literal] Whom does Zoli encourage the boys to trust during this frightening time? (God) [BATs: 8a Faith in God's promises; 8d Courage]
- ▶ [literal] How long have Zoli's family and the reserves been traveling? (two months)
- [interpretive] Why is it taking Zoli's family and the reserves so long to get out of the country? (They can travel only at night so that the Russians won't see them.)

Read aloud how Zoli and the others have to travel during the war.

- ▶ [interpretive] How does Zoli feed the soldiers and his family? (He trades items for food.)
- [interpretive] Why does Zoli stop at the second farmhouse? (He does not have enough food for everyone.)

Read aloud with confidence what the woman tells Zoli about soldiers.

A little boy, about eight, put his head on his knees and sobbed. Ilona went to sit beside him and stroked his hair.

"Any of you who are sixteen," I hesitated and then went on, "can do what you will."

"Can't we go with you, Zoli bacsi?" said Dani.

I shook my head. "I'm sorry. I can't take you."

He looked as though he might cry as well.

"I love you, boys, but God loves you more. And I must trust Him to look after you. I want you to trust Him too."

* * *

"Where are we?" Henrik asked.

He sat in the front of the wagon.

I reined Alexander near.

"Somewhere west of Bratislava, I think," I said.

We made such little headway, traveling slowly in the dark, hiding in the woods all day. Two months of this dodging, and still no Hungarian fighting units had appeared.

I held Alexander in and let the next wagon come abreast of me.

The driver said. "Yes, sir?"

"I'm going to take a blanket off the wagon and ride to that farm over there and see if I can make a trade for our breakfast."

He nodded.

"Keep moving. I'll catch up with you."

The farmer's wife gladly parted with some eggs and milk for the heavy wool blanket. It hardly would feed twenty-seven men and my family. But it was the best deal I could make.

There was another farmhouse in the distance. I could still see the wagons to the left. I turned Alexander to the house. A stout woman there looked me up and down.

"What do I want with eggs?" she said. "I have chickens myself."

"Please," I said, "I have children with me."

"No soldier has children with him."

208

"If I bring my son here, will you believe me?"

"I might."

I looked at the sky. The sun was nearly full up.

My assistant, Pataki, took the eggs gingerly, and then the milk. I reached for Henrik, and he came flying. He took his place in front of me and grabbed into the mane.

"Let's go, Papa."

"Pull off in that woods over there," I told Pataki. "We won't be long."

Alexander snorted to a halt in the farmyard. The woman leaned out the window.

"Well, I'll be," she said.

"Hello," said Henrik. His blond hair shone in the early sun.

"Hello yourself."

He laughed. "Papa and I rode over from the wagon. Alexander is one good horse."

She came out of the house then and up to Henrik. She looked at me. "I might have some extra around here," she said.

She returned with a sack of bread and vegetables and cheese.

I offered her money.

"What good does that do anybody? Just see this little one gets out of this."

Evacuating a city

When the War Is Over   209

Follow-up discussion: page 209

▶ [interpretive] What bold idea does Zoli use to get more food? (He takes Henrik off the wagon and brings him to the woman to see.)

[critical] Whom do you think gave Zoli this idea? (Elicit that God gave Zoli wisdom as he cared for his family through danger.)

Read aloud in a surprised voice what the woman says when she sees Henrik.

[interpretive] Why does the woman say money is of little use to anyone? (Trading items is more valuable because war affects the value of money.)

Looking ahead

▶ How will the war continue to affect Zoli and his family?

Worktext Objectives

The student will

- Divide words into syllables between the base word and suffix.
- Place the accent mark on the syllable preceding the ending *-sion* or *-tion*.

Structural Analysis: Worktext page 84

◀ Complete teaching of these skills was presented in Lessons 49 and 56.

Use Teaching Visuals 9 and 12, *Ponies Carry the Mail* and *A Special Mailbag*, to review the syllable division rule 4 and accent rule 4 before the students complete the page independently.

COMPREHENSION

The student will

- Discern the motives of characters.
- Recognize the author's use of simile.
- Demonstrate understanding of the author's message: Obstacles can be overcome through faith in God.

 Use the prepared sentences to introduce the vocabulary words in context.

Head note

Read aloud the head note on reader page 210.

▶ Where do Zoli and his family go now that the war is almost over? (home to Hungary)

Who is waiting for Zoli at the old orphanage? (Dani)

What is the war situation like in Hungary? (Russia is taking over Hungary by force.)

Before silent reading: pages 210-13

Motivation

▶ What important decision does Zoli make?

After silent reading

Overview discussion: pages 210-13

▶ [intrepretive] How is Hungary changing now that World War II is over? (Hungary is being completely overtaken by Russian forces and Russia will set up its own form of government.)

▶ [literal] What obstacles does Zoli have to overcome before reaching Austrian soil? (search lights, guards, rain, and land mines)

▶ [critical] Do you think it is an easy or difficult decision for Zoli to decide to leave Hungary? Why? (Answers may vary, but elicit that it was a difficult decision because of the risk he put himself, Dani, and his family through.)

[interpretive] Why does Zoli decide to run for his freedom rather than stay in Hungary? (If he stays in Hungary, the country will be under Russian control. By fleeing to Austria, he will have freedom to make his own decisions and choices and to serve God.)

Zoli and his men were stopped by American soldiers but were released because the war was nearly over. Zoli and his family go home to Hungary where Dani has been waiting for them near the old orphanage. But the Russians are taking Hungary by force, and once again Zoli must flee an enemy. He, Ilona, their sons, and Dani pretend to have a picnic near the Austrian border. Then they must decide if they will make a run for freedom through a farmer's fields.

A Run for Freedom
1947

The corn rustled around us. I gathered Ilona, Henrik, Kalman, and Dani to me.

"I love you," I said to them. "Remember that."

We started down the rows, planted so as to lead those who dared to freedom.

"Just keep walking straight down the corn rows. Follow the row, Henrik."

I picked Kalman up and carried him.

The lifeless stalks rattled in the rain and with our passing. The darkness deepened. The searchlights from the guard towers at the end of the field switched on and passed over the corn.

"Papa, look at the lights!"

Zoli and his family escaped through a field like this.

210

Follow-up discussion: page 210

▶ [literal] Why are Zoli, his family, and Dani in a cornfield? (They are leaving the country to gain their freedom.)

[critical] Why does Zoli tell the others to remember that he loves them? (Accept any answer, but emphasize that Zoli realizes that they may be captured by soldiers and never see each other again; he also wants them to know that he is taking this risk because he loves them and desires freedom for them.)

Read aloud what Zoli says to his family and Dani, showing his love for them.

"Shhh."

"Why?"

"Shhh."

The lights came over us and we froze. The white beams flowed on by, and we moved again. The rain was like silver needles in the lights.

Water ran down my face, down inside my shirt. Dani, a gray movement just two rows over, held his hand over his eyes to block the flow. My heart pounded now—not from the walking, but from the last terror I had not told them of.

The leaves of the corn scraped by my face, rasped on my ears. Kalman fell asleep on my shoulder.

Suddenly I was aware that Henrik was not beside me.

"Stop!"

I thrust Kalman into Ilona's arms. I started back through the row, looking with more than normal sight into that black and muddy world.

"Henrik!"

I ran then, beating the stalks away from me.

"Son!"

Between my gasps for air, I heard, "Papa, Papa."

I went across the rows toward the sound.

"Henrik! Call to me!"

Suddenly he was ahead of me, running toward the station again. I overran him and grabbed him.

"Henrik, what are you doing?"

"Oh, Papa," he said, "I was running after you!"

I held him to me until thought I would crush him. "You got turned around, son."

"I fell, Papa."

His tears were heavier than the rain.

"It's all right now. Papa found you. Papa found you."

We went on again. I carried Kalman and held Henrik's hand. At last the corn thinned out, and we were at the edge of a great plowed field. On the other side was the wire—the flimsy, terrible border.

Follow-up discussion: page 211

▶ [interpretive] What simile does the author use to describe the rain in the cornfield? ("like silver needles in the lights")

[appreciative] How does this simile make you think the rain felt?

[critical] Zoli's heart is pounding with terror. What do you think the terror is that Zoli is referring to? (Accept any answer, but elicit that they may not reach their freedom due to the obstacles they have to face.)

▶ [literal] Whom is Zoli carrying on his shoulders? (Kalman)

Read aloud the paragraphs describing who gets lost in the cornfield. Read it with fear and desperation in your voice.

▶ [literal] What does the border of Austria look like? (It is a flimsy wire in a plowed field.)

[critical] Why does Zoli refer to the wire as "terrible"? (Answers may vary, but point out that the wire keeps people inside a country that has no freedom and that living without freedom is a terrible thing.)

[appreciative] What would it be like to live in a country with no freedom?

Follow-up discussion:
page 212

▶ [interpretive] How do the guards prevent people from escaping? (Possible answers: They shine searchlights over the cornfields to spot anyone who may be trying to cross the border; they watch the border from guard towers.)

▶ [interpretive] What could be in the ground to keep people from crossing a country's border? (Soldiers sometimes buried land mines along the border; if a person stepped on a mine, the mine would explode, killing or injuring the person.)

[interpretive] How do you know Dani is trusting in God? (As they think about the possibility of land mines, Dani says, "As God wills.") [BATs: 8a Faith in God's promises; 8d Courage]

[critical] What does Dani mean? (Elicit that Dani knows they are in God's care and he desires God's will for their lives, whether it be freedom or death.) [Bible Promise: I. God as Master]

[appreciative] If you had been with Zoli, would you have continued with Zoli or would you have turned back?

Read aloud Zoli's instructions to everyone. Read the instructions with trust and courage in your voice.

We crouched in the corn. They waited for me to speak. The rain drove down on us, splattering and rattling on the stalks. When the lights passed over a second time, I drew in a deep breath.

"Some borders have land mines. Some don't."

There was no answer from anyone. Finally, Ilona's voice came to me, hardly above the noise of the rain.

"How do we know?"

"We don't."

Again there was no speaking.

At last Dani said, "As God wills, I say."

"Yes," said Ilona.

I felt for their hands, one then the other.

"When I say to go, we all go together. Henrik, do you understand?"

"Yes, Papa."

Dani said, "I've got him."

The rain was pounding now. We were soaked, the water running into our shoes. The army kept the

212

ground plowed smooth, to look for footprints, but I was sure this rain would take our secret to the streams.

I watched for the lights to pass once more.

"Now!"

We ran. The mud caked to our shoes and our legs, slowing us down. Ilona struggled, and I took her by the arm and lifted her. The lights arced on the far end of the field and started back for us. We were but seconds from the border.

"God," I cried out, "help us!"

The lights swept through again, but this time we were behind their range. We were over the wire, all of us.

I dropped to my knees in the Austrian soil, holding my sons to me. And in the pouring rain, I wept.

The Gaal family in America

▶ [literal] What does Zoli wait for before he tells everyone to run? (for the lights from the guard tower to pass by them one more time)

Read aloud Zoli's desperate cry to God as they near the border.

[interpretive] When are Zoli, his family, and Dani safe? (Once they cross over the wire they are safe; the soldiers cannot harm them because they are now in another country with different laws.)

[critical] What is Zoli thinking as he holds his sons, kneeling and weeping on Austrian soil? (Answers may vary, but elicit that he is grateful to God for protecting his family from the guards and land mines and for the freedom they will now enjoy.) [BAT: 7c Praise]

▶ [appreciative] What can you learn from the life of Zoli? (Answers may vary, but emphasize that Zoli overcame many obstacles in his life because he trusted in God. As Zoli put his faith in God, God protected and blessed him.)

Worktext Objectives

The student will

■ Match words and definitions.

■ Determine word meaning from context.

■ Identify solutions to problems in the story.

Vocabulary:
Worktext page 85

Instruct the students to find each word on the reader page given to help them determine which definition is correct. Encourage the students to write their own sentences to show the meaning of the word in the story. Guide them through the first one, which is done for them.

Comprehension:
Worktext page 86

Teaching of problems and solutions was presented in Lesson 14.

Read and answer the first problem on the page together.

SOMETHING EXTRA

Find It: A promise from God

Assign one of the following words to each student: *strength, afraid, trouble, courage, trust, help.* Instruct the student to look up the word in the Bible concordance to find a promise from God that contains the word.

Provide an index card for each student to copy the reference and the entire verse on. Encourage each student to attach the verses to the corner of his desk or somewhere at home to remind him of God's promises to him.

Read It: More about Zoli

Invite the student to read more about Zoli. *Zoli's Legacy, Book I: Inheritance* tells the story of Zoli's early life. *Zoli's Legacy, Book II: Bequest* continues with the story of his adult life. Both books are available from JourneyForth.

SKILL LESSON: ENCYCLOPEDIAS

Materials
- Encylopedia volume containing an article about Canada
- Vocabulary sentences for display

INTRODUCTION

Vocabulary
Use the prepared sentences to introduce the vocabulary words in context.

Research
▶ Experts who want to help people learn about many interesting topics write articles for encyclopedias. Although it is impossible for an encyclopedia to contain all the facts about all topics, encyclopedias contain many articles on many subjects.

▶ What keywords would we look up in the encyclopedia to find information about World War II? (possible answers: World War II, Germany, Hitler)

Besides using encyclopedias, what other sources can we use to find information? (library books on specific topics, computers, videos)

Have you wanted to learn more about a certain topic?

Lesson	Reader pages	Worktext pages
68	214-15	87-88

VOCABULARY

LESSON 68

*†A volume is one book of a whole encyclopedia set. (p. 214)

*The long magazine article had many subtitles. (p. 214)

*†Do you like to look at illustrations as you read? (p. 214)

†I did not have much time, so I had to skim through the book quickly. (p. 214)

Correlated Activities
- **Vocabulary Box, Activity 5: Puzzle Pastime**
- **Spelling Practice, Activity 4: Secret Code Spelling**
See "Classroom Management for Grouping" in the Appendix.

Objectives

COMPREHENSION

The student will

- Recognize the parts of an encyclopedia article.
- Skim to locate information.
- Determine a keyword for a given idea.
- Understand the use of subtitles in expository writing.
- Develop skill for reading expository text.

Before silent reading: pages 214-15

Motivation

▶ What is a quick and easy way to research a topic?

How can information be found on a page quickly?

After silent reading

Overview discussion: pages 214-15

▶ [literal] What do you use first to find information in an encyclopedia? (keywords)

[literal] Why do some topics have subtitles on a page? (The topic is broad, so the author organizes it into smaller sections with subtitles.)

▶ [literal] What are two purposes of a caption? (to give an explanation of a picture and help the reader skim an article)

▶ [literal] What technology today provides a quick and easy way to do research? (computers)

[literal] What may a computer encyclopedia offer that a book encyclopedia cannot? (possible answers: media pictures, sounds, videos)

[appreciative] How do you like to learn more about a topic? Why?

SKILL LESSON:
Encyclopedias

The word *encyclopedia* literally means "many feet." A person has to "walk through" all the sciences to know everything. Ancient scholars thought that anything encyclopedic would contain all knowledge. Today, books that provide general information are called encyclopedias. Most encyclopedias list their information alphabetically.

• Using a Keyword

You might want to learn more about the war that changed the lives of the children in "When the War Is Over." An encyclopedia could help you. First you would have to decide what keywords to use. You might try *World War II* or *Hungary*. The letter on the spine of each volume tells the part of the alphabet that it contains. *World War II* would be in the *W* volume.

• Using Titles and Subtitles

Some subjects are so broad that encyclopedia writers organize them with subtitles. Usually major subtitles appear in the center of the column or are capitalized. Minor subtitles are usually in dark print, but they are of normal size and are not centered.

• Using Illustrations and Captions

Illustrations give you an idea of how a certain person, place, or event looked. The sentence underneath an illustration is called the caption. It explains what is going on in the picture. Captions provide an idea of what the article will cover. A careful reader can skim through an encyclopedia article by reading the captions.

• Using Computers

Computers offer a quick and easy way to access information. Once you load your program, you can type in your keyword. This will take you to the encyclopedia article. The article may offer a variety of media-pictures, sounds, or videos relating to the topic. Also,

Follow-up discussion: page 214

▶ [literal] What does the word *encyclopedia* mean? ("many feet")

[critical] Why is *encyclopedia* a good name for books that contain general information? (Answers may vary, but elicit that encyclopedias take you many places and help you learn about many things.)

[interpretive] How can information be found quickly in an encyclopedia volume? (It is listed alphabetically.)

▶ [literal] How can you tell major and minor subtitles apart on a page? (Major subtitles are usually in the center of the column and capital-ized; minor subtitles are usually in dark print, normal size, and not centered.)

Read aloud the subtitles on this page.

▶ [interpretive] Why is there no caption on this page? (because there are no pictures)

Read aloud the purposes for captions.

▶ [critical] If you want to find out about polar bears, what keywords might you use to find information? (possible answers: bears, polar bears, Alaska, Arctic)

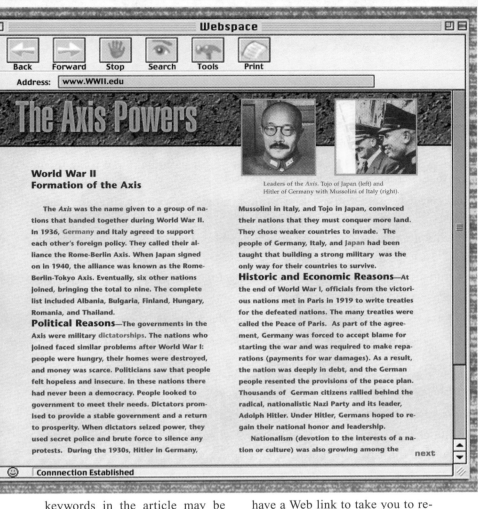

The Axis Powers

World War II
Formation of the Axis

The *Axis* was the name given to a group of nations that banded together during World War II. In 1936, Germany and Italy agreed to support each other's foreign policy. They called their alliance the Rome-Berlin Axis. When Japan signed on in 1940, the alliance was known as the Rome-Berlin-Tokyo Axis. Eventually, six other nations joined, bringing the total to nine. The complete list included Albania, Bulgaria, Finland, Hungary, Romania, and Thailand.

Political Reasons—The governments in the Axis were military dictatorships. The nations who joined faced similar problems after World War I: people were hungry, their homes were destroyed, and money was scarce. Politicians saw that people felt hopeless and insecure. In these nations there had never been a democracy. People looked to government to meet their needs. Dictators promised to provide a stable government and a return to prosperity. When dictators seized power, they used secret police and brute force to silence any protests. During the 1930s, Hitler in Germany,

Mussolini in Italy, and Tojo in Japan, convinced their nations that they must conquer more land. They chose weaker countries to invade. The people of Germany, Italy, and Japan had been taught that building a strong military was the only way for their countries to survive.

Historic and Economic Reasons—At the end of World War I, officials from the victorious nations met in Paris in 1919 to write treaties for the defeated nations. The many treaties were called the Peace of Paris. As part of the agreement, Germany was forced to accept blame for starting the war and was required to make reparations (payments for war damages). As a result, the nation was deeply in debt, and the German people resented the provisions of the peace plan. Thousands of German citizens rallied behind the radical, nationalistic Nazi Party and its leader, Adolph Hitler. Under Hitler, Germans hoped to regain their national honor and leadership.

Nationalism (devotion to the interests of a nation or culture) was also growing among the

Leaders of the Axis. Tojo of Japan (left) and Hitler of Germany with Mussolini of Italy (right).

next

keywords in the article may be highlighted. By clicking on them, you will be able to access corresponding articles.

If you have Internet access, your encyclopedia software may have a Web link to take you to related information on the Web. Some companies offer an online encyclopedia. This would give you current information about your topic.

Encyclopedias   215

Follow-up discussion: page 215

▶ [interpretive] What keywords might have been typed to access the computer article shown? (Axis powers)

▶ [interpretive] What are the subtitles in the article shown? (possible answers: Political Reasons, Historic and Economic Reasons, World War II, Formation of the Axis)

▶ [literal] What words in a computer encyclopedia article provide access to related articles? (highlighted keywords)

[interpretive] What words in the computer article shown provide access to related articles? (Germany, dictatorships, Japan)

[interpretive] If you are skimming this computer article, what information can you gain from the caption? (the names of the key Axis leaders and their countries)

Read aloud the caption in this article.

▶ [appreciative] Have you done research on the Internet? What did you research?

The student will

- Use an encyclopedia.
- Identify parts of an encyclopedia article.
- Determine a keyword for a given idea.
- Identify the encyclopedia volume containing a keyword.
- Match subtitles with information.

STUDY SKILLS
Encyclopedia articles

Write *keyword* and *volume* for display.

▶ What do you do first when you want to find information about a topic in an encyclopedia? (decide what keywords to use)

What keyword would you use first to find information about cities in Canada? (Canada)

In which volume would you find an article about Canada? (the volume labeled *C* or *Ca*)

Allow a student to look up *Canada* in the encyclopedia volume.

Write *guidewords* for display.

▶ Where are the guidewords on the encyclopedia page? (at the top of the page)

Choose a student to point out the guidewords on the pages where the article about Canada begins.

▶ What do the guidewords tell us? (articles with titles listed alphabetically between the two guidewords are on these pages)

Write *title* and *subtitle* for display.

Choose students to identify the title and several subtitles in the *Canada* article.

▶ Can you find information about the cities in Canada?

Guide the students in locating the subtitle about cities.

Also point out and discuss other features such as illustrations, captions, maps, and charts, as well as the information at the end of the article that gives related topics.

Study Skills: Worktext pages 87-88

SOMETHING EXTRA
Find It: A favorite topic

Provide each student with an opportunity to use an encyclopedia to locate information. Direct the student to choose a topic of interest and to look it up in an encyclopedia. Allow each student to read aloud a selected paragraph from the article.

JOHN 3:16—A TRUE STORY

Gladys Aylward responds to the plea of young Chinese believers for someone to take the gospel to the interior of China. When Gladys arrives at the farthest settlement—a lamasery—she finds that the Word of God has preceded her. The monks have a copy of John 3:16 and have been waiting for years for someone to come tell them about the God who loves.

Lesson	Reader pages	Worktext pages
69	216-20	89-90
70	221-26	91-92

Materials
- Pillow or cushion for each student
- World map or globe
- Vocabulary sentences for display

Background information
Gladys Aylward—While China was experiencing war in the 1940s, Gladys Aylward went to China as a missionary. For several years she ran an orphanage. When invaders came too close, she evacuated her orphanage. She traveled for weeks on foot with the children, taking them to safety. "John 3:16—A True Story" takes place several months after Gladys's journey with the children. The story begins at a Christian conference where Gladys is recuperating from an illness.

INTRODUCTION

Vocabulary
Use the prepared sentences to introduce the vocabulary words in context.

Traditions
Ask the students to sit on the pillows during the reading lesson.

▶ Do we usually sit on pillows in school?

We are sitting on pillows today because we will be reading a story about Tibetan and Chinese people. During the time of this story it was a tradition for these people to sit on the floor on pillows instead of on chairs.

Display the world map.

▶ Where are Tibet and China?

Point out your location and then the locations of Tibet and China.

Head note
Read the head note on reader page 216 aloud.

▶ What did Gladys Aylward do earlier in her life before this story takes place? (She escaped from a war-torn area of China with many Chinese children.)

Briefly share the background information about Gladys Aylward's work in China.

▶ How do you know that the story will be about events that really happened to Gladys Aylward? (The title says, "A True Story," and the head note says the story is an experience Gladys had later in her life.)

VOCABULARY

LESSON 69

*†The state in which I live is about the same size as the province in which he lives. (p. 217)

*†The farmers and other peasants worked under the hot sun all day. (p. 217)

†She waved her arms back and forth, gesturing for him to come over. (p. 217)

*†The lack of grass and bushes made the land look barren. (p. 218)

†Christians believe the Bible is sacred, or holy, because it is God's Word. (p. 220)

LESSON 70

†Holes and cracks in the sidewalk are recesses for weeds to grow. (p. 221)

†The tour guide escorted us back to the hotel. (p. 221)

†By asking over and over again, his persistence got him an answer. (p. 224)

†Communists believe the government should own everything. (p. 226)

Correlated Activities
- **Word Work, Activity 2: Blooper Blurbs**
- **Spelling Practice, Activity 1: Spell Check**
See "Classroom Management for Grouping" in the Appendix.

Objectives

COMPREHENSION

The student will

- Compare and contrast information.
- Draw conclusions.
- Use context to determine word meaning.
- Demonstrate understanding of the author's messages: Missionaries desire to follow God's leading; missionaries are not "perfect" Christians.

Before silent reading: pages 216-18

Motivation

▶ Will Gladys continue her missionary work?

How do Gladys and other story characters show faithfulness to the Lord?

After silent reading

Overview discussion: pages 216-18

▶ [literal] Why are the students praying for a place on the map they have never been to? (God laid it on their hearts to pray for someone to take the gospel to the people there.) [BATs: 6b Prayer; 5c Evangelism and missions]

[literal] How does God answer the students' prayers? (Gladys decides to go to the province.) [BAT: 2b Servanthood; 8a Faith in God's promises]

▶ [critical] Is it easy for Gladys to go on a mission when she does not know if she will have a place to sleep or food to eat? Why or why not? (Answers may vary, but elicit that she is following the Lord's leading and so trusts the Lord to provide for her and protect her.) [BAT: 2c Faithfulness; Bible Promise: H. God as Father]

[interpretive] How does the Lord provide for and protect Gladys on her journey? (In each village, she finds Christians who provide shelter for the night and a guide who takes

John 3:16

A True Story

Milly Howard
illustrated by Roger Bruckner

A biography of Gladys Aylward, These Are My People, *written by the author of this story, ended as the English missionary escaped from a war-torn area of China with many Chinese children. This is the story of an experience that Gladys had later in her life.*

A Place on the Map

Gladys Aylward got out of bed and pulled on her robe. Quietly she walked to the doorway and stood still, listening. There again was the sound that had awakened her. She moved slowly down the hall and stopped at an open door. Inside, a group of fifteen Chinese students knelt around a map. The sound of praying had awakened Gladys.

Gladys waited as student after student prayed for a town or village on the map. When the meeting was over, she approached the leader of the group.

216

her to the next village, and Dr. Huang guides her into the mountains.)

▶ [interpretive] How does Dr. Huang show his dedication to the Lord? (Possible answer: He guides Gladys into the mountains, walks farther than planned, shares God's Word with everyone they meet, and prays for someone to whom they can witness.)

[interpretive] Why is Gladys ashamed after she hears Dr. Huang's prayer on the tenth day of walking? (Dr. Huang prays for the chance to witness to someone, but Gladys prays only for her own needs.) [BAT: 5b Unselfishness]

Follow-up discussion: page 216

▶ [literal] What awakens Gladys? (the sound of students praying)

[critical] What time do you think it is? Why? (Answers may vary, but discuss that Gladys might be sleeping during the day because she is sick or the students might be praying all through the night.)

"Is that a map of your home province?" she asked.

"No, we have never been to this place," the leader replied. "But God has laid it on our hearts to pray for someone to carry the gospel there."

"Why doesn't one of you go?"

"We have not yet finished our studies," the young man replied. "Our special prayer is for someone to go ahead of us to prepare the way."

During the next few weeks Gladys thought often about the map and the students as she rested from the illness that had drained her strength. Finally, when she felt much better, she sought out the leader again. "I'll go," she said.

Two days later, with the blessings and praises of the young Chinese Christians ringing in her ears, Gladys set off on her journey.

The sky was a sharp, clear blue, and the light breeze that bent the long grasses was warm. Gladys walked slowly but steadily, enjoying the brightness of the sun. Cheerfully she called greetings in Chinese to the travelers on the road. In the villages, she found Christians who provided her with shelter during the nights. Then, after days of travel, she began to cover land that was not familiar to her. At each village she asked for a guide to take her as far as the next village. In this way she reached the village of Tsin Tsui, the last village known to the Chinese peasants.

"You cannot go on," the villagers told her, gesturing toward rough-looking mountains. "There is nothing else."

"Well, it can't be the end of the world," Gladys said with a smile. "There must be other people out there."

A Chinese doctor stepped forward. "I've always wanted to see what lies beyond the mountains," he said. "I'll go five days with you."

The other villagers shook their heads as Gladys and Dr. Huang started up the dusty trail that led out of the village. As they walked, Dr. Huang and Gladys began to talk about the Bible. Dr. Huang was a Christian and had many questions to ask Gladys. Frequently they read passages

Follow-up discussion: page 217

▶ [literal] Why are the students not able to go to the province now? (They have not yet finished their studies.)

Read aloud the dialogue between Gladys and the leader of the students. Read to show the students' dedication to the Lord.

▶ [interpretive] What makes Gladys decide to go? (She thinks about the map and the students for the weeks she rests from her illness.)

[interpretive] How does the author let you know Gladys is happy to be on her mission in China? (She enjoys the sunshine and cheerfully greets people.)

Read aloud the description of what Gladys sees and feels when she begins her journey.

▶ [interpretive] Why do the people of Tsin Tsui think Gladys should stop her journey? (They do not think there is anything else beyond their village.)

[interpretive] Why doesn't Gladys take the villagers' advice? (She knows there must be other people farther out who need to hear about God's love.) [BAT: 2a Obedience]

[appreciative] How would you feel if you were in Gladys's place with all the villagers shaking their heads at you as you walk on into the unknown?

**Follow-up discussion:
page 218**

▶ [literal] Why do Gladys and Dr. Huang stop to pray on the tenth day of the journey? (They have met no one all day and are concerned they might not find food and shelter or anyone to witness to for the rest of the trip.)

Read aloud both Gladys's and Dr. Huang's prayers. Read to show the seriousness of their situation.

[critical] After hearing Dr. Huang's prayer, Gladys is ashamed. Is it wrong to pray for food and shelter? Why or why not? (Answers may vary, but elicit that praying for your own needs is not wrong, but thinking only of yourself is wrong.)

▶ [critical] What is Gladys doing while she kneels in silence? (Answers may vary, but elicit that she is praying and confessing her selfishness to the Lord.) [BAT: 6b Prayer]

[interpretive] How does the author let you know that Gladys is happy and wants to praise the Lord after confessing her selfishness? (She suggests that they sing.)

[appreciative] Would you feel like singing? Why or why not?

aloud as they walked. The five days became nine, and still, they walked on, sharing God's Word with each other and with everyone they met on the trail. The tenth day they met no one at all. On and on they walked into what looked like a wilderness. Ahead of them stretched mountain after mountain, barren and dry. The sun passed slowly overhead, and the shadows began to lengthen.

At last, tired and thirsty, Gladys dropped her pack on the trail. "Dr. Huang, we must stop and pray."

The doctor knelt beside Gladys as she began to pray. "Oh, Lord, we have no water and no food. Please take care of us. Give us a place to rest and shelter for the night."

When Gladys had finished, the doctor began to pray. "Lord, we have seen no one today. Send us someone to whom we can witness. Send us someone with whom we can talk about Your Son."

Gladys was ashamed. Here she was thinking only of herself! For a few minutes she knelt in silence; then she said quietly, "Shall we sing?"

218

Softly they began an old hymn. Then their voices became stronger as the words rolled out into the clear mountain air. When the notes faded away, they began another song. Suddenly Dr. Huang stopped.

"There he is!" he shouted.

"What? Who?" Gladys peered into the dusty distance.

But Dr. Huang had already raced off down the path and was soon out of sight. Gladys sat on her pack, feeling very alone in the sudden silence.

Finally she saw two tiny figures moving toward her across the rocks. She shaded her eyes. As

John 3:16—A True Story   219

Follow-up discussion: page 219

▶ [interpretive] What makes Dr. Huang stop singing? (He sees someone in the distance.)

[interpretive] How does the author let you know Gladys cannot see the man Dr. Huang sees? (Gladys asks, "What? Who?" and peers into the distance.)

[interpretive] Why does Gladys feel very alone? (It is very quiet after Dr. Huang stops singing and runs off to meet the man.)

Read aloud the paragraph describing the sudden silence.

Before silent reading: pages 219-20

Motivation

▶ Will Gladys and Dr. Huang have the opportunity to witness to someone on the journey?

After silent reading

Overview discussion: pages 219-20

▶ [interpretive] Why does Dr. Huang shout, "There he is!" and run to meet the person as if he had been expecting that person? (Elicit that he believes the person is the Lord's answer to his prayer for someone to whom he can witness.) [BAT: 8a Faith in God's promises]

[interpretive] Why doesn't Gladys run to meet this person too? (Elicit that she does not see the person and is tired from the journey.)

[literal] Who is the person Dr. Huang meets? (a Tibetan lama, or monk)

Explain that in Tibet, *lama* is the word used for a monk, one who lives with other monks in a monastery away from the rest of the world while depriving himself of possessions and doing good works in an effort to know God. (Note: You may need to point out that the lamas in this story are people while the llamas in the story in Unit 1 are animals. Note the difference in spelling.)

▶ [literal] Why is Gladys surprised when she sees that the man is a lama, or monk? (Tibetan monks usually do not have anything to do with women.)

▶ [interpretive] Why does the lama invite Gladys into the lamasery when women are usually not allowed into their sacred building? (Elicit that the lama knows Dr. Huang and Gladys can tell him about the God who loves.) [BAT: 6a Bible study]

[interpretive] What do you think a lamasery is? (a monastery for Tibetan lamas)

Follow-up discussion: page 220

▶ [interpretive] What does Dr. Huang mean when he says, "This is the man"? (He is certain the Lord has sent this man for Gladys and him to witness to.)

[interpretive] How does Gladys know the man is a lama? (Answers may vary, but suggest that he must have the clothing and hairstyle of a lama.)

[interpretive] Why is Gladys surprised when she finds out that the lama has invited Dr. Huang and her to the lamasery? (It is against the religious rules of a lamasery to allow a woman to enter.)

Read aloud Gladys and Dr. Huang's conversation about the unusual situation. Read to show Gladys's surprise.

[literal] How does the lama end Gladys's questioning? (He says that they have waited a long time to hear about the God who loves.)

Read aloud the last paragraph, showing how the lama calmly answers Gladys's questions.

[critical] How does Gladys feel after she finds out the lama has been waiting to hear about God? (Answers may vary, but elicit that she must be glad as she is reminded of God's ability to answer prayer.) [BAT: 6b Prayer; 8a Faith in God's promises]

Looking ahead

▶ Will the lama accept what Dr. Huang and Gladys have to say?

they came closer, she recognized Dr. Huang. The two figures stopped above her, and she realized they were on a higher trail.

"Come up here," Dr. Huang called. "This is the man!"

Gladys looked at the steep, rocky slope and shook her head. "I can't," she said. "I'm too tired."

Dr. Huang scrambled down the slope. When he reached Gladys, he said, "Leave the packs here. I'll help you up."

Together they struggled up to the other trail. A Tibetan lama, or monk, was waiting. He stood patiently beside a large rock.

Gladys stared. "Did you tell him I was a woman?"

she asked, knowing that the monks had nothing to do with women.

Dr. Huang nodded. "Yes, but he still invited us to spend the night in the lamasery."

"Me? In a lamasery?" Gladys hesitated. "Why would they invite a woman into their sacred building?"

Suddenly the monk spoke. His accent was strange, but Gladys could understand him. "We have waited a long time to hear about the God who loves."

220

Worktext Objectives

The student will

- Locate information explicitly stated.
- Develop sentence closure.
- Read a map.

Comprehension: Worktext page 89

Explain that Gladys Aylward could have written a letter like this. Allow the students to use their readers to complete the letter.

Study Skills: Worktext page 90

Discuss *inset* as defined on the page. Instruct the students to read carefully as they complete the page.

The God Who Loves

Without another word, Gladys followed the two men. They crossed the mountain ridge, and Gladys gasped in amazement. The other side of the barren mountain they had been climbing was lush and green. Thick grass grew along the slopes, and water ran over the rocks. Brightly flowered vines drooped from the walls of a beautiful temple on the crest of a slope.

Gladys and Dr. Huang followed the monk down a trail to the temple gates. As the huge carved gates closed behind them, Gladys stared in amazement. They were standing in a large courtyard. Sunlight patterned the cool shadows of the courtyard and gleamed off golden statues in recesses along the walls. A movement in the shadows caught Gladys's attention. A group of yellow-clad lamas came forward and bowed. They led Gladys and Dr. Huang to rooms that had been prepared for them. Gladys rested comfortably on tiger rugs and silk cushions as water and dish after dish of delicious food were brought to her.

Later, two monks escorted Gladys and Dr. Huang through several courtyards to a large room near the center of the lamasery. Nearly five hundred lamas were seated there in half circles. Gladys and Dr. Huang were taken to the front.

"Whatever shall we do?" Gladys whispered.

"You must sing," Dr. Huang said.

Gladys began to sing.

John 3:16—A True Story   221

COMPREHENSION

The student will

■ Recognize the author's use of description and imagery to create setting.

■ Demonstrate understanding of biblical truths: God is love; God is sovereign; God answers prayer.

 Use the prepared sentences to introduce the vocabulary words in context.

Before silent reading: pages 221-26

Motivation

▶ Why are the lamas waiting for someone to tell them about the God who loves?

After silent reading

Overview discussion: pages 221-26

▶ [interpretive] How does the author help you see what Gladys and Dr. Huang see as they enter the courtyard? (Accept any answers describing the setting, such as the sunlight patterning cool shadows, golden statues, lamas in yellow robes, tiger rugs, and silk cushions.)

▶ [literal] What do Gladys and Dr. Huang do in the large room with the lamas? (Gladys sings and talks, and Dr. Huang speaks of Jesus' birth, life, and death.) [BATs: 5c Evangelism and missions; 7b Exaltation of Christ]

▶ [literal] In what ways has the Lord prepared the lamas to hear the gospel? (A lama took a tract containing John 3:16 to the lamasery, the lamas found someone who told them more information and gave them the four Gospels, and the lamas read the Gospels and have been waiting for God to send a messenger to tell them more.) [Bible Promise: I. God as Master]

Follow-up discussion: page 221

▶ [interpretive] How does the author let you know that Gladys is pleasantly surprised by what she sees on the other side of the mountain? (Gladys gasps and stares in amazement at what she sees.)

Read aloud the paragraph describing the beautiful lamasery.

▶ [interpretive] How does Gladys feel when she and Dr. Huang are led in front of five hundred lamas? How do you know? (She feels uncomfortable because she asks Dr. Huang what they should do.)

[appreciative] How would you feel if you had to sing in front of five hundred people you did not know?

Follow-up discussion: page 222

▶ [critical] Why are the lamas silent the entire time Gladys and Dr. Huang are talking and singing? (They are eager to hear all that Gladys and Dr. Huang have to say about God.)

[literal] Why do Gladys and Dr. Huang stop witnessing in the large room? (Gladys is tired.)

[literal] Why does Gladys not go to sleep right away? (Several lamas come to her room throughout the night to hear more about God.) [BAT: 5a Compassion]

▶ [literal] What amazes the lamas the most about God? (His love) [BAT: 7a Grace]

[critical] Why do the lamas want to hear about Calvary over and over? (Elicit that Christ's death is the ultimate act of God's love for sinners.) [Bible Promise: E. Christ as Sacrifice]

Read aloud the paragraph describing the events at Gladys's room. Read to show the lamas' great desire to hear about God.

▶ [literal] How long do Gladys and Dr. Huang stay at the lamasery? (one week)

[literal] On the last day of Gladys's visit, where do the lamas take her? (to the head lama)

When she finished, there was a deathly silence. She looked at Dr. Huang.

Dr. Huang stood up and began to speak. He told about the birth of Jesus, of His life, and how He died on the cross at Calvary.

Gladys sang again, and then she talked. When she finished, Dr. Huang spoke again. Gladys sang another song and talked; then it was Dr. Huang's turn. And so it went.

Gladys couldn't see the faces of the lamas. The silence was unbroken except for the sound of Dr. Huang's voice as he spoke. Finally Gladys said, "I must rest. I'm afraid I'm going to fall off this seat."

"Then we will finish," said Dr. Huang. They rose and walked straight out into the hall. Behind them they heard the first sounds of movement since they had entered the room.

They reached their rooms, and a tired Gladys began to prepare for bed. A knock sounded at the door. When she opened it, two monks stood outside. "Woman, are you too tired to tell us more?"

"Are you allowed to enter?" Gladys asked.

"If there are two of us," they answered.

"Then come in."

Far into the night more lamas kept on coming. They sat around the room, listening. They accepted without question God's creation of the world, the virgin birth, the miracles. It was God's love that amazed them. Over and over they asked to be told about Calvary.

Gladys and Dr. Huang stayed for a week, answering questions. On the last day of their visit, Gladys was taken before the head lama. She sat on a stool beside him and listened as he told her his story.

"For many years," he explained, "the monks of this lamasery have collected an herb that grows on the mountainside. The herb is much desired in the cities and has always brought a good price. Some years ago, after the herb had been harvested and dried, it was taken to the city as usual. As the monks passed through a village on the way, a

John 3:16—A True Story   223

**Follow-up discussion:
page 223**

▶ [interpretive] What event does the picture show? (several lamas listening, either in the large room or in Gladys's room)

[appreciative] What do the expressions on the lama's faces tell you?

Follow-up discussion: page 224

▶ [literal] What is written on the tract the lama had taken from the missionary? (John 3:16)

[interpretive] How do you know the verse is important to the lamas? (They keep the tract with the verse and put it on the wall. They also search for many years to find out more about the meaning of the verse.)

[interpretive] Why does Gladys murmur "The God who loves . . ."? (She realizes that the lamas got the phrase "the God who loves" from the verse on the tract.)

Read aloud the sentence that tells what Gladys murmurs. Read to show her understanding of the saying.

▶ [literal] How many years did the lamas hear nothing more about God than what was written on the tract? (five)

[appreciative] Would it be difficult to wait five years to learn about something very important to you?

▶ [literal] After five years, how did the lamas finally learn more about the God who loves? (They were persistent in their search and finally found someone who told them more and gave them the four Gospels.) [BAT: 5c Evangelism and missions]

Read aloud the last paragraph, showing the lamas' eagerness to learn about the Gospels.

man stood on the side of the road waving a piece of paper."

"Curious, a monk stopped and took the piece of paper. He tucked it inside his robe and brought it back after the herbs had been sold."

The lama interrupted his story and pointed to a worn piece of paper stuck on the wall behind him. Leaning closer, Gladys saw an ordinary tract on which was written in Chinese the words of John 3:16: "For God so loved the world that he gave his only begotten Son, that whosoever believeth in him should not perish but have everlasting life."

"The God who loves . . ." Gladys murmured softly.

The lama nodded. "Yes," he said as he continued his story. "When we sent the herbs to be sold the next year, the men were instructed to find out more about the God who loved the world, but for five years they heard nothing. Finally, one year they decided to keep going until they found someone who could tell them more about this God. When they reached the city of Len Chow, their persistence was rewarded. They found a man who told them to go to the building that had 'Faith, Hope, and Charity' carved above the door. In that building they found someone who told them more and gave them the four Gospels, Matthew, Mark, Luke, and John.

"The men hurried back to share their news. Eagerly we read the Gospels and believed what we read. However, there was much that was not clear to us. Over and over we read the verse, 'Go ye into all the world and preach the gospel.'

224

"At last we realized all we had to do was wait. This God would send a messenger to tell us more. So for another three years we waited.

"Last week two of our lamas were out on the hillside, gathering sticks. They heard you sing. Believing that only those who know God will sing as you did, they knew that God's messengers had arrived. One hurried back to the lamasery with the news of your arrival, and we began preparations for you as our guests. The other hurried down to meet you and bring you back to us."

Gladys listened to the end of the story in awe of God's power, knowing she was listening to an account of the working of the Holy Spirit. "Truly, Lord," she thought as she remembered the tracts, the mission, and the young

John 3:16—A True Story   225

▶ [literal] What did the lamas finally realize they had to do? (They had to wait for God to send a messenger.) [BAT: 8a Faith in God's promises]

[interpretive] How did the lamas know that God would send a messenger to them? (They had read the verse, "Go ye into all the world and preach the gospel," so they knew that someone would obey God's command and come to tell them more about God's love.)

[literal] Why did the lamas know Gladys and Dr. Huang were God's messengers? (The lamas heard Gladys and Dr. Huang singing and believed that only people who know God would sing as they did.)

[critical] What parts of Gladys and Dr. Huang's singing might make them sound like God's messengers? (Accept any answer, but elicit that the words of the song, the tune of the song, and the attitude with which they were singing made them sound like God's messengers.)

[interpretive] Why did the priests hurry to meet Gladys and Dr. Huang and bring them to the lamasery? (The lamas had been waiting many years for God's messengers and were eager to learn more about God.) [BATs: 6a Bible study; 6a Reverence for the Bible]

▶ [literal] How does Gladys feel about the lamas' story? (She is in awe of God's power.)

Read aloud the paragraph telling Gladys's thoughts about the story. Read to show her amazement with the power of God.

[interpretive] How is the lama's story "an account of the working of the Holy Spirit"? (Elicit that the Holy Spirit worked in many people's hearts and directed many events to prepare the lamas for God's Word and to bring God's Word to the lamas.)

Follow-up discussion:
page 226

▶ [interpretive] What does Gladys mean when she says, "it is as Paul said, 'I have planted, Apollos watered; but God gave the increase'!"? (The students' prayers, the man who gave the tract, the person at the mission, and the doctor and Gladys all had a part in reaching the lamas for Christ, but it was God who worked in the lamas' hearts.) [BAT: 3e Unity of Christ and the church]

▶ [interpretive] What words tell you that Gladys and Dr. Huang are encouraged by their experience with the lamas? ("enriched in mind and spirit")

▶ [literal] Years after Gladys's trip, what does she hear about the lamas? (that the Communists destroyed the lamasery and drove the lamas away)

[critical] Though Gladys does not know what finally happened to the lamas, why is she not concerned? (She trusts the Lord and realizes that He can bring the lamas to know Him and can protect and care for them.) [Bible Promise: I. God as Master]

Read aloud the last sentence, showing Gladys's comfort in knowing that God is in control of everything.

[critical] What would have happened to the lamas if Gladys had never gone on her mission? (Answers may vary, but elicit that God could have used another means to reach the lamas; however, Gladys would not have had the blessing of being used by God.)

Christians who had been so faithful in their prayers, "it is as Paul said, 'I have planted, Apollos watered; but God gave the increase'!"

Gladys and Dr. Huang began their long trip back, enriched in mind and spirit. Years later, Gladys learned that the Communists had destroyed the lamasery and driven the lamas away. She never discovered what happened to those five hundred lamas. Gladys trusted the Lord, knowing that He could finish what He had begun in His own way, in His own time.

226

> ## Worktext
> ## Objectives

The student will

■ Recall facts and details.
■ Infer unstated supporting details.
■ Draw conclusions.

Comprehension:
Worktext page 91

Comprehension:
Worktext page 92

SOMETHING EXTRA

Tell About It: The God who loves

Provide tracts for the students to distribute to unsaved friends and acquaintances. Encourage the students to give out the tracts and speak to those they give them to. Allow them to tell about their opportunities they had to tell others about the God who loves and any known results of their witnessing.

Lesson	Worktext pages
71	246-47

Objectives

The student will

- Recognize that adding suffixes to some words may cause the primary accent to shift to the syllable before the suffix (ac´·ci·dent, ac•ci•den´•tal).
- Recognize that a shift in accent often occurs when the meaning of a word changes (per´•fect, per•fect´).

Background information

Accent Rule 5—Adding suffixes to some words may affect where the primary accent falls. It often shifts to the syllable before the suffix.

A shift in accent often occurs when the meaning of a word changes.

Materials

- Teaching Visual 15: *The Greatest Ride*

WORDS WITH SHIFTING ACCENTS

① **Introduction: Making the Connection**

▶ For what main purpose was the pony express begun? (to improve communication between California and the Eastern states)

▶ In March of 1861, a month before the Civil War began, it seemed that Lincoln's inaugural address would help Californians decide whether to stay in the Union or to join the Confederate states in secession. Plans were made to rush Lincoln's speech by pony express to Sacramento as fast as possible. His words and reasoning might convince Californians to stay in the Union. Listen to find out if the plan succeeded.

Read the following account to the students.

Bob Haslam was chosen to carry Lincoln's speech over the most dangerous stretch of the pony express route. Numerous hazards lurked here. The only express rider who was ever killed on duty received his injuries on this part of the trail.

At first the 118-mile section in Nevada from Smith's Creek to Fort Churchill was very quiet; but Bob, suspecting that trouble was still ahead, refused the fast horse waiting for him at Cold Spring station and chose instead Old Buck, a slower mount. Old Buck had once been owned by Indians who must have treated him harshly. Old Buck hated Indians and would alert Bob if he sensed any nearby.

It was dark, so Bob watched Old Buck carefully as they rode westward toward Middle Gate remount station. Several miles out, Old Buck snorted, and his ears stood straight up. A little farther on, Old Buck snorted again and began to shake his head. His ears still pointed ahead. But when they passed through one patch of brush, Old Buck's ears flicked to the sides. Bob knew this was it!

The attack came suddenly. Wild yells and flying arrows did not keep Bob and Old Buck from pressing onward. Bob drew out his revolvers and returned fire. Old Buck broke into a run and bit any warriors who got close to him. Several warriors were riding swift horses that were stolen from remount stations. Old Buck could not outrun them. Though Bob hated to do it, he shot the swifter horses to save his life and to help save the Union.

Bob was also injured that night. An arrow hit his left arm, leaving it useless. A second arrow broke his jaw and knocked out five teeth. Pain almost caused him to lose consciousness, but he struggled to overcome the dizziness. Old Buck carried him on, successfully reaching Middle Gate.

Though he was covered in blood and barely recognizable, Bob not only reached Middle Gate but completed the rest of his ride that night. Lincoln's speech reached California in record time, and California remained in the Union.

Discuss the following.

▶ How was the pony express a great service to the U.S.? (by delivering the news needed to help strengthen the Union)

▶ Why was it wiser to choose the slower horse to carry the mail over the most dangerous part of the trail? (possible answer: because the slower horse, Old Buck, would be able to show where danger was)

Farther Along

▶Move It

Read the pairs of words. Mark the accented syllables in each word to show the shift in the accent.

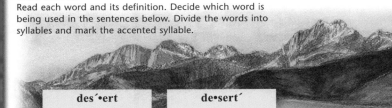

ex•claim´ ex•cla•ma´•tion	na´•tion na•tion•al´•i•ty	pub´•lic pub•lic´•i•ty
des´•tine des•ti•na´•tion	sac´•ri•fice sac•ri•fi´•cial	pos´•si•ble pos•si•bil´•i•ty

When a suffix is added to some words, the accent shifts to the syllable before the suffix.

▶Choose It

Read each word and its definition. Decide which word is being used in the sentences below. Divide the words into syllables and mark the accented syllable.

des´•ert
A very dry region covered with sand or pebbles.

de•sert´
To leave or abandon.

1. Some express stations were located in the **d e s´•e r t.**
2. "I don't want to **d e•s e r t´** you, but the mail can't wait."

min´•ute
A unit of time equal to sixty seconds.

mi•nute´
Very, very small; tiny.

3. Riders stopped at express stations for no more than three **m i n´•u t e s.**
4. **M i•n u t e´** grains of sand could blow into the riders' eyes.

The accent often shifts when the meaning of a word changes.

246

③ Skill application:
Worktext page 246

Move It
Ask a student to read aloud the pair of words in the first box.

▶ What happens to the accent when the suffix *-tion* is added to *exclaim?* (The accent shifts to another syllable.)

Where should the accent mark appear in *exclamation?* (at the end of the syllable *ma*)

Add the accent mark.

Complete the section together, using a similar procedure with each pair of words.

Skill Station Day

Choose It
Ask students to read the first pair of sentences aloud.

▶ What two words in these sentences look the same but have different meanings? (desert, desert)

Ask students to read aloud the words and definitions in the first two boxes and to identify which word is used in each sentence.

Guide the students in dividing the words into syllables and inserting the accent marks according to their meaning.

Complete the activity together.

② Skill development:
Visual 15—*The Greatest Ride*

▶ The job of the pony express was to move the mail farther along. Keep this fact in mind as we examine some changes in these words.

Read aloud the first three pairs of words.

▶ What has been added to each base word? (the suffix *-tion*)

As I read each pair of words again, listen to what happens to the accent. (The accent shifts to a different syllable.)

Adding suffixes to some words may affect where the primary accent falls. It often shifts to the syllable before the suffix.

▶ Listen to some words with other suffixes added.

Read aloud the second set of word pairs.

▶ Does the accent shift farther along in these words also? (yes)

▶ Accents can also shift when the meaning of a word changes.

Ask students to read the pair of words and the sentences at the bottom of the visual. Discuss the shift in accent and the difference in the words' meanings.

④ Skill application:
Worktext page 247

Photograph Credits

The following agencies and individuals have furnished materials to meet the photographic needs of this textbook. We wish to express our gratitude to them for their important contribution.

Suzanne R. Altizer
J. Bean
Bob Jones University
   Classic Players
George R. Collins
Corel Corporation
Creation Science Foundation,
   Ltd., Australia
Eastman Chemicals Division

Beverly Factor
Zoltan Gaal
Brian D. Johnson
Breck P. Kent
Sam Laterza
Library of Congress
Miriam Mitchem
NASA (National Aeronautics
   and Space Administration)

National Archives
John Nesbit
PhotoDisc, Inc.
Roper Mountain Science
   Center
Unusual Films
John Wolsieffer
www.arttoday.com

Front and Back Cover
PhotoDisc, Inc. (background)

Title Page
PhotoDisc, Inc.

Unit Openers
Exploits PhotoDisc, Inc.; **Encounters** Breck P. Kent; **Quests** George R. Collins (war men and cannon), Unusual Films (U.S. Constitution); **Creatures** Breck P. Kent; **Potpourri** Corel Corporation; **Heroes** PhotoDisc, Inc.

Unit 1
PhotoDisc, Inc. 23 (background), 48, 50; Corel Corporation 46, 47; John Wolsieffer 49

Unit 2
National Archives 90; PhotoDisc, Inc. 91; Unusual Films 133

Unit 3
Corel Corporation 168, 185; Library of Congress 194, 196; Courtesy of Zoltan Gaal 199, 202, 206 (both), 213; www.arttoday.com 200, 207, 209, 212, 215 (both); Eastman Chemicals Division 210

Unit 4
Creation Science Foundation, Ltd. Australia, photo by J. Bean 238 (moth); Miriam Mitchem 238 (butterfly); Corel Corporation 239 (both), 240 (toad), 241 (Canada goose); PhotoDisc, Inc. 240 (frog and duck), 241 (chimpanzee, monkey, and white goose); © 1996 Beverly Factor 242 (dolphin); Unusual Films 262 (both)

Unit 5
PhotoDisc, Inc. 352, 359, 360, 362 (background), 397 (both), 398-99 (background); Unusual Films 353, 356 (both); John Nesbit 355 (Jolly Roger flag); Sam Laterza 402, 404, 405, 406, 408, 409; NASA 411; Roper Mountain Science Center, photo by Suzanne R. Altizer 412; Corel Corporation 394 (background)

Unit 6
Brian D. Johnson 436, 437, 438 (both), 439, 441, 442; Unusual Films 477

Glossary
www.arttoday.com 544

Glossary

This glossary has information about selected words found in this reader. You can find meanings of words as they are used in the stories. Certain unusual words such as foreign names are included so that you can pronounce them correctly when you read.

The pronunciation symbols below show how to pronounce each vowel and several of the less-familiar consonants.

ă	pat	ĕ	pet	îr	fierce
ā	pay	ē	be	ŏ	pot
âr	care	ĭ	pit	ō	go
ä	father	ī	pie	ô	paw, for, ball

oi	oil	ŭ	cut	zh	vision
o͝o	book	ûr	fur	ə	ago, item,
o͞o	boot	*th*	the		pencil, atom,
yo͞o	abuse	th	thin		circus
ou	out	hw	which	ər	butter

529

A

a·bound | ə **bound´** | —*verb* To be plentiful or to have plenty of.

ac·cel·er·a·tor | ăk **sĕl´** ə rā´ tər | —*noun* Anything that increases speed. In a car the accelerator is a pedal the driver steps on to make the car go faster.

ac·count | ə **kount´** | —*noun* A written or spoken description; a report.

ad·join | ə **join´** | —*verb* To be next to; be side by side.

ad·mis·sion | ăd **mĭsh´** ən | —*noun* A price charged or paid to enter a place.

ad·mon·ish | ăd **mŏn´** ĭsh | —*verb* To kindly correct or instruct against a certain action.

a·do·be | ə **dō´** bē | —*noun* A house built with bricks made of clay and straw that dry and harden in the sun.

ad·vance | ăd **văns´** | —*verb* To move forward, onward, or upward.

a·feared or **a·feard** | ə **fîrd´** | —*adjective* Afraid; frightened; scared.

al·bi·no | ăl **bī´** nō | —*noun* An animal or person that is white because it or he has no skin pigmentation.

al·le·giance | ə **lē´** jəns | —*noun* Loyal and faithful devotion to someone or something.

am·bu·lance | **ăm´** byə ləns | —*noun* A large vehicle that is used to rush people who are sick or hurt to a hospital. An ambulance has special medical equipment and trained people to help on the way to the hospital.

am·mu·ni·tion | ăm´ yə **nĭsh´** ən | —*noun* Bullets, explosives, bombs, grenades, or anything else that can be fired from a gun or weapon or can explode and cause damage.

am·phib·i·ous | ăm **fĭb´** ē əs | —*adjective* Able to travel on land or in water.

an·noy | ə **noi´** | —*verb* To bother; irritate; pester.

an·ten·na | ăn **tĕn´** ə | —*noun* One of a pair of long, thin feelers on the head of some animals.

an·tic | **ăn´** tĭk | —*noun* A game, prank, or stunt.

anx·ious·ly | **ăngk´** shəs lē | or | **ăng´** shəs lē | —*adverb* With worry.

a·pol·o·gize | ə **pŏl´** ə jīz | —*verb* To say one is sorry; make an apology.

ap·prov·al | ə **pro͞o´** vəl | —*noun* A favorable opinion; praise.

aq·ua·ma·rine | ăk wə mə **rēn´** | or | ä kwə mə **rēn´** | —*noun* A blue-green gemstone.

a·quar·i·um | ə **kwâr´** ē əm | —*noun* A water-filled tank in which sea life is kept and observed.

arc·tic | **ärk´** tĭk | or | **är´** tĭk | —*noun* The north polar region.

as·cend | ə **sĕnd´** | —*verb* To go or move upward; rise.

as·cen·sion | ə **sĕn´** shən | —*noun* A going up.

as·pen | **ăs´** pən | —*noun* A poplar tree with leaves that flutter in even the slightest breeze.

a·ston·ished | ə **stŏn´** ĭshd | —*adjective* Extremely surprised.

a·stound | ə **stound´** | —*verb* To fill or strike with surprise or sudden wonder; astonish.

as·tro·naut | **ăs´** trə nôt | —*noun* A person who is trained to fly in a spacecraft.

at·tain·able | ə **tān´** ə bəl | —*adjective* Capable of being gained or accomplished.

at·tempt | ə **tĕmpt´** | —*noun* An effort or try.

at·ten·tion | ə **tĕn´** shən | —*noun* Mental concentration; thinking, watching, or listening carefully to or about someone or something.

au·di·tion | ô **dĭsh´** ən | —*verb* To perform on a trial basis; to show one's skill in acting or singing.

au·thor | **ô´** thər | —*noun* A person who writes a book, story, article, play, or other work.

av·a·lanche | **ăv´** ə lănch | or | **ăv´** ə länch | —*noun* A large mass of material that falls or slides down the side of a mountain. An avalanche is usually made up of snow, ice, earth, or rocks.

awe | ô | —*noun* A feeling of wonder, fear, or respect about something that is mighty or majestic.

awed | ôd | —*adjective* Full of wonder.

az·ure | **ăzh´** ər | —*adjective* A light to medium blue, like that of the sky on a clear day.

B

balk | bôk | —*verb* To stop short and refuse to go on.

ban·is·ter | **băn´** ĭ stər | —*noun* A handrail.

bar·ren | **băr´** ən | —*adjective* Not producing anything.

bar·ter | **bär´** tər | —*verb* To trade one thing for another without using money.

base | bās | —*noun* The lowest part; the bottom.

bash·ful | **băsh´** fəl | —*adjective* Timid and embarrassed with other people; shy.

aspen

astronaut

adobe

ă	pat	ĕ	pet
ā	pay	ē	be
âr	care	ĭ	pit
ä	father	ī	pie
îr	fierce	oi	oil
ŏ	pot	o͞o	book
ō	go	o͞o	boot
ô	paw, for	yo͞o	abuse
		ou	out
ŭ	cut	ə	ago,
ûr	fur		item,
th	the		pencil,
th	thin		atom,
hw	which		circus
zh	vision	ər	butter

birthstone

ă	pat	ĕ	pet
ā	pay	ē	be
âr	care	ĭ	pit
ä	father	ī	pie
îr	fierce	oi	oil
ŏ	pot	ŏŏ	book
ō	go	ōō	boot
ô	paw,	yōō	abuse
	for	ou	out
ŭ	cut	ə	ago,
ûr	fur		item,
th	the		pencil,
th	thin		atom,
hw	which		circus
zh	vision	ər	butter

bronc

bay | bā | —*noun* A reddish brown horse.

ba·zaar | bə zär´ | —*noun* A market made up of a street lined with shops and stalls.

bill | bĭl | —*noun* The hard, projecting mouth parts on the head of a bird.

birch | bûrch | —*noun* A tree with smooth bark that peels off easily. There are several kinds of birch trees.

birth·stone | bûrth´ stōn | —*noun* A jewel associated with a certain month, worn by people born in that month.

bit | bĭt | —*noun* A shaped piece of metal that is part of a horse's bridle. The bit goes into the horse's mouth and is used to help control the animal.

bluff | blŭf | —*noun* A steep cliff, hill, or riverbank.

bog | bôg | or | bŏg | —*noun* A soft, wet area of land; marsh; swamp.

bois·ter·ous | boi´ stər əs | or | boi´ strəs | —*adjective* Overactive and noisy.

bored | bôrd | or | bōrd | —*adjective* Made weary by lack of interest.

bot·tle·neck | bŏt´ l nĕk | —*noun* A narrow or blocked section of a river or stream.

bound | bound | —*verb* To run by leaping.

bow out | bou out | —*verb* To gracefully withdraw, usually from a contest or game.

brack·ish | brăk´ ĭsh | —*adjective* Stagnant, sour, or salty.

brand | brănd | —*noun* A piece of burning wood.

bran·dish | brăn´ dĭsh | —*verb* To wave or swing about either as a weapon or as a symbol of triumph.

brawn·y | brô´ nē | —*adjective* Heavily muscled; strong.

bread·board | brĕd´ bôrd | or | brĕd´ bōrd | —*noun* A board on which breads and pastries are prepared.

bronc | brŏngk | —*noun* A wild or partly tamed horse of western North America.

broth | brôth | or | brŏth | —*noun* The water in which meat, fish, or vegetables have been boiled or simmered.

bru·in | brōō´ ĭn | —*noun* A bear.

bush·el bas·ket | bōōsh´ əl băs´ kĭt | —*noun* A basket capable of holding a bushel of grain.

bus·tle[1] | bŭs´ əl | —*noun* A frame used to fill out the back of a skirt or dress.

bus·tle[2] | bŭs´ əl | —*verb* To hurry and move around in a busy and excited way.

---

ca·ble | kā´ bəl | —*noun* A thick, strong rope made of twisted wire or fiber.

cai·man | kā´ mən | —*noun* An animal that looks like an alligator but is a little smaller.

calm | käm | —*verb* To make or become peacefully quiet.

cam·o·mile or **cham·o·mile** | kăm´ ə mīl | —*noun* An aromatic plant used to make a soothing tea.

can·o·py | kăn´ ə pē | —*noun* A covering like a tent held up over a bed, entrance, or important person.

can·vass | kăn´ vəs | —*verb* To walk door to door for sales purposes or advertising.

car·da·mom | kär´ də məm | or **car·da·mon** | kär´ də mən | —*noun* An edible seed that comes from an Asian plant.

cast | kăst | or | käst | —*verb* To throw or fling.

cau·tious | kô´ shəs | —*adjective* Showing or having caution; careful.

cau·tious·ly | kô´ shəs lē | —*adverb* Showing caution in order to avoid danger or trouble.

cav·al·cade | kăv əl kăd´ | or | kăv´ əl kăd | —*noun* A loud, colorful parade or procession using horses.

chafe | chāf | —*verb* To feel annoyed or irritated.

chan·nel | chăn´ əl | —*noun* A body of water that connects two larger bodies.

char·ac·ter | kăr´ ĭk tər | —*noun* A person in a book, story, or play.

char·ac·ter·is·tic | kăr ĭk tər ĭs´ tĭk | —*noun* A special feature of a person or thing.

charm | chärm | —*verb* To please or delight.

check[1] | chĕk | —*noun* In chess, the result of a move that places the opponent's king in danger.

check[2] | chĕk | —*interjection* An idiom indicating "yes" or "all set."

chron·i·cle | krŏn´ ĭ kəl | —*noun* A history of events.

cinch | sĭnch | —*noun* A strap for a saddle, usually fastened along a horse's or other animal's belly.

civ·il | sĭv´ əl | —*adjective* Concerning the events happening within a country or community.

clerk | klûrk | —*noun* A person who works in an office and keeps records and other papers in correct order.

cli·ché | klē shā´ | —*noun* A well-known saying or expression.

cable

caiman

canopy

cli·max | **klī´** măks | —*noun* The most exciting part or the turning point in a story.

coax | kōks | —*verb* To try in a gentle or pleasant way to get a person or an animal to do something.

cobblestones

cob·ble·stone | **kŏb´** əl stŏn | —*noun* A round stone once used to pave streets.

cock·pit | **kŏk´** pĭt | —*noun* The part of an airplane where the pilot and copilot sit.

col·lide | kə **līd´** | —*verb* To strike or bump together violently; crash.

com·bi·na·tion | kŏm´ bə **nā´** shən | —*noun* The joining of two or more elements.

com·mence | kə **mĕns´** | —*verb* To begin; start.

cockpit

com·men·tar·y | **kŏm´** ən tĕr ē | —*noun* A book containing explanations and illustrations of an important book, play, or poem.

com·mit | kə **mĭt´** | —*verb* To give over to another person or place; give into another's care; entrust to.

com·pass¹ | **kŭm´** pəs | or | **kŏm´** pəs | —*noun* An instrument used to show directions.

com·pass² | **kŭm´** pəs | or | **kŏm´** pəs | —*verb* To encircle or surround.

compass

com·pound | **kŏm´** pound | —*noun* A unit of buildings often

set apart by a fence, wall, or ditch.

con·ceal | kən **sēl´** | —*verb* To keep from being seen, noticed, or known; hide.

con·duct | kən **dŭkt´** | —*verb* To act as a path for electricity, heat, or other forms of energy.

con·fi·dence | **kŏn´** fĭ dəns | —*noun* Trust or faith in others.

con·fi·dent | **kŏn´** fĭ dənt | —*adjective* Trusting; being certain; assured; especially in oneself.

con·firm | kən **fûrm´** | —*verb* To give or get definite evidence.

con·se·quence | **kŏn´** sĭ kwĕns´ | —*noun* Something that happens as a result of another action or condition.

con·sul | **kŏn´** səl | —*noun* A government representative who lives in a foreign country to ensure fair business and legal practices there for the people of his own citizenship.

con·su·late | **kŏn´** sə lĭt | —*noun* The office or building of a consul.

con·tempt | kən **tĕmpt´** | —*noun* A feeling that someone or something is of little value, worthless, or not wanted; scorn; disdain.

con·tent | kon **tĕnt´** | —*adjective* Pleased with what one has or is; satisfied.

con·ti·nent | **kŏn´** tə nənt | —*noun* One of the main land masses of the earth. The seven continents are Africa, Antarctica, Asia, Australia, Europe, North America, and South America.

con·tri·bute | kən **trĭb´** yŏŏt | —*verb* To give, supply, or donate.

cor·ral | kə **răl´** | —*noun* A pen or place for keeping cattle or horses.

cot | kŏt | —*noun* A narrow bed, usually made of canvas stretched over a folding frame.

coun·sel·or | **koun´** sə lər | or | **koun´** slər | —*noun* A person who advises or guides; advisor.

cou·pon | **kŏŏ´** pŏn | or | **kyŏŏ´** pŏn | —*noun* A small certificate that can be exchanged for money, food, or other goods.

dash·ing | **dăsh´** ĭng | —*adjective* Brave, bold, and daring.

daze | dāz | —*noun* A state of not realizing what is going on around oneself, a confused condition.

de·bris | də **brē´** | or | **dā´** brē | —*noun* The scattered pieces or remains of something that has been broken, destroyed, or thrown away; rubble.

de·fense | dĭ **fĕns´** | —*noun* The act of defending or protecting.

court·ship | **kôrt´** shĭp | or | **kōrt´** shĭp | —*noun* The period of time when a man tries to persuade a woman to marry him.

crack shot | krăk shot | —*noun* A person who is an excellent marksman with a gun.

crest | krĕst | —*noun* The top of something, such as a mountain or wave.

cot

cross-ref·er·ence | **krôs´ rĕf´** ər əns | —*noun* A reference from one part of a book to related information in another part.

cup | kŭp | —*noun* Any land formation in the shape of a cup.

cu·ri·ous | **kyŏŏr´** ē əs | —*adjective* 1. Eager to learn or know. 2. Unusual or remarkable.

cur·rent | **kûr´** ənt | or | **kŭr´** ənt | —*noun* Moving liquid or gas.

cup

de·fi·ant | dĭ **fī´** ənt | —*adjective* The attitude of refusing to obey authority.

del·e·ga·tion | **dĕl´** ĭ **gā´** shən | —*noun* A person or group of people who speak in behalf of an organization or government.

de·lir·i·ous | dĭ **lîr´** ē əs | —*adjective* Out of one's senses; raving.

de·pend·a·ble | dĭ **pĕn´** də bəl | —*adjective* Able to be depended upon; reliable.

ă	pat	ĕ	pet
ā	pay	ē	be
âr	care	ĭ	pit
ä	father	ī	pie
îr	fierce	oi	oil
ŏ	pot	ŏŏ	book
ō	go	ŏŏ	boot
ô	paw,	yŏŏ	abuse
	for	ou	out
ŭ	cut	ə	ago,
ûr	fur		item,
th	the		pencil,
th	thin		atom,
hw	which		circus
zh	vision	ər	butter

534

disk drive

de·scrip·tion | dĭ **skrĭp´** shən | —*noun* An account in words describing something.

de·sign | dĭ **zīn´** | —*noun* 1. A plan or a specific purpose. 2. An arrangement of lines, figures, or objects into a pattern.

de·ter·mine | dĭ **tûr´** mĭn | —*verb* To decide or settle.

de·vel·oped | dĭ **vĕl´** əpt | —*adjective* Grown; every detail complete.

die·sel | dē´ zəl | —*noun* A type of fuel high in oil. The oil is burned by hot air in an engine instead of by an electric spark.

dis·ap·point·ed | dĭs ə **poin´** tĭd | —*adjective* Feeling a failure in hopes or wishes.

dis·card | dĭs **kärd´** | —*verb* To throw away.

dis·con·so·late | dĭs **kŏn´** sə lĭt | —*adjective* Sorrowful; unable to be consoled.

disk drive | dĭsk drĭv | —*noun* The device within a computer that operates the diskette in order to store or transmit information.

dis·mal | **dĭz´** məl | —*adjective* Causing gloom or depression; dreary.

dis·may | dĭs **mā´** | —*noun* A sudden loss of courage or confidence in the face of danger or trouble.

dis·suade | dĭ **swād´** | —*verb* To persuade a person against his chosen course of action; convince otherwise.

doorman

drum

dis·tress | dĭ **strĕs´** | —*noun* Serious danger or trouble.

di·vine | dĭ **vīn´** | —*adjective* Of or from God.

door·man | **dôr´** măn | —*noun* A man hired by a hotel, apartment, or business to open the door for patrons and provide other small services.

dor·mi·to·ry | **dôr´** mĭ tôr ē | or | **dôr´** mĭ tōr ē | —*noun* A building containing many bedrooms.

dou·blet | **dŭb´** lĭt | —*noun* A jacket, sometimes sleeveless, fitted to the body. Doublets were worn during Shakespeare's time.

doubt·ful | **dout´** fəl | —*adjective* Not sure or certain.

dra·mat·i·cal·ly | drə **măt´** ĭk lē | —*adverb* In a bold, impressive way; showing a strong flair and enthusiasm.

drip tray | drĭp trā | —*noun* The tray for catching condensation at the bottom of an old-fashioned freezer or refrigerator.

drought | drout | —*noun* A long period with little or no rain.

drove | drōv | —*noun* A crowd.

drum | drŭm | —*noun* A container shaped like a barrel.

dust dev·il | dŭst **dĕv´** əl | —*noun* A small whirlwind.

dwin·dle | **dwĭn´** dəl | —*verb* To become smaller or less; diminish.

---

ec·sta·sy | **ĕk´** stə sē | —*noun* A condition of delight, joy, or happiness.

e·di·tion | ĭ **dĭsh´** ən | —*noun* One out of a number of copies of a book, all printed at the same time.

Eif·fel Tow·er | ī´ fəl tou´ ər | —*noun* A tourist attraction in Paris, France. The Eiffel Tower is almost 1,000 feet high.

el·e·ment | **ĕl´** ə mənt | —*noun* A basic part of something.

em·bank·ment | ĕm **băngk´** mənt | —*noun* A mound of earth or stone built up to hold back water or hold up a road.

em·bar·rass | ĕm **băr´** əs | —*verb* To cause to feel uncomfortable and nervous.

em·broi·der | ĕm **broi´** dər | —*verb* To decorate cloth by sewing on designs.

en·chi·la·da | ĕn chə **lä´** də | —*noun* A tortilla stuffed with meat and cheese and served in a hot sauce.

en·coun·ter | ĕn **koun´** tər | —*noun* A meeting or confrontation, usually for a purpose.

en·dure | ĕn **door´** | or | ĕn **dyoor´** | —*verb* To put up with; stand; bear.

en·gi·neer | ĕn jə **nîr´** | —*noun* A person who is trained to build such things as bridges, canals, and oil wells.

en·list | ĕn **lĭst´** | —*verb* To join or cause to join the armed forces.

er·rand | **ĕr´** ənd | —*noun* A short trip taken to perform a task.

et cet·er·a | ĕt **sĕt´** ər ə | or | ĕt **sĕt´** rə | And other things of the same kind; and so forth. A Latin phrase meaning "and the rest." Used chiefly in abbreviated form: *etc.*

ex·ag·ger·ate | ĭg **zăj´** ə rāt´ | —*verb* To describe something as larger or more interesting than it really is.

ex·pense | ĭk **spĕns´** | —*noun* Something that requires the spending of money.

ex·per·i·ment | ĭk **spĕr´** ə mənt | —*noun* Something done to show a fact, test a theory, or find out what might happen.

ex·ploit | **ĕk´** sploit´ | —*noun* A heroic or brave deed.

Eiffel Tower

embroider

ă	pat	ĕ	pet	îr	fierce	oi	oil	ŭ	cut	ə	ago,
ā	pay	ē	be	ŏ	pot	oo	book	ûr	fur		item,
âr	care	ĭ	pit	ō	go	oo	boot	*th*	the		pencil,
ä	father	ī	pie	ô	paw,	yoo	abuse	th	thin		atom,
					for	ou	out	hw	which		circus
								zh	vision	ər	butter

flank

ă	pat	ĕ	pet
ā	pay	ē	be
âr	care	ĭ	pit
ä	father	ī	pie
îr	fierce	oi	oil
ŏ	pot	oŏ	book
ō	go	oō	boot
ô	paw,	yoō	abuse
	for	ou	out
ŭ	cut	ə	ago,
ûr	fur		item,
th	the		pencil,
th	thin		atom,
hw	which		circus
zh	vision	ər	butter

foal

fab·ric | făb´ rĭk | —*noun* A piece of cloth.

fal·ter | fôl´ tər | —*verb* To move unsteadily; stumble.

fa·nat·ic | fə năt´ ĭk | —*noun* A person who believes in or loves something so much that he does foolish things for it.

fare | fâr | —*noun* The price of a ride on a bus, train, or other vehicle.

fas·ci·nate | făs´ ə nāt´ | —*verb* To attract and interest very strongly.

fas·ci·nat·ed | făs´ ə nāt´ əd | —*adjective* Attracted and interested very strongly.

fate·ful | fāt´ fəl | —*adjective* Life-changing; unavoidable.

feat | fēt | —*noun* An act or deed, especially a skillful one.

fend | fĕnd | —*verb* To provide for oneself; survive.

fidg·et | fĭj´ ĭt | —*verb* To move some part of the body restlessly.

fig·ure | fĭg´ yər | —*verb* To work out by using numbers.

file | fīl | —*noun* A tool with a rough surface, used for smoothing, scraping, and cutting.

fit[1] | fĭt | —*noun* A sudden onset of a strong emotional or physical reaction.

fit[2] | fĭt | —*adjective* To be in the proper condition for a task; physically fit.

flank | flăngk | —*noun* The part between the hip and the ribs on either side of the body of an animal or person; the side.

flan·nel | flăn´ əl | —*noun* A soft cloth made of cotton or wool.

floun·der | floun´ dər | —*verb* To move in a clumsy way or with difficulty; struggle.

flus·tered | flŭs´ tərd | —*adjective* Nervous, excited, confused.

foal | fōl | —*noun* A young horse, zebra, or donkey.

fore·shad·ow | fôr shăd´ ō | or | fŏr shăd´ ō | —*verb* To hint at or suggest in advance.

for·lorn | fôr lôrn´ | —*adjective* Sad; without hope.

for·sake | fôr sāk´ | —*verb* To give up; leave; abandon.

for·tune | fôr´ chən | —*noun* A person's life's work and social standing; success; wealth.

frame | frām | —*noun* A form that holds something; a supporting structure.

fraz·zle | frăz´ əl | —*verb* To fluster.

fret | frĕt | —*verb* To worry; usually to worry out loud or to show by restlessness that one is worried.

---

fruit·less | froōt´ lĭs | —*adjective* Without success or results.

fu·gi·tive | fyoō´ jĭ tĭv | —*noun* A person running away, especially from the law.

gadg·et | găj´ ĭt | —*noun* A small, unusual tool or mechanical device.

gal·le·on | găl´ ē ən | or | găl´ yən | —*noun* A large sailing ship with three masts that was used mainly during the sixteenth century.

gap·ing | gā´ pĭng | —*adjective* Wide open, exposing depth.

gar·ret | găr´ ĭt | —*noun* An attic or loft at the top of a house.

gen·darme | zhän´ därm´ | —*noun* A French policeman.

ge·ra·ni·um | jĭ rā´ nē əm | —*noun* A plant with rounded clusters of red, pink, or white flowers. Geraniums are often grown in flowerpots.

girth | gûrth | —*noun* A strap that encircles a horse's belly.

glare | glâr | —*verb* To stare angrily.

glaze | glāz | —*noun* A thin, shiny coating.

gloat | glōt | —*verb* To feel or show great satisfaction.

gloom | gloōm | —*noun* Sadness; low spirits.

gor·geous | gôr´ jəs | —*adjective* Extremely beautiful; magnificent.

gra·cious | grā´ shəs | —*adjective* Courteous and kind; well-mannered.

grant | grănt | —*verb* To give or allow.

grin·go | grĭng´ gō | —*noun* A foreigner.

guf·faw | gə fô´ | —*noun* Hoarse laughter; a short, sudden laugh.

guild | gĭld | —*noun* A union of merchants or craftsmen in the Middle Ages. Guilds set standards of workmanship and looked after the welfare of their members.

guild chap·el | gĭld chăp´ əl | —*noun* (Medieval) A chapel owned by a guild and used for its religious ceremonies.

guise | gīz | —*noun* A disguise.

galleon

geranium

herald

H

hal·ter | hôl′ tər | —*noun* A set of ropes or straps for leading or tying an animal. A halter fits around an animal's nose and its neck just behind the ears.

har·mon·i·ca | här **mŏn**′ ĭ kə | —*noun* A small rectangular musical instrument containing one or more rows of metal reeds. It is played by blowing in and out through a set of holes.

haugh·ty | hô′ tē | —*adjective* Too proud of oneself; superior in one's own mind; arrogant.

hav·oc | **hăv**′ ək | —*noun* Destruction or terrible waste.

heed | hēd | —*noun* Close attention or consideration.

her·ald | **hĕr**′ əld | —*noun* A crier or messenger who reads official declarations.

husk

her·e·tic | **hĕr**′ ĭ tĭk | —*noun* One who holds false religious beliefs.

hes·i·tate | **hĕz**′ ĭ tāt′ | —*verb* To stop or wait because one is not sure.

hoist | hoist | —*verb* To raise up or lift, often with the help of a machine.

hum·ding·er | **hŭm**′ **dĭng**′ ər | —*noun* Something that is very special or amazing.

hu·mil·i·ate | hyo͞o **mĭl**′ ē āt′ | —*verb* To hurt the pride or self-respect of; make ashamed.

husk | hŭsk | —*noun* The dry outer covering of an ear of corn and of some other seeds and fruits.

I

i·dle | **īd**′ l | —*adjective* Not working or busy; doing nothing.

il·lus·tra·tor | **ĭl**′ ə strāt ər | —*noun* A person who makes pictures or diagrams for printed and other visual material.

im·pact | **ĭm**′ păkt | —*noun* The action of one object striking against another; collision.

im·pres·sion | ĭm **prĕsh**′ ən | —*noun* An effect, image, or feeling that stays in the mind.

in·dig·nant | ĭn **dĭg**′ nənt | —*adjective* Feeling or showing anger about something that is unfair, mean, or bad.

in·di·vis·i·ble | ĭn də **vĭz**′ ə bəl | —*adjective* Not capable of being divided.

in·hab·it·ed | ĭn **hăb**′ ĭ tĭd | —*adjective* Lived in; made to be home.

in·quis·i·tive | ĭn **kwĭz**′ ĭ tĭv | —*adjective* Eager to learn.

in·sane | ĭn **sān**′ | —*adjective* Of, showing, or affected by a serious mental illness; crazy; mad.

in·stinc·tive·ly | ĭn **stĭngk**′ tĭv lē | —*adverb* Automatically; without thought.

in·stru·ment pan·el | **ĭn**′ strə mənt **păn**′ əl | —*noun* A board of controlling devices and scales used to operate a complicated machine.

in·ter·cede | **ĭn**′ tər **sēd**′ | —*verb* To plead on behalf of another.

in·ter·mis·sion | **ĭn**′ tər **mĭsh**′ ən | —*noun* An interruption or recess in activity; a break.

J

jus·ti·fy | **jŭs**′ tə fī′ | —*verb* To show or prove to be just, fair, and right.

K

kit | kĭt | —*noun* Shortened form of *kitten*. The young of certain animals such as foxes or squirrels.

L

la·dle | **lād**′ l | —*verb* To dip out a liquid using a cup-shaped spoon that has a long handle; to use a ladle.

in·ter·na·tion·al | **ĭn**′ tər **năsh**′ ə nəl | —*adjective* Of or between two or more nations or their people.

in·ter·state | **ĭn**′ tər stāt′ | —*adjective* Between states.

in·va·sion | ĭn **vā**′ zhən | —*noun* The act of forcefully entering a country by military power.

in·vent | ĭn **vĕnt**′ | —*verb* To think up and make; create something that did not exist before.

i·tal·ic | ĭ **tăl**′ ĭk | or | ī **tăl**′ ĭk | —*noun* A style of printing with the letters slanting to the right.

I

italic

knapsack

knap·sack | **năp**′ săk′ | —*noun* A canvas or leather bag made to be worn on the back. A knapsack is used to carry clothing, equipment, or supplies on a hike or march.

la·goon | lə **go͞on**′ | —*noun* A shallow body of water that is usually connected to a larger body of water, such as an ocean. A lagoon is often surrounded by coral reefs.

ladle

lariat

lever

land·ing | lăn´ dĭng | —*noun* A place where boats can unload; a wharf or pier.

lar·i·at | lăr´ ē ət | —*noun* A long rope with a sliding noose at one end, used especially to catch horses or cattle.

lar·va | lär´ və | —*noun* An insect in an early form, when it has just hatched from an egg. A larva has a soft body and looks like a worm. A caterpillar is a larva.

las·so | lăs´ ō | or | lă sōō´ | —*verb* To catch with a lasso or lariat.

lav·ish | lăv´ ĭsh | —*adjective* To give generously.

lay·out | lā´ out´ | —*noun* The arrangement of furniture or other structures in a room or building.

leath·er | lĕth´ ər | —*noun* A material made from animal skin or hide that has been cleaned and tanned.

leg·end | lĕj´ ənd | —*noun* A story that has been handed down from earlier times.

ă	pat	ĕ	pet
ā	pay	ē	be
âr	care	ĭ	pit
ä	father	ī	pie
îr	fierce	oi	oil
ŏ	pot	ŏŏ	book
ō	go	ōō	boot
ô	paw,	yōō	abuse
	for	ou	out
ŭ	cut	ə	ago,
ûr	fur		item,
th	the		pencil,
th	thin		atom,
hw	which		circus
zh	vision	ər	butter

mag·net | măg´ nĭt | —*noun* A piece of metal or rock that attracts iron, steel, and some other substances.

make·shift | māk´ shĭft´ | —*adjective* A quick substitute, usually invented in an emergency.

male | māl | —*noun* A person who is a man or a boy.

lev·er | lĕv´ ər | or | lē´ vər | —*noun* A simple machine made up of a strong, stiff bar that rests on a fixed point on which it turns. It is used to lift heavy things.

limb | lĭm | —*noun* One of the larger branches of a tree.

Lim·burg·er cheese | lĭm´ bûr´ gər chēz | —*noun* A cheese with a strong smell.

lo·co | lō´ kō | —*adjective* Crazy; insane.

loft | lôft | or | lŏft | —*noun* An open space under a roof; an attic.

loop·hole | lōōp´ hōl | —*noun* A mistake in a written or verbal contract that allows one party to avoid his obligation.

lope | lōp | —*verb* To run with a rolling stride.

low·er·ing | lou´ ər ĭng | or | lour´ ĭng | —*adjective* Dark, with gathering clouds.

lunge | lŭnj | —*verb* A sudden, forceful movement forward.

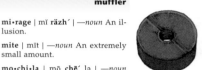
M

mal·e·mute | măl´ ə myōōt´ | —*noun* An Alaskan sled dog that looks like a husky.

man·gy | măn´ jē | —*adjective* Having bare or dirty spots; shabby.

man·ta ray | măn´ tə rā | —*noun* A fish with a long, flat body shaped like wings or like a mantle.

---

man·u·script | măn´ yə skrĭpt´ | —*noun* A book written by hand or by typewriter. Often a writer sends a manuscript to a publisher, who makes it into a printed book.

mar·i·gold | măr´ ĭ gōld | or | mâr´ ĭ gōld | —*noun* A garden plant that has orange, yellow, or reddish flowers.

mar·ma·lade | măr´ mə lād´ | —*noun* A jam made from sugar and the pulp and rind of fruits.

mas·sive | măs´ ĭv | —*adjective* Very large and heavy; huge.

mat·ted | măt´ ĭd | —*adjective* Thick, tangled, or twisted.

me·chan·ic | mə kăn´ ĭk | —*noun* A person who is skilled in making, using, or repairing machines.

men·tal | mĕn´ tl | —*adjective* Of, in, or done by the mind.

mer·chan·dise | mûr´ chən dīz´ | or | mûr´ chən dīs´ | —*noun* Things bought and sold; goods.

mer·chant | mûr´ chənt | —*noun* A person who makes money by buying and selling goods.

mill·stone | mĭl´ stōn | —*noun* One of two large, round, flat stones used to grind grain.

min·i·a·ture | mĭn´ ē ə chər | or | mĭn´ ə chər | —*adjective* Much smaller than the usual size.

mi·rac·u·lous | mĭ răk´ yə ləs | —*adjective* Like a miracle.

mi·rage | mĭ räzh´ | —*noun* An illusion.

mite | mīt | —*noun* An extremely small amount.

mo·chi·la | mō chē´ lə | —*noun* (Spanish). A leather knapsack, sometimes made to fit over a saddle.

moist | moist | —*adjective* Slightly wet; damp.

mold | mōld | —*noun* A hollow container that is made in a particular shape. A liquid or soft material, such as wax, gelatin, or plaster, is put into a mold. When the material hardens, it takes the shape of the mold.

moor·ing | mōōr´ ĭng | —*noun* A stable, secure place where a boat can be tied.

Mo·ra·vi·an | mə rā´ vē ən | —*noun* A Protestant denomination.

mo·sey | mō´ zē | —*verb* To move or stroll along.

mount | mount | —*noun* A horse or other animal for riding.

mount·ed | mount´ əd | —*adjective* Put in a suitable place for display or use.

move·ment | mōōv´ mənt | —*noun* The work, membership, or cause of a group of people who are trying to achieve a social or political goal.

muf·fler | mŭf´ lər | —*noun* A long scarf worn around the neck.

millstone

mochila

mold

muffler

Glossary

mush[1] | mŭsh | —*noun* A journey by sled dog; a command to a dog sled to go.

mush[2] | mŭsh | —*verb* To travel by dogsled.

nar·ra·tor | năr´ ăt ər | —*noun* One who tells a story or makes a report.

ne·glect | nĭ glĕkt´ | —*verb* To fail to care for or give proper attention to.

ne·go·ti·ate | nĭ gō´ shē āt | —*verb* To discuss or talk over in order to reach an agreement or settlement.

noose | nōōs | —*noun* A loop formed in a rope with a kind of knot that lets the loop tighten as the rope is pulled.

nurse

no·tice | nō´ tĭs | —*noun* An announcement in a public place or publication.

no·tion | nō´ shən | —*noun* A sudden idea or desire.

no·to·ri·ous | nō tôr´ ē əs | or | nō tōr´ ē əs | —*adjective* Well known for something bad or unpleasant.

nurse | nûrs | —*noun* A woman who is hired to take care of someone else's child or children.

o·blige | ə blīj´ | —*verb* To make grateful or thankful.

o·le·o | ō´ lē ō´ | —*noun* A food made as a substitute for butter; margarine.

o·pin·ion | ə pĭn´ yən | —*noun* A judgment based on special knowledge and given by an expert.

o·ral | ôr´ əl | or | ōr´ əl | —*adjective* Spoken instead of written.

or·dain | ôr dān´ | —*verb* To install as a minister, priest, or rabbi by means of a formal ceremony.

or·ner·y | ôr´ nə rē | —*adjective* Stubborn and high-spirited; mischievous.

or·phan | ôr´ fən | —*noun* A child whose parents are dead.

ă pat	ĕ pet	îr fierce	oi oil	ŭ cut	ə ago,
ā pay	ē be	ŏ pot	ŏŏ book	ûr fur	item,
âr care	ĭ pit	ō go	ōō boot	*th* the	pencil,
ä father	ī pie	ô paw,	yōō abuse	th thin	atom,
		for	ou out	hw which	circus
				zh vision	ər butter

---

pal·met·to | păl mĕt´ ō | or | păl mĕt´ ō | —*noun* A palm tree with leaves shaped like fans.

pan | păn | —*verb* To wash dirt or gravel in a pan in search of gold.

par·ka | pär´ kə | —*noun* A warm jacket with a hood. Parkas are often lined with fur.

pars·ley | pär´ slē | —*noun* A plant with feathery or curly leaves that are used to flavor or decorate food.

pas·sage | păs´ ĭj | —*noun* 1. A journey or trip, especially on a ship. 2. A part of a written work.

pas·ture | păs´ chər | or | păs´ chər | —*noun* A piece of land covered with grass and other plants that are eaten by horses, cattle, sheep, or other animals that graze.

pau·per | pô´ pər | —*noun* A common man who is very poor.

peal | pēl | —*noun* A loud ringing of a set of bells.

peas·ant | pĕz´ ənt | —*noun* A person who belongs to the group or class of small farmers and farm workers in Europe.

pe·des·tri·an | pə dĕs´ trē ən | —*noun* A person who travels on foot.

peer | pîr | —*verb* To look closely in order to see something clearly; stare.

per·form·ance | pər fôr´ məns | —*noun* The way in which something or someone works.

Per·sian cat | pûr´ zhən kăt | —*noun* A cat with long, silky fur, often kept as a pet.

pe·so | pā´ sō | —*noun* A Mexican unit of money similar to the American dollar bill but of less value.

phar·ma·cist | fär´ mə sĭst | —*noun* A person who is trained to prepare drugs and medicines; a druggist.

phi·los·o·pher | fĭ lŏs´ ə fər | —*noun* A person who is a scholar; one who prefers to think rather than to resort to force or action.

pi·ty | pĭt´ ē | —*noun* A feeling of sorrow for another's suffering.

play·wright | plā´ rīt | —*noun* A person who writes plays.

plot | plŏt | —*noun* The sequence of events in a story or play.

plumb | plŭm | —*adverb* Totally.

pneu·mo·nia | nōō mōn´ yə | or | nyōō mōn´ yə | —*noun* A serious disease of the lungs.

po·li·o | pō´ lē ō´ | —*noun* Poliomyelitis. A disease that can cause paralysis, damage to the muscles, and sometimes death. Poliomyelitis affects mainly children and young people, but a vaccine can now prevent it.

palmetto

parka

peso

porch

portico

pupa

po·lit·i·cal | pə lĭt´ ĭ kəl | —*adjective* Concerning the affairs or activities of government.

porch | pôrch | or | pōrch | —*noun* A section with a roof that is attached to the outside of a house.

port | pôrt | or | pōrt | —*noun* A harbor and the area of a harbor where boats are loaded and unloaded.

por·ti·co | pôr´ tĭ kō | or | pōr´ tĭ kō | —*noun* A porch or walk whose roof is held up by columns.

post | pōst | —*noun* A straight piece of wood or metal set up in the ground.

post·man | pōst´ mən | —*noun* A letter carrier; mailman.

pot·pour·ri | pō pʊ̄ rē´ | —*noun* A collection of pretty or fragrant odds and ends.

pre·mi·um | prē´ mē əm | —*noun* A high-quality gasoline.

pre·serves | prĭ zûrvz´ | —*noun* Fruit cooked with sugar to keep it from spoiling.

prim | prĭm | —*adjective* Overly proper.

pri·or·i·ty | prī ôr´ ĭ tē | —*noun* Something of first importance.

priv·i·lege | prĭv´ ə lĭj | —*noun* A special right or permission given to a person or group.

pros·per | prŏs´ pər | —*verb* To be successful; do well; thrive.

prov·ince | prŏv´ ĭns | —*noun* A big division of a country.

pro·vi·sion | prə vĭzh´ ən | —*noun* The act of giving what is needful or useful.

pub·lish·er | pŭb´ lĭ shər | —*noun* A person or company that produces and sells printed materials, such as books, magazines, or newspapers.

pu·pa | pyʊ̄´ pə | —*noun* An insect during a resting stage while it is changing from a larva into an adult. A pupa is protected by an outer covering such as a cocoon.

Q

quar·rel | kwôr´ əl | or | kwŏr´ əl | —*noun* An angry argument.

quar·ry | kwôr´ ē | or | kwŏr´ ē | —*noun* An open place where stone is taken out by cutting or blasting.

quar·ry·men | kwôr´ ē mĕn | or | kwŏr´ ē mĕn | —*noun* Laborers who work in a quarry for stone cutting or blasting.

qua·ver | kwā´ vər | —*verb* To speak in a trembling, unsteady way.

quea·sy | kwē´ zē | —*adjective* Nauseated.

quest | kwĕst | —*noun* A pursuit or search for something greatly desired and worthwhile.

quick·sil·ver | kwĭk´ sĭl´ vər | —*noun* The element mercury or something that looks like it.

R

rad·ish | răd´ ĭsh | —*noun* A plant with a white root that has a strong, sharp taste. The skin of the root may be red or white.

rake | rāk | —*verb* To scrape with a hard object, such as a spur.

ranch | rănch | —*noun* A large farm on which cattle, sheep, or horses are raised.

ran·som | răn´ səm | —*noun* The amount of money demanded or paid so that a person being held prisoner may be set free.

re·act | rē ăkt´ | —*verb* To act in response to something else or because something else has happened; respond.

read·i·ness | rĕd´ ē nĭs | —*noun* A state of preparation or alertness.

re·cep·tion | rĭ sĕp´ shən | —*noun* A social gathering in honor of someone.

reck·less | rĕk´ lĭs | —*adjective* Without care or caution.

reck·on | rĕk´ ən | —*verb* To consider or to compute.

quilt | kwĭlt | —*noun* A covering for a bed. A quilt is made of two layers of cloth sewn together with a padding of cotton, feathers, or other material between.

quiv·er | kwĭv´ ər | —*verb* To shake with a slight vibrating motion; tremble.

quilt

rec·tor | rĕk´ tər | —*noun* A minister in charge of a church and parish.

reel | rēl | —*verb* To stagger.

re·flec·tion | rĭ flĕk´ shən | —*noun* Serious thought.

re·gret | rĭ grĕt´ | —*verb* To feel sorry about.

re·lay | rē´ lā | —*noun* A crew, group, or team that relieves another; a shift.

re·li·a·ble | rĭ lī´ ə bəl | —*adjective* Able to be relied or depended upon.

re·luc·tant·ly | rĭ lŭk´ tənt lē | —*adverb* Lacking inclination; not willingly.

re·plen·ish | rĭ plĕn´ ĭsh | —*verb* To refill.

rep·tile | rĕp´ tĭl | —*noun* Any of a group of animals that are cold-blooded and creep or crawl on the ground. Reptiles have a backbone and are covered with scales or hard plates. Snakes, turtles, and dinosaurs are reptiles.

radish

ă	pat	ĕ	pet
ā	pay	ē	be
âr	care	ĭ	pit
ä	father	ī	pie
îr	fierce	oi	oil
ŏ	pot	ʊ̄	book
ō	go	ʊ̄	boot
ô	paw,	yʊ̄	abuse
	for	ou	out
ū	cut	ə	ago,
ûr	fur		item,
th	the		pencil,
th	thin		atom,
hw	which		circus
zh	vision	ər	butter

rhododendron

re·pub·lic | rĭ **pŭb´** lĭk | —*noun* A form of government in which the power of government rests with the voters, who elect representatives to govern the country. A republic is usually headed by a president rather than a monarch.

rep·u·ta·tion | rĕp´ yə **tā´** shən | —*noun* The general worth or quality of someone or something as judged by others.

re·search | rĭ **sûrch´** | or | **rē´** sûrch´ | —*noun* The carefully organized study of a subject or problem.

re·spect·a·ble | rĭ **spĕk´** tə bəl | —*adjective* Proper in behavior or appearance.

re·spon·si·ble | rĭ **spŏn´** sə bəl | —*adjective* Being dependable or reliable; trustworthy.

rowel

rho·do·den·dron | rō´ də **dĕn´** drən | —*noun* A shrub with evergreen leaves and clusters of white, pinkish, or purplish flowers.

rhythm | **rĭth´** əm | —*noun* A regular repeating of a movement, action, or sounds.

rutabaga

sac·ri·fice | **săk´** rə fīs | —*noun* The act of giving up something valuable or desired for the sake of someone else.

sal·vage | **săl´** vĭj | —*verb* To save something from being damaged or destroyed.

ri·val | **rī´** vəl | —*noun* Someone who tries to do as well as or better than another; competitor.

roam | rōm | —*verb* To travel through an area without a goal or purpose.

ro·de·o | **rō´** dē ō | or | rō **dā´** ō| —*noun* A public show in which cowboys display their skills in horseback riding and compete in riding broncos or steers, roping cattle, and similar events.

row·el | **rou´** əl | —*noun* A wheel with sharp spikes around it.

rud·der | **rŭd´** ər | —*noun* A plate of wood or metal attached to the back of a boat beneath the waterline. The rudder is used to steer the boat.

run·way | **rŭn´** wā´ | —*noun* A smooth lane of level ground that airplanes use to take off and land.

ru·ta·ba·ga | rōō´ tə **bā´** gə | or | rōō´ tə bā´ gə | —*noun* An edible plant, something like a turnip.

sand·bar | **sănd´** bär | —*noun* A shoal or bar of sand built up by the current of a river. Small boats or fish are often caught on sandbars.

sap·ling | **săp´** lĭng | —*noun* A slender tree.

ă	pat	ĕ	pet	îr	fierce	oi	oil	ŭ	cut	ə	ago,
ā	pay	ē	be	ŏ	pot	ŏŏ	book	ûr	fur		item,
âr	care	ĭ	pit	ō	go	ōō	boot	*th*	the		pencil,
ä	father	ī	pie	ô	paw,	yōō	abuse	th	thin		atom,
					for	ou	out	hw	which		circus
								zh	vision	ər	butter

---

sap·phire | **săf´** īr | —*noun* A hard, deep-blue stone used as a gemstone.

saun·ter | **sôn´** tər | —*verb* To stroll or walk leisurely.

scep·ter | **sĕp´** tər | —*noun* A rod or staff that is held by a queen or king. It is a symbol of authority.

schol·ar | **skŏl´** ər | —*noun* A person who has a great deal of knowledge.

scold·ing | **skōl´** dĭng | —*noun* A long, sustained rebuke.

scow | skou | —*noun* A flat-bottomed boat used for big loads.

scrap | skrăp | —*noun* A tiny piece; a little bit.

scraw·ny | **skrô´** nē | —*adjective* Thin and bony.

scythe | sīth | —*noun* A tool with a long, curved blade attached to a long, bent handle. It is used for mowing and reaping.

se·cure | sĭ **kyōor´** | —*adjective* Strongly fastened; not likely to fall or break.

se·cu·ri·ty | sĭ **kyōor´** ĭ tē | —*noun* A system of guards, locks, and restrictions that ensures peace or secrecy.

sen·try | **sĕn´** trē | —*noun* A soldier or other person who is posted to watch for attacks and to check people coming and going; a guard.

se·quel | **sē´** kwəl | —*noun* A book or story that can be understood

as a separate work but also continues the story of another work.

shack·le | **shăk´** əl | —*noun* A metal bracelet, usually on the end of a chain, used for restraining a captive by the arm or leg.

shin·gle | **shĭng´** gəl | —*noun* One of many thin pieces of wood or other material laid in rows that overlap. Shingles are used to cover roofs of houses.

siege | sēj | —*noun* The act of surrounding a fort, city, or position for a long time by an enemy trying to capture it. During a siege food and supplies are cut off from those enclosed to force them to surrender.

sim·i·le | **sĭm´** ə lē | —*noun* A figure of speech that uses *like* or *as* to compare two different things.

sim·mer | **sĭm´** ər | —*verb* To cook below or just at the boiling point.

sit·u·a·tion | sĭch ōō **ā´** shən | —*noun* A condition or combination of circumstances; the way events or things are at a certain time.

skid | skĭd | —*verb* To slip or slide on a surface.

skit·ter | **skĭt´** ər | —*verb* Touched lightly, quickly, and repeatedly.

slack | slăk | —*adjective* Not tight; loose.

slaugh·ter | **slô´** tər | —*noun* The cruel and brutal murder of many persons.

sapphire

scythe

shackle

sorghum

sorrel

spire

spur

sleigh | slā | —*noun* A light vehicle or carriage on metal runners. It is usually drawn by a horse and used for traveling on ice or snow.

slen·der | slĕn´ dər | —*adjective* Having little width; thin; slim.

slick·er | slĭk´ ər | —*noun* A shiny, waterproof raincoat or poncho.

smug·gle | smŭg´ əl | —*verb* To bring into or take out of a country secretly or illegally.

snout | snout | —*noun* The long nose, jaws, or front part of the head of an animal. Pigs and alligators have snouts.

so·cia·ble | sō´ shə bəl | —*adjective* Liking other people; liking company; friendly.

sol·emn | sŏl´ əm | —*adjective* Very serious and grave.

sol·i·tar·y | sŏl´ ĭ tĕr ē | —*adjective* Existing or living alone.

so·lu·tion | sə lōō´ shən | —*noun* The solving of a problem.

sor·ghum | sôr´ gəm | —*noun* A grain often used to make syrup or to feed animals.

sor·rel | sôr´ əl | —*noun* A horse whose color is slightly orange to light brown.

source | sôrs | or | sōrs | —*noun* A place or thing from which something comes.

sour·dough | sour´ dō | —*noun* A settler in the Yukon who had to make his bread with sourdough instead of with yeast.

spar·row | spăr´ ō | —*noun* Any of several small brownish or grayish birds that are very common in cities.

spat | spăt | —*noun* A short quarrel.

spire | spīr | —*noun* The highest part of a building that tapers upward above a steeple or other structure.

spoil | spoil | —*verb* To become rotten or damaged so as to be bad to use.

spook | spōōk | —*verb* To startle or make nervous.

sprint | sprĭnt | —*verb* To run at top speed.

spur | spûr | —*noun* A sharp metal piece in the shape of a small wheel with spikes, worn on the heel of a person's boot. It is used to make a horse go faster.

stake | stāk | —*noun* A stick or post with a sharp end for driving into the ground as a marker, support, or part of a fence.

star·tle | stär´ tl | —*verb* 1. To cause to jump in surprise or fright. 2. To cause to be afraid; to cause wonder.

stead | stĕd | —*noun* A position or purpose held by one person as an exchange or replacement for another.

sten·cil | stĕn´ səl | —*noun* A sheet of paper or other material in which letters or figures have been cut so that when ink is applied to the sheet, the patterns will appear on the surface beneath.

still | stĭl | —*adjective* Without noise; quiet; silent.

stout | stout | —*adjective* Strong; firm; sturdy.

strad·dle | străd´ l | —*verb* To sit or stand so that each leg is on either side of something, as when sitting on a horse.

strait | strāt | —*adjective* (Archaic) Tight, confined.

strut | strŭt | —*verb* To walk in a proud manner.

stud | stŭd | —*verb* To dot onto a surface; sprinkle about.

stud·y | stŭd´ ē | —*noun* A room used for studying, reading, or working.

stu·por | stōō´ pər | —*noun* A daze; a state of confused inactivity.

sub·merged | səb mûrjd´ | —*adjective* Covered with water.

sub·mit | səb mĭt´ | —*verb* To yield to the control, influence, or authority of another.

sub·ti·tle | sŭb´ tīt l | —*noun* A second title used to explain a heading.

sul·len | sŭl´ ən | —*adjective* Showing bad humor; silent or angry; glum.

sul·try | sŭl´ trē | —*adjective* Very hot and humid.

sure·foot·ed | shōōr´ fŏŏt´ ĭd | —*adjective* Able to walk on steep surfaces without stumbling.

STENCIL

stencil

surf | sûrf | —*noun* The waves of the sea as they break upon the shore or the white foam that is on the beach.

sus·pend | sə spĕnd´ | —*verb* To halt any action for a period of time.

sus·pi·cious | sə spĭsh´ əs | —*adjective* Causing lack of trust or doubt in others.

swap | swŏp | —*verb* To trade items.

sym·bol·ize | sĭm´ bə līz | —*verb* To be a symbol of; represent; stand for.

sym·pa·thet·ic | sĭm pə thĕt´ ĭk | —*adjective* Showing or feeling understanding, pity, or kindness toward others.

syn·a·gogue | sĭn´ ə gŏg | or | sĭn´ ə gôg | —*noun* A building or place used by Jews for worship and religious instruction.

ă	pat	ĕ	pet
ā	pay	ē	be
âr	care	ĭ	pit
ä	father	ī	pie
îr	fierce	oi	oil
ŏ	pot	ŏŏ	book
ō	go	ōō	boot
ô	paw, for	yōō	abuse
		ou	out
ŭ	cut	ə	ago, item, pencil, atom, circus
ûr	fur		
th	the		
th	thin		
hw	which		
zh	vision	ər	butter

tad·pole | tăd´ pōl | —*noun* A frog or toad when it has just been hatched and lives underwater. In this stage it has gills, a tail, and no legs. The gills and tail disappear as the legs develop and the frog or toad becomes fully grown.

tadpole

tai·lor | tā´ lər | —*noun* A person who makes, repairs, or alters clothing.

tal·ent·ed | tăl´ ən tĭd | —*adjective* Having a natural ability to do something well.

tan·gled | tăng´ gəld | —*adjective* Mixed together in a confused or twisted mass.

ta·per | tā´ pər | —*verb* To make or become gradually thinner at one end.

taunt | tônt | —*verb* To ridicule.

taw·ny | tô´ nē | —*noun* The color of tanned leather; a light shade of brown.

toll

tel·e·graph | tĕl´ ə grăf | —*noun* A system of sending messages over wire or radio to a special receiving station.

ten·or | tĕn´ ər | —*noun* A man's singing voice, higher than a baritone and lower than an alto.

ter·ror | tĕr´ ər | —*noun* 1. Great or intense fear.   2. A person or thing that causes such fear.

Thames Riv·er | tĕmz rĭv´ ər | —*noun* A large river in England that flows through London.

ther·a·py | thĕr´ ə pē | —*noun* A sustained treatment of a disability or injury to bring about a cure.

thick·et | thĭk´ ĭt | —*noun* A dense growth of shrubs or small trees.

thong | thŏng | or | thŏng | —*noun* A thin strip of leather used to fasten something, such as a sandal.

thor·ough·bred | thûr´ ō brĕd | or | thər´ ə brĕd | —*noun* A purebred animal.

thread·bare | thrĕd´ bâr | —*adjective* Frayed or worn.

til·ler | tĭl´ ər | —*noun* A lever or handle used to turn a rudder or steer a boat.

tol·er·ate | tŏl´ ə rāt | —*verb* To put up with; endure.

toll | tōl | —*verb* (archaic) To pull something.

top·ic | tŏp´ ĭk | —*noun* A single subject or theme within a larger work.

tow | tō | —*verb* To pull along behind with a chain, rope, or cable.

trade lan·guage | trād lăng´ gwĭj | —*noun* A well-known language from one set of people used by other nations, tribes, or races because it has been spread through the market industry of a certain large area.

tra·di·tion | trə dĭsh´ ən | —*noun* The practice of passing down ideas, customs, and beliefs from one generation to the next.

trag·e·dy | trăj´ ĭ dē | —*noun* A serious play that ends badly for the main character or characters.

tramp | trămp | —*verb* To go on foot.

tram·po·line | trăm´ pə lēn´ | or | trăm´ pə lĭn | —*noun* A sheet of canvas stretched across a metal frame and fastened with springs. Trampolines are used for jumping and other gymnastics.

trans·con·ti·nen·tal | trăns kŏn tə nĕn´ tl | —*adjective* Across the continent.

tran·scribe | trăn skrīb´ | —*verb* To write out completely.

trans·form | trăns fôrm´ | —*verb* To change very much in appearance or characteristics.

trans·gress | trăns grĕs´ | or | trănz grĕs´ | —*verb* To disobey a law or command; sin; do what God forbids.

trans·mit·ter | trăns mĭt´ ər | or | trănz mĭt´ ər | —*noun* A device that sends out electrical, radio, or television signals.

treach·er·ous | trĕch´ ər əs | —*adjective* Not dependable; dangerous.

trel·lis | trĕl´ ĭs | —*noun* A framework used for training climbing plants.

tri·al run | trī´ əl rŭn | —*noun* A preliminary test of a machine or vehicle that simulates actual use.

trop·i·cal | trŏp´ ĭ kəl | —*adjective* Of, like, or found in the very hot regions of the earth that are near the equator.

trampoline

trun·dling | trŭn´ dlĭng | —*verb* Moving or pulling along on wheels.

tum·ble·weed | tŭm´ bəl wēd | —*noun* A plant that, when it dies, breaks free and is blown about by the wind.

tun·dra | tŭn´ drə | —*noun* A large plain without trees in arctic regions. Mosses and small shrubs are the only kinds of plant life that grow on it. The ground beneath the surface of tundra remains frozen all year round.

tumbleweed

ty·ran·ni·cal | tĭ răn´ ĭ kəl | or | tī răn´ ĭ kəl | —*adjective* Cruel or unjust.

ă	pat	ĕ	pet	îr	fierce	oi	oil	ŭ	cut	ə	ago,
ā	pay	ē	be	ŏ	pot	ōō	book	ûr	fur		item,
âr	care	ĭ	pit	ō	go	ōō	boot	th	the		pencil,
ä	father	ī	pie	ô	paw,	yōō	abuse	th	thin		atom,
					for	ou	out	hw	which		circus
								zh	vision	ər	butter

U

vehicles

un·der·brush | ŭn′ dər brŭsh | —*noun* Small trees, shrubs, and other plants that grow thickly beneath tall trees in a forest or wooded area.

un·in·tel·li·gi·ble | ŭn ĭn **tĕl′** ĭ jə bəl | —*adjective* Not able to be understood.

un·tame | ŭn **tām′** | —*adjective* Not able to be subjected; not gentle.

ur·chin | **ûr′** chĭn | —*noun* A small, playful child; a child with no money or home.

V

veranda

val·our or **val·or** | **văl′** ər | —*noun* Courage and strength in battle.

val·u·a·ble | **văl′** yŏŏ ə bəl | or | **văl′** yə bəl | —*adjective* Worth much money.

ve·hi·cle | **vē′** ĭ kəl | —*noun* Anything used for moving people or goods; a means of transportation. Cars, trucks, trains, wagons, bicycles, airplanes, rockets, sleds, and ships are all vehicles.

ven·i·son | **vĕn′** ĭ sən | —*noun* Deer or elk when used for food.

ven·ture | **vĕn′** chər | —*verb* To take a risk with; expose to possible loss or danger.

ve·ran·da | və **răn′** də | —*noun* A porch or balcony with a roof.

ver·sion | **vûr′** zhən | or | **vûr′** shən | —*noun* A new form of something, based on an original model.

ves·ti·bule | **vĕs′** tə byŏŏl | —*noun* The area immediately inside the doorway of a building; a lobby.

vol·ume | **vŏl′** yŏŏm | or | **vŏl′** yəm | —*noun* One book of a set.

vol·un·teer | vŏl ən **tîr′** | —*verb* To give or offer, usually without being asked.

W

waistcoat

waist·coat | **wĕs′** kĭt | or | **wăst′** kōt | —*noun* A vest.

walk | wôk | —*noun* A place set apart or designated for walking.

wal·low | **wŏl′** ō | —*verb* To move in a rolling manner.

war·i·ly | **wâr′** ĭ lē | —*adverb* Carefully; cautiously.

watch | wŏch | —*noun* Someone who guards or protects.

---

wharf | hwôrf | or | wôrf | —*noun* A landing place or pier at which ships may tie up and load or unload.

whey | hwā | or | wā | —*noun* The watery part of milk that separates from the curds when milk turns sour.

whirl·wind | **hwûrl′** wĭnd | or | **wûrl′** wĭnd | —*noun* A wind or current of air that turns round and round, often violently, as a tornado.

whoop | hŏŏp | or | hwŏŏp | or | wŏŏp | —*noun* A loud cry or shout.

wid·owed | **wĭd′** ōd | —*adjective* Left without a husband or wife because of death.

wield | wēld | —*verb* To handle or swing a weapon or tool with great skill and power.

wince | wĭns | —*verb* To move or pull back quickly from something that is painful, dangerous, or frightening.

won·der·ful | **wŭn′** dər fəl | —*adjective* Causing wonder; marvelous; impressive.

work·out | **wûrk′** out | —*noun* Exercise or practice, especially in athletics.

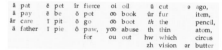

whirlwind

Y

yarn | yärn | —*noun* A long tale; a story, often adventurous or funny.

year·ling | **yîr′** lĭng | —*noun* An animal whose age is between one and two years.

Yu·kon | **yŏŏ′** kŏn | —*noun* A northern territory of Canada next to Alaska.

ă pat	ĕ pet	îr fierce	oi oil	ŭ cut	ə ago,
ā pay	ē be	ŏ pot	ŏŏ book	ûr fur	item,
âr care	ĭ pit	ō go	ŏŏ boot	th the	pencil,
ä father	ī pie	ô paw,	yŏŏ abuse	th thin	atom,
		for	ou out	hw which	circus
				zh vision	ər butter

Glossary

Appendix

Contents

The Classroom Management for Grouping games, Evaluation Materials, and Lesson Materials are intended to be used for making photocopies and student worksheets. See copyright page for limited license to copy.

Pages A24-A27 and A37-A38 are not used in Part 1 and appear only in Part 2.

Bible Action Truths

The quality and consistency of a man's decisions reflect his character. Christian character begins with justification, but it grows throughout the lifelong process of sanctification. God's grace is sufficient for the task, and a major part of God's gracious provision is His Word. The Bible provides the very "words of life" that instruct us in salvation and Christian living. By obeying God's commands and making godly decisions based on His Word, Christians can strengthen their character.

Too often Christians live by only vague guidance—for instance, that we should "do good" to all men. While doing good is desirable, more specific guidance will lead to more consistent decisions.

Consistent decisions are made when man acts on Bible principles—or Bible Action Truths. The thirty-seven Bible Action Truths (listed under eight general principles) provide Christians with specific goals for their actions and attitudes. Study the Scriptures indicated for a fuller understanding of the principles in Bible Action Truths.

Thousands have found this format helpful in identifying and applying principles of behavior. Yet, there is no "magic" in this formula. As you study the Word, you likely will find other truths that speak to you. The key is for you to study the Scriptures, look for Bible Action Truths, and be sensitive to the leading of the Holy Spirit.

1. **Salvation-Separation Principle**

   Salvation results from God's direct action. Although man is unable to work for this "gift of God," the Christian's reaction to salvation should be to separate himself from the world unto God.

   a. **Understanding Jesus Christ** (Matthew 3:17; 16:16; I Corinthians 15:3-4; Philippians 2:9-11) Jesus is the Son of God. He was sent to earth to die on the cross for our sins. He was buried but rose from the dead after three days.

   b. **Repentance and faith** (Luke 13:3; Isaiah 55:7; Acts 5:30-31; Hebrews 11:6; Acts 16:31) If we believe that Jesus died for our sins, we can accept Him as our Savior. We must be sorry for our sins, turn from them, confess them to God, and believe that He will forgive us.

   c. **Separation from the world** (John 17:6, 11, 14, 18; II Corinthians 6:14-18; I John 2:15-16; James 4:4; Romans 16:17-18; II John 10-11) After we are saved, we should live a different life. We should try to be like Christ and not live like those who are unsaved.

2. **Sonship-Servant Principle**

   Only by an act of God the Father could sinful man become a son of God. As a son of God, however, the Christian must realize that he has been "bought with a price"; he is now Christ's servant.

   a. **Authority** (Romans 13:1-7; I Peter 2:13-19; I Timothy 6:1-5; Hebrews 13:17; Matthew 22:21; I Thessalonians 5:12-13) We should respect, honor, and obey those in authority over us. (attentiveness, obedience)

   b. **Servanthood** (Philippians 2:7-8; Ephesians 6:5-8) Just as Christ was a humble servant while He was on earth, we should also be humble and obedient. (attentiveness, helpfulness, promptness, teamwork)

   c. **Faithfulness** (I Corinthians 4:2; Matthew 25:23; Luke 9:62)

We should do our work so that God and others can depend on us. (endurance, responsibility)

   d. **Goal setting** (Proverbs 13:12, 19; Philippians 3:13; Colossians 3:2; I Corinthians 9:24) To be faithful servants, we must set goals for our work. We should look forward to finishing a job and going on to something more. (dedication, determination, perseverance)

   e. **Work** (Ephesians 4:28; II Thessalonians 3:10-12) God never honors a lazy servant. He wants us to be busy and dependable workers. (cooperativeness, diligence, initiative, industriousness, thoroughness)

   f. **Enthusiasm** (Colossians 3:23; Romans 12:11) We should do *all* tasks with energy and with a happy, willing spirit. (cheerfulness)

3. **Uniqueness-Unity Principle**

   No one is a mere person; God has created each individual a unique being. But because God has an overall plan for His creation, each unique member must contribute to the unity of the entire body.

   a. **Self-concept** (Psalm 8:3-8; 139; II Corinthians 5:17; Ephesians 2:10; 4:1-3, 11-13; II Peter 1:10) We are special creatures in God's plan. He has given each of us special abilities to use in our lives for Him.

   b. **Mind** (Philippians 2:5; 4:8; II Corinthians 10:5; Proverbs 23:7; Luke 6:45; Proverbs 4:23; Romans 7:23, 25; Daniel 1:8; James 1:8) We should give our hearts and minds to God. What we do and say really begins in our minds. We should try to think of ourselves humbly as Christ did when He lived on earth. (orderliness)

   c. **Emotional control** (Galatians 5:24; Proverbs 16:32; 25:28; II Timothy 1:7; Acts 20:24) With the help of God and the power of the Holy Spirit, we should have control over our feelings. We must be careful not to act out of anger. (flexibility, self-control)

   d. **Body as a temple** (I Corinthians 3:16-17; 6:19-20) We should remember that our bodies are the dwelling place of God's Holy Spirit. We should keep ourselves pure, honest, and dedicated to God's will.

   e. **Unity of Christ and the church** (John 17:21; Ephesians 2:19-22; 5:23-32; II Thessalonians 3:6, 14-15) Since we are saved, we are now part of God's family and should unite ourselves with others to worship and grow as Christians. Christ is the head of His church, which includes all believers. He wants us to work together as His church in carrying out His plans, but He forbids us to work in fellowship with disobedient brethren.

4. **Holiness-Habit Principle**

   Believers are declared holy as a result of Christ's finished action on the cross. Daily holiness of life, however, comes from forming godly habits. A Christian must consciously establish godly patterns of action; he must develop habits of holiness.

   a. **Sowing and reaping** (Galatians 6:7-8; Hosea 8:7; Matthew 6:1-8) We must remember that we will be rewarded according to the kind of work we have done. If we are faithful, we will be rewarded. If we are unfaithful, we will not be rewarded. We cannot fool God. (thriftiness)

   b. **Purity** (I Thessalonians 4:1-7; I Peter 1:22) We should try to live lives that are free from sin. We should keep our minds, words, and deeds clean and pure.

c. **Honesty** (II Corinthians 8:21; Romans 12:17; Proverbs 16:8; Ephesians 4:25) We should not lie. We should be honest in every way. Even if we could gain more by being dishonest, we should still be honest. God sees all things. (fairness)

d. **Victory** (I Corinthians 10:13; Romans 8:37; I John 5:4; John 16:33; I Corinthians 15:57-58) If we constantly try to be pure, honest, and Christlike, with God's help we will be able to overcome temptations.

5. Love-Life Principle

We love God because He first loved us. God's action of manifesting His love to us through His Son demonstrates the truth that love must be exercised. Since God acted in love toward us, believers must act likewise by showing godly love to others.

a. **Love** (I John 3:11, 16-18; 4:7-21; Ephesians 5:2; I Corinthians 13; John 15:17) God's love to us was the greatest love possible. We should, in turn, show our love for others by our words and actions. (courtesy, compassion, hospitality, kindness, thankfulness to men, thoughtfulness)

b. **Giving** (II Corinthians 9:6-8; Proverbs 3:9-10; Luke 6:38) We should give cheerfully to God the first part of all we earn. We should also give to others unselfishly. (hospitality, generosity, sharing, unselfishness)

c. **Evangelism and missions** (Psalm 126:5-6; Matthew 28:18-20; Romans 1:16-17; II Corinthians 5:11-21) We should be busy telling others about the love of God and His plan of salvation. We should share in the work of foreign missionaries by our giving and prayers.

d. **Communication** (Ephesians 4:22-29; Colossians 4:6; James 3:2-13; Isaiah 50:4) We should have control of our tongues so that we will not say things displeasing to God. We should encourage others and be kind and helpful in what we say.

e. **Friendliness** (Proverbs 18:24; 17:17; Psalm 119:63) We should be friendly to others, and we should be loyal to those who love and serve God. (loyalty)

6. Communion-Consecration Principle

Because sin separates man from God, any communion between man and God must be achieved by God's direct action of removing sin. Once communion is established, the believer's reaction should be to maintain a consciousness of this fellowship by living a consecrated life.

a. **Bible study** (I Peter 2:2-3; II Timothy 2:15; Psalm 119) To grow as Christians, we must spend time with God daily by reading His Word. (reverence for the Bible)

b. **Prayer** (I Chronicles 16:11; I Thessalonians 5:17; John 15:7, 16; 16:24; Psalm 145:18; Romans 8:26-27) We should bring all our requests to God, trusting Him to answer them in His own way.

c. **Spirit-filled** (Ephesians 5:18-19; Galatians 5:16, 22-23; Romans 8:13-14; I John 1:7-9) We should let the Holy Spirit rule in our hearts and show us what to say and do. We should not say and do just what we want to do, for those things are often wrong and harmful to others. (gentleness, joyfulness, patience)

d. **Clear conscience** (I Timothy 1:19; Acts 24:16) To be good Christians, we cannot have wrong acts or thoughts or words bothering our consciences. We must confess them to God and to those people against whom we have sinned. We cannot live lives close to God if we have guilty consciences.

e. **Forgiveness** (Ephesians 4:30-32; Luke 17:3-4; Colossians 3:13; Matthew 18:15-17; Mark 11:25-26) We must ask forgiveness of God when we have done wrong. Just as God forgives our sins freely, we should forgive others when they do wrong things to us.

7. Grace-Gratitude Principle

Grace is unmerited favor. Man does not deserve God's grace. However, after God bestows His grace, believers should react with an overflow of gratitude.

a. **Grace** (I Corinthians 15:10; Ephesians 2:8-9) Without God's grace we would be sinners on our way to hell. He loved us when we did not deserve His love and provided for us a way to escape sin's punishment by the death of His Son on the cross.

b. **Exaltation of Christ** (Colossians 1:12-21; Ephesians 1:17-23; Philippians 2:9-11; Galatians 6:14; Hebrews 1:2-3; John 1:1-4, 14; 5:23) We should realize and remember at all times the power, holiness, majesty, and perfection of Christ, and we should give Him the praise and glory for everything that is accomplished through us.

c. **Praise** (Psalm 107:8; Hebrews 13:15; I Peter 2:9; Ephesians 1:6; I Chronicles 16:23-36; 29:11-13) Remembering God's great love and goodness toward us, we should continually praise His name. (thankfulness to God)

d. **Contentment** (Philippians 4:11; I Timothy 6:6-8; Psalm 77:3; Proverbs 15:16; Hebrews 13:5) Money, houses, cars, and all things on earth will last only for a little while. God has given us just what He meant for us to have. We should be happy and content with what we have, knowing that God will provide for us all that we need. We should also be happy wherever God places us.

e. **Humility** (I Peter 5:5-6; Philippians 2:3-4) We should not be proud and boastful but should be willing to be quiet and in the background. Our reward will come from God on Judgment Day, and men's praise to us here on earth will not matter at all. Christ was humble when He lived on earth, and we should be like Him.

8. Power-Prevailing Principle

Believers can prevail only as God gives the power. "I can do all things through Christ." God is the source of our power used in fighting the good fight of faith.

a. **Faith in God's promises** (II Peter 1:4; Philippians 4:6; Romans 4:16-21; I Thessalonians 5:18; Romans 8:28; I Peter 5:7; Hebrews 3:18; 4:11) God always remains true to His promises. Believing that He will keep all the promises in His Word, we should be determined fighters for Him.

b. **Faith in the power of the Word of God** (Hebrews 4:12; Jeremiah 23:29; Psalm 119; I Peter 1:23-25) God's Word is powerful and endures forever. All other things will pass away, but God's Word shall never pass away because it is written to us from God, and God is eternal.

c. **Fight** (Ephesians 6:11-17; II Timothy 4:7-8; I Timothy 6:12; I Peter 5:8-9) God does not have any use for lazy or cowardly fighters. We must work and fight against sin, using the Word of God as our weapon against the Devil. What we do for God now will determine how much He will reward us in heaven.

d. **Courage** (I Chronicles 28:20; Joshua 1:9; Hebrews 13:6; Ephesians 3:11-12; Acts 4:13, 31) God has promised us that He will not forsake us; therefore, we should not be afraid to speak out against sin. We should remember that we are armed with God's strength.

Bible Promises

A. Liberty from Sin—Born into God's spiritual kingdom, a Christian is enabled to live right and gain victory over sin through faith in Christ. (Romans 8:3-4—"For what the law could not do, in that it was weak through the flesh, God sending his own Son in the likeness of sinful flesh, and for sin, condemned sin in the flesh: that the righteousness of the law might be fulfilled in us, who walk not after the flesh, but after the Spirit.")

B. Guiltless by the Blood—Cleansed by the blood of Christ, the Christian is pardoned from the guilt of his sins. He does not have to brood or fret over his past because the Lord has declared him righteous. (Romans 8:33—"Who shall lay any thing to the charge of God's elect? It is God that justifieth." Isaiah 45:24—"Surely, shall one say, in the Lord have I righteousness and strength: even to him shall men come; and all that are incensed against him shall be ashamed.")

C. Basis for Prayer—Knowing that his righteousness comes entirely from Christ and not from himself, the Christian is free to plead the blood of Christ and to come before God in prayer at any time. (Romans 5:1-2—"Therefore being justified by faith, we have peace with God through our Lord Jesus Christ: by whom also we have access by faith into this grace wherein we stand, and rejoice in hope of the glory of God.")

D. Identified in Christ—The Christian has the assurance that God sees him as a son of God, perfectly united with Christ. He also knows that he has access to the strength and the grace of Christ in his daily living. (Galatians 2:20—"I am crucified with Christ: nevertheless I live; yet not I, but Christ liveth in me: and the life which I now live in the flesh I live by the faith of the Son of God, who loved me, and gave himself for me." Ephesians 1:3—"Blessed be the God and Father of our Lord Jesus Christ, who hath blessed us with all spiritual blessings in heavenly places in Christ.")

E. Christ as Sacrifice—Christ was a willing sacrifice for the sins of the world. His blood covers every sin of the believer and pardons the Christian for eternity. The purpose of His death and resurrection was to redeem a people to Himself. (Isaiah 53:4-5—"Surely he hath borne our griefs, and carried our sorrows: yet we did esteem him stricken, smitten of God, and afflicted. But he was wounded for our transgressions, he was bruised for our iniquities: the chastisement of our peace was upon him; and with his stripes we are healed." John 10:27-28—"My sheep hear my voice, and I know them, and they follow me: and I give unto them eternal life; and they shall never perish, neither shall any man pluck them out of my hand.")

F. Christ as Intercessor—Having pardoned them through His blood, Christ performs the office of High Priest in praying for His people. (Hebrews 7:25—"Wherefore he is able also to save them to the uttermost that come unto God by him, seeing he ever liveth to make intercession for them." John 17:20—"Neither pray I for these alone, but for them also which shall believe on me through their word.")

G. Christ as Friend—In giving salvation to the believer, Christ enters a personal, loving relationship with the Christian that cannot be ended. This relationship is understood and enjoyed on the believer's part through fellowship with the Lord through Bible reading and prayer. (Isaiah 54:5—"For thy Maker is thine husband; the Lord of hosts is his name; and thy Redeemer the Holy One of Israel; The God of the whole earth shall he be called." Romans 8:38-39—"For I am persuaded, that neither death, nor life, nor angels, nor principalities, nor powers, nor things present, nor things to come, nor height, nor depth, nor any other creature, shall be able to separate us from the love of God, which is in Christ Jesus our Lord.")

H. God as Father—God has appointed Himself to be responsible for the well-being of the Christian. He both protects and nourishes the believer, and it was from Him that salvation originated. (Isaiah 54:17—"No weapon that is formed against thee shall prosper; and every tongue that shall rise against thee in judgment thou shalt condemn. This is the heritage of the servants of the Lord, and their righteousness is of me, saith the Lord." Psalm 103:13—"Like as a father pitieth his children, so the Lord pitieth them that fear him.")

I. God as Master—God is sovereign over all creation. He orders the lives of His people for His glory and their good. (Romans 8:28—"And we know that all things work together for good to them that love God, to them who are the called according to his purpose.")

Phonics Generalizations

Broad Phonics Generalizations

1. Closed syllable generalization: When the only vowel letter in a word (or syllable) is followed by one or more consonant letters, usually the vowel letter is short *(lamp, bed, inn, rod, cup)*.

2. Silent *e* generalization: A vowel letter is usually long when it is followed by one consonant letter and a silent *e* *(name, slide, hope, rule)*.

3. Open syllable generalization: When the only vowel letter in a word (or syllable) comes at the end of the word (or syllable), often that vowel letter is long *(me, ta•ble)*.

4. *R*-influenced vowel generalization: An *r* following a vowel letter usually changes the sound of the vowel letter. (See Special Phonics Generalizations.)

5. Semivowel generalization: When a *w* or *y* follows a vowel letter, it acts as a vowel letter, helping to make the vowel sound *(pray, snow, new, obey)*.

6. Two-vowel (first vowel letter long) generalization: When two vowel letters are together in a word, often the first one is long and the second one is silent *(pail, seed, dream, pie, boat, blue)*.

7. Two-vowel (special sound) generalization: Two vowel letters sometimes work together to make a special sound. (See Special Phonics Generalizations.)

8. Unaccented syllable generalization: In an unaccented syllable, the vowel sound is often schwa, /ə/, regardless of what vowel letters are used *(snug´•gle, beg´•gar, doc´•tor, peach´•es, base´•ment, kind´•ness, short´•er, short´•est, a•bove´, un•lock´)*.

Special Phonics Generalizations

/ĕ/ ea *(head)*

/ĭ/ y *(myth)*

/ā/ ei *(veil)*

/ē/ ie *(piece)*
  y in an unaccented syllable at the end of a word *(ba´•by, neat´•ly)*
  i at the end of a syllable *(ski)*

/ī/ y at the end of an accented syllable *(my, sup•ply)*
  i in a closed syllable *(wild, find)*
  i before *gh* *(light)*

/ō/ o in a closed syllable *(gold, colt, roll)*

/ū/, /ōō/ ew at the end of a word *(stew)*
  oo *(broom)*

/ûr/ er, ir, ur *(clerk, dirt, turn)* or after *w* *(worm)*

/är/ ar *(shark)*

/or/ or *(stork, more)*

/âr/ are, air *(care, hair)*
  ear *(bear)*

/îr/ ear, eer *(hear, deer)*

/ô/ au, aw *(Paul, law, lawn)*
  a before *l* *(ball, salt)*
  o in some closed syllable words *(cost, toss, cloth, soft, song)*

/ou/ ou, ow *(cloud, how, tower)*

/ōō/ oo *(cook)*

/oi/ oi, oy *(boil, boy)*

/s/ c before *e*, *i*, and *y* *(cent, city, cyclone)*

/j/ g before *e*, *i*, and *y* *(gentle, giant, gym)*
  ge at the end of a one-syllable word, usually signaling a long vowel sound *(page, range)*
  dge at the end of a one-syllable word, usually signaling a short vowel sound *(budge)*

/ch/ tch at the end of a one-syllable word, signaling a short vowel sound *(match)*

/f/ ph *(phone)*

Consonant letters are sometimes silent *(w* in *write; l* in *walk; gh* in *light; b* in *climb; k* in *knife; d* in *edge;* and *t* in *batch)*.

Structural Generalizations

Aural clues

- Every vowel sound in a word is in a separate syllable.

Syllable division rules

Rule 1: *VC/CV* pattern

Divide words with the *VC/CV* pattern into syllables between consonants, even when one of the consonants is written as a consonant digraph (*bas•ket, dol•phin*).

(Introduced in Lesson 22 with Visual 4, *California Challenge.*)

Rule 2: Compound words

Divide compound words into syllables between the base words (*base•ball, bas•ket•ball*).

(Introduced in Lesson 27 with Visual 5, *Dangerous Trails.*)

Rule 3: Words ending with a consonant + *le*

In most words ending with a consonant + *le*, divide into syllables before the consonant (*lit•tle, Bi•ble*).

In words ending with the consonant digraph *ck* + *le*, divide into syllables after the *ck* (*pick•le*).

(Introduced in Lesson 39 with Visual 8, *Eighty Stables.*)

Rule 4: Words with affixes

a. In words with prefixes, divide into syllables between the prefix and the base word (*un•load*).

b. In words with suffixes, sometimes divide into syllables between the base word and the suffix.

    If the base word ends with /d/ or /t/, the suffix *-ed* is in a separate syllable (*hand•ed, plod•ded, rest•ed*).

    If the base word ends with *ch, sh, s, x,* or *z,* the suffix *-es* is a separate syllable (*church•es, wish•es, dress•es, box•es, buzz•es*).

(Introduced in Lesson 49 with Visual 9, *Ponies Carry the Mail.*)

Accent rules

Rule 1: Compound words

In compound words the primary accent falls on or within the first base word (*base´•ball*).

In compound words the secondary accent falls on or within the second base word (*bas´•ket •ball´*).

(Introduced in Lesson 27 with Visual 5, *Dangerous Trails.*)

Rule 2: Words with affixes

In words with affixes, the accent usually falls on or within the base word (*un•lock´•ing, ham´•mer•ing*).

(Introduced in Lesson 49 with Visual 10, *End of a Hard Ride.*)

Rule 3: Two-syllable words without affixes

In two-syllable words without affixes, the accent usually falls on the first syllable (*bas´•ket*).

In two-syllable words without affixes, the accent falls on the second syllable when that syllable contains two vowels (*col•lapse´*).

(Introduced in Lesson 49 with Visual 10, *End of a Hard Ride.*)

Rule 4: Schwa syllables

The accent never falls on a syllable with a vowel sound called a schwa—ə.

    The schwa sound can be spelled many ways. Some common schwa syllables are *a-* (*again*), *con-* (*content*), *-le* (*little*), *-er* (*never*), *-ain* (*captain*), *-ous* (*famous*), and *-tion* (*nation*).

    In words with the schwa ending /shən/, the accent usually falls on the syllable that precedes the ending (*va•ca´•tion*).

(Introduced in Lesson 56 with Visual 12, *A Special Mailbag.*)

Rule 5: Shift in accent

a. Adding suffixes to some words may affect where the primary accent falls. The accent often shifts to the syllable before the suffix (*ac´•ci•dent, ac•ci•den´•tal*).

b. A shift in accent often occurs when the meaning of a word changes (*per´•fect, per•fect´*).

(Introduced in Lesson 71 with Visual 15, *The Greatest Ride.*)

Remedial Service Word List

As the irregular, frequently-used words on the Remedial Service Word List are encountered in the reading selections, they may require review. These words are best practiced in context because a strong sentence provides both syntax and semantic cues for the reader. You may want to make cards for your struggling readers; or, if you prefer, you could purchase the set prepared for grade 2 available from BJU Press (product number 115469). To make this teaching strategy convenient for the teacher, each card in the set has three suggested context sentences on the back. Do remember, however, that a personalized sentence will meet the same need.

above	color	give	Mr.	shoe	want
against	coming	gone	Mrs.	should	war
among	country	great	music	son	warm
another	dear	group	neighbor	special	wash
answer	does	hear	nothing	straight	watch
any	done	heard	obey	sure	water
beautiful	don't	heart	off	their	were
been	door	hour	often	they	whose
both	during	laugh	once	they're	woman
break	early	learn	only	though	women
brother	earth	live	picture	thought	wonderful
brought	enough	love	pretty	through	won't
built	every	many	pull	together	word
busy	eye	minute	push	touch	work
buy	father	money	put	toward	world
care	friend	month	quiet	trouble	would
children	front	mother	says	usual	you're
Christ	full	move	several	very	

Teaching Visuals Index

Book Reports

Promote reading with your students by providing imaginative ways for them to tell others about the books they have read. Avoid the book report that requires the same standard information from each student—title, author, and description. This discourages independent reading and stifles creativity.

Scrapbook

Provide cardstock or construction paper pages and a binder or ready-made photo album or scrapbook.

The student imagines himself as a main character in the book and collects memorabilia that the character might collect for a scrapbook. Objects might include pictures from magazines and newspapers, objects mentioned in the book, hand-drawn illustrations, photographs of things related to the book, prize ribbons, scraps of cloth, and so forth. He makes a scrapbook using cardstock or construction paper pages collected in a binder with a decorated front cover or uses a ready-made photo album or scrapbook.

On the cover of the scrapbook or the first page, he writes the title of the book, the name of the author, and the name of the chosen main character. The scrapbook should contain at least five pages with 1-3 items per page. For each item, the student writes a short caption, including a quote from the book, explaining its significance. He displays the scrapbook.

Bulletin Board

Provide a sign-up sheet of available days and times for students to use a small bulletin board or section of a larger board to promote a book. Supply basic materials such as construction paper, writing paper, background paper, borders, and letters.

Students work alone or in teams of two or three to design a bulletin board to promote a book they have read. Students include the following elements: title of the book, name of the author, illustration of a cover for the book, outstanding quotes or excerpts, and illustration of a favorite scene with a one- or two-line caption. Students prepare all materials for the board before the scheduled display day. Give guidelines on how to display objects neatly on the board. With supervision at the scheduled time, the students arrange the bulletin board display.

Character Postcard

Provide 4" × 6" index cards or heavy paper to simulate a postcard.

The student writes on one side of the card a message to himself from a main character in the book, pretending he and the character know each other. In the message, the character tells the student about an event happening in his life from a selected part of the book, including quotes from the book. The student illustrates the described event or the setting from the book on the other side of the card. He displays the postcard.

Award Winner

Prepare a supply of blank award certificates. Provide writing and drawing paper.

The student writes a short citation to nominate a main character in the book for an award. He includes the title of the award, the title of the book, the name of the author, and the name of the character. In his speech, he expresses the character's worthiness of the award by giving examples of the character's traits and actions from the book, including quotes from the book. Award titles could include The Most Mission Minded, The Funniest, The Character I Would Want as a Friend the Most, and The Overcomer. He displays the citation along with an illustration of the character and a completed award certificate for the character.

News Report

Two students who have read the same book prepare a news report together. One student pretends to be the reporter covering the most exciting or important event in the book. The other student pretends to be a character or several characters from the book. The report includes the title of the book, the name of the author, and the reporter's interview with the character, using some quotes from the book. The students can make costumes, posters, maps, or props to enhance interest and understanding of the event. They present their news report for others.

Reading Contests

A reading contest is a good way to motivate students to use the reading skills they are learning. Using a team approach to a reading contest helps provide encouragement to all students.

Reach New Heights!

1. Make or draw two large mountains on each side of a bulletin board or chalkboard. Prepare two mountain-climbing figures and two scales. Make each mountain climber a different color. Attach a scale to the middle of each mountain so that it touches the highest point on the mountain. Use a paper clip to attach each mountain climber to a scale.

2. Divide the class into two teams. As you assign the students to teams, consider their reading abilities so that the two teams will be evenly matched.

3. Send home an information sheet and a "page total" form with the students to inform the parents about the reading contest. Each time the student returns a signed form, he takes home a new form. The form should include the following:

   My child, (name) , has read (number) pages from (book title). Parent's signature_____

4. As the forms are returned, each day total the number of pages read by each team. For every hundred pages read per team, move the team's mountain climber up the mountain one notch. Add the number of pages beyond an even hundred (100, 200, 300, etc.) to the next day's total.

5. The team whose mountain climber reaches the top of the mountain first wins. (You may want to give special recognition to individuals with high totals within each reading group or team.)

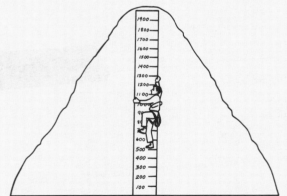

Pack the Shelves

1. Before starting the contest, send home a letter to inform the parents about the reading contest and to ask them to donate empty food boxes. (Suggest one size, such as 16 oz. elbow macaroni boxes.) Collect 2-3 boxes per student in your class. Have one empty shelf available for each team.

2. Divide the class into two teams. As you assign the students to teams, consider their reading abilities so that the two teams will be evenly matched.

3. Send home an information sheet and a "page total" form with the students to inform the parents about the reading contest. Each time the student returns a signed form, he takes home a new form. The form should include the following:

   My child, (name) , has read (number) pages from (book title). Parent's signature_____

4. For every hundred pages read by a team, cover the side of a box with construction paper to make it look like the spine of a book when placed on a shelf. Place the "book" on the team's shelf.

5. The team who "packs the shelf" first wins. (You may want to give special recognition to individuals with high totals within each reading group or team.)

Classroom Management for Grouping

The classroom management activities that follow are provided to give students meaningful activities that will reinforce skills they are learning. Each activity needs to be carefully explained to the students. Once the students become familiar with the various activities, write for display the titles of the management activities for the lesson and allow the students to complete them without further direction. If your class has three reading groups, one group could be working on seatwork and a second group could be completing the management activities while you give reading instruction to the third group. Students should keep a library book in their desks in order to have reading material available in the event they complete seatwork or management activities early. You may want to read through all of the management activities before the beginning of the school year in order to familiarize yourself with the activities and to make special note of any advance preparations that are necessary.

Vocabulary Box

1. Word Hunt

Advance teacher preparation: Cut blank paper into 3" × 5" sheets.

Materials
- File box for each student (This will become his vocabulary box.)
- A-Z tabbed card dividers for each student
- Student reader for each student
- 3" × 5" sheets of paper
- Three to five vocabulary words from the story, including the page number where each word appears in the student reader. (Write the words on an index card and store for later use, or write them for display.)

astounded	p. 27
scepter	p. 28
fend	p. 30

Word Hunt (continued)

Activity
The student reads the three to five words written on the index card or on display and copies one word and its corresponding page number on the front of each 3" × 5" sheet of paper. Using his reader, the student finds each word in context and copies the sentence from the reader onto the back of each sheet of paper. When all of the sentences are copied, the student underlines the vocabulary word in each sentence and writes what he thinks the underlined word means below the sentence. When this activity is complete, the student files each paper (by the first letter of the vocabulary word) behind the correct letter divider in his vocabulary box. (This is not a graded activity, but each student may bring his vocabulary box to the reading group periodically for you to check for accuracy.)

2. Study Buddies

Materials
- Vocabulary box for each student

Activity
Two students work together. Each student chooses ten words from his vocabulary box. One student reads the underlined word and the context sentence from one of his papers to his study buddy, and the study buddy gives a definition for the given word. The students take turns reading words and sentences and giving definitions.

3. Glossary Day

Advance teacher preparation: Cut blank paper into 3" × 5" sheets.

Materials
- Vocabulary box for each student
- Student reader for each student
- 3" × 5" sheets of paper
- Three to five vocabulary words from the story, written on an index card or for display

Activity
The student reads the words that are written on the index card or for display and copies one word onto the front of each 3" × 5" sheet of paper. The student looks up each word in the glossary of his student reader and writes the meaning of the word on the back of each sheet of paper. He also writes on the back of each sheet a sentence of his own for each word and underlines the vocabulary word in each sentence. When this activity is complete, the student files each paper behind the correct letter divider in his vocabulary box.

Note: This activity works best with the lessons it is recommended with—"Yukon Trail," "Hamlet, Augusta Jones, and Me," "Pony Penning Day," "Night Ride to River Station," "When the Wind Blows from the South," and "Friend or Foe."

4. War of the Words

Materials
- Vocabulary boxes from two students

Activity
Two students work together. One student is player A and the other is player B. Each player brings his vocabulary box: player A has box A, and player B has box B. The players swap boxes and choose 15-20 word cards from the box, each card from a different letter category. Word cards from box A become stack A, and word cards from box B become stack B. The two stacks of word cards are kept separate from each other throughout the game, and these stacks are called "battle piles." The players shuffle the word cards they have chosen and place the cards word-side-down in front of them (stack A in front of player B and stack B in front of player A). The pile in front of each player is that player's battle pile.

Each player turns over the top card of his battle pile at the same time.

The player whose word card comes first alphabetically gets the opportunity to "fight" the battle. This player fights the battle by giving a correct definition for the word on his opponent's card after the opponent reads the word aloud.

War of the Words
(continued)

- If the fighting player gives the correct definition, he wins the word card from his opponent's battle pile and places it in his "victory pile"—a pile separate from his battle pile. The word card that the fighting player drew at the beginning of the round is place on the bottom of the fighting player's battle pile.
- If the fighting player does not give the correct definition, the opponent reads the correct definition aloud. The opponent then becomes the fighting player and gets the opportunity to define the word from his opponent's card, using the same fighting procedure.
- If both words start with the same letter, the first player who says "War" first gets the chance to "fight."

Continue turning over the cards and giving definitions until all the cards in one player's battle pile are gone or until a specified time is up. The player with the most cards in his victory pile wins the war. The students then give the word cards back to the original owner, who places them alphabetically behind the correct letter divider in the vocabulary box.

5. Puzzle Pastime

Advance teacher preparation: Collect and display examples of crossword puzzles for the students to refer to.

Materials
- Vocabulary box for each student
- Sheets of graph paper and writing paper
- Examples of crossword puzzles (optional)

Activity
The student chooses ten words from his vocabulary box. The student arranges the words to make a crossword puzzle. For each word, the student makes up a clue that is a synonym, rhyming word, antonym, riddle, or definition. The student makes a copy of the clues for each word and the puzzle without the words in it. The clues and the first box for each word should have corresponding numbers. The student exchanges puzzles with a classmate and solves the classmate's puzzle.

Computer variation: The student creates the crossword puzzle and clues on a computer.

Connections

1. Fact or Fiction Destinations

Advance teacher preparation: *Collect travel information (from magazines, travel stores, the Internet, books, etc.) and display for students to reference.*

Materials
- 9" × 12" or larger sheets of drawing paper
- Travel information
- Encyclopedia, magazines, newspapers

Activity
The student creates a travel brochure for a real place or a fictional place. He folds a 9" × 12" sheet of drawing paper into a three-panel travel brochure. On the front cover, the student illustrates and writes the name of his destination. Then he fills the brochure with interesting facts and information about the destination or activities at the destination. He can include a schedule of events, activities to do at the destination, costs, and so forth. Encourage students to look up places in the encyclopedia, magazines, newspapers, and other travel materials provided.

Computer variation: *The student creates the brochure on a computer and looks up information on the Internet or a computer encyclopedia.*

2. Dreamy Domains

Advance teacher preparation: *Write varying budget amounts on strips of paper, and store the strips in a resealable bag.*

Materials
- Various catalogs containing home furnishings (remove unwanted sections)
- Resealable bag containing budget strips
- Sheets of writing paper
- Sheets of drawing paper

Activity
Students work in pairs or individually. The students choose a budget strip from the resealable bag. Then the students use the catalog index to find in the catalog items to decorate and furnish a dream place—such as a dream room, castle, tree house, private train car, jet, underground cave, or space station. The students list the cost of each item, adding up the costs while trying to stay within their budget, and draw a picture of their dream place.

Computer variation: *The student looks up items and prices on the Internet.*

3. Amazing Ads

Advance teacher preparation: *Collect and display grocery store advertisements (optional).*

Materials
- Grocery store advertisements
- Sheets of writing paper
- Sheets of drawing paper

Activity
Each student designs an advertisement for his favorite food or for an imaginary food. Students can display their products and advertisements in the classroom.

Computer variation: *The student creates advertisements using a computer.*

4. Recipe Reconstruction

Advance teacher preparation: *Collect and record easy and nutritionally balanced recipes for a child's snack or lunch, and write one recipe on each card. Write the list of ingredients on one piece of paper and each step of the directions on separate strips of paper. Put the original recipe card along with the list of ingredients and the strips of directions in a resealable bag.*

Materials
- Sheets of writing paper
- Resealable bags, each containing a recipe card, a paper listing ingredients, and recipe steps on paper strips
- Actual ingredients and utensils for recipes (optional)

Recipe Reconstruction (cont.)

Activity
Students work in pairs. Each pair chooses a resealable bag and removes only the list of ingredients and the strips of recipe directions from the bag. While referring to the list of ingredients, the students decide how to best arrange the recipe directions in proper sequence. When finished arranging the directions, they check the sequence with the original recipe card. Each student then copies the original recipe and takes the recipe home for his family to try.

(Optional: students can make the recipe for a class snack.)

5. Treasure Hunt

Advance teacher preparation: *Collect and store small objects in a box.*

Materials
- Box of objects
- Sheets of writing paper

Activity
Two students work together. The first partner chooses an object from the box and hides it in the room while the other partner closes his eyes. Then the other partner chooses and hides an object while the first partner closes his eyes. Each student writes directions or clues to find the object he hid. The partners swap directions and try to find the hidden objects.

Computer variation: *The student creates clues on a computer.*

Word Work

1. Comic Connection

Advance teacher preparation: Collect appropriate newspaper comic strips. Mount each strip on construction paper and number the backs of the frames to show the correct order. Cut apart the individual frames and laminate them. Store the entire comic strip in an envelope labeled with a title.

Materials
• Envelopes containing laminated comic strip frames

Activity
The student chooses an envelope and reads each comic strip frame. He places the frames in sequence and then checks the order by looking on the back of the frames.

Variations:
• The student creates a comic strip to go with a story from the reader.
• Supply the student with one frame from the middle of a comic strip. The student creates frames to complete the comic strip.

2. Blooper Blurbs

Advance teacher preparation: Prepare short paragraphs about historical events, famous people, classroom events, or reader stories. Put errors in each paragraph, such as omitting punctuation or capitalization, misspelling words, or incorrectly using a grammar skill students need to practice, and indicate the number of errors in the paragraph. Provide the paragraph with the corrections for the student to use to check his corrections.

Materials
• Sheets of writing paper
• Paragraphs about historical events, famous people, classroom events, or reader stories, containing errors

Activity
The student chooses a paragraph and copies it, correcting the errors. He checks his copied paragraph with the corrected paragraph provided.

Variation: The student writes a sentence or paragraph containing errors and indicates the number of errors. A classmate corrects the errors as he copies it.

3. The Title Match

Advance teacher preparation: Collect (from reader stories, newspapers, classroom or library books) or write short paragraphs. Write a corresponding title for each paragraph. Mount each paragraph and title on a sheet of construction paper. Write the title on the back of the paragraph for self-checking. Cut apart the title from the paragraph and laminate them. Store paragraphs and titles in resealable bags, placing several paragraphs and corresponding titles in each bag.

Materials
• Resealable bags, each containing several paragraphs and their corresponding titles

Activity
The student chooses a bag and separates the paragraphs and titles into two piles. He reads the paragraphs and matches them with their corresponding titles.

4. Worn Words

Advance teacher preparation: Prepare a chart of several undescriptive, overused words. Write the words across the top of the chart, leaving additional columns so that more overused words can be added. Display the chart. Cut blank paper into 3" × 5" sheets.

Materials
- Chart with overused words at the top of columns
- Sheets of writing paper
- 3" × 5" sheets of white paper
- 3" × 5" sheets of colored paper

said	walked	good		

Worn Words
(continued)

Activity
As students read and listen to literature, they notice descriptive words that replace nondescriptive, overused words. When a student finds such a word he writes it under the corresponding overused word on the chart. Limit each student to one word per day for each overused word.

After many words have been added to the chart, the students may do the following activities.

1. Two students work together. Each student writes sentences using the descriptive words and gives the sentences to his partner. The partner figures out what overused words the descriptive words replaced.

2. Two students work together. Each student chooses five overused words from the chart and writes each one on a sheet of colored paper; he chooses three descriptive words for each overused word chosen and writes each one on a sheet of white paper. The student mixes up the words and swaps them with his partner. He matches the descriptive words with the corresponding overused words.

3. Two students work together. They prepare and play a traditional concentration game by making one descriptive card per corresponding overused word card. The students mix up the cards, place them word-side down, and turn over two cards at a time to find matching words.

5. Dictionary Challenge

Advance teacher preparation: Cut blank paper into 3" × 5" sheets.

Materials
- Dictionary for each student or pair
- 3" × 5" sheets of paper

Activity
Two students work together. Each student looks up in the dictionary three words that he thinks his partner does not know. On a sheet of paper, the student writes the words at the top and three numbered definitions below the word, one definition correct, and the other two incorrect but close to the correct definition. The student then circles the number of the correct definition. Taking turns, each student reads one word and the three definitions to his partner. The partner guesses which definition is correct. If his guess is correct, he gets a point. The student with the most points wins. After the students prepare and use the sheets of paper, collect the papers for future Dictionary Challenges.

Recreational Reading

1. Board Game

Advance teacher preparation: Prepare the board games according to the directions given on Appendix pages A20 (Part 1) and A24 (Part 2). The game board and game pieces may be laminated and each game stored in a file folder.

Materials
- Licorice Bits game (Appendix pages A20-A23)
- Brave the Badge game (Appendix pages A24-A27)

Activity
The directions for playing Licorice Bits are included on Appendix page A20. The directions for playing Brave the Badge are included on Appendix page A24.

2. Design a Game

Advance teacher preparation: Collect and display examples of various kinds of games for students to refer to, such as board games, crossword puzzles, and word searches.

Materials
- Various weights and colors of drawing paper
- Markers and crayons
- Game pieces (counters, beans, buttons)

Activity
The student designs a game to go with a story he has read in the reader. The game can be a board game, a crossword puzzle, a word search, or another type of game or activity that can be played in the classroom. The student uses questions or vocabulary related to the story to make the game and writes the directions for playing the game. Provide game pieces if necessary. Allow students to play the finished game. Store the game for repeated use.

Computer variation: The student uses a computer to create games, directions, and questions.

3. Frantic Antics

Advance teacher preparation: Write characters' names and corresponding story titles (from reader stories that the students have already read) on slips of paper, one name and corresponding title per slip. Mix up the slips and put them in a box with a lid.

Materials
- Box with a lid containing names and titles
- Timer

Activity
Three or four students work together. One student picks a slip of paper from the box. Without showing any other students, he looks at the slip he picked and sets the timer for two minutes. The student tries to get his classmates to say the name of the character and the story. To do this, the student silently acts out any part of the story without saying the name of the character or story title. The student acknowledges a correct guess of the character's name or story title but continues acting out parts of the story until both the character's name and story title are guessed correctly.

Frantic Antics (continued)

A point is awarded to the student who correctly guesses the character's name and a point to the student who correctly guesses the story title. The student actor receives one point each for the character's name and the story title if they are guessed correctly.

Play continues until each student has had at least one turn to act out part of a story.

Variation: Two students work together but do not award points.

4. Touchable Tales

Advance teacher preparation: *Collect magazines and a variety of craft materials including shoe boxes, fabric, construction paper, and other items useful in creating a miniature scene.*

Materials
- Magazines
- Craft materials
- Scissors
- Glue
- Paints, markers, and crayons

Activity
After the student reads a story from the reader, he prepares a diorama of an important event, a character, or a favorite scene from the story. The student uses magazine photos and craft materials to create the diorama and includes the title of the book and the author's name. Display the diorama.

Computer variation: *The student uses a computer to create a diorama with clip art or pictures from the Internet.*

5. Grab It, Read It, Pass It

Materials
- Timer
- Sheets of writing paper

Activity
Three or four students work together. Each student chooses a book to read from the classroom library.

The students sit in a circle. One student sets the timer for five minutes. Each student reads his book until the timer goes off. At that time, each student stops reading and writes the title of the book, author, genre (if he knows), subject, and a short sentence about whether he would like to continue reading this book and why.

Then each student passes his book to the classmate on his right. The timer is again set for five minutes, and each student begins reading the book just passed to him. Repeat the cycle as time allows or until each student has read from each book.

Spelling Practice

1. Spell Check

Materials
- List of current spelling words
- Sheets of writing paper

Activity
Two students work together. One student gives the other a written practice test of the spelling words for the week. The child who is the test giver says the word, uses it in a sentence, and repeats the word. The other child writes the list of spelling words. The students then switch roles.

2. Spelling Makes Cents

Materials
- List of current spelling words
- Timer
- Sheets of writing paper
- Dictionary

Activity
Two students work together. Using the current spelling list, each student writes the same spelling word on a sheet of paper. One student sets the timer for two minutes. Each student uses the letters of the word to write as many other words as possible until the timer goes off. At that time, the students swap papers and check the words written by their partner. They count the number of letters in each word. Each letter is worth one cent. Next to the spelling word at the top of the paper, each student writes how much the spelling word is worth, which is the total number of letters used in all the words made from the original word. The student with the most cents wins.

Each student can challenge his partner if he thinks one of his partner's words is not spelled correctly or is not a real word. The word in question is looked up in the dictionary. If the word is incorrect, the partner does not receive any cents for that word.

Repeat the process with three more spelling words.

3. Softball Sluggers

Advance teacher preparation: Prepare the Softball Sluggers game according to the directions given on Appendix page A28. The game board, word cards, and game pieces may be laminated and the entire game stored in a file folder.

Materials
- Softball Sluggers game (Appendix pages A28-30)

Activity
The directions for playing Softball Sluggers are included on Appendix page A28.

4. Secret Code Spelling

Materials
- Sheets of writing paper
- List of current spelling words

Activity
Two students work together. At the top of the paper, each student writes each letter of the alphabet. Under each letter he writes or draws a symbol to stand for each letter. Any kind of symbol can be used, including numbers, pictures, lines, dots, and letters. He then writes the spelling words in random order on the page, using his secret code symbols. He exchanges his secret code spelling words with his partner, solves his partner's secret code spelling words, exchanges the deciphered secret code spelling words, and checks his partner's words.

Computer variation: The student creates secret codes using a computer for symbols, pictures, fonts, and so forth. He prints out the secret coded spelling words for his partner to solve.

5. Pen a Pyramid

Materials
- Sheets of writing paper
- Dictionary

Activity
Students work in pairs or individually. Each student writes a given vowel in the top block of the pyramid. The student uses the vowel to make a two-letter word that includes the vowel for the second level of blocks. He continues working down the pyramid, using the vowel to make four-, six-, eight-letter words, and so on. Each new word is a new level of blocks in the pyramid. The student tries to make the tallest pyramid possible. He may use the dictionary to check the spelling of words as he makes the pyramid.

Creative Writing

1. Runaway Writings

Advance teacher preparation: Prepare story starter sentences, write them on strips of paper, and keep them in a resealable bag.

Materials
- Resealable bag containing story starter sentences
- Sheets of writing paper

Activity
Two students work together. Each student chooses a story starter sentence, copies it onto writing paper, and writes two more sentences of the story. The students swap the stories and each student reads what has been written and then writes two more sentences of the story. Continue this process until each student has written six sentences for each story. Each student reads aloud a finished story to his partner.

Computer variation: Story starters are typed on a computer and the students take turns adding two sentences to the story. The finished story is printed out and read aloud to the partner.

2. Senses in Setting

Advance teacher preparation: Collect pictures of scenes (from magazines, calendars, etc.) depicting various settings and moods, mount them on construction paper, and laminate them. Display several pictures for the student to choose from. Display on a sheet of posterboard a list of questions for brainstorming: While making believe that you are in this place, (1) What do you see? smell? hear? feel? taste? (2) Where is this place? (3) What's happening in this picture? (4) If the person in this picture could talk, what do you think he or she would say? (5) How does this picture make you feel?

Materials
- Pictures of scenes
- List of questions for brainstorming
- Sheets of writing paper

Senses in Setting (continued)

Activity
The student chooses one picture and uses the list for brainstorming to develop ideas. Using the ideas he has developed, he writes a short story that is set in the place pictured. He displays his story with the picture.

Computer variation: The student types his story on a computer.

3. Life and Times in 4th Grade

Advance teacher preparation: Take photographs of the class on special days or during special activities and place them in a resealable bag.

Materials
- Resealable bag containing photographs of the class
- Sheets of writing paper
- Sheets of drawing paper
- Three-ring binder
- Glue

Activity
The student chooses a photograph and glues it to the top of a sheet of writing paper. Below the photograph, the student writes a paragraph about the special time. He puts the photograph and paragraph in the binder. Display the continually growing book for students to read other students' writings and for parents or visitors who come to the classroom. Photocopy the book for each student at end of the year as a fourth-grade memories book.

Computer variation: The student uses a computer to type and illustrate stories.

4. Roll-a-Sentence

Advance teacher preparation: Prepare and laminate four cube patterns, cut them out, fold them, and secure them with tape. Use an overhead marking pen to write one word on each side of each cube. Use nouns, verbs, adverbs, adjectives, and prepositions.

Materials
- Four word cubes
- Sheets of writing paper

Activity
Two students work together. Provide four word cubes per pair. The students roll all four cubes at the same time. Each student writes a sentence using the four words that have come up on the cubes and any other words that are needed to complete the sentence. Each student receives one point for each of the four words used. Repeat the process several times. The student with the most points wins.

Note: The word cubes can be wiped off with a damp cloth or paper towel, and new words can be written on them.

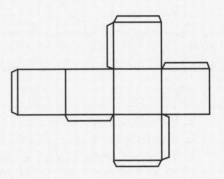

5. Story-in-a-Bag

Advance teacher preparation: Collect small objects and paper bags (lunch or grocery size). Put five objects in each bag.

Materials
- Paper bags, each containing five small objects
- Sheets of writing paper

Activity
The student chooses a bag and writes or tells a story that includes all the objects in the bag.

Computer variation: The student types the story on a computer.

Licorice Bits

Advance teacher preparation

- **Game board**—Enlarge onto heavyweight paper the Licorice Bits game board on Appendix page A21. Color and laminate the game board.
- **Question-answer cards**—Copy onto one side of heavyweight paper the question cards on Appendix pages A22-A23. Cut the cards apart. Write a large question mark on the back of each card. Laminate the cards.

- **Game pieces**—Copy onto heavyweight paper the pictures of the characters from "An Emergency" and the stands below. Color, cut out, and laminate the characters and stands and assemble them to be used as game pieces on the Licorice Bits game board.
- **Provide a number cube.**

Licorice Bits game

Players: 2-4
Playing instructions

1. Set up the game by mixing up the question-answer cards and putting them in a pile question-mark up on the licorice bits bin on the game board. Each player chooses a game piece and places it on the start space on the game board.

2. Each player rolls the number cube once. The player who rolls the highest number begins the game. Play continues with the player to the left until the game is completed.

3. As the game progresses, each player rolls the number cube.

   - The person to the player's left picks up the card on the top of the pile and reads the question to the player. (The answer is in italics.)

     a. If the player's answer is correct, he moves the number of spaces indicated on the number cube.

     b. If the player's answer is incorrect, the player to his left begins his turn.

   - If the person to the player's left picks up a Wild Card, he gives it to the player. Then he picks up another question card and reads it to the player. The player can save the Wild Card to use when he gives an incorrect answer; at that time he may "turn in" the Wild Card and then have another turn.

   - When a player lands on a space with special directions on it, he reads the directions and follows them.

   - When a player lands on a blank space, his turn is over; the next player begins his turn.

   4. The player who reaches the Finish space first is the winner.

    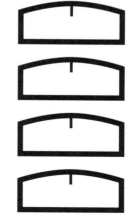

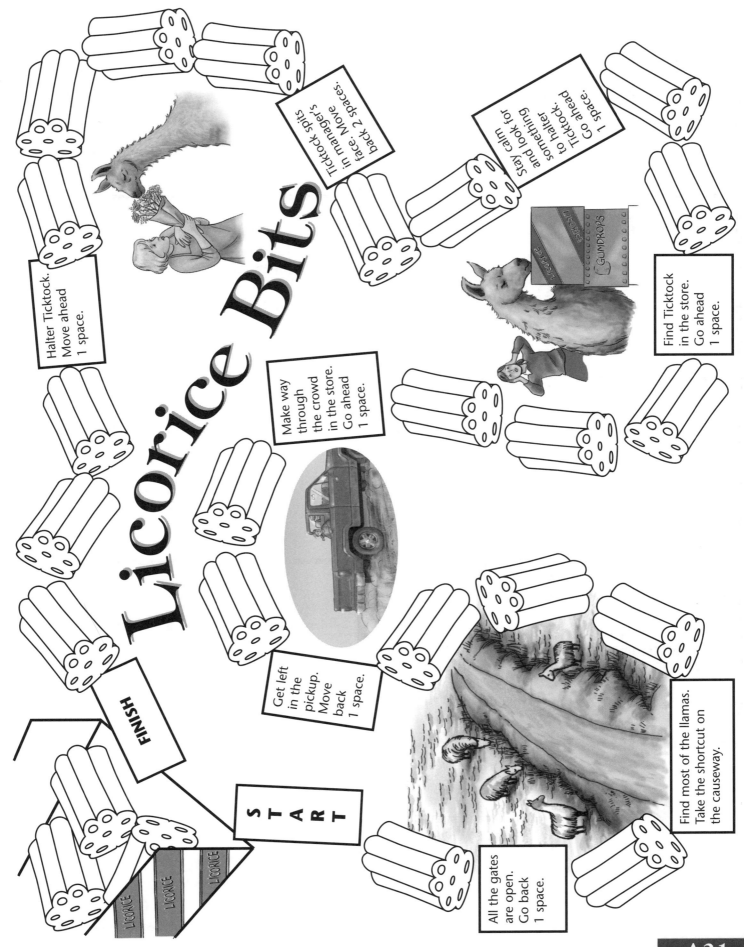

Licorice Bits

START
S
T
A
R
T

FINISH

Halter Ticktock. Move ahead 1 space.

Ticktock spits in manager's face. Move back 2 spaces.

Stay calm and look for something to halter Ticktock. Go ahead 1 space.

Find Ticktock in the store. Go ahead 1 space.

Make way through the crowd in the store. Go ahead 1 space.

Get left in the pickup. Move back 1 space.

Find most of the llamas. Take the shortcut on the causeway.

All the gates are open. Go back 1 space.

What is the name of the game Jack says Ticktock is playing? *Kill the Kid*	**Which two people get out of the truck when it stops at the causeway?** *Mrs. Ericson and Jack*	**Who finds Ticktock?** *Penny*	**Doc Ericson could qualify for a research *grant*. What is a *grant*?** *funds* or *money given for research or study*
What is Ticktock doing in the store when Penny finds her the first time? *She has her muzzle in the black licorice bits.*	**What does Penny use instead of a rope to halter Ticktock?** *a dog leash*	**Why does Ticktock spit on the store manager?** *He is scaring her with his yelling.*	**Why does Ticktock let Penny halter her in the store?** *Ticktock is sniffing and nibbling a bouquet of flowers.*
Whom does Doc Ericson go to get in town? *the sheriff*	**What town does Doc Ericson drive into?** *Winneca*	**Which llama is in the store?** *Ticktock*	**Name one of the three animals that the people think Ticktock is.** *(1) Shetland pony* *(2) camel* *(3) giraffe*
Name one of the three chores Jack and Penny do besides working with the llamas. *(1) pick up rocks* *(2) scrape paint* *(3) weed the garden*	**What do Jack and Penny say when the dinner gong bangs?** *"Trouble!"*	**How do the llamas get out of the pasture?** *The gates are open.*	**Where are most of the llamas found after they get loose?** *on either side of the causeway (knee-deep in shallow water)*
Who tells this story? *Penny*	**Which llama is the boss of the herd?** *Jock*	**Name one of the three ways llamas defend themselves.** *(1) spit* *(2) males bite* *(3) slash with hooves*	**What part of an intruder does a llama aim its spit at?** *face* or *the eyes*

WILD CARD	Why is the farm hog-wired? *so the llamas do not get out and to keep the llamas safe from other animals*	Who pays for the items Ticktock ruins? *Doc Ericson*	Are Jack and Penny taller or shorter than a llama? *shorter*
WILD CARD	How could Doc Ericson qualify for a research grant? *by making Penny and Jack's visit educational*	The llamas are lifting their *muzzles* to catch the smells. What is a *muzzle?* *the nose and mouth of an animal's face*	Doc and Penny drive down the dirt road, headed for the *causeway.* What is a *causeway?* *a raised road*
What store items is Ticktock interested in? *things that have a strong smell* or *candy and flowers*	What does the manager think is wrong with Ticktock when she spits on him? *He thinks Ticktock has rabies.*	What does Penny do to the dog leash so it will not choke Ticktock? *fastens it above the knot she ties*	Which gate opens to the dirt road? *the barnyard gate*
Why does Mrs. Ericson want Scruggs and Jean to come to the farm? *so there will be two boys and two girls* or *so no one will get picked on or left out*	Why is everything silent on the farm? *The llamas are gone.*	What food does the author compare Ticktock's behavior to when she is taken out of the store? *milk ("Ticktock was as mild as milk.")*	How does Penny get Ticktock to go out of the store with her? *with the flowers and the leash*
Jock sometimes fights with the *yearling* males. What is a *yearling?* *a one-year-old animal*	Ticktock snorts *indignantly,* as though she thinks Penny is cheating. What does the word *indignantly* mean? *feeling or showing anger about something unfair, mean, or bad*	Penny and Jack learn how to *halter* a llama. To *halter* is to do what? *put a halter on*	Penny and Jack learn how to *groom* the llamas. To *groom* is to do what? *clean and brush* or *make neat*

Appendix ... A23

Softball Sluggers

Advance teacher preparation

- **Game board**—Enlarge onto heavyweight paper the Softball Sluggers game board on Appendix page A29. Color and laminate the game board.

- **Word cards**—Copy onto one side of heavyweight paper the Single, Double, Triple, or Home Run cards from Appendix page A30. Cut them apart and laminate them. Use an overhead marking pen to write the spelling words on the blank side of the cards. On each Single card write a word from a past word list; on each Double card write a word from the current word list; on each Triple card write a word from a future word list; on each Home Run card write a word from a fifth grade word list or a challenge word.

- **Game pieces**—Copy onto heavyweight paper the softball players and stands below, three girl and three boy softball player pieces for each team. Color, cut out, and laminate the players and stands and assemble them to be used as game pieces on the Softball Sluggers game board.

- **Provide a coin for the coin toss.**

- **Provide a sheet of paper and a pencil for keeping score.**

SOFTBALL SLUGGERS GAME

Players: 2-6
Playing instructions

1. Set up the game by placing the word cards word-side down in piles on the appropriate labels (Single, Double, Triple, Home Run) on the game board.

2. The players divide into two teams: A and B. Each player chooses a game piece and places it in the Team A or Team B dugout. One player is chosen to keep score.

3. A coin toss determines which team goes first: heads—Team A goes first; tails—Team B goes first.

4. The batter (a player on the first team) tells the pitcher (a player on the other team) whether he wants a single, double, triple, or home run. The pitcher picks up the card on the top of the chosen pile, reads the word to the batter, and uses the word in a sentence. The batter spells the word. (As the game progresses, if all the players on a team are on a base, the player on the base closest to home plate spells the word.)

   - If the batter spells the word correctly, he and any other players on a base move the number of bases indicated by the type of card.
   - If the batter misspells the word, he is out.

5. The first team continues until it misspells three words (three outs). Then the other team has a turn. When both teams have had three outs, the first inning is over.

6. The game continues for nine innings (or the number of innings time allows). The team with the most points wins the game.

SOFTBALL SLUGGERS

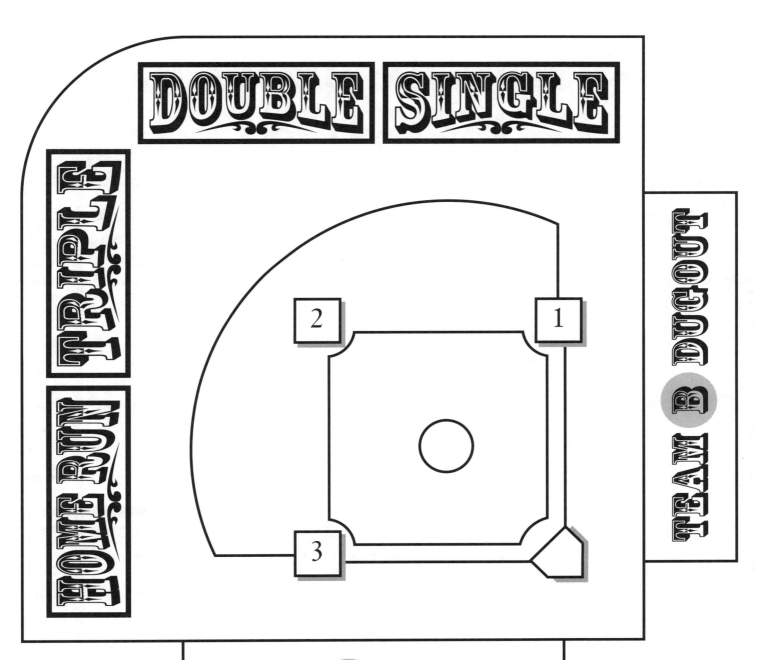

DOUBLE SINGLE

TRIPLE

HOME RUN

2

1

3

TEAM B DUGOUT

TEAM A DUGOUT

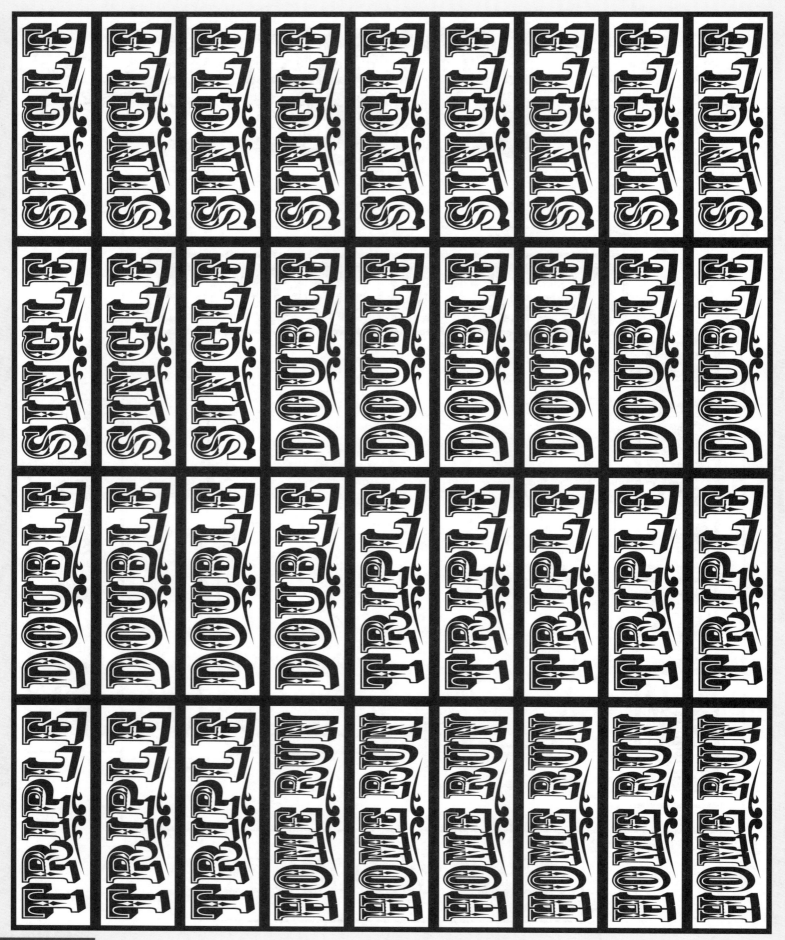

Informal Checklist of Reading Behaviors

Name _____   Grade _____   Reading Group _____

Date	Skill	Task	Rating (10 is excellent)	Comments
SILENT READING				
	Literal thinking	Recalls explicitly stated facts, ideas, details, and sequence of events	1 2 3 4 5 6 7 8 9 10	
	Interpretive thinking (vocabulary)	Explains word meaning in own words. Uses the four cuing systems to gain meaning of unknown words	1 2 3 4 5 6 7 8 9 10	
	Interpretive thinking	Infers main ideas and key concepts in paragraphs and stories. Logically predicts coming events	1 2 3 4 5 6 7 8 9 10	
	Critical thinking	Makes perceptive judgments about character thoughts, feelings, actions, and motives. Compares actions and thoughts of characters to biblical principles	1 2 3 4 5 6 7 8 9 10	
	Appreciative thinking	Relates story events and characters to real life	1 2 3 4 5 6 7 8 9 10	
	Appreciative thinking	Is increasingly aware of the author's literary skill. Notices figurative language, vivid description, or compelling action	1 2 3 4 5 6 7 8 9 10	
ORAL READING				
	Word recognition	Reads without defaults and self-corrects miscues smoothly	1 2 3 4 5 6 7 8 9 10	
	Communication	Conveys meaning of the text to listener(s) through appropriate phrasing, inflection, pace, and emotional tone	1 2 3 4 5 6 7 8 9 10	
WRITTEN RESPONSES				
	Comprehension skills	Worktext pages (average of several recommended pages)	1 2 3 4 5 6 7 8 9 10	
	Skills: literature, structural analysis, study skills	Worktext pages (average of several recommended pages)	1 2 3 4 5 6 7 8 9 10	

Conversion Table

	Very Good	Good	Satisfactory	Needs Improvement	Needs Remedial
Silent Reading	54-60	48-53	42-47	36-41	0-35
Oral Reading	18-20	16-17	14-15	12-13	0-11
Written Responses	18-20	16-17	14-15	12-13	0-11

Percentages (points)	
90-100	A
80-89	B
70-79	C
60-69	D
0-59	failing

© 2000 BJU Press. Limited license to copy granted on copyright page.

Individual Anecdotal Record

Name _____   Grade _____   Reading Group _____

Date	Comments	Prescription

NOTE:

▶ Comments do not need to be made in complete sentences, but they should be complete enough to be easily interpreted. Whenever possible, tie the behavior observed to a skill. *(Example: Jason evaluated character's statement . . . decided it was opinion rather than fact: critical level of comprehension.)*

▶ Improvements in motivation, attitude, skills, and applications should be noted, and deficiencies and prescriptive measures indicated. All comments should be written in positive terms with the student's reading progress in mind.

▶ You may find it helpful to keep the individual anecdotal records on a clipboard for easy access during reading instruction.

Student's name _____

Backpacking in Yellowstone National Park

Imagine camping in grizzly bear country. Bob and Sam Perry did. They went on a backpacking trip into the wilderness. The park ranger told them to hide all their food in a tree several hundred yards away from their tent. He also suggested that they sleep near a good climbing tree. Bob and Sam adhered to the ranger's advice and looked for good climbing trees. They never met a bear, but they did see bighorn sheep, elk, and three moose.

Each man carried a thirty-pound backpack while walking twelve miles a day. They had to battle rain and slick rocks. They faced light snow and winds up to forty miles per hour.

After a week in the wilderness, both were glad to see the ranger station. They could rest their sore muscles and aching feet. It was nice to get back to the comforts of modern life, but the backpacking trip was a great experience they will never forget.

Oral Reading Level Form

Oral Reading Level	Miscues Allowed	Actual Miscues
Independent	0–4	
Instructional: High	5–10	
Instructional: Average	11–16	
Instructional: Low	17–20	
Frustration	21+	

Comprehension Questions

_____ 1. *[literal]* Who goes backpacking in grizzly bear country? *(Bob and Sam)*

_____ 2. *[literal]* What advice does the park ranger give to Bob and Sam before they start their trip? *(hide their food in a tree far from their tent and sleep near a good climbing tree)*

_____ 3. *[interpretive]* Why would they need to put their food far from their tent and sleep near a good climbing tree? *(to protect them from bears)*

_____ 4. *[literal]* What is one of the animals Bob and Sam see? *(possible answers: bighorn sheep, elk, and moose)*

_____ 5. *[interpretive]* When the selection says that Bob and Sam adhere to the ranger's advice, what does that mean? *(They follow his advice.)*

_____ 6. *[interpretive]* What are two of the hardships the men face on their trip? *(possible answers: rain, slick rocks, light snow, strong winds, carrying thirty-pound backpacks for twelve miles a day)*

_____ 7. *[critical]* Why do you think it was nice to get back to the comforts of modern life? *(Answers may vary but should include the use of modern conveniences—e.g., running water, soft bed, electricity.)*

_____ 8. *[interpretive]* How do you know the men enjoy their backpacking trip? *(The selection says that it was a great experience they will never forget.)*

Comprehension Level Form

# of incorrect answers	Comprehension Level
0	Independent at 4.0
1–2	Instructional at 4.0
3+	Frustration at 4.0

Comments _____

Student's name _____

Night Hunters

An owl's food source comes from hunting live prey. Rats, mice, and other small animals make up the owl's diet. Owls can eat over 2,000 rodents per square mile each year.

Part of the owl's success in hunting depends on its ability to fly silently. An owl's wings are very broad, allowing it to flap slowly while still maintaining speed. Slow-moving wings make very little sound. In addition, the main wing feathers have fringed edges to muffle any noise that might be made. These silent night hunters give no warning to the helpless animals, as they become the next meal.

Once captured, the small prey is swallowed whole by the owl. A larger rodent is torn to pieces before being swallowed. Owls spit up the fur and bones that cannot be digested. This ball of fur and bones is called a casting. By studying the castings, we can learn about the owl's eating habits.

Oral Reading Level Form

Oral Reading Level	Miscues Allowed	Actual Miscues
Independent	0-4	
Instructional: High	5-10	
Instructional: Average	11-16	
Instructional: Low	17-20	
Frustration	21+	

Comprehension Questions

_____ 1. *[literal]* What does an owl eat? *(rodents, rats, mice, small animals)*

_____ 2. *[interpretive]* Why does an owl need to be silent when hunting? *(to give no warning to the animals)*

_____ 3. *[literal]* What two parts of the owl's body aid in silent flight? *(broad wings and fringed edges on the main feathers)*

_____ 4. *[interpretive]* When the selection says that the fringed edges muffle any noise, what does *muffle* mean? *(to keep from making noise)*

_____ 5. *[interpretive]* Why would an owl tear its prey before swallowing it? *(the prey is too large to swallow whole)*

_____ 6. *[interpretive]* Can an owl digest the entire prey? How do you know? *(No; they spit up balls of bones and fur called castings.)*

_____ 7. *[literal]* What can we learn by studying castings? *(We can learn about an owl's eating habits.)*

_____ 8. *[critical]* Why is it helpful to man that owls kill such a large number of rodents? *(Answers may vary, but should express that owls keep the rodent population down. Rodents carry diseases.)*

Comprehension Level Form

# of incorrect answers	Comprehension Level
0	Independent at 4.5
1-2	Instructional at 4.5
3+	Frustration at 4.5

Comments _____

Lesson Materials

Copy and cut out the three letters.

Dear Granddad,

I am enjoying my summer so much that I don't want to go to school yet! I've heard that there are going to be five sixth-grade classes this year! It is still very hot here. I'm glad there's air conditioning in school now!

I think that for my science project this year I'm going to catch a baby alligator in my aquarium and study it. I haven't asked Mom yet. That might be a good idea, don't you think? Write again soon!

Love,
Kyle

Dearest Grandpa,

School has started once again in the one-room schoolhouse. I attend classes only twice each week as I am busy helping Pa bring in the last cuttings of hay. The weather is turning quite cold, though we've seen no snow yet. Write soon.

Your grandson,
Joel

Dearest Grandpa,

School started last Monday. I have finally made it to the fifth grade. We have ten students in our class this year. Although it is only September, heaps of snow have prevented us from attending school for the past three days. Tomorrow I shall try to ski to school if Mother will let me. Write again soon!

Love,
Shawn

Use with Lesson 4.

Name _____

A limerick is a poem with five lines.

Lines 1, 2, and 5 rhyme.

Lines 3 and 4 rhyme.

Complete the limerick.

There was a bright girl from _____

Who could never remember her _____ .

So she bought a computer

And hired a tutor,

_____ .

Illustrate the limerick.

Use with Lesson 24.